The Corporate Responsibility Code Book
Revised Second Edition

Deborah Leipziger

Deborah Leipziger advises companies, governments and UN agencies on corporate responsibility (CR) issues. She has advised leading multinational companies on strategic and supply chain issues, as well as a wide range of CR initiatives, including the UN's Global Compact, the Global Reporting Initiative, the UN Environment Programme, the Human Rights Impact Assessment, and Social Accountability International. She serves as a member of several boards including the Advisory Committee on Socially Responsible Investment for Aviva Investors in the UK and the Center for Ethics at Manhattanville College, USA.

She is a co-author of *Living Corporate Citizenship* (FT, 2002) and *Corporate Citizenship: Successful Strategies of Responsible Companies* (FT, 1998). She is the author of *Social Accountability 8000: The Definitive Guide to the New Social Standard* (FT Prentice Hall, 2001). Her books have been translated into Portuguese, French, Korean and Chinese.

Born in Brazil, Ms. Leipziger has a Masters in Public Administration from Columbia University and a Bachelor of Arts from Manhattanville College in Economics and International Studies. She can be reached at www.deborahleipziger.com.

THE CORPORATE RESPONSIBILITY code book

REVISED SECOND EDITION

Deborah Leipziger

Viva Books

New Delhi | Mumbai | Chennai | Kolkata | Bengaluru | Hyderabad | Kochi | Guwahati

This book is dedicated to my three daughters, Natasha Lara, Alexandra Nicole and Jacqueline Lucia, my triple bottom line.

First Indian Edition 2011

VIVA BOOKS PRIVATE LIMITED

- 4737/23 Ansari Road, Daryaganj, New Delhi 110 002
  E-mail: vivadelhi@vivagroupindia.net, Tel. 42242200
- 76, Service Industries, Shirvane, Sector 1, Nerul, Navi Mumbai 400 706
  E-mail: vivamumbai@vivagroupindia.net, Tel. 27721273, 27721274
- Jamals Fazal Chambers, 26 Greams Road, Chennai 600 006
  E-mail: vivachennai@vivagroupindia.net, Tel. 28290304, 28294241
- B-103, Jindal Towers, 21/1A/3 Darga Road, Kolkata 700 017
  E-mail: vivakolkata@vivagroupindia.net, Tel. 22836381, 22816713
- 7, Sovereign Park Apartments, 56-58, K. R. Road, Basavanagudi, Bengaluru 560 004
  E-mail: vivabangalore@vivagroupindia.net, Tel. 26607409, 26607410
- 101-102 Mughal Marc Aptt., 3-4-637 to 641, Narayanguda, Hyderabad 500 029
  E-mail: vivahyderabad@vivagroupindia.net, Tel. 27564481, 27564482
- First Floor, Beevi Towers, SRM Road, Kaloor, Kochi 682 018, Kerala
  E-mail: vivakochi@vivagroupindia.net, Tel: 0484-2403055, 2403056
- 232, GNB Road, Beside UCO Bank, Silpukhuri, Guwahati 781 003
  E-mail: vivaguwahati@vivagroupindia.net, Tel: 0361-2666386

Published by arrangement with

Greenleaf Publishing Limited
Aizlewood's Mill
Nursery Street
Sheffield S3 8CG
UK

ISBN : 978-81-309-1921-8

Published by Vinod Vasishtha for Viva Books Private Limited, 4737/23, Ansari Road, Daryaganj New Delhi - 110 002.

Printed and bound by Sanat Printers, Kundli - 131 028, Sonepat, Haryana.

Contents

Foreword

Kishor A. Chaukar
Managing Director, Tata Industries Limited
Chairman, Tata Council for Community Initiatives

Corporate responsibility is becoming increasingly important as running a business becomes more complex. While generating investment and managing short-term issues are quite well understood, business understanding of the long-term contribution towards human well-being and environmental preservation is far lower than is desirable. However, this aspect is beginning to be recognised by an increasing number of enlightened businesses and their communities. There is also a surge in the number of processes, systems and specific standards to guide them towards their aspirations to become better global citizens.

Today we are grappling with a large number of these systemic outcomes and a global convergence has begun towards codifying and 'standardising' responsible business practice. While new ideas and the world-view of thought leaders in sustainability will continue to prove influential, we can undoubtedly witness a critical space consisting of an aggregation of well-catalogued material: processes and procedures to guide an increasing number of champions and business practioners in their daily work-especially heads of strategy, marketing, operations, supply chain managers, finance, community builders and so on.

Deborah Leipziger has had a long association with voluntary standard bodies and has been a part of the contemporary sustainability wave. Deborah's work particularly in the area of human rights and social accountability is well known, as is much as her previous work on corporate responsibility. I particularly welcome this Indian edition of *The Corporate Responsibility Code Book*, revised specifically for our practitioners, which unites in one single book a huge spectrum of practice and bandwidth of knowledge on this important but relatively less well-known subject.

My hope is that *The Corporate Responsibility Code Book* reaches every committed and serious sustainability practioner, whether she or he is a CEO, head of a business vertical function, facilitator, journalist, student, faculty in business schools, investor community, government official or policy-maker. It is a must-read for all those engaged in shaping tomorrow's business.

Best wishes
Kishor A. Chaukar
Mumbai, 8 June 2011

A note to readers

What's in a name?

As I wrote this book I was constantly reminded of the phrase 'things are seldom what they seem'. Corporate responsibility (CR) codes and standards are seldom what they seem. The reader should be advised that the terminology of CR tools is still being developed. The terms 'code', 'standard' and 'norm' are often used interchangeably and imprecisely. Another example of this imprecision is in the use of the term 'voluntary'. Although many company codes on labour issues are described as 'voluntary', they often require companies to conform to existing laws. Even the use of terms such as 'sustainable development' and 'accountability' within the title of codes and standards can be imprecise. The International Chamber of Commerce (ICC) Charter on Sustainable Development is far more about environment than sustainable development writ large. Social Accountability 8000 is more about labour rights than social accountability writ large. The field of corporate responsibility is still evolving and developing its own *lingua franca*.

Codes are in the eye of the beholder

Much of what is written about CR tools is public relations and marketing—an attempt to gain more members and attain critical mass. In this book, I seek to break through the 'spin' to objectively describe principles and codes; but, in reading my descriptions of the strengths and weaknesses of the initiatives, keep in mind that for some a code might be too rigorous and yet for others the same code might be too lenient.

This book seeks to provide clarity in a very broad and complex field, by offering manageable and useful information. *The Corporate Responsibility Code Book* is a reference guide for companies, non-governmental organisations (NGOs), trade unions and students. This book will be useful for companies trying to decide between several different approaches; for NGOs or civil-society groups trying to decide which codes to lobby companies to adhere to; and for activists, who can use this volume to call attention to cases where companies are not living up to the standards that they have committed themselves to in writing. But, mostly, this is a useful reference book to check what issues are included in which tools, and which are absent. Each profile is meant to stand alone so in some cases there may be some repetition.

It has been a challenge to narrow the field from the thousands of codes and standards into 34 key tools. There are a great many useful tools that are not included here but that may be included in a future edition. Another challenge has been to describe a constantly moving target, as each of the initiatives described herein are evolving.

Deborah Leipziger

Acknowledgements

This book is based on interviews with a wide range of experts from various countries and sectors. I am grateful to the following people for their time and wisdom:

Adrian Henriques
Shareen Hertel
Geoffrey Chandler
Gemma Crijns
Laura Donovan
John Elkington
Jan Jonker
Hilary Sutcliffe
Deborah Smith
Rory Sullivan
Simone de Colle
Malcolm McIntosh
Dorothy Mackenzie
Andrew Wilson
Katherine Hagen
Reino Fridh
David Vidal
Anita Normark
Eileen Kaufman
Sumi Dhanarajan
Jane Nelson
Mark Wade
Allen White

The following people reviewed the profiles of their organisations:

Mats Isaksson, OECD
Jonathan Cohen, AccountAbility
Mattias Stausberg, Global Compact
Kathryn Gordon, OECD
Mark Wade, Shell
Reg Green, ICEM
Dan Rees, Ethical Trading Initiative
Ineke Zeldenrust, Clean Clothes Campaign
Anne Lally, Fair Labor Association
David Weissbrodt, UN Working Group on the Working Methods and Activities of Transnational Corporations
Eileen Kaufman, Social Accountability International
Teodorina Lessidrenska, Global Reporting Initiative
Susan Cote-Freeman, Transparency International
Jill Rosenblum, The Natural Step

The following people assisted in the preparation of the second edition:

John Elkington
Dr Sandra Waddock, Boston College
Dr Craig Murphy, Wellsley
Brooke Barton, Ceres
Georg Kell, UN Global Compact
Steve Waygood, Aviva
Anders Tunold Kråkenes, EITI
Roger Frost, ISO
Sam Hoskins, Equator Principles
Beatrice de Montleau, ABN Amro

I am thankful to the standard-setters who have allowed Greenleaf Publishing to reproduce the standards in this volume. Each of the standard-setters was invited to comment on the introductory remarks that precede its principles, code or standard. I am grateful to them for their feedback.

My friends have supported me through this endeavour and deserve recognition. A special thank you goes to Shareen Hertel for her thoughtful advice, encouragement and wisdom. I am also very grateful to Jan Jonker for his encouragement and introductions.

I am grateful to my dear friends, Monica Sallouti, Jessica Holmes, Robin Schaap, Nancy Bennet, Oshani Perera, Gail Whiteman, Nancy Combs, Ann Marie Armbruster, Alice Winkler, Marie Kagaju, Maritza Saxon and Karin Green, for their faith in me.

I am grateful to my daughters, Natasha Lara, Jacqueline Lucia and Alexandra Nicole, for illustrating the recycled early drafts of this book. I am, as always, grateful to my parents for teaching me to love books and the written word.

Finally, I would like to thank John Stuart, Dean Bargh and their team at Greenleaf Publishing for their support and sound advice.

Acknowkedgements for the Indian edition

I am grateful to Anant G. Nadkarni, VP Group Corporate Sustainability at the Tata Council for Community Initiatives, who has been a strong advocate for the Indian edition of *The Corporate Responsibility Code Book*. Many people have played a role in the Indian edition, including:

- Georg Kell, UN Global Compact
- Matthias Stausberg, UN Global Compact
- Eileen Kaufman, Social Accountability International
- Joleen Ong, Social Accountability International
- Rishi Singh, Social Accountability International
- Joe Phelan, International Business Leaders Forum
- Dr Bimal Arora, Scaling up Indian CSR initiatives, GIZ

Introduction

There is no single code or standard, no panacea that will lead to corporate responsibility. Each company is different, with its own challenges, corporate culture, unique set of stakeholders and management systems. Corporate responsibility is a journey for which there is no single map but hundreds of guides. Codes and standards are maps that can be combined in new ways for different journeys. In my lectures around the world, I am asked the question, 'What are the best standards for companies seeking to be socially responsible?' Over the course of more than a decade, I have analysed hundreds of codes of conduct and standards to answer that question. This book is a result of 12 years of inquiry into corporate responsibility.

The Corporate Responsibility Code Book is a guide for companies trying to understand the landscape of corporate responsibility. This book is a valuable tool not only for companies developing their own code but also for companies with a strong track record in corporate responsibility, seeking to understand the interrelationships among codes and standards in order to create their own vision.

Companies are seeking to integrate codes of conduct and guidelines into their corporate cultures and management systems. The challenge for corporate responsibility is that each company is different; each sector has different priorities. The very same company in one region may face different challenges in other parts of the world. And yet stakeholders, especially consumers and investors, are keen for some degree of comparability with which they can evaluate corporate performance. There are countervailing forces at work within corporate responsibility: on the one hand is the need for convergence to simplify the large numbers of codes and standards; and on the other hand there is the need to foster diversity and innovation.

Code paradoxes

It is a paradox that many of the best codes of conduct and standards are not well known and that some corporate responsibility instruments that are well disseminated are not terribly effective. The purpose of this book is to disseminate some of the best corporate responsibility instruments available and to comment on their role. Another paradox is that it is possible to have comprehensive codes of conduct that achieve nothing, and quite vague codes of conduct that are well embedded into the organisation and that foster innovation and change.

Information overload is nowhere more apparent than in the field of corporate responsibility. There are millions of pages and web pages written on codes and standards, but most of it is 'spin' put out by organisations punting to sell their code or standard. The reality is that corporate responsibility is an emerging field, a new terrain for which maps are much needed but often imprecise. Just as the early cartographers drew imaginary creatures on their maps when they came up against the edge of what they knew, there is much *terra incognita* in the field of corporate responsibility. The weaving together of codes and standards in this volume points out the *terra incognita*, the vacuums within corporate responsibility, and also the duplication.

The need for a code book

In my consulting practice I advise companies about codes of conduct and their implementation. On many occasions I am brought in after a company has already developed a policy or code and disseminated it. Disseminating a code that is poorly crafted can lead to confusion and inefficiency, causing a 'domino effect' of misunderstanding and apathy.

My clients ask, 'What is the difference between Social Accountability 8000 [SA8000] and AccountAbility 1000 [AA1000]? Which should I use?' The answer is that each code and standard is a product of the organisation that crafted it and that each of the 34 codes in this book offer valuable lessons in corporate responsibility. There is no Holy Grail in the field of corporate responsibility, only different approaches and views of the field. *The Corporate Responsibility Code Book* distils the most valuable elements of each corporate responsibility instrument in a balanced and concise way.

The Corporate Responsibility Code Book will guide companies through a critical turning point in the field of social responsibility, from rhetoric to action on codes of conduct. The goal of the book is to help companies select, develop and implement social and environmental codes of conduct. One of the first steps a company can take to become more socially responsible is to adopt a code of conduct—but taking this step without clear implementation strategies leaves companies exposed. This book will demonstrate how the world's leading companies are implementing global codes of conduct, including the Global Compact of the United

Nations, the Guidelines for Multinational Enterprises of the Organisation for Economic Co-operation and Development (OECD), SA8000 and AA1000. The codes in this book cover a wide range of issues, including human rights, labour rights, environmental management, corruption and corporate governance. This book also includes 'how-to' (or 'process') codes focusing on reporting, stakeholder engagement and assurance.

Albert Einstein wrote that 'Not everything that counts can be counted; and not everything that can be counted counts.'[1] This sentence provides a useful commentary on codes of conduct and principles and a useful refrain for readers who should question the tools presented in this volume. Do these tools allow an organisation to count and consider what is most relevant in its sector, to its stakeholders? Do the tools count that which does not need to be counted?

The instruments and tools described in this book can be seen as a dialogue between different actors in society. As the book indicates, there have been several waves of dialogue, from the 1970s, in which multinational companies were seen as the enemy to be tamed, to the 1990s where a number of leading companies became far more engaged in a process of dialogue with stakeholders. The codes and principles described in this work have served to institutionalise dialogue and to create fora for discussion among actors who had never been in discussion or between whom there was hostility. It may well be that these dialogues are the most significant contribution of these tools, and yet such contributions cannot be 'counted'.

In this book, I will answer the following questions:

- What distinguishes an outstanding code of conduct from a mediocre code of conduct?
- How can we implement an existing code of conduct?
- What are the pitfalls to avoid in implementing the code of conduct?
- How can we build on work already taking place in this field?

Dr Samuel Johnson once said 'A man may be very sincere in good principles without having good practice' (Boswell 1765: 403); the same is true for companies. At best, codes of conduct and standards can promote corporate responsibility, but they can also be used as a 'fig leaf', as an automatic response to deflect criticism. It is ironic that many of the companies involved in corporate scandals, such as Enron and Royal Ahold, have excellent statements on social policies. If the corporate responsibility movement is to progress, it must shun hollow statements.

This book is based on interviews with the standard-setters, with the implementers of standards, with academics, with activists and with other key stakeholders from around the world. Each of the standards and codes described has been shared with the promulgators of the instrument to ensure that the information is as up to date as possible. To those standards-setters whose standards are not profiled in this

1 This quote was featured on the integrityworks website: www.integrityworks.com/about/about.htm, last accessed 20 April 2010.

book, I apologise. It is possible that further editions of this book will be published with additional codes and standards. I welcome your thoughts on emerging standards that might be useful in such a volume.

Reference

Boswell, J. (1765) *Life of Johnson* (G.B. Hills edn; rev. L.F. Powell; New Haven, CT: Yale University Press [1995]).

Introduction to the second edition

The field of corporate responsibility has changed considerably since the publication of the first edition of *The Corporate Responsibility Code Book* in late 2003. This second edition reflects these changes, with the formation of new initiatives, the improvement of others and the gradual decline of several initiatives that influenced the field.

This second edition includes:

- New initiatives such as the UN Principles for Responsible Investment, the Equator Principles, ISO 26000 and the Extractive Industry Transparency Initiative
- Updated versions of the UN Global Compact and the Global Reporting Initiative
- The addition of codes and principles that have become more relevant, such as the ILO Code of Practice on HIV/AIDS
- The deletion of codes and guidelines that have fallen into disuse, such as the Global Sullivan Principles and SIGMA, despite their impact in the emergence of CR
- The description of linkages between initiatives and the complex web of alliances spawning in the field of CR

A review of the first *Code Book* allows for an analysis of where the vacuums lie within the field. The corporate responsibility field has provided little guidance for companies on how to address health issues within the community and within the workplace. While initiatives such as the ETI and SA8000 provide guidance on how to address health and safety issues, issues of wellness and disease prevention are not addressed in codes and principles for companies. The ILO Code of Practice on HIV/AIDS in the workplace provides orientation on managing diseases in the workplace, and is therefore included in this second edition, even though it dates back to 2001.

The language of CR has evolved considerably since the first publication. Use of the terms 'corporate responsibility' and 'sustainability' has become more common. And the economic crisis of 2008–2009 has heightened awareness about many of the central themes of his book: transparency, sustainability and trust.

As with the first edition of the *Code Book*, this second edition provides a road map for companies to navigate risk and complexity.

Deborah Leipziger
March 2010

Introduction to the Indian edition

The eyes of the world are upon India as it ushers in a new phase of development, assuming a greater role on the global stage. The world's largest democracy, India has a great deal to teach the world about corporate responsibility. 'As Indian companies are going global their stakes in improving social and environmental conditions in their home country have increased. Competitiveness can only be sustained if the enabling environment for doing business improves. Corporate responsibility and the willingness to cooperate is one way of making it happen,' says Georg Kell, Executive Director of the UN Global Compact.

It is very fitting that the first country-specific edition of *The Corporate Responsibility Code Book* is a special edition for India. Crushing poverty and corruption continue to plague India, making the principles and norms in this book relevant and *de rigueur*. India is a crucible in which the initiatives profiled in this book will be tested and put into practice.

This Introduction describes how some of the key initiatives in this book are taking root in India. The UN Global Compact, the Global Reporting Initiative, the Guiding Principles on Business and Human Rights, and Social Accountability 8000 are profiled, and the Tata Index is introduced. Although not in the first or second edition, the Tata Index has a great deal to teach the world.

The UN Global Compact

The UN Global Compact is a global initiative supported by more than 90 national and regional networks. As the world's largest voluntary corporate responsibility (CR) initiative, the Global Compact seeks to advance human rights, labour standards, environmental stewardship and anti-corruption in business. The Indian Global Compact Network (GCN) was launched in 2003 and has nearly 100 members (out of 230 Global Compact signatories in India), including business as well as civil society. It is important to note that the Global Compact is widely seen as consistent with Indian-led initiatives, including those developed by the Ministry of Corporate Affairs. The CSR initiative developed by the Department of Public Enterprises in India includes a reference to the Global Compact.

By participating in the GCN, Indian companies are part of both a national policy debate and of an international platform. The GCN also plays a role in regional meetings of the Global Compact. The Indian network provides its members with capacity building, assisting them in preparing their communication on progress, a key component of membership in the UN Global Compact. GCN members are also encouraged to share examples of best practice. The GCN comprises a diverse group of members, including Tata Global Beverages, Hindustan Unilever and civil society groups such as Transparency International and CARE India. Georg Kell, Executive Director of the UN Global Compact reports that 'over the past decade the network has refined its approaches. It has grown not only in numbers, but has built a strong track record of innovative learning methodology and is now supporting collective action of like-minded participants to tackle corruption. CR is deeply embedded in the culture of many Indian corporations.'

The Global Reporting Initiative

The Global Reporting Initiative (GRI) has pioneered the most widely used sustainability reporting framework, used by thousands of companies around the world. The GRI encourages companies to report on their social and environmental impact and systems, and also works with multinational companies to promote reporting by suppliers, many of whom are small and medium enterprises.

In India, the GRI has created a GRI Focal Point, funded by the German Development Ministry (GIZ). The Focal Point promotes capacity building and also seeks to align the Indian voluntary disclosure framework with the GRI. To date, nearly 50 Indian companies and over 5,000 individuals have been trained in GRI Reporting.

The Guiding Principles for Business and Human Rights

The Guiding Principles for Business and Human Rights are a landmark in the field of corporate responsibility. Developed by Professor John Ruggie, a Special Representative for Business and Human Rights, appointed by the UN Secretary General, the Guiding Principles are one of the newest initiatives in the field. On 16 June 2011, the UN Human Rights Council in Geneva endorsed the Principles after an extensive process of research and consultation lasting six years. Previously known as the Ruggie Framework, the Principles establish a framework known as Protect, Respect and Remedy. States have a duty to protect human rights and the Principles recommend that governments should provide greater clarity on what is expected of business; companies have a duty to respect human rights and must demonstrate that they 'know and show' that they are respecting human rights. Where people are harmed by business activities, there must be access to remedy, including 'adequate accountability and effective redress, judicial and non-judicial'.

The Principles require that companies:

- Develop a human rights policy commitment
- Conduct human rights due diligence to understand the risks they face
- Establish a remediation process when abuses are committed

The Principles are relevant for Indian companies operating in India and around the world and for multinational corporations operating in India.

Social Accountability 8000 (SA8000)

SA8000 is a certification standard that addresses human rights in the workplace, including issues such as child and forced labour, discrimination, health and safety, and other issues. India is the world leader in SA8000 certifications, with 586 facilities certified, covering 380,000 workers. SA8000 training is offered throughout India. Recently, SAI has brought out the Hindi translation of SA8000 to reach out to the SMEs down the supply chain.

In 2010, Social Accountability International (SAI) opened up an office in Bangalore, with funding from the German development organization GIZ, to oversee a public–private partnership between SAI, the Business for Social Compliance Initiative (BSCI) and GIZ. According to SAI Project Director Rishi Singh, 'as India moves forward with its growth and emergence on the world stage, it's important we develop and set the right practices to support and enable human rights. Especially as a democracy, we want to put forth a high degree of responsibility to re-engineer new supply chain systems to support sustainability practices.'

There is a constructive dialogue between SAI, the owner of the SA8000 standard, and public officials and policy-makers in India. In 2002, the Textiles Committee (Ministry of Textiles, Government of India) convened meetings for manufacturers in 26 cities, to support industry certification to SA8000, ISO 14000 and ISO 9000. The Committee provides technical assistance to companies to adopt different standards.

The Tata Index for Sustainable Human Development

Tata has long been an inspiration in its commitment to corporate responsibility principles. Tata has developed the following statement on CR:

Tata Purpose Statement on Corporate Responsibility

1. Serving the Community is the purpose of business.
2. Enhancing human excellence and Improving the Quality of Life is our endeavor.
3. Conserving the Environment, Restoring Biodiversity and Social Development are integrated into one.
4. Core competence, expertise and technology reach the common people, especially the underprivileged.
5. Tata Companies are Partners in Development.
6. The culture of Volunteering is pervasive throughout the Tata Group.
7. Working with People brings Organizational and Personal Learning.
8. Tata Companies and their business process are environmentally and socially sustainable.

According to Anant G Nadkarni, Vice President, Group Corporate Sustainability at TATA,

> Jamsetji Tata, founder of the Tata group believed that the community or people at large are central to the purpose of business and that corporations exist solely for enriching the lives of those connected with the enterprise. It was also believed that wealth gathered by the Tata enterprises should be held in trust exclusively for the people rather than be held by individuals in their name. Large portions of profit went into the Tata Trusts who now hold around sixty six percent ownership in Tata Sons, the apex company of the Tata group. Therefore, all business processes have come under one framework of an integrated business model to ensure that what comes from the people can go back to them to enhance their well being and build trust in the communities in which they operate.

In 2002, Tata partnered with the UN Development Programme (UNDP) to benchmark the contributions of Tata corporations in social and environmental sustainability. The result is the Tata Index for Sustainable Human Development. Launched in 2003, the Tata Index provides a framework or context for understanding how companies can co-create sustainable value.

The Tata Index asks a key question: what is the impact of a company on the community? How can we understand our actions, processes and systems so as to understand our impact on society? How does our impact transform society? In this

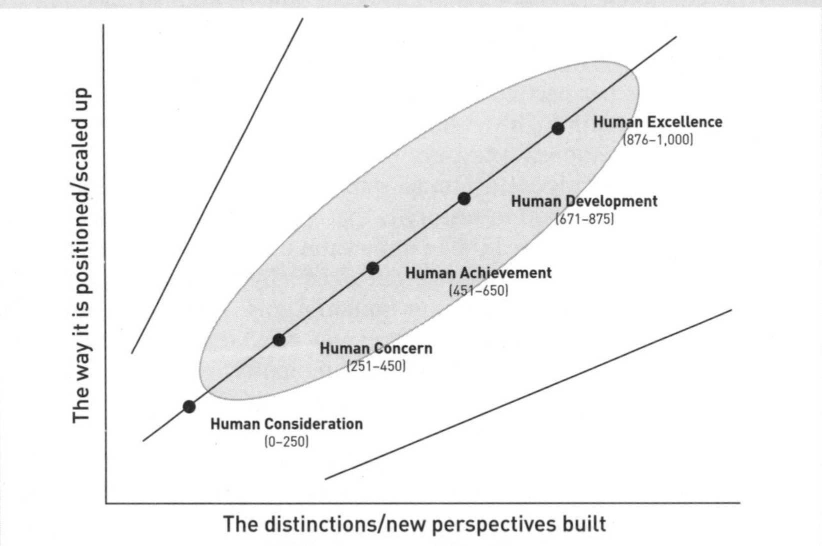

Human Consideration: The company's intervention may be one-off or temporary or represent just an initial phase. People in the community remain marginalised.

Human Concern: In this phase, we begin to see improvement in living conditions among the local community. The company has a commitment to promoting the needs of women and children, or the disabled.

Human Achievement: In this phase there is evidence of collective action. According to a Tata publication: human achievement is characterised by 'conventions, arrangements, systems and processes to progressively improve living conditions'.

Human Development is characterised by 'achievement in terms of income generation, leadership, growth of assets and access to technology'.

Human Excellence is characterised by 'meeting the needs of people first. There are systems of good governance, procedures for maintaining order, arrangements for revisiting and evolving the development agenda, a high degree of maturity in the analysis of information, integration of learning, a high degree of capability for reconciliation and reflection, in resolution of conflict, and towards creating best and world-class practices for leadership in building community.'

Each of these phases is assigned a range of points, the first from 0–250, and increasing in increments up to 1,000, the score for Human Excellence.

> **The Tata Index is a useful mechanism for companies within India and beyond to consider the impact of their standards and actions on the local community. The Index brings together processes and outcomes in a way that can be useful for considering each of the initiatives in this book. The very underpinning of the Tata Index, that sustainability is something that is co-created between a company and the community or society, is a fundamental concept applicable to all CR codes, standards, and initiatives.**

Figure i.1: Tata Program is a Journey towards Human Development

context, the Tata Index provides a framework for understanding codes and standards, a lens with which to understand a company's journey towards corporate responsibility.

Figure i.1 provides perspective on how to understand and map a company's progress towards CR. Although developed by Tata and UNDP, it is relevant for companies and organisations worldwide.

I conclude with the words of the human rights pioneer Mary Robinson: 'One of the great ironies of this period in history is that, just as technology remakes our world, the need to maintain the human dimension of our work, and a company's sense of its social responsibility, is growing at an equally rapid pace. Harmonizing economic growth with the protection of human rights is one of the great challenges we face today. It is a challenge which, if met, can harness the great power of economic growth to the great principle of human dignity.'

In India we see technology, human rights, corporate and public governance, combating corruption and the environment at the forefront of the agenda of many CEOs of major corporations and also, increasingly, for small and medium-sized enterprises and the government. My hope is that *The Corporate Responsibility Code Book* can serve as a map for Indian companies on the journey to becoming more responsible.

Deborah Leipziger
29 July 2011

Executive summary of corporate responsibility initiatives

The following list provides the web addresses at which the code, principle or standard may be found, the part and chapter in which it is discussed in this book, keywords and a brief description of the code, principle or standard.

AA1000 Series: AccountAbility Principles Standard 2008

www.accountability.org

Part X, 'Implementation', Chapter 26, page 444

Keywords Principles • Inclusivity • Materiality • Responsiveness • Accountability • Assurance

The AccountAbility 1000 (AA 1000) Series defines best practice in accountability and assurance. The AA1000 Series consists of: (1) the AA1000 AccountAbility Principles, (2) the AA1000 Assurance Standard and (3) the AA1000 Stakeholder Engagement Standard. Launched in 1999, AA 1000 is designed to assist companies, stakeholders, assurance providers, consultants and standard-setting bodies. The AccountAbility Principles Standard 2008 (AA1000APS) defines key principles in the field of accountability.

AA1000 Assurance Standard

www.accountability.org

Part X, 'Implementation', Chapter 27, page 455

Keywords Assurance • Assurance providers • Accountability • Principles • Competence

The AA1000 Assurance Standard includes core assurance principles, practice and quality standards, guidelines for organisations and qualifications for assurance providers. Developed by AccountAbility, the AA1000 Assurance Standard is compatible with the Global Reporting Initiative.

Business Principles for Countering Bribery

www.sa-intl.org/index.cfm?fuseaction=Page.viewPage&pageID=609

www.transparency.org

Part VI, 'Combating corruption', Chapter 18, page 334

Keywords Bribery • Transparency International • Social Accountability International • Multi-stakeholder • Consultation • Non-governmental organisations • Policies • Procedures • Facilitation payments

Published in December 2002, the Business Principles for Countering Bribery were developed through a multi-stakeholder dialogue, including trade unions, companies, non-governmental organisations (NGOs) and academics from many countries. The convenors of the dialogue are Transparency International and Social Accountability International (SAI). Transparency International was founded in 1993 to build coalitions to fight corruption. Companies are encouraged to apply (rather than adopt) the Business Principles by initiating their own internal process of setting policies and procedures within the company through consultation with stakeholders.

Ceres Principles

www.ceres.org/Page.aspx?pid=416

Part V, 'From environment to sustainability', Chapter 14, page 295

Keywords Multi-stakeholder • Environment • Sustainability • Waste • Energy conservation • Protection of whistle-blowers • Valdez Principles

Founded in 1989, the Coalition for Environmentally Responsible Economies (Ceres) is a network of more than 80 environmental, investor and advocacy groups promoting sustainability. Ceres is best known for the Ceres Principles, a set of ten principles covering the major environmental concerns facing companies, including energy conservation, reduction and disposal of waste, and risk reduction. Companies endorsing the Principles must commit publicly to those Principles, address issues raised by the Ceres network and other stakeholders and report annually on their progress in meeting the Ceres Principles.

EMAS (Eco-Management and Audit Scheme)

http://ec.europa.eu/environment/emas/documents/guidance_en.htm

Part V, 'From environment to sustainability', page 251

Keywords European • Environmental management systems • Training • Accreditation • Verification • Environmental reports

Developed in 2001 by the European Parliament and the Council of the European Union, EMAS is a voluntary initiative that seeks to promote environmental performance by organisations. A systems-based approach, EMAS requires participating organisations to regularly produce a public report on their environmental performance. These reports are verified by an independent verifier. The goal of EMAS is continuous improvement.

EMAS includes the following management systems: policies, planning, training communication, documentation, emergency preparedness, records, audit and management review.

The Equator Principles

www.equator-principles.com

Part IX, 'Framework, sectoral and regional agreements', Chapter 24, page 425

Keywords Social • Environmental assessment • Project financing • Financial Institution

The Equator Principles (EPs) are a set of guidelines for financial institutions which provide a benchmark on social and environmental issues for project financing. Adopted in 2003, by ten international banks, the Equator Principles apply across all sectors and countries, addressing all project financing with capital costs over $10 million. Adopters of the Equator Principles are known as Equator Principles Financial Institutions (EPFIs). Under the Principles, borrowers must conduct a Social and Environmental Assessment of a proposed project. For projects with significant adverse impacts on affected communities, the consultation process will be free, prior and informed. To ensure that consultation, disclosure and community engagement continues throughout construction and operation of the project, the borrower establishes a grievance mechanism to address and resolve community concerns and complaints. The Equator Principles require an independent review of all Category 'A' projects, and, as appropriate, for Category 'B' projects. EPFIs must report to the public annually on their progress in meeting the Principles.

Ethical Trading Initiative: Base Code

www.ethicaltrade.org/eti-base-code

Part III, 'Labour rights', Chapter 10, page 208

Keywords Labour rights • Tripartite • Good practice • Development

The Ethical Trading Initiative (ETI) seeks to improve the lives of workers in global supply chains by creating a forum to identify and promote good practice in the implementation of codes of conduct. The initiative is tripartite, consisting of membership groups from three sectors: companies, NGOs and trade unions. The ETI is funded by the UK government's

Department for International Development and by its members, who pay dues. In pursuit of its aims, the ETI conducts experimental projects into aspects of code implementation, hosts seminars, events and conferences and has a research and publications programme.

Extractive Industry Transparency Initiative

www.eiti.org

Part VI, 'Combating corruption', Chapter 17, page 329

Keywords Transparency • Oil • Gas • Mining • Governments • Validation • Multi-stakeholder • Independent assessment

The EITI has created a global standard for transparency in oil, gas and mining. Through a consultative process with companies, governments and civil society in 2003, the EITI has developed a list of principles that describe how companies and governments can promote transparency. Companies publish what they pay to resource-rich governments in taxes and other payments. Receiving governments then publish what they receive. An independent auditor then compares the two figures. To achieve compliant status, countries must complete an EITI Validation, which is the quality assurance mechanism of the EITI process. The independent assessment reviews the country's progress and delineates which steps need to be taken to improve the process, and makes a recommendation to the EITI Board on whether or not the country has met the requirements for becoming Compliant. A national multi-stakeholder group selects the Independent Validator, according to the EITI Validation Guide.

Fair Labor Association: Workplace Code of Conduct

www.fairlabor.org/about_us_code_conduct_e1.html

Part III, 'Labour rights', Chapter 9, page 200

Keywords Labour rights • Brands • Independent monitoring • Verification

The Fair Labor Association (FLA) is a network of companies, human rights and labour organisations, colleges and universities seeking to improve working conditions. The FLA accredits independent monitors to inspect factories. It works with companies to improve internal monitoring systems. Companies are expected to implement systems to ensure that the FLA Workplace Code of Conduct is upheld throughout their supply chains. The FLA accredits, selects, hires and pays monitors to conduct independent and external monitoring visits in 5% of participating company factories.

Global Compact

www.unglobalcompact.org/AboutTheGC

Part I, 'Global initiatives', Chapter 3, page 76

Keywords UN Secretary-General • Environment • Human rights • Labour • UN agencies • Development • Partnerships • Learning network

The UN Global Compact is an initiative of UN Secretary-General, Kofi Annan, 'to give a human face to globalisation' (Annan 1999). Launched in July 2000, the Compact addresses environment, human rights and workers' rights. The Global Compact unites global principles with local networks. The Compact is a global, multi-stakeholder, multi-issue network with more than 40 regional and national sub-networks. As a voluntary initiative, the Global Compact convenes all key social actors: companies, labour, civil-society organisations and governments.

Global Reporting Initiative

www.globalreporting.org/ReportingFramework/G3Guidelines

Part X, 'Implementation', Chapter 28, page 470

Keywords Sustainability • Guidelines • Reporting • Social reports • Environment • Framework • Indicators • Multi-stakeholder

The Global Reporting Initiative (GRI) has pioneered sustainability reporting guidelines that serve as a framework for economic, social and environmental reporting. The GRI's mission is 'to elevate the quality of reporting to a higher level of comparability, consistency and utility' (GRI 2002: 9). In 1997, Ceres, in collaboration with the Tellus Institute, convened the GRI.

ICC Business Charter for Sustainable Development

www.bsdglobal.com/tools/principles_icc.asp

Part V, 'From environment to sustainability', page 246

Keywords Integrated management • Education • Research • Prior assessment • Precautionary approach • Transfer of technology • Compliance • Reporting • Emergency preparedness

Launched in 1991, the International Chamber of Commerce (ICC) Business Charter was developed by business leaders. The Charter includes 16 principles which focus on how to make the environment a corporate priority. Among the key issues are: integrated management, education, research, prior assessment, precautionary approach, transfer of technology, compliance, reporting and emergency preparedness.

International Labour Organisation: Code of Practice on HIV/AIDS

www.ilo.org/public/english/protection/trav/aids/code/languages/hiv_a4_e.pdf

Part IV, 'Health issues', Chapter 12, page 218

Keywords HIV/AIDS • Gender equality • Social dialogue • Tripartite • Government • Trade unions • Employers

The ILO Code of Practice on HIV/AIDS is a useful tool for companies, governments and trade unions on dealing with HIV/AIDS in the workplace. The Code was developed in partnership between the tripartite bodies of the ILO: employers, employers' organisations and governments. The Code provides guidance to these diverse groups to allow for coherent and integrated implementation. The key principles include: (a) recognising that HIV/AIDS is a workplace issue; (b) non-discrimination in employment; (c) gender equality; (d) screening and confidentiality; (e) social dialogue; and (f) prevention and care and support. In its stated objective, the ILO Code of Practice seeks to prevent HIV/AIDS, manage and mitigate the impact of HIV/AIDS on the world of work, allow for the care of workers infected and affected by HIV/AIDS, and eliminate the stigma and discrimination on the basis of real or perceived HIV status.

International Labour Organisation: Tripartite Declaration of Principles concerning Multinational Enterprises and Social Policy

www.ilo.org/empent/Whatwedo/Publications/lang--en/docName--WCMS_094386/index.htm

Part III, 'Labour rights', Chapter 7, page 165

Keywords Labour rights • Development • Training • International Labour Organisation (ILO) • ILO conventions

Launched in 1977, the Tripartite Declaration of Principles Concerning Multinational Enterprises and Social Policy is directed towards companies, governments, trade unions and employers' organisations. The Declaration refers to 28 ILO conventions and 28 recommendations negotiated within a multilateral frame-work.

ISO 14001

www.iso.org/iso/iso_catalogue/management_standards/iso_9000_iso_14000/iso_14000_essentials.htm

Part X, 'Implementation', Chapter 29, page 491

Keywords Environmental management systems • International Organisation for Standardisation (ISO) • Auditors • Certification • Standard

ISO 14001 is the key element in a family of standards for creating environmental management systems (EMSs). An EMS is 'the part of the overall management system that includes organisational structure, planning activities, responsibilities, practices, procedures, processes and resources for developing, implementing, achieving, reviewing and maintaining the environmental policy'.[1]

The International Organisation for Standardisation (ISO) has developed over 13,000 standards, working with standard-setting bodies in 145 countries. As with all ISO standards, companies that have successfully undergone an ISO 14001 audit by a trained auditor receive an ISO 14001 certificate. Elements of the ISO series—particularly ISO 14001—can also be used internally, without external auditors.

ISO 26000

www.iso.org

Part I, 'Global Initiatives', Chapter 4, page 89

Keywords Governance • Environment • Human rights • Labour practices • Fair operating practices • Consumer issues • Community involvement

The new draft of ISO 26000 provides guidance on the key themes of social responsibility, including governance, environment, human rights, labour practices, fair operating practices, consumer issues, community involvement, and societal development. The standard will be applicable to all organisations wherever they operate. This voluntary Guidance is not meant for use in certification, but rather provides guidance on a wide range of issues. Companies will be able to use ISO 26000 in several ways: first, the guidelines will provide a common language and framework for companies; second, companies can adopt the guidelines or use them to orient their own policies. Third, companies can use the list of issue areas to report on their activities.

Johnson & Johnson Credo

www.jnj.com/connect/about-jnj/jnj-credo

Part VIII, 'Company codes of conduct', Chapter 21, page 397

Keywords Customers • Employees • Communities • Environment • Compensation • Stockholders • Suppliers • Distributors

Written in 1943, the Johnson & Johnson Credo contains the key values of the company, including equal opportunity, environmental protection and quality.

The Credo defines the company's stakeholders, including doctors, nurses, patients, mothers, fathers and other customers, as well as employees, communities, stockholders, suppliers and distributors. The Credo has been translated into 36 languages.

1 www.iso14000.com, accessed 2003.

The Natural Step Principles

www.naturalstep.org/en/usa/principles-sustainability

Part V, 'From environment to sustainability', Chapter 15, page 301

Keywords Sustainability • Environment • Human needs • Systems • Redesign • Sweden • Thermodynamics • Vision • Assessment

The Natural Step Principles were developed by scientists and are based on the laws of thermodynamics.[2] The Principles focus on systems, requiring the organisations working with The Natural Step to redefine their relationship to the environment. The Natural Step provides companies with tools for visioning and assessment and with a framework for action.

Global Agreement between the ICEM and Statoil

www.icem.org/index.php?id=107&la=EN

Part IX, 'Framework, sectoral and regional agreements', Chapter 22, Section 22.6, page 409

Keywords Labour • Human rights • Environment • Trade unions • Global Compact • Global union federation • Petroleum • ILO conventions • Subcontractors

In 1998, Statoil signed an agreement with the Norwegian Oil and Petrochemical Workers' Union (NOPEF) on behalf of the International Federation of Chemical, Energy, Mine and General Workers' Unions (ICEM). The agreement covers labour, human rights and the environment. The goal of the agreement is 'to create an open channel of information between ICEM and Statoil management about industrial relations issues in order to continuously improve and develop good work practice in Statoil's world-wide operations' (Statoil undated). The most significant aspect of the agreement is that it sets a global policy to guide and empower decisions at the local level.

OECD Convention for Combating Bribery of Foreign Officials in International Business Transactions

www.oecd.org/document/21/0,2340,en_2649_34855_2017813_1_1_1_1_,00.html

Part VI, 'Combating corruption', Chapter 16, page 311

Keywords Bribery • Foreign public officials • Criminalise • Facilitation payments • Functional equivalence

Launched in 1997, the OECD Convention on Combating Bribery is a landmark agreement, defining key terms and developing a legal framework for addressing bribery. The Convention has been ratified by all 30 members of the OECD and by a growing number of non-members as well. The Convention applies to bribery of foreign government officials anywhere, regardless of where the incident takes place.

2 For more on the history of The Natural Step, see Robèrt 2002.

OECD Guidelines for Multinational Enterprises

www.oecd.org/department/0,2688,en_2649_34889_1_1_1_1_1,00.html

Part I, 'Global initiatives', Chapter 2, page 60

Keywords Environment • Technology • Science • Taxation • Labour rights • National Contact Points

The OECD Guidelines for Multinational Enterprises are among the most comprehensive of corporate responsibility (CR) tools, addressing a range of issues unparalleled in any single CR instrument. The Guidelines address science, technology and taxation—issues that are not common denominators among CR tools. Given their comprehensive nature, the Guidelines are useful in setting a context for companies on CR. In a sense, they provide for companies a map of the CR issues they may encounter.

OECD Principles of Corporate Governance

www.oecd.org/dataoecd/32/18/31557724.pdf

Part VII, 'Corporate governance', Chapter 19, page 376

Keywords Shareholders • Stakeholders • Disclosure • Transparency • Board of directors • Corporate governance

Endorsed in 1999 by the OECD, and last revised in 2004, the Principles of Corporate Governance represent the first initiative by an intergovernmental organisation to develop guiding principles in the field of corporate governance. The OECD Principles are directed to a wide audience, including governments, companies, investors and business groups.

Principles for Responsible Investment

www.unpri.org

Part IX, 'Framework, sectoral and regional agreements', Chapter 25, page 437

Keywords Investment • Environmental • Social • Governance • Principles • Engagement • Disclosure • Reporting

The Principles for Responsible Investment (PRI) provide a framework for investors on how to incorporate environmental, social and governance (ESG) issues into investment decisions. The goal of the PRI is to affect change throughout the mainstream investment community, not only within the socially responsible investment community. The PRI contains six principles which address a broad range of issues, from implementing environmental, social and governance issues to disclosure and reporting. The PRI uses investment as leverage to drill ESG aims into companies across the board. The aim of the PRI is to promote active engagement among investors. Rather than exclude or divest from socially and environmentally irresponsible companies, the PRI creates opportunities for engagement across a wide range of investment categories.

Responsible Care®

www.responsiblecare.org/flashpresenation.html

Part IX, 'Framework, sectoral and regional agreements', Chapter 23, Section 23.6.2, page 421

Keywords Chemical industry • Policy • Employee involvement • Experience sharing • Safety • Product stewardship • Resource conservation • Stakeholder engagement • Management systems • Self-assessment

The chemical industry's voluntary initiative, Responsible Care, was first conceived in Canada in 1985 to address public concern about the manufacture, distribution and use of chemicals. Since 1992, when Agenda 21 was adopted, the number of national chemical industry associations embracing the initiative has grown from 6 to 53. Under Responsible Care, the worldwide chemical industry is committed to continual improvement in all aspects of health, safety and environmental performance and to open communication about its activities and achievements.

Rio Declaration on Environment and Development

www.un.org/documents/ga/conf151/aconf15126-1annex1.htm

Part V, 'From environment to sustainability', Chapter 13, page 287

Keywords Sustainable development • Poverty • Sovereignty • Technology transfer • Compensation • Precautionary principle • Environmental impact assessment • Women • Youth • Indigenous peoples

In 1992 the Earth Summit (UN Conference on Environment and Development [UNCED]) was held in Rio de Janeiro, where heads of state adopted the Rio Declaration. The Rio Principles enshrined in the declaration define the right of people to development and gives signatories the responsibility to safeguard the environment for future generations.

Shell Business Principles

www.shell.com/home/content/aboutshell/who_we_are/our_values/sgbp/sgbp_30032008.html

Part VIII, 'Company codes of conduct', Chapter 20, page 390

Keywords Economic principles • Business integrity • Political activities • Health, safety and environment • Community • Competition • Stakeholders

First published in 1976, but since amended, Shell's Business Principles cover a very wide range of issues, including economic principles, business integrity, political activities, health, safety, environment, community and competition. One of the most significant aspects of the Principles is the section on 'responsibilities', in which Shell identifies its five key stakeholders: shareholders, customers, employees, those with whom they do business and society.

Social Accountability 8000

www.sa-intl.org/index.cfm?pageId=937

Part III, 'Labour rights', Chapter 8, page 183

Keywords Labour rights • Accreditation • Certification • Management systems • Multi-sectoral • Multi-stakeholder

Social Accountability 8000 (SA8000) is a global and verifiable standard designed to make workplaces more humane. The standard combines key elements of the International Labour Organisation (ILO) conventions with the management systems of ISO. SA8000 is a certification standard developed, overseen and updated through multi-stakeholder dialogue with trade unions, companies, NGOs and academics.

Universal Declaration of Human Rights

www.un.org/Overview/rights.html

Part II, 'Human rights', Chapter 5, page 139

Keywords United Nations • Human rights • Foundation standard • Slavery • Freedom of opinion • Freedom of expression

The Universal Declaration of Human Rights (UDHR) is one of the most significant documents ever drafted. It enshrines the concept of human rights broadly, to include not only political rights but also social and economic rights. Universally accepted, the UDHR has formed the basis of many constitutions around the world. Moreover, the UDHR is cited in many of the corporate responsibility codes and principles contained in this book as a foundation standard. Adopted by the UN General Assembly in 1948, the UDHR was unanimously adopted by the then 48 member states of the United Nations.

Voluntary Principles on Security and Human Rights

www.state.gov/www/global/human_rights/001220_fsdrl_principles.html

Part II, 'Human rights', Chapter 6, page 149

Keywords Governments • Extractive sector • Private security forces • Non-governmental organisations • Human rights

The Voluntary Principles on Security and Human Rights represent an unprecedented step in the field of corporate responsibility. Convened by the US and UK governments, a consensus was reached by NGOs, companies and a trade union on principles in the difficult area of human rights and security in the extractive sector (i.e. in the mining and petroleum sector). The agreement sets an important precedent for other sectoral discussions. First released in December 2000, the agreement is noteworthy because it was convened by governments and included key stakeholders.

References

Annan, K. (1999) Speech made by the UN Secretary-General, Kofi Annan, at the World Economic Forum in Davos, Switzerland, on 31 January 1999 (www.un.org/News/Press/docs/1999/19990201.sgsm6881.html).

GRI (Global Reporting Initiative) (2002) *Sustainability Reporting Guidelines* (Boston, MA: GRI).

Robèrt, K.-H. (2002) *The Natural Step Story: Seeding a Quiet Revolution* (Gabriola Island, BC, Canada: New Society Publishers).

Statoil (undated) *The Exchange of Information and the Development of Good Working Practice within Statoil Worldwide Operations* (submission to the Global Compact Learning Forum; Stavanger, Norway: Statoil).

1 Values, principles, norms, codes and standards

Corporate social responsibility is a journey, and codes and standards can serve as a map to guide companies towards greater transparency and accountability. Statements of values and principles serve as a magnetic north for companies, orienting companies in times of crisis as well as through times of opportunity.[1] Such tools are not an end in themselves, but a beginning. Creation of a code of conduct without implementation is a dangerous pursuit, raising expectations among company stakeholders, such as consumers, investors, employees and local communities. A statement of values or principles or the creation of a code or standard represents the proverbial line in the sand for a company, a call to action.

In this book, a wide range of voluntary corporate responsibility (CR) instruments are examined, including:

- Principles
- Codes of conduct
- Standards
- Norms
- Guidelines
- Framework agreements

There are many other types of CR instruments, including labelling initiatives, stakeholder dialogue and so on, but in this book we look at documents that guide behaviour.

1 I am grateful to Mark Wade, of Shell, for this metaphor, which he credits to the World Business Council for Sustainable Development.

1.1 Definitions

In corporate responsibility, there is a continuum from values, through principles and codes, to standards (see Fig. 1; Box 1.1): it is necessary to delineate values and principles before articulating codes and standards.

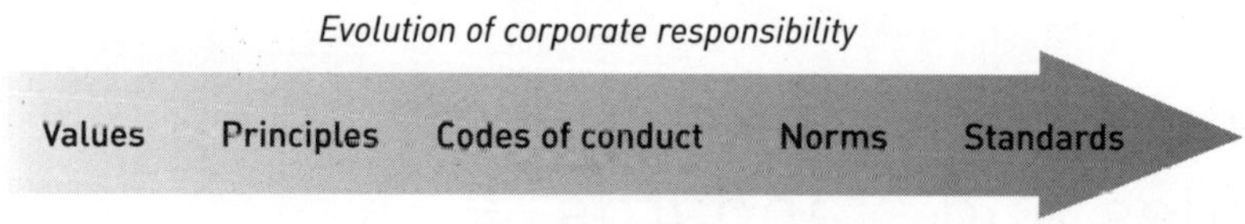

Figure 1.1 **The corporate responsibility continuum**

- ***Value:*** 'any object or quality desirable as a means or as an end in itself' (*American College Dictionary* 1970); for example: corporate responsibility values include diversity and honesty
- ***Principle:*** 'fundamental truth or law as the basis of reasoning or action; a personal code of conduct' (*Concise Oxford Dictionary* 1995).
- ***Code of conduct:*** 'a set of rules' (*Concise Oxford Dictionary* 1995) or a 'formal statement of the values and business practices of a corporation. A code may be a short mission statement, or it may be a sophisticated document that requires compliance with articulated standards and have a complicated enforcement mechanism' (www.codesofconduct.org, accessed 2003).
- ***Norm:*** 'model or pattern' (*American College Dictionary* 1970); norms tend to be internationally agreed.
- ***Standard:*** 'an authoritative model or measure, a pattern for guidance, by comparison with which the quality, excellence, correctness, etc. of other things [e.g. the corporate responsibility of a company] may be determined' (*American College Dictionary* 1970); or 'a set of principles, code of conduct or process system established by a third party whereby adoption of that standard leads to a prescribed level of performance being achieved' (Smith 2002: 21).

Box 1.1 **The corporate responsibility continuum: definitions**

Codes and standards differ in several ways. A code of conduct is specific to a firm or industry, whereas a standard is applicable across a wide range of sectors and geographic regions. Another major difference is the degree to which monitoring, auditing and reporting occur in companies adhering to codes and in those adopting standards. A code of conduct is generally subject only to internal scrutiny by the company, whereas companies adhering to standards are accountable to a broader constituency. According to Shareen Hertel of Columbia University, who has studied workers' rights in Mexico and Bangladesh, 'with standards, governments, firms and civil society can institutionalise the standard, as it is amenable to varying governance and implementation frameworks'.[2] A standard generally includes some form of consensus forged among different stakeholders. In this analysis, codes and standards are voluntary (for a comparison of codes and standards, see Table 1.1).

Code of conduct	***Standard***
Internal or firm-specific	Applied broadly, across geographic regions and/or sectors
Entails limited accountability	Entails greater accountability (i.e. in terms of reporting and scrutiny)
Requires internal consensus and possibly some external consultation	Requires some degree of consensus among stakeholders, and, therefore, is more accountable

Table 1.1 **A comparison of codes of conduct and standards**

Although the term 'standard' is used frequently in the field of corporate responsibility, a better term might be 'norm'. In its technical definition, the term 'standard' implies that companies can and should achieve a uniform output. For example, there are standards that specify the gauge for train tracks to ensure uniformity. Given the significant differences between companies, arising from sectoral, regional, cultural and historical differences, it is unlikely that standardisation is possible or even desirable. According to Gemma Crijns of Nyenrode University, the majority of the so-called CR standards are, in fact, a series of norms.[3] The ability of norms to catalyse and encourage different approaches among companies is a theme of this book and a challenge for the field of corporate responsibility.

1.2 Categories of codes and standards

Given that the definitions of codes and standards are often vague and blurred, one of the best ways to define codes is to categorise them (see Fig. 1.2). It is important to note that, throughout this book, codes and standards may fall into more than

2 Interview with Shareen Hertel, Columbia University, New York, 8 January 2003.
3 Gemma Crijns, Nyenrode University, Breukelen, The Netherlands, communication with the author, 2003.

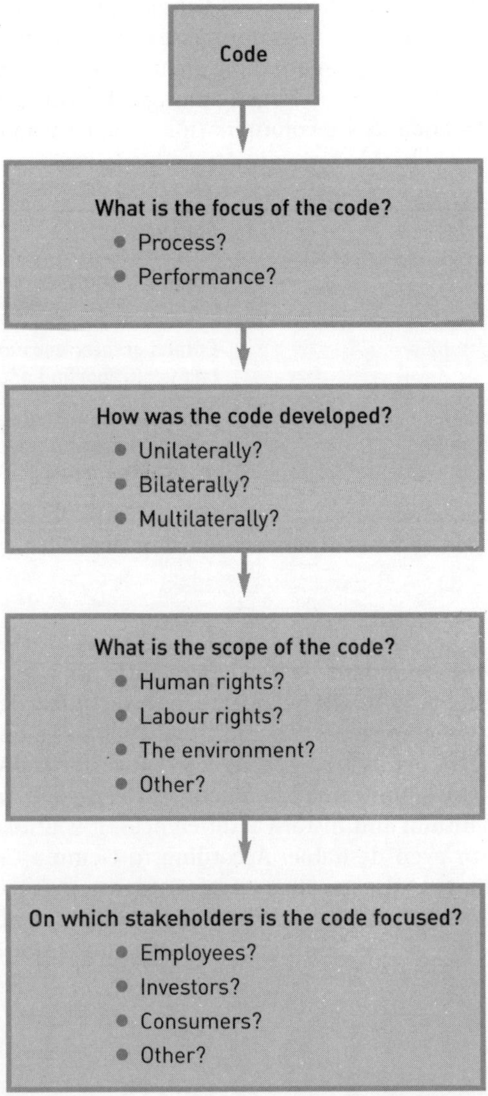

Figure 1.2 **Classification of codes**

one category, given their complexity and cross-cutting nature. Codes and standards can be distinguished by:

- Their focus or purpose (i.e. whether they are focused on process and/or performance)
- The way in which they were developed (i.e. unilaterally, bilaterally or multilaterally)
- Their scope (i.e. whether they cover human rights, labour and/or environment)
- Their stakeholder focus (i.e. whether they are focused on employees, investors, consumers and so on, or whether they are multi-stakeholder tools)

These different types of category are important in comparing codes and standards, in gaining an understanding of how codes complement one another and in determining which may be considered as competitive.

1.2.1 Classification by focus

CR codes and standards can be divided into two key categories—those that focus on performance (or outcome) and those that focus on process (or method) (see Fig. 1.3):

- **Performance-oriented codes** define minimum standards of what constitutes socially responsible behaviour. For example, companies should prohibit child labour and discrimination. Among the key performance instruments are the OECD Guidelines for Multinational Enterprises (also a foundation standard) and the Global Compact. These tools relate to the focus of corporate responsibility and the desired outcomes that companies are working towards.
- **Process-oriented standards and guidelines** define the procedures a company should follow, such as social reporting and stakeholder consultation. Among the key examples of process-oriented tools are the Global Reporting Initiative (GRI), the AccountAbility 1000 series (AA1000) and ISO 14001. These instruments relate to the 'how' of corporate social responsibility.

However, it is important to note that these categories are not mutually exclusive. Some standards, such as Social Accountability (SA8000), may include both process and performance requirements (see the area of overlap between the two circles in Fig. 1.3).

Among the process-oriented and performance-oriented, some standards may be regarded as being foundation and/or certification standards:

- **Foundation standards** lay the groundwork for a new field, defining best practice in an emerging area. The various ILO conventions and the OECD

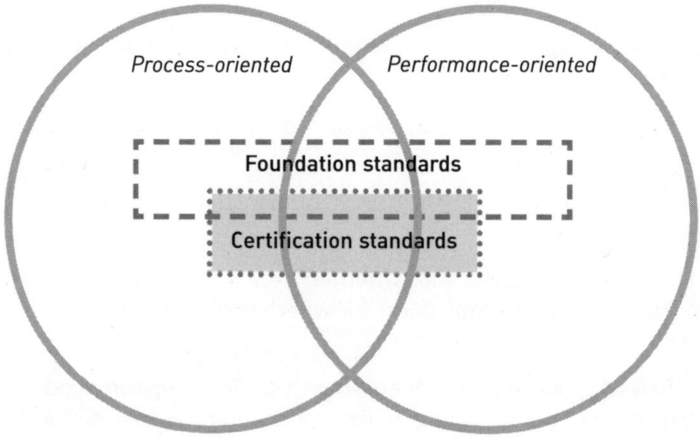

Figure 1.3 **Classification of codes, standards and guidelines according to focus**

Guidelines for Multinational Enterprises are examples of foundation standards.

- **Certification standards** are systems that award a certificate to organisations that comply with certain criteria and that pass an external and independent audit. SA8000 and ISO 14001 are examples of certification standards.

In this book, the discussions of codes and standards will utilise this terminology.

1.2.2 Classification by method of development

As illustrated in Figure 1.2, codes, standards and guidelines may be classified according to the way in which they have been crafted:

- **Unilateral codes** are developed by a company. Usually, there is some level of dialogue with key stakeholders, but the company has ultimate responsibility for the code. These 'branded' codes include Nike's Code of Conduct[4] and the Shell Business Principles (Chapter 20).
- **Bilateral codes** are signed between two parties. A framework agreement between a trade union and a company is an example of a bilateral code.

4 www.nikebiz.com/responsibility/documents/Nike_Code_of_Conduct.pdf

The Ikea Framework Agreement (see page 408) and the Inditex Framework Agreement are examples.

- **Multilateral or multi-stakeholder codes** are developed by a network of organisations through extensive negotiations. Examples are SA8000 and the Ethical Trading Initiative Base Code.

With regard to multilateral codes, according to the World Bank (2003: 12):

> Multi-stakeholder initiatives are efforts that bring diverse stakeholders together around a set of agreed principles in the area of labour, human rights or the environment. These initiatives vary in their mission, some focusing on shared learning around best practice and others with more focused monitoring or certification programmes.

1.2.3 Classification by scope

Corporate responsibility includes a very wide range of issues; however, most CR initiatives address only a portion of them. The following provides a listing of some of the key issues in CR, with a sample of the tools that address them:

Corporate governance

- OECD Principles of Corporate Governance

Combating bribery

- OECD Convention on Countering Bribery
- Business Principles for Countering Bribery

Environment

- Ceres Principles
- The Natural Step

Labour

- ILO Tripartite Declaration of Principles Concerning Multinational Enterprises and Social Policy
- Social Accountability 8000

Human rights

- Universal Declaration of Human Rights

Health

- ILO Code of Practice on HIV/AIDS and the World of Work

1.2.4 Classification by stakeholder focus

Different standards and codes are targeted at different groups of stakeholders. Most of the initiatives addressed in this book focus on employees and suppliers. However, companies can choose to apply a code or norm among one group of stakeholders but not others. For example, a company may implement a code of conduct in its supply chain but not in its own facilities

The following is a partial listing of the diversity of stakeholders referenced within the key tools presented within this book:

Employees

- SA8000
- Shell's Business Principles
- Johnson & Johnson Credo
- ILO Code of Practice on HIV/AIDS and the World of Work

Suppliers

- SA8000
- Workplace Code of Conduct of the Fair Labor Association
- Base Code of the Ethical Trading Initiative
- Model Code of the Clean Clothes Campaign

Customers

- Shell's Business Principles
- Johnson & Johnson Credo

Trade unions

- SA8000
- Global Agreement between ICEM and Statoil
- Workplace Code of Conduct of the Fair Labor Association
- Base Code of the Ethical Trading Initiative
- Model Code of the Clean Clothes Campaign

Governments

- OECD Convention on Countering Bribery
- Business Principles for Countering Bribery
- ILO Code of Practice on HIV/AIDS and the World of Work

- Extractive Industries Transparency Initiative
- ISO 26000

Society/community

- Shell's Business Principles
- Global Reporting Initiative
- Johnson & Johnson Credo
- Equator Principles
- ISO 26000

Shareholders

- Shell's Business Principles
- Johnson & Johnson Credo

1.2.5 Classification by sector

Different sectors face different types of issues, constraints and pressure from stakeholders. As a result, many industries are developing sectoral initiatives; for example, the Voluntary Principles on Security and Human Rights were developed by the extractive sector in a multi-stakeholder setting (see Chapter 6). Responsible Care® addresses the CR issues within the chemical industry (see Chapter 23, Section 23.6.2).

1.2.6 Classification by region

There are some CR tools developed for and within a regional context. One example is the Asia–Pacific Economic Co-operation Code of Business Conduct (see Chapter 23, Section 23.7). While these initiatives can be useful in galvanising support from a region, global tools, because of their universality, tend to be more useful in a globalised world.

1.3 How can codes of conduct help companies?

Codes and guidelines can serve different goals, in the short, medium and long term. In the short term, codes can assist with crisis management; in the medium term, codes can prevent a crisis; in the long term, a code that is effectively implemented can enhance stakeholder (including shareholder) value, promote trust, enhance business performance and help to forestall crises.[5]

An effective code of conduct or standard can:

5 Interview with Shareen Hertel, Columbia University, New York, 8 January 2003.

- Raise awareness about corporate responsibility within the company
- Help companies to set strategies and objectives
- Assist companies with implementation and control of values
- Help companies avoid risk
- Foster dialogue and partnerships between companies and key stakeholders
- Enhance unity and identity among divergent companies

1.3.1 Raising awareness of corporate responsibility

A code of conduct can raise consciousness about corporate responsibility within a company, serving as an important signal to employees, investors and consumers.[6] Codes are essential for communicating consistently with employees, in that codes clarify expectations,[7] especially on bribery and corruption issues. According to John Elkington, founder of SustainAbility, codes can make organisations 'pay attention and think. They can legitimise new demands that would otherwise be dismissed, and help codify and simplify complex issues whose very complexity is an alibi for inaction'.[8]

Most companies use their websites to communicate their values, principles and codes. Like an outstanding CR policy, a well-implemented code of conduct can serve to differentiate a company in a crowded marketplace.

1.3.2 Setting strategies and objectives

A code of conduct or standard can assist a company in managing change in a highly complex business environment. Companies such as Aviva[9] in the United Kingdom are looking to their business principles to guide them in creating social and environmental goals and objectives.

1.3.3 Assisting with implementation and control

Codes of conduct and standards oriented towards process contain useful guides for implementing and controlling social and environmental standards. SA8000 provides useful management systems which are helpful in implementing codes and social standards, including 'training programmes, communications, elected representatives, management representatives with adequate budgets, clear lines of authority, management reviews, control of suppliers, and planning as well as policies, procedures, forms, checklists for recording compliance with each portion

6 Part X provides more information on effective tools for raising awareness.
7 Interview with Hilary Sutcliffe, Director of Shared View Social Responsibility, 17 January 2003
8 Interview with John Elkington, SustainAbility, 2 February 2003.
9 www.aviva.com/responsibility/index.htm

of the standard. By integrating SA8000 into these systems, SA8000 becomes part of the culture of the company' (Leipziger 2001: 59). Among the process tools discussed in this book are: AA1000, the Global Reporting Initiative and ISO 14001.

1.3.4 Avoiding risk

Codes can assist a company in limiting its risk of being caught in a scandal, but only if the code is well implemented. An code that is no more than ornamental can actually increase risk. In the words of Geoffrey Chandler, formerly with Shell and Amnesty International's Business Group:

> Genuine codes, genuinely implemented, reduce risk in today's critical world. A code that is no more than a public relations front increases risk because its fraudulence will readily be exposed. Companies complain that when they proclaim what they are trying to do in terms of principles they are more vigorously scrutinised to see if they live up to them. Well that's life. If they don't want scrutiny, try hiding and see what that leads to. If their actions stand up to scrutiny they will gain greatly in terms of reputation.[10]

1.3.5 Fostering dialogue and partnerships with key stakeholders

One of the most valuable aspects of developing a code of conduct concerns the dialogue and consultations with trade unions, non-governmental organisations (NGOs) and employees that may occur in such a process. Opening up the channels of communication is a valuable by-product of code development. This type of sustained dialogue between a company and its stakeholders is essential for developing trust. According to Shareen Hertel, 'a code can assist a company in building an invaluable reservoir of goodwill'.[11]

1.3.6 Enhancing unity and identity among divergent companies

In a global world, principles and values can contribute to a company's brand and corporate culture. For example, Nokia states that:

> the values and principles incorporated into the Nokia Way are at the very heart of our distinctive culture—and they unite our whole company, across the world (www.nokia.com).

The Nokia Values include customer satisfaction, respect for the individual, achievement and continuous learning.

For multinational companies with global operations, the setting of values,

10 Interview with Geoffrey Chandler, 8 January 2003.

11 Interview with Shareen Hertel, Columbia University, New York, 8 January 2003.

principles and codes can be a mechanism for building a common, shared, sense of identity within the company.

Holcim, one of the world's largest cement companies, has operations in over 70 countries. Holcim management viewed the development of a code of conduct to implement its CR policy as an opportunity to build bridges between its far-flung operations at a time when the company was re-branding from Holderbank to Holcim (www.holcim.com).

1.4 The DNA of an outstanding code of conduct or standard

An outstanding code of conduct or standard has several characteristics:

- It is clear and concise, not complex.
- It is flexible and dynamic.
- It must be written with implementation in mind.
- It should reference key standards.
- It should elicit strong support from stakeholders.
- It should contain mechanisms for addressing complaints and resolving disputes.
- It should be based on a genuine desire to change.

1.4.1 Clarity and conciseness

An outstanding code does not seek to do too much. Clear and concise, it provides definitions for key terms. Clarity is one of the key variables, as the people tasked with implementing the code in a factory itself may not have a formal education. Clarity is essential for successful implementation of a code, as people will often see what they want to see in it. (This is also why companies need to invest in high-quality translations of codes into local languages, as is the case with Shell's Business Principles, which are now available in 51 languages, covering the first languages of 99% of its employees.[12])

1.4.2 Flexibility and dynamism

CR instruments need to be flexible and responsive. Thus, it is important not only that there be revisions to codes and standards but that the revisions do not occur too frequently. An outstanding code will promote innovation and 'breakthrough

12 Personal communication with Mark Wade, Shell.

approaches'[13] in the workplace, and, as such, it too must be open to change. Flexibility need not be interpreted only in terms of changes to the standard itself; sometimes, highlighting issues in training or in guidance materials is a useful substitute to altering the standard (for more on training, see Part X).

1.4.3 Written with implementation in mind

A standard should define a clear process for achieving compliance and for demonstrating how this compliance is to be achieved.[14] Standard-setters need to develop clear guidance material for people implementing standards. Likewise, a company that sets a code of conduct for its suppliers should also provide guidance and training on implementation. When it comes to standards, 'the devil is in the details'.

1.4.4 Reference to key standards

A code of conduct or standard should benefit from the experience of other standards, including normative standards such as the Universal Declaration of Human Rights and specific conventions of the International Labour Organisation. Standards do not occur in a vacuum.

1.4.5 Stakeholder support

Stakeholders need to be involved in the development of the code. Stakeholder participation is necessary not only to make the code or standard more legitimate but also to enhance its implementation. Stakeholders need to feel a sense of ownership of the code and its success.

According to Jane Nelson of the International Business Leaders' Forum, a strong code or standard must involve the private sector in its development.[15]

1.4.6 Complaints and dispute resolution

Disputes will arise in most CR systems, given different cultures and different interpretations of CR instruments. The existence of disputes may be an indicator that the system is in fact being taken seriously by stakeholders. Complaints may constitute important feedback for the system and can signal a need to address issues differently. However, few standards and codes contain formal, written procedures for addressing complaints or for resolving disputes.

An effective system for handling problems can avoid negative publicity, which can seriously threaten an emerging standard.

13 I am indebted to John Elkington for this useful phrase.

14 Interview with Deborah Smith, EQ Management Ltd, Shoreham Beach, West Sussex, UK, 14 January 2003.

15 Interview with Jane Nelson, International Business Leaders' Forum, London, 11 April 2003.

1.4.7 Desire to change

An outstanding code or standard is not enough in itself to make a difference. The key variable for a successful implementation process is the desire of the company to change. According to human rights expert Rory Sullivan:

> It is not the code itself that determines success. The key variable is the commitment of the company to change. If the company wants to be leading-edge a code can help it to achieve leading-edge results. If a company is just adopting a code in order to quell the concerns of the press or a pressure group, then the results will be mediocre.[16]

1.5 Bringing a code of conduct or guidelines to life

To bring a code of conduct to life there is a need to:

- Train to raise awareness
- Gain strong support at a senior level
- Provide text in appropriate translations
- Provide incentives to implement the code or guidelines

1.5.1 Training to raise awareness

Training is necessary at all levels in implementing a code or guidelines. Workers, managers, auditors and suppliers will all benefit from training. Training creates a supporting scaffold for change.

1.5.2 Strong support from senior leadership

In order to succeed, codes and principles must have the support of the chief executive officer (CEO) and/or the board of directors. CR initiatives that emerge from external or public relations are of questionable value. Because of this, Responsible Care and the Global Compact require a letter of personal commitment from the CEO.

1.5.3 Translation of text

In order to be effective, codes need to be accessible to stakeholders. Companies, standard-setters and governments need to invest in translating codes and stan-

16 Interview with Rory Sullivan, Director of Investor Responsibility, Insight Investment (Member of the Amnesty International Business Group, United Kingdom), London, 21 January 2003.

dards into key languages. In some cases, workers may be illiterate. Some companies, such as Chiquita, have developed easy-to-understand versions of their codes, with cartoon drawings that explain issues to workers with little formal education.[17]

1.5.4 Incentives

Incentives are critical. Incentives to embed CR policies include factoring CR goals into a manager's performance evaluation and use of CR performance as a criteria for bonuses and wage rises. These types of incentives send a powerful signal that the company is changing.

1.6 Guidelines for reviewing corporate responsibility tools

The following chapters of this book contain the text of 34 CR instruments. In analysing these codes and standards, there are several factors to consider:

- The origins
- The date
- The focus
- The signatories

1.6.1 The origins

The nature of the organisation (or organisations) that developed or launched the code is a very important consideration. Foremost among these considerations is the type of organisation. For example, an employers' organisation will have to satisfy a wide range of companies, which can result in a watered-down code that meets the lowest common denominator. Yet such standards developed through a multi-stakeholder process will demonstrate that consensus has been reached.

1.6.2 The date

There are several waves of codes. Codes and standards dating from the 1970s were developed at a time when multinational corporations were 'under fire', in part for their activities in countries such as Chile and South Africa. The OECD Guidelines and the ILO Tripartite Declaration were greatly influenced by the era in which they were developed.

17 www.chiquita.com, accessed 2003

1.6.3 The focus

We need to look at who is at the centre of the code. Employees? Customers? Investors? Stakeholders in general? The driving forces behind the code are very important factors in understanding the DNA of a code.

1.6.4 Signatories

Here, we need to look at whether the standard has reached a critical mass and what the signatories reveal about the standard. For example, are all of the signatories located in certain regions or specific sectors? Are the companies at risk in some way?

* * *

In the following chapters, readers will encounter 34 sets of principles, codes, standards, norms and other initiatives. While they are all different, they represent important markers on the journey to make companies responsible.

References

American College Dictionary (1970) *The American College Dictionary* (New York: Random House).

Concise Oxford Dictionary (1995) *The Concise Oxford Dictionary* (Oxford, UK: Clarendon Press, 9th edn).

Leipziger, D. (2001) *SA8000: The Definitive Guide to the New Social Standard* (London: FT).

Smith, D. (2002) *Demonstrating Corporate Values: Which Standard for your Company?* (London: Institute of Business Ethics).

World Bank (2003) *Terms of Reference: Study of Options for Strengthening CSR Implementation among Suppliers in Global Supply Chains* (Washington, DC: World Bank Group, 25 March 2003).

Part I
Global initiatives

This part covers global principles that are being adopted around the world and that address a wide range of issues. These principles serve as a useful framework for companies on some of the major issues within the field of corporate responsibility.

The major global initiatives examined in this part are, in the order in which they were launched:

- OECD Guidelines for Multinational Enterprises
- UN Global Compact
- ISO 26000

The Millennium Development Goals are also included at the end of Chapter 3 as a reference to the UN Global Compact.

A number of other initiatives have developed a global following, including the AccountAbility 1000 series (AA1000), Social Accountability 8000 (SA8000), ISO 14001, the Global Reporting Initiative (GRI) and others. These initiatives will be addressed in subsequent parts of the book, either by issue area or by focus (SA8000 can be found in Chapter 8, in Part III, on labour rights; AA1000, the GRI, and ISO 14001 can be found in Chapters 26, 28 and 29, respectively, in Part X, on process standards [implementation]).

2
The OECD Guidelines for Multinational Enterprises

This is the value added of the Guidelines for all: for enterprises as a useful point of reference, for stakeholders as a high quality vehicle for dialogue, and for developing countries as a partnership and co-operation-building instrument.

Corrine Dreyfus, European Commission[1]

The basic approach of the Guidelines is that internationally agreed guidelines can help to prevent misunderstandings and build an atmosphere of confidence and predictability between business, labour, and governments.

OECD[2]

Type Foundation and performance standard

Strength Comprehensiveness

Keywords Environment • Technology • Science • Taxation • Labour rights • National contact points

2.1 Background

The OECD Guidelines for Multinational Enterprises (hereinafter referred to as the Guidelines), part of the OECD Declaration on International Investment and Multinational Enterprises (OECD 2000), feature recommendations from governments to

1 Dreyfus 2001: 120.
2 OECD 2002.

companies. Unique among corporate responsibility (CR) tools in its comprehensive nature, the set of Guidelines addresses all aspects of corporate behaviour, from taxation and competition to consumer interests and science and technology. The Guidelines are voluntary and non-binding.

To understand the objectives of the Guidelines, it is necessary to review the role of the OECD. The Organisation for Economic Co-operation and Development (OECD) promotes policies that contribute to economic growth and development. Founded in 1961, the OECD is a membership organisation for governments from 30 countries.[3] The OECD has made a significant contribution to corporate social responsibility by developing several CR-related principles, including the OECD Principles of Corporate Governance (see Part VII, Chapter 19) and the OECD Convention on Combating Bribery of Foreign Public Officials in International Business Transactions (see Part VI, Chapter 16).

The objectives of the Guidelines are (see page 65):

1. To ensure that the operations of these enterprises are in harmony with government policies
2. To strengthen the basis of mutual confidence between enterprises and the societies in which they operate
3. To help improve the foreign investment climate
4. To enhance the contribution to sustainable development made by multinational enterprises

The Guidelines were adopted in 1976; as such they are part of the first wave of CR tools. Since then, the Guidelines have been revised to include sustainable development issues and the core labour standards. The Guidelines provide an important foundation for many codes and standards.

2.2 Strengths and weaknesses

The Guidelines are among the most comprehensive of CR tools, addressing a range of issues unparalleled in any single CR instrument. The Guidelines address science, technology and taxation—issues that are not common denominators among CR tools. Given their comprehensive nature, the Guidelines are useful in setting a context on CR for companies. In a sense, the Guidelines are a map for companies of the CR issues they may encounter.

3 The member countries are, in alphabetical order: Australia, Austria, Belgium, Canada, the Czech Republic, Denmark, Finland, France, Germany, Greece, Hungary, Iceland, Republic of Ireland, Italy, Japan, Korea, Luxembourg, Mexico, The Netherlands, New Zealand, Norway, Poland, Portugal, the Slovak Republic, Spain, Sweden, Switzerland, Turkey, the United Kingdom, and the USA. The European Commission also takes part in the work of the OECD. In addition, Argentina, Brazil and Chile have declared their commitment to the Guidelines but are not OECD members.

The Guidelines encourage companies to 'observe standards of employment and industrial relations not less favourable than those observed by comparable employers in the host country' (see page 71). In many regions, observance of local norms would be insufficient to meet basic standards set by the International Labour Organisation (ILO). The ILO participated in the negotiations and views the Guidelines as being compatible with its own conventions and declarations. The words 'not less favourable' mean that companies are asked to observe the other recommendations on human rights, core labour standards and supply chain codes.

The OECD requires each member state to appoint a National Contact Point (NCP) to promote the Guidelines. The NCP also addresses issues that may arise from the Guidelines, by assessing the problem and assisting the parties to reach an agreement through mediation. The Committee on International Investment and Multinational Enterprises (CIME) reviews the reports of the NCPs.

The institutional capacity of the CIME and the NCPs enhances the potential of the Guidelines to be used effectively. For example, when a major multinational corporation abruptly announced its decision to close its French operations, the French trade union contacted the NCP. According to Corrine Dreyfus of the European Commission,

> The architecture of this follow-up mechanism [NCPs] is unique, especially inasmuch as it involves the public authorities stepping in to promote dialogue and to help find solutions. This architecture is embedded in the commitment of adhering countries (Dreyfus 2001: 120).

Although the NCPs provide local infrastructure to the Guidelines, Anne-Christine Habbard of the International Federation for Human Rights (FIDH) states that the FIDH in France is disappointed in the NCPs' enforcement of the Guidelines (Habbard 2001: 101).

2.3 Companies to which the Guidelines for Multinational Enterprises apply

The Guidelines are a useful starting point and checklist for all companies, but they are especially so for multinational corporations. However, as the Guidelines do not contain management systems, it is best they be used in conjunction with process standards.

2.4 Questions posed and answered

The Guidelines answer the following questions:

- How can multinational corporations operate in harmony with local practice?
- Which common principles for corporate behaviour of multinational corporations will promote sustainable economic growth?

2.5 The promise and the challenge

The revisions to the Guidelines in 2000 re-energised the CIME and the NCPs, making the Guidelines more relevant than ever. However, a great deal of work still needs to be done to make the Guidelines better known. The Polish NCP stated that:

> despite many efforts aimed at making the Guidelines better known by the parties concerned, they are still not widely recognised in Poland as an effective instrument for assuring the appropriate standards of business conduct (quoted in OECD 2001: 17).

In the same OECD report (OECD 2001: 17) it was concluded that 'the same observation would probably be valid for many other adhering countries as well'. In the 'Summary Report of the Chair of the Meeting on the Activities of the NCPs' in the 2002 Annual Report on the Guidelines (OECD 2002) it is suggested that the visibility of the instrument is growing but that much remains to be done to ensure that the Guidelines reach their full potential as a vital tool for the international community and for host societies.

There are signs that more OECD member states are using the Guidelines in new ways. Although it is common for member states to inform investors about the Guidelines, the Dutch government is the first to require companies seeking export credits to take notice of the Guidelines. Also, the French organisation in charge of managing export credits and investment guarantees (COFACE [Compagnie Française pour l'Assurance du Commerce Extérieur] asks companies to sign a letter acknowledging that they are aware of the Guidelines.

References

Dreyfus, C. (2001) 'Enhancing the Contribution of the OECD Guidelines for Multinational Enterprises: Lessons to be Learned', in *OECD Annual Report 2001* (Paris: OECD): 120.

Habbard, A.C. (2001) 'The Integration of Human Rights in Corporate Principles: OECD Guidelines for Multinational Enterprises: Global Instruments for Corporate Responsibility', in *OECD Annual Report 2001* (Paris: OECD): 101.

OECD (Organisation for Economic Co-operation and Development) (2000) *OECD Declaration on International Investment and Multinational Enterprises* (Paris: OECD, 27 June 2000).

—— (2001) 'OECD Guidelines for Multinational Enterprises: Global Instruments for Corporate Responsibility', in *OECD Annual Report 2001* (Paris: OECD): 17.

—— (2002) *OECD Guidelines for Multinational Enterprises: Global Instruments for Corporate Responsibility* (Paris: OECD).

Additional resources

Further reading

OECD (Organisation for Economic Co-operation and Development) (2000) *The OECD Guidelines for Multinational Enterprises: Meeting of the OECD Council at Ministerial Level* (Paris: OECD).

Website

OECD (Organisation for Economic Co-operation and Development): www.oecd.org.

Note: Many National Contact Points have developed handbooks for implementation of the Guidelines. These range from simple to very in-depth guides. For a list of National Contact Points, go to the OECD website.

The OECD Guidelines for Multinational Enterprises*

PART I: THE OECD GUIDELINES FOR MULTINATIONAL ENTERPRISES

Preface

1. The OECD *Guidelines for Multinational Enterprises* (the *Guidelines*) are recommendations addressed by governments to multinational enterprises. They provide voluntary principles and standards for responsible business conduct consistent with applicable laws. The *Guidelines* aim to ensure that the operations of these enterprises are in harmony with government policies, to strengthen the basis of mutual confidence between enterprises and the societies in which they operate, to help improve the foreign investment climate and to enhance the contribution to sustainable development made by multinational enterprises. The *Guidelines* are part of the OECD *Declaration on International Investment and Multinational Enterprises* the other elements of which relate to national treatment, conflicting requirements on enterprises, and international investment incentives and disincentives.

2. International business has experienced far-reaching structural change and the *Guidelines* themselves have evolved to reflect these changes. With the rise of service and knowledge-intensive industries, service and technology enterprises have entered the international marketplace. Large enterprises still account for a major share of international investment, and there is a trend toward large-scale international mergers. At the same time, foreign investment by small- and medium-sized enterprises has also increased and these enterprises now play a significant role on the international scene. Multinational enterprises, like their domestic counterparts, have evolved to encompass a broader range of business arrangements and organisational forms. Strategic alliances and closer relations with suppliers and contractors tend to blur the boundaries of the enterprise.

3. The rapid evolution in the structure of multinational enterprises is also reflected in their operations in the developing world, where foreign direct investment has grown rapidly. In developing countries, multinational enterprises have diversified

* The Preface and the ten guidelines reprinted with permission from *The OECD Guidelines for Multinational Enterprises*, © OECD 1994.

beyond primary production and extractive industries into manufacturing, assembly, domestic market development and services.

4. The activities of multinational enterprises, through international trade and investment, have strengthened and deepened the ties that join OECD economies to each other and to the rest of the world. These activities bring substantial benefits to home and host countries. These benefits accrue when multinational enterprises supply the products and services that consumers want to buy at competitive prices and when they provide fair returns to suppliers of capital. Their trade and investment activities contribute to the efficient use of capital, technology and human and natural resources. They facilitate the transfer of technology among the regions of the world and the development of technologies that reflect local conditions. Through both formal training and on-the-job learning enterprises also promote the development of human capital in host countries.

5. The nature, scope and speed of economic changes have presented new strategic challenges for enterprises and their stakeholders. Multinational enterprises have the opportunity to implement best practice policies for sustainable development that seek to ensure coherence between social, economic and environmental objectives. The ability of multinational enterprises to promote sustainable development is greatly enhanced when trade and investment are conducted in a context of open, competitive and appropriately regulated markets.

6. Many multinational enterprises have demonstrated that respect for high standards of business conduct can enhance growth. Today's competitive forces are intense and multinational enterprises face a variety of legal, social and regulatory settings. In this context, some enterprises may be tempted to neglect appropriate standards and principles of conduct in an attempt to gain undue competitive advantage. Such practices by the few may call into question the reputation of the many and may give rise to public concerns.

7. Many enterprises have responded to these public concerns by developing internal programmes, guidance and management systems that underpin their commitment to good corporate citizenship, good practices and good business and employee conduct. Some of them have called upon consulting, auditing and certification services, contributing to the accumulation of expertise in these areas. These efforts have also promoted social dialogue on what constitutes good business conduct. The *Guidelines* clarify the shared expectations for business conduct of the governments adhering to them and provide a point of reference for enterprises. Thus, the *Guidelines* both complement and reinforce private efforts to define and implement responsible business conduct.

8. Governments are co-operating with each other and with other actors to strengthen the international legal and policy framework in which business is conducted. The post-war period has seen the development of this framework, starting with the adoption in 1948 of the Universal Declaration of Human Rights. Recent instruments include the ILO Declaration on Fundamental Principles and Rights at Work, the Rio Declaration on Environment and Development and Agenda 21 and the Copenhagen Declaration for Social Development.

9. The OECD has also been contributing to the international policy framework. Recent developments include the adoption of the Convention on Combating Bribery of Foreign Public Officials in International Business Transactions and of the OECD Principles of Corporate Governance, the OECD Guidelines for Consumer Protection in the Context of Electronic Commerce, and ongoing work on the OECD Guidelines on Transfer Pricing for Multinational Enterprises and Tax Administrations.

10. The common aim of the governments adhering to the *Guidelines* is to encourage the positive contributions that multinational enterprises can make to economic, environmental and social progress and to minimise the difficulties to which their various operations may give rise. In working towards this goal, governments find themselves in partnership with the many businesses, trade unions and other non-governmental organisations that are working in their own ways toward the same end. Governments can help by providing effective domestic policy frameworks that include stable macroeconomic policy, non-discriminatory treatment of firms, appropriate regulation and prudential supervision, an impartial system of courts and law enforcement and efficient and honest public administration. Governments can also help by maintaining and promoting appropriate standards and policies in support of sustainable development and by engaging in ongoing reforms to ensure that public sector activity is efficient and effective. Governments adhering to the *Guidelines* are committed to continual improvement of both domestic and international policies with a view to improving the welfare and living standards of all people.

I. Concepts and Principles

1. The *Guidelines* are recommendations jointly addressed by governments to multinational enterprises. They provide principles and standards of good practice consistent with applicable laws. Observance of the *Guidelines* by enterprises is voluntary and not legally enforceable.

2. Since the operations of multinational enterprises extend throughout the world, international co-operation in this field should extend to all countries. Governments adhering to the *Guidelines* encourage the enterprises operating on their territories to observe the *Guidelines* wherever they operate, while taking into account the particular circumstances of each host country.

3. A precise definition of multinational enterprises is not required for the purposes of the *Guidelines*. These usually comprise companies or other entities established in more than one country and so linked that they may co-ordinate their operations in various ways. While one or more of these entities may be able to exercise a significant influence over the activities of others, their degree of autonomy within the enterprise may vary widely from one multinational enterprise to another. Ownership may be private, state or mixed. The *Guidelines* are addressed to all the entities within the multinational enterprise (parent companies and/or local entities). According to the actual distribution of responsibilities among them, the different entities are expected to co-operate and to assist one another to facilitate observance of the *Guidelines*.

4. The *Guidelines* are not aimed at introducing differences of treatment between multinational and domestic enterprises; they reflect good practice for all. Accordingly, multinational and domestic enterprises are subject to the same expectations in respect of their conduct wherever the *Guidelines* are relevant to both.

5. Governments wish to encourage the widest possible observance of the *Guidelines*. While it is acknowledged that small- and medium-sized enterprises may not have the same capacities as larger enterprises, governments adhering to the *Guidelines* nevertheless encourage them to observe the *Guidelines* recommendations to the fullest extent possible.

6. Governments adhering to the *Guidelines* should not use them for protectionist purposes nor use them in a way that calls into question the comparative advantage of any country where multinational enterprises invest.

7. Governments have the right to prescribe the conditions under which multinational enterprises operate within their jurisdictions, subject to international law. The entities of a multinational enterprise located in various countries are subject to the laws applicable in these countries. When multinational enterprises are subject to conflicting requirements by adhering countries, the governments concerned will co-operate in good faith with a view to resolving problems that may arise.

8. Governments adhering to the *Guidelines* set them forth with the understanding that they will fulfil their responsibilities to treat enterprises equitably and in accordance with international law and with their contractual obligations.

9. The use of appropriate international dispute settlement mechanisms, including arbitration, is encouraged as a means of facilitating the resolution of legal problems arising between enterprises and host country governments.

10. Governments adhering to the *Guidelines* will promote them and encourage their use. They will establish National Contact Points that promote the *Guidelines* and act as a forum for discussion of all matters relating to the *Guidelines*. The adhering Governments will also participate in appropriate review and consultation procedures to address issues concerning interpretation of the *Guidelines* in a changing world.

II. General Policies

Enterprises should take fully into account established policies in the countries in which they operate, and consider the views of other stakeholders. In this regard, enterprises should:

1. Contribute to economic, social and environmental progress with a view to achieving sustainable development.

2. Respect the human rights of those affected by their activities consistent with the host government's international obligations and commitments.

3. Encourage local capacity building through close co-operation with the local community, including business interests, as well as developing the enterprise's activities in domestic and foreign markets, consistent with the need for sound commercial practice.

4. Encourage human capital formation, in particular by creating employment opportunities and facilitating training opportunities for employees.

5. Refrain from seeking or accepting exemptions not contemplated in the statutory or regulatory framework related to environmental, health, safety, labour, taxation, financial incentives, or other issues.

6. Support and uphold good corporate governance principles and develop and apply good corporate governance practices.

7. Develop and apply effective self-regulatory practices and management systems that foster a relationship of confidence and mutual trust between enterprises and the societies in which they operate.

8. Promote employee awareness of, and compliance with, company policies through appropriate dissemination of these policies, including through training programmes.

9. Refrain from discriminatory or disciplinary action against employees who make bona fide reports to management or, as appropriate, to the competent public authorities, on practices that contravene the law, the *Guidelines* or the enterprise's policies.

10. Encourage, where practicable, business partners, including suppliers and subcontractors, to apply principles of corporate conduct compatible with the *Guidelines*.

11. Abstain from any improper involvement in local political activities.

III. Disclosure

1. Enterprises should ensure that timely, regular, reliable and relevant information is disclosed regarding their activities, structure, financial situation and performance. This information should be disclosed for the enterprise as a whole and, where appropriate, along business lines or geographic areas. Disclosure policies of enterprises should be tailored to the nature, size and location of the enterprise, with due regard taken of costs, business confidentiality and other competitive concerns.

2. Enterprises should apply high quality standards for disclosure, accounting, and audit. Enterprises are also encouraged to apply high quality standards for non-financial information including environmental and social reporting where they exist. The standards or policies under which both financial and non-financial information are compiled and published should be reported.

3. Enterprises should disclose basic information showing their name, location, and structure, the name, address and telephone number of the parent enterprise and

its main affiliates, its percentage ownership, direct and indirect in these affiliates, including shareholdings between them.

4. Enterprises should also disclose material information on:
   a) The financial and operating results of the company.
   b) Company objectives.
   c) Major share ownership and voting right.
   d) Members of the board and key executives, and their remuneration.
   e) Material foreseeable risk factors.
   f) Material issues regarding employees and other stakeholders.
   g) Governance structures and policies.

5. Enterprises are encouraged to communicate additional information that could include:
   a) Value statements or statements of business conduct intended for public disclosure including information on the social, ethical and environmental policies of the enterprise and other codes of conduct to which the company subscribes. In addition, the date of adoption, the countries and entities to which such statements apply and its performance in relation to these statements may be communicated.
   b) Information on systems for managing risks and complying with laws, and on statements or codes of business conduct.
   c) Information on relationships with employees and other stakeholders.

IV. Employment and Industrial Relations

Enterprises should, within the framework of applicable law, regulations and prevailing labour relations and employment practices:

1. a) Respect the right of their employees to be represented by trade unions and other bona fide representatives of employees, and engage in constructive negotiations, either individually or through employers' associations, with such representatives with a view to reaching agreements on employment conditions;
   b) Contribute to the effective abolition of child labour.
   c) Contribute to the elimination of all forms of forced or compulsory labour.
   d) Not discriminate against their employees with respect to employment or occupation on such grounds as race, colour, sex, religion, political opinion, national extraction or social origin, unless selectivity concerning employee characteristics furthers established governmental policies which specifically promote greater equality of employment opportunity or relates to the inherent requirements of a job.

2. a) Provide facilities to employee representatives as may be necessary to assist in the development of effective collective agreements.

b) Provide information to employee representatives which is needed for meaningful negotiations on conditions of employment.

c) Promote consultation and co-operation between employers and employees and their representatives on matters of mutual concern.

3. Provide information to employees and their representatives which enables them to obtain a true and fair view of the performance of the entity or, where appropriate, the enterprise as a whole.

4. a) Observe standards of employment and industrial relations not less favourable than those observed by comparable employers in the host country.

   b) Take adequate steps to ensure occupational health and safety in their operations.

5. In their operations, to the greatest extent practicable, employ local personnel and provide training with a view to improving skill levels, in co-operation with employee representatives and, where appropriate, relevant governmental authorities.

6. In considering changes in their operations which would have major effects upon the livelihood of their employees, in particular in the case of the closure of an entity involving collective lay-offs or dismissals, provide reasonable notice of such changes to representatives of their employees, and, where appropriate, to the relevant governmental authorities, and co-operate with the employee representatives and appropriate governmental authorities so as to mitigate to the maximum extent practicable adverse effects. In light of the specific circumstances of each case, it would be appropriate if management were able to give such notice prior to the final decision being taken. Other means may also be employed to provide meaningful co-operation to mitigate the effects of such decisions.

7. In the context of bona fide negotiations with representatives of employees on conditions of employment, or while employees are exercising a right to organise, not threaten to transfer the whole or part of an operating unit from the country concerned nor transfer employees from the enterprises' component entities in other countries in order to influence unfairly those negotiations or to hinder the exercise of a right to organise.

8. Enable authorised representatives of their employees to negotiate on collective bargaining or labour-management relations issues and allow the parties to consult on matters of mutual concern with representatives of management who are authorised to take decisions on these matters.

V. Environment

Enterprises should, within the framework of laws, regulations and administrative practices in the countries in which they operate, and in consideration of relevant international agreements, principles, objectives, and standards, take due account of the need to protect the environment, public health and safety, and generally to conduct their activities in a manner contributing to the wider goal of sustainable development. In particular, enterprises should:

1. Establish and maintain a system of environmental management appropriate to the enterprise, including:
   a) Collection and evaluation of adequate and timely information regarding the environmental, health, and safety impacts of their activities.
   b) Establishment of measurable objectives and, where appropriate, targets for improved environmental performance, including periodically reviewing the continuing relevance of these objectives; and
   c) Regular monitoring and verification of progress toward environmental, health, and safety objectives or targets.
2. Taking into account concerns about cost, business confidentiality, and the protection of intellectual property rights:
   a) Provide the public and employees with adequate and timely information on the potential environment, health and safety impacts of the activities of the enterprise, which could include reporting on progress in improving environmental performance; and
   b) Engage in adequate and timely communication and consultation with the communities directly affected by the environmental, health and safety policies of the enterprise and by their implementation.
3. Assess, and address in decision-making, the foreseeable environmental, health, and safety-related impacts associated with the processes, goods and services of the enterprise over their full life cycle. Where these proposed activities may have significant environmental, health, or safety impacts, and where they are subject to a decision of a competent authority, prepare an appropriate environmental impact assessment.
4. Consistent with the scientific and technical understanding of the risks, where there are threats of serious damage to the environment, taking also into account human health and safety, not use the lack of full scientific certainty as a reason for postponing cost-effective measures to prevent or minimise such damage.
5. Maintain contingency plans for preventing, mitigating, and controlling serious environmental and health damage from their operations, including accidents and emergencies; and mechanisms for immediate reporting to the competent authorities.
6. Continually seek to improve corporate environmental performance, by encouraging, where appropriate, such activities as:
   a) Adoption of technologies and operating procedures in all parts of the enterprise that reflect standards concerning environmental performance in the best performing part of the enterprise.
   b) Development and provision of products or services that have no undue environmental impacts; are safe in their intended use; are efficient in their consumption of energy and natural resources; can be reused, recycled, or disposed of safely.

c) Promoting higher levels of awareness among customers of the environmental implications of using the products and services of the enterprise; and
d) Research on ways of improving the environmental performance of the enterprise over the longer term.

7. Provide adequate education and training to employees in environmental health and safety matters, including the handling of hazardous materials and the prevention of environmental accidents, as well as more general environmental management areas, such as environmental impact assessment procedures, public relations, and environmental technologies.

8. Contribute to the development of environmentally meaningful and economically efficient public policy, for example, by means of partnerships or initiatives that will enhance environmental awareness and protection.

VI. Combating Bribery

Enterprises should not, directly or indirectly, offer, promise, give, or demand a bribe or other undue advantage to obtain or retain business or other improper advantage. Nor should enterprises be solicited or expected to render a bribe or other undue advantage. In particular, enterprises should:

1. Not offer, nor give in to demands, to pay public officials or the employees of business partners any portion of a contract payment. They should not use subcontracts, purchase orders or consulting agreements as means of channelling payments to public officials, to employees of business partners or to their relatives or business associates.

2. Ensure that remuneration of agents is appropriate and for legitimate services only. Where relevant, a list of agents employed in connection with transactions with public bodies and state-owned enterprises should be kept and made available to competent authorities.

3. Enhance the transparency of their activities in the fight against bribery and extortion. Measures could include making public commitments against bribery and extortion and disclosing the management systems the company has adopted in order to honour these commitments. The enterprise should also foster openness and dialogue with the public so as to promote its awareness of and co-operation with the fight against bribery and extortion.

4. Promote employee awareness of and compliance with company policies against bribery and extortion through appropriate dissemination of these policies and through training programmes and disciplinary procedures.

5. Adopt management control systems that discourage bribery and corrupt practices, and adopt financial and tax accounting and auditing practices that prevent the establishment of "off the books" or secret accounts or the creation of documents which do not properly and fairly record the transactions to which they relate.

6. Not make illegal contributions to candidates for public office or to political parties or to other political organisations. Contributions should fully comply with public disclosure requirements and should be reported to senior management.

VII. Consumer Interests

When dealing with consumers, enterprises should act in accordance with fair business, marketing and advertising practices and should take all reasonable steps to ensure the safety and quality of the goods or services they provide. In particular, they should:

1. Ensure that the goods or services they provide meet all agreed and legally required standards for consumer health and safety, including health warnings and product safety and information labels.
2. As appropriate to the goods or services, provide accurate and clear information regarding their content, safe use, maintenance, storage, and disposal sufficient to enable consumers to make informed decisions.
3. Provide transparent and effective procedures that address consumer complaints and contribute to fair and timely resolution of consumer disputes without undue cost or burden.
4. Not make representations or omissions, nor engage in any other practices, that are deceptive, misleading, fraudulent, or unfair.
5. Respect consumer privacy and provide protection for personal data.
6. Co-operate fully and in a transparent manner with public authorities in the prevention or removal of serious threats to public health and safety deriving from the consumption or use of their products.

VIII. Science and Technology

Enterprises should:

1. Endeavour to ensure that their activities are compatible with the science and technology (S&T) policies and plans of the countries in which they operate and as appropriate contribute to the development of local and national innovative capacity.
2. Adopt, where practicable in the course of their business activities, practices that permit the transfer and rapid diffusion of technologies and know-how, with due regard to the protection of intellectual property rights.
3. When appropriate, perform science and technology development work in host countries to address local market needs, as well as employ host country personnel in an S&T capacity and encourage their training, taking into account commercial needs.
4. When granting licenses for the use of intellectual property rights or when otherwise transferring technology, do so on reasonable terms and conditions and

in a manner that contributes to the long term development prospects of the host country.

5. Where relevant to commercial objectives, develop ties with local universities, public research institutions, and participate in co-operative research projects with local industry or industry associations.

IX. Competition

Enterprises should, within the framework of applicable laws and regulations, conduct their activities in a competitive manner. In particular, enterprises should:

1. Refrain from entering into or carrying out anti-competitive agreements among competitors:
    a) To fix prices.
    b) To make rigged bids (collusive tenders).
    c) To establish output restrictions or quotas; or
    d) To share or divide markets by allocating customers, suppliers, territories or lines of commerce.
2. Conduct all of their activities in a manner consistent with all applicable competition laws, taking into account the applicability of the competition laws of jurisdictions whose economies would be likely to be harmed by anti-competitive activity on their part.
3. Co-operate with the competition authorities of such jurisdictions by, among other things and subject to applicable law and appropriate safeguards, providing as prompt and complete responses as practicable to requests for information.
4. Promote employee awareness of the importance of compliance with all applicable competition laws and policies.

X. Taxation

It is important that enterprises contribute to the public finances of host countries by making timely payment of their tax liabilities. In particular, enterprises should comply with the tax laws and regulations in all countries in which they operate and should exert every effort to act in accordance with both the letter and the spirit of those laws and regulations. This would include such measures as providing to the relevant authorities the information necessary for the correct determination of taxes to be assessed in connection with their operations and conforming transfer pricing practices to the arm's length principle.

3
The UN Global Compact

> **Amnesty International [AI] believes initiatives like the UN Global Compact are worthwhile because, at a minimum, they encourage companies to make a commitment to human rights. This gives AI—and other [non-governmental organisations]—a clear opportunity to hold these companies to that commitment. We also believe that the possibilities for dialogue on human rights issues within the Global Compact framework have some value.**
>
> *Amnesty International, Economic Relations Briefing*[1]

> **UBS supports the Global Compact and is convinced that by adopting its principles it not only contributes to its stated objectives, but also creates value for its shareholders.**
>
> *UBS*[2]

Type Performance-oriented tool

Strength Its global scope

Keywords UN Secretary-General • Environment • Labour • Human rights • UN agencies • Development • Partnerships • Learning network

3.1 Background

The UN Global Compact is an initiative of UN Secretary-General, Kofi Annan, 'to give a human face to globalisation' (Annan 1999). Launched in 2000, the Compact

1 Quoted on the Amnesty International website, http://web.amnesty.org, accessed 2003.
2 Quoted on the UBS website, www.ubs.com, accessed 2003.

addresses the environment, human rights and workers' rights. The Compact unites global principles with local networks to create fluid networks. The Compact is a global multi-stakeholder, multi-issue network with more than 40 regional and national sub-networks. As a voluntary initiative, the Global Compact convenes all the key social actors: companies, labour, civil-society organisations and governments. At the time of writing (mid-2003), more than 1,000 companies were participating in the initiative. Participating companies are asked to communicate in their annual reports and/or other prominent public reports (e.g. sustainability reports) on progress made in implementing the nine principles.

The Global Compact is the first initiative on corporate responsibility aimed at companies to emerge from the UN Secretary-General's office. The initiative benefits from the engagement of several UN bodies, including the ILO, The UN Development Programme (UNDP), the UN Environment Programme (UNEP), and the Office of the UN High Commissioner for Human Rights. In May 2003, the UN Industrial Development Organisation (UNIDO) joined the Global Compact as the fifth UN core agency. These core agencies provide expertise and operational support (see Fig. 3.1).

The Global Compact differs from nearly all other corporate responsibility (CR) initiatives in that it seeks to promote development through good corporate citizenship. Members of the Global Compact commit 'to join with the United Nations in partnership projects of benefit to developing countries, particularly the least developed, which the forces of globalisation have largely marginalised' (Ruggie 2002: 31).

The Global Compact is a voluntary initiative, with a clear focus on learning and dialogue; it is not a code or a system for verification. In the words of one of its key architects, John Ruggie, the Global Compact has 'explicitly adopted a learning approach to inducing corporate change, as opposed to a regulatory approach; and it comprises a network form of organisation, as opposed to the traditional hierarchic/bureaucratic form' (Ruggie 2002: 28).

The ten principles of the Global Compact are derived from the Universal Declaration of Human Rights, the ILO's Fundamental Principles on Rights at Work (ILO 1998) and the Rio Declaration on Environment and Development.

3.2 Strengths and weaknesses

No other CR initiative has the moral authority and convening power of the UN Secretary-General. With these assets, the Global Compact has succeeded in promoting corporate responsibility broadly through networks around the world. The Compact has also mobilised an impressive database of corporate activities on corporate responsibility. Perhaps its greatest achievement has been to rally support for corporate responsibility in many countries where this is a relatively new concept. The Global Compact is a truly global initiative, with the majority of participating companies coming from the South, and with a large number of active networks in developing countries.

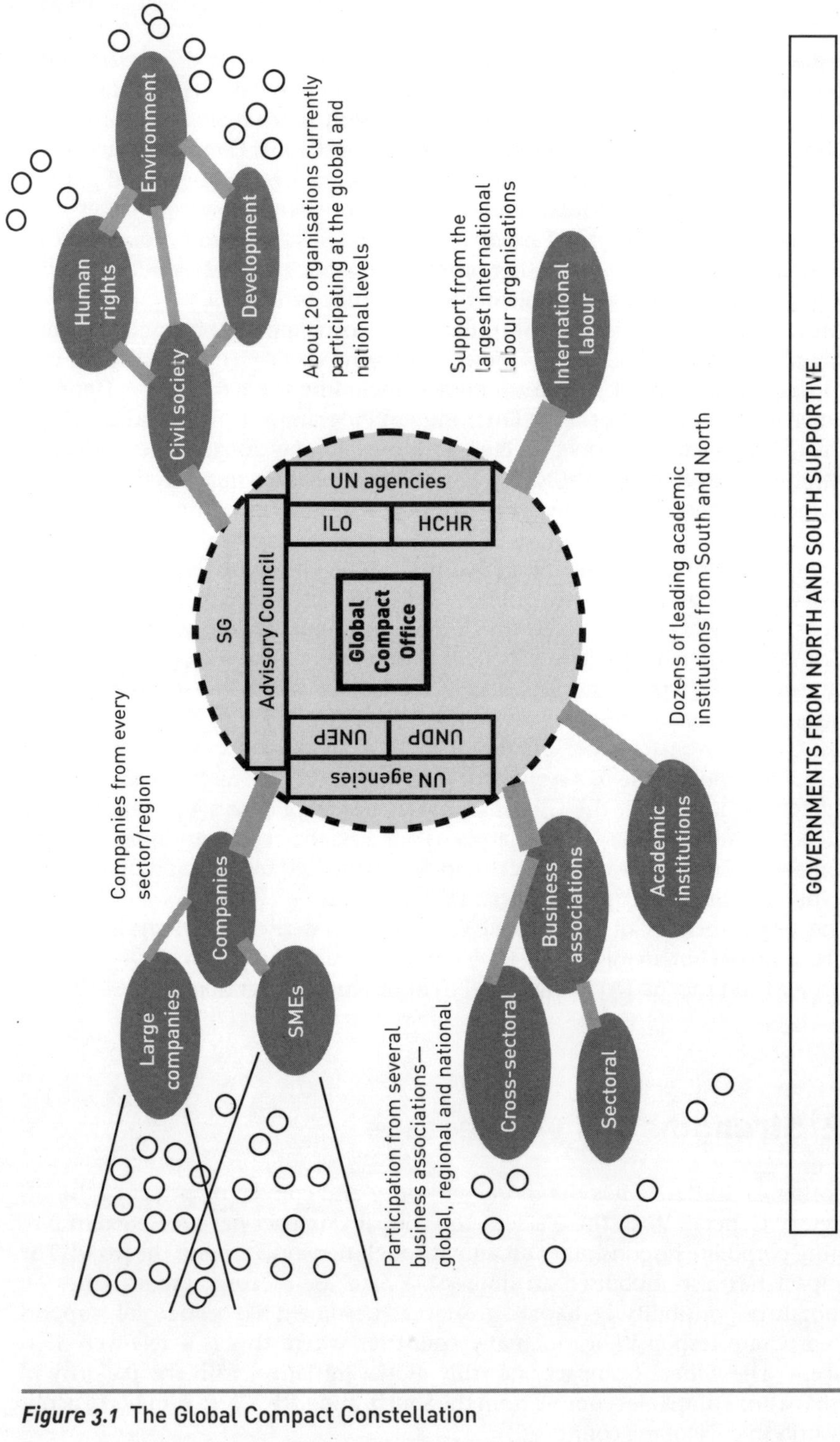

Figure 3.1 **The Global Compact Constellation**

By focusing on development, the Compact provides a new direction for corporate responsibility, giving voice to the poor and tackling such issues as the digital divide and HIV/AIDS. The partnership projects should contribute to the Millennium Development Goals, to which all 189 member states of the US have committed themselves by 2015 (these appear at the end of this chapter, on page 87). The support of key UN bodies in this regard provides legitimacy and significant expertise.

The Compact has produced accessible handbooks for companies, available on its website. *A Guide to the Global Compact* (see 'Additional resources' on page 84) is an excellent tool for all companies seeking to implement CR policies, including useful definitions and examples.

If the principles of the Global Compact lack the specificity of AA1000 and SA8000 it is because they were designed to meet the needs of a very global and diverse constituency of governments and businesses. The key difference is that the Compact was never intended to supplant any regulatory initiatives. Instead, it complements them. The Global Compact Office does not have the mandate or the resources to monitor company activity. The general nature of the principles can be perceived as both a strength and a weakness. It is easier to attract a critical mass of companies with general principles than with highly specialised criteria. Moreover, general principles make it easier for companies to integrate the Compact into their own internal codes or policies. By developing a general standard, and by forging alliances with highly specialised initiatives such as SA8000 and GRI, the Compact is able to build a critical mass.

The flexible structure of the Compact is both a source of great strength and a source of weakness. As a series of 'nested networks', it is a flexible instrument for promoting corporate responsibility at a global level. Figure 3.2 demonstrates the architecture of the Global Compact. It is a useful framework for other initiatives to co-ordinate with, an umbrella under which many actors and initiatives can be united. Its critics question whether companies submitting case studies to the UN Secretariat are, in fact, creating new CR projects or are submitting initiatives that were already under way before the Compact was announced. Other critics are concerned that companies with poor social and environmental records will be able to benefit from their association with the Compact, in effect 'blue-washing' their image (HRW 2000: 1-2). For example, Nestlé, which has long been criticised for marketing infant formula to mothers in the developing world, has joined the Compact. This presents a dilemma in that UNICEF, a UN body, has been one of the critics of Nestlé (Freedman and Stecklow 2000; www.babymilkaction.org), but it also represents an opportunity for dialogue.

Another criticism of the Compact is its lack of assurance systems (Roth 2000). However, its architect, John Ruggie, responds that large-scale verification by the United Nations is not feasible (Ruggie 2002: 32). The Global Compact has developed strong partnerships with other key initiatives, such as SA8000 (Chapter 8), to promote independent certification, and with the Global Reporting Initiative (Chapter 28), to promote reporting.

<table>
<tr><th>Engagement mechanisms</th><th colspan="2">Operational concepts</th></tr>
<tr><td rowspan="5">Learning forums</td><td colspan="2">• Example submission (mandatory)</td></tr>
<tr><td colspan="2">• Business case studies</td></tr>
<tr><td colspan="2">• Supportive research/analytical work</td></tr>
<tr><td colspan="2">• Informal, issue-specific networks</td></tr>
<tr><td colspan="2">• Annual conferences</td></tr>
<tr><td rowspan="3">Policy dialogues</td><td>Annual topic</td><td>Working groups</td></tr>
<tr><td>Role of business in zones of conflict</td><td>• Transparency
• Conflict impact assessment and risk management
• Multi-stakeholder partnerships
• Revenue-sharing regimes</td></tr>
<tr><td>Business and sustainable development</td><td>• Sustainable investment (LDCs)
• Sustainable entrepreneurship
• Corporate management and sustainability
• Investors and sustainability</td></tr>
<tr><td rowspan="6">Partnership projects</td><td colspan="2">Suggested parameters</td></tr>
<tr><td colspan="2">• Should be inspired by the Global Compact</td></tr>
<tr><td colspan="2">• Should contribute to the Millennium Development Goals</td></tr>
<tr><td colspan="2">• Should be carried out with other actors such as UN agencies, labour, NGOs and public-sector entities</td></tr>
<tr><td colspan="2">• Should allow network participants to offer a substantial example of how they enact the principles (thus providing added incentives for them to do so)</td></tr>
<tr><td colspan="2">• Projects involving several companies are particularly encouraged</td></tr>
<tr><td>Outreach and network building</td><td colspan="2">Replication of global structure
• National Learning Forums
• National Policy Dialogues
• National Partnership Projects</td></tr>
<tr><td>Global Compact governance</td><td colspan="2">• Building strategic alliances
• Innovating operational concepts
• Inter-agency co-ordination
• Advocacy and policy coherence of UN officials
• Global Compact Advisory Council
i) protecting integrity
ii) issue leadership</td></tr>
</table>

Figure 3.2 **Summary of Global Compact activities**

3.3 Companies to which the Global Compact applies

The Global Compact is well suited to companies making their first inroads into the field of CR. Companies with a well-established record in CR may seek to join the UN Global Compact to further promote their work in CR. The Global Compact is creating strong networks in Brazil and India and throughout Eastern Europe.

3.4 Questions posed and answered

The UN Global Compact poses several questions (McIntosh *et al.* 2003: 115):

- What are the principles that define responsible corporate behaviour?
- How can corporate citizenship promote development?
- How can the United Nations and governments begin to create mechanisms to address the governance of a globalised world?
- What constitutes best practice in corporate citizenship?

3.5 The promise and the challenge

The Global Compact has one of the most ambitious objectives of any of the initiatives described in this book: to make the world economy more sustainable and inclusive (United Nations 2003: 4). The brainchild of the very popular UN Secretary-General Kofi Annan, the Global Compact has the ability to convene CEOs from around the world to promote corporate responsibility and development. The Compact is forging new types of alliances and partnerships while promoting corporate responsibility globally.

Like any new, global, initiative, the Compact faces challenges. One of the questions it must address is whether or not all companies can join the Compact or whether there should be some kind of a screen. Could a tobacco company join the Compact? At this point, none is on the list, but it is not clear whether the Compact will develop exclusion criteria. According to Georg Kell of the UN Secretary-General's Office:

> the Global Compact is not about sinners and saints. There will always be companies that lead and companies that follow. We want to keep the door open. But we need some safeguards (quoted in United Nations 2003: 8).

According to *Ethical Performance* (2002), companies that have signed up to the UN Global Compact but have not delivered on their pledge to implement the ten principles may face expulsion. The Global Compact explains that this article was controversial as it misrepresented several issues (see www.unglobalcompact.org). The integrity of the Global Compact initiative is critically important to its mission. Therefore, the Global Compact Office is continuing to build in integrity measures. Efforts are under way to handle dilemmas through dialogue (www.unglobalcompact.org).

Another key challenge for the Global Compact, and for many of the initiatives described in this book, is the need to promote the principles among small and medium-sized enterprises (SMEs). SMEs have fewer resources to devote to corporate responsibility than do multinational corporations, and may face less pressure from consumers and investors than do large enterprises.[3] UNIDO's role as the Compact's fifth core agency will be to address the specific concerns and needs of SMEs.

The Global Compact has had only partial success in attracting US-based companies. This may be due, in part, to the cynicism that many Americans feel towards the United Nations.

3.6 Update[4]

Since its inception, the Global Compact has grown dramatically to include 7,700 corporate participants with networks in 80 countries. In 2008, the Global Compact grew by 30%.

Strengths and weaknesses

Professor Sandra Waddock of Boston College believes it is the aspirational nature of the Global Compact that has made it so important. 'The Global Compact has legitimised discussions within corporations on issues such as human rights and corruption. The Global Compact was among the first initiatives to address the issues of violence and water.'

The Global Compact has been a catalyst for many of other CR initiatives. Professor Waddock, who holds the Galligan Chair of Strategy at Boston College, believes the Global Compact has become a model for how to create other aspirational initiatives. For example, it has played a role in the development of the Principles for Responsible Investment, the Principles for Responsible Management in Education and the Global Responsible Leadership Fund.

The Global Compact is a good complement to many of the specialised codes and standards profiled in this book. It provides an overarching framework which can be supplemented with other more detailed codes, such as Social Accountability 8000.

3 ILD (Institute for Leadership Development), 'SMEs in the Global Compact', www.ildglobal.org, accessed 2003.

4 Based on interviews with Professor Sandra Waddock, 11 June 2009.

The Global Compact is not a service provider, nor is it able to accept earmarked funding from within the UN system. These specific modalities are necessary to maintain its credibility, but also challenge its ability to grow. According to Georg Kell, the Global Compact has adopted a system its director terms the 'Obama model' of accepting many small contributions, rather than become beholden to large funders.[5]

The promise and the challenge

The Global Compact has created a new space—an opportunity for public-private interface—which did not previously exist within the United Nations. Negotiating this space has been a challenge in that it requires the private sector to accept the goals of the UN as well as the constraints of operating within the UN system; and governments have to accept that the process is non-political.

Like many CR initiatives, the Global Compact faces the challenge of managing growth with very limited resources. With applicants numbering 100–150 per month, meeting expectations of new companies is not easy. According to Georg Kell, there is a need to balance quality and growth, to ensure both the pace and the direction. It is important to motivate the front-runners, so that they do not slow down. Likewise, it is important to attract additional funding.

References

Annan, K. (1999) Speech made by the UN Secretary-General, Kofi Annan, at the World Economic Forum in Davos, Switzerland, 31 January 1999 (www.un.org/News/Press/docs/1999/19990201.sgsm6881.html).

Ethical Performance (2002) News Alert, 8 April 2002, www.ethicalperformance.com.

Freedman, A.M., and S. Stecklow (2000) 'Bottled up: As Unicef battles baby-formula makers, African infants sicken', *Wall Street Journal*, 12 December 2000: A1.

HRW (Human Rights Watch) (2000) 'Business and Human Rights: The Role of the International Community', in *World Report 2000* (New York: HRW, www.hrw.org): 1-2.

ILO (International Labour Organisation) (1998) *Fundamental Principles on Rights at Work* (Adopted by the International Labour Conference at its 86th session, Geneva, 18 June 1988; Geneva: ILO).

McIntosh, M., D. Leipziger and G. Coleman (2003) *Living Corporate Citizenship: Strategic Routes to Socially Responsible Business* (London: FT Pearson).

Roth, K. (2000) Letter from Human Rights Watch to Kofi Annan, 28 July 2000, www.hrw.org, accessed 2003.

Ruggie, J.G. (2002) 'The Theory and Practice of Learning Networks: Corporate Social Responsibility and the Global Compact', *Journal of Corporate Citizenship* 5 (Spring 2002): 27-36.

United Nations (2003) 'Guide to the Global Compact: A Practical Understanding of the Vision and Nine Principles', United Nations, www.unglobalcompact.org.

5 Interview with Georg Kell, 1 July 2009.

Waddock, S. (2002) 'Learning from Experience: The UN Global Compact Learning Forum 2002', available at www.unglobalcompact.org.

Additional resources

Further reading

McIntosh, M., S. Waddock and G. Kell (2004) *Learning to Talk: The Early Years of the UN Global Compact* (Sheffield, UK: Greenleaf Publishing, forthcoming).

Website

UN Global Compact: www.unglobalcompact.org. This website contains the following publications online:

- *The Comprehensive Guide to the Global Compact*
- *A Guide to the Global Compact: A Practical Understanding of the Vision and Nine Principles*
- *The Global Compact Performance Model*
- *Reports from Learning Fora*

The Global Compact's Ten Principles

The UN Global Compact's ten principles in the areas of human rights, labour, the environment and anti-corruption enjoy universal consensus and are derived from:

- The Universal Declaration of Human Rights;
- The International Labour Organization's Declaration on Fundamental Principles and Rights at Work
- The Rio Declaration on Environment and Development
- The United Nations Convention Against Corruption

The Global Compact asks companies to embrace, support and enact, within their sphere of influence, a set of core values in the areas of human rights, labour standards, the environment, and anti-corruption:

Human Rights

- **Principle 1:** Businesses should support and respect the protection of internationally proclaimed human rights; and
- **Principle 2:** make sure that they are not complicit in human rights abuses.

Labour

- **Principle 3:** Businesses should uphold the freedom of association and the effective recognition of the right to collective bargaining;
- **Principle 4:** the elimination of all forms of forced and compulsory labour;
- **Principle 5:** the effective abolition of child labour; and
- **Principle 6:** the elimination of discrimination in respect of employment and occupation.

Environment

- **Principle 7:** Businesses should support a precautionary approach to environmental challenges;
- **Principle 8:** undertake initiatives to promote greater environmental responsibility; and

- **Principle 9:** encourage the development and diffusion of environmentally friendly technologies.

Anti-Corruption

- **Principle 10:** Businesses should work against corruption in all its forms, including extortion and bribery.

The Millennium Development Goals

1. Eradicate extreme poverty and hunger

- Reduce by half the proportion of people living on less than a dollar a day
- Reduce by half the proportion of people who suffer from hunger

2. Achieve universal primary education

- Ensure that all boys and girls complete a full course of primary schooling

3. Promote gender equality and empower women

- Eliminate gender disparity in primary and secondary education preferably by 2005, and at all levels by 2015

4. Reduce child mortality

- Reduce by two thirds the mortality rate among children under five

5. Improve maternal health

- Reduce by three quarters the maternal mortality ratio

6. Combat HIV/AIDS, malaria and other diseases

- Halt and begin to reverse the spread of HIV/AIDS
- Halt and begin to reverse the incidence of malaria and other major diseases

7. Ensure environmental sustainability

- Integrate the principles of sustainable development into country policies and programmes; reverse loss of environmental resources
- Reduce by half the proportion of people without sustainable access to safe drinking water
- Achieve significant improvement in lives of at least 100 million slum dwellers, by 2020

8. Develop a global partnership for development

- Develop further an open trading and financial system that is rule-based, predictable and non-discriminatory. Includes a commitment to good governance, development and poverty reduction—nationally and internationally
- Address the least developed countries' special needs. This includes tariff- and quota-free access for their exports; enhanced debt relief for heavily indebted poor countries; cancellation of official bilateral debt; and more generous official development assistance for countries committed to poverty reduction
- Address the special needs of landlocked and small island developing States
- Deal comprehensively with developing countries' debt problems through national and international measures to make debt sustainable in the long term
- In cooperation with the developing countries, develop decent and productive work for youth
- In cooperation with pharmaceutical companies, provide access to affordable essential drugs in developing countries
- In cooperation with the private sector, make available the benefits of new technologies—especially information and communications technologies

By the year 2015, all 191 United Nations Member States have pledged to meet the above goals

4
ISO 26000

> **The main impact of ISO 26000 lies in the education and awareness-raising which surrounds it. This applies to its development as well as to its actual use.**
>
> *Adrian Henriques, Chair of the ISO 26000 UK Mirror Committee, Professor of Accountability, Middlesex University, Representative of Forum for the Future and Amnesty International (UK) to ISO 26000 consultations*

Type Guidelines, process and performance

Strength Comprehensive, broad scope of issues, breadth and depth, broad consultation process

Weakness Complex and without significant innovation

Keywords Governance • Environment • Human rights • Labour practices • Fair operating practices • Consumer issues • Community involvement

4.1 Overview

The new Draft International Standard, ISO 26000 Guidance on Social Responsibility, provides guidance on the key themes of social responsibility, including governance, environment, human rights, labour practices, fair operating practices, consumer issues, community involvement, and societal development. The standard will be applicable to all organisations wherever they operate. This voluntary Guidance is not meant for use in certification, but rather provides guidance on a wide range of issues.

Companies will be able to use ISO 26000 in several ways. First, the guidelines will provide a common language and framework for companies. Second, companies can adopt the guidelines or use them to orient their own policies. Third, companies can use the list of issue areas to report on their activities.

It is likely that ISO 26000 will be launched formally in 2010. Several countries are considering setting up national standards that could be used as a certification standard. For example, both Portugal and Denmark are contemplating developing a standard for certification based on ISO 26000.

4.2 Development of ISO 26000

Ninety-two countries and 42 organisations have participated in the process of developing ISO 26000. The Guidelines have developed through a series of international meetings with stakeholders from:

- Industry
- Trade unions
- Government
- Consumer groups
- Non-governmental organisations

These stakeholders met with organisations known as D-liaison organisations to draft the first edition of the standard. The development of ISO 26000 included the formation of national committees, some of which were multi-stakeholder. The US formulated a national committee with representatives from a wide range of interests. Some countries were not able to afford to send representatives. D-liaisons included groups such as the UN Global Compact, the Global Reporting Initiative, Social Accountability International and Transparency International. These organisations can comment but cannot vote in the proceedings. D-liaisons can lobby relevant national committees to effect change.

Each participating country develops a mirror committee made up of individuals from each stakeholder group, wherever possible. The mirror committee's role during this process is to provide feedback and share positions with the entire working group as well as with their stakeholder group representatives. The review process has been extensive with more than 7,000 organisations commenting throughout this process.

4.3 Strengths and weaknesses

ISO 26000 makes an important contribution to the field by defining the scope of corporate responsibility. ISO 26000's comprehensive description of what constitutes CR provides an important framework for companies grappling with their ethical, social and environmental responsibilities. The definition of CR forged within the ISO 26000 process gives this emerging definition legitimacy. However, the comprehensive nature of ISO 26000 may make it a bit daunting for some companies.

The ISO 26000 process is to be commended for providing translations into a very wide range of languages.

ISO 26000's current definition of 'stakeholder' has been deemed 'non-standard' by CR advisor Adrian Henriques, who has participated in the ISO 26000 process representing Amnesty International. According to the ISO 26000 definition, a stakeholder is 'an individual or group that has an interest in any activities or decisions of an organisation'. The more traditional definition of a stakeholder is anyone who is impacted by or impacts an organisation.

4.4 Companies to which ISO 26000 applies

ISO 26000 applies to all organisations in all sectors. As with many standards, small and medium-sized organisations may face more of a challenge with implementation than larger companies.

4.5 Questions posed and answered

ISO 26000 poses and answers many questions, including the following:

- What are the key areas within the field of CR that companies need to address?
- How are stakeholders defined?
- How should a company engage with stakeholders?
- How far does the responsibility of an organisation extend?

4.6 The promise and the challenge

An attractive aspect of ISO 26000 is the ability to combine it with existing systems for other ISO standards, such as ISO 9000 and 14001. Memoranda of understanding have been signed with several key other standards and guidelines to facilitate co-implementation of ISO 26000 with other initiatives, such as the Global Compact and the Organisation for Economic Co-operation and Development. Plans are under way to develop streamlined systems for companies seeking to implement both ISO 26000 and SA8000.

As ISO 26000 remains a Draft International Standard at the time of writing, it is still early to report on its full implementation.

Additional resources

Website

www.iso.org

Draft International Standard ISO 26000: Guidance on Social Responsibility*

Table 1: ISO 26000 outline

Clause title	Clause number	Description of clause contents
Scope	Clause 1	Defines the content and scope of this International Standard and identifies certain limitations and exclusions.
Terms, definitions and abbreviated terms	Clause 2	Identifies and provides the definition of key terms that are of fundamental importance for understanding social responsibility and for using this International Standard.
Understanding social responsibility	Clause 3	Describes the important factors and conditions that have influenced the development of social responsibility and that continue to affect its nature and practice. It also describes the concept of social responsibility itself - what it means and how it applies to organizations. The clause includes guidance for small and medium-sized organizations on the use of this International Standard.
Principles of social responsibility	Clause 4	Introduces and explains the generic principles of social responsibility.
Recognizing social responsibility and engaging with stakeholders	Clause 5	Addresses two practices of social responsibility: an organization's recognition of its social responsibility, and its identification of and engagement with its stakeholders. It provides guidance on the relationship between an organization, its stakeholders and society, recognizing the core subjects and issues of social responsibility and an organization's sphere of influence.
Guidance on social responsibility core subjects	Clause 6	Explains the core subjects and associated issues relating to social responsibility (see Table 2). For each core subject, information has been provided on its scope, its relationship to social responsibility, relevant principles and considerations, and related actions and expectations.

Clause title	Clause number	Description of clause contents
Guidance on integrating social responsibility throughout an organization	Clause 7	Provides guidance on putting social responsibility into practice in an organization. This includes guidance related to: understanding the social responsibility of an organization, integrating social responsibility throughout an organization, communication related to social responsibility, improving the credibility of an organization regarding social responsibility, reviewing progress and improving performance and evaluating voluntary initiatives for social responsibility.
Annex on voluntary initiatives and tools related to social responsibility	Annex A	Presents a non-exhaustive list of voluntary initiatives and tools related to social responsibility that address aspects of one or more core subjects or the integration of social responsibility throughout an organization.
Bibliography		Includes references to authoritative international instruments and ISO Standards that are referenced in the body of this International Standard as source material.
Index		Provides direction to references to topics, concepts and terms in this International Standard as source material.

Table 2: Core subjects and issues of social responsibility

Core subjects and issues	Addressed in sub-clause
Core subject: Organizational governance	6.2
Core subject: Human rights	6.3
Issue 1: Due diligence	6.3.3
Issue 2: Human rights risk situations	6.3.4
Issue 3: Avoidance of complicity	6.3.5
Issue 4: Resolving grievances	6.3.6
Issue 5: Discrimination and vulnerable groups	6.3.7
Issue 6: Civil and political rights	6.3.8
Issue 7: Economic, social and cultural rights	6.3.9
Issue 8: Fundamental rights at work	6.3.10
Core subject: Labour Practices	6.4
Issue 1: Employment and employment relationships	6.4.3
Issue 2: Conditions of work and social protection	6.4.4

Issue 3: Social dialogue	6.4.5
Issue 4: Health and safety at work	6.4.6
Issue 5: Human development and training in the workplace	6.5
Core subject: The environment	6.5.3
Issue 1: Prevention of pollution	6.5.4
Issue 2: Sustainable resource use	6.5.5
Issue 3: Climate change mitigation and adaptation	6.5.6
Issue 4: Protection and restoration of the natural environment	6.5.7
Core subject: Fair operating practices	6.6
Issue 1: Anti-corruption	6.6.3
Issue 2: Responsible political involvement	6.6.4
Issue 3: Fair competition	6.6.5
Issue 4: Promoting social responsibility in the sphere of influence	6.6.6
Issue 5: Respect for property rights	6.6.7
Core subject: Consumer issues	6.7
Issue 1: Fair marketing, information and contractual practices	6.7.3
Issue 2: Protecting consumers' health and safety	6.7.4
Issue 3: Sustainable consumption	6.7.5
Issue 4: Consumer service, support, and dispute resolution	6.7.6
Issue 5: Consumer data protection and privacy	6.7.7
Issue 6: Access to essential services	6.7.8
Issue 7: Education and awareness	6.7.9
Core subject: Community involvement and development	6.8
Issue 1: Community involvement	6.8.3
Issue 2: Education and culture	6.8.4
Issue 3: Employment creation and skills development	6.8.5
Issue 4: Technology development	6.8.6
Issue 5: Wealth and income creation	6.8.7
Issue 6: Health	6.8.8
Issue 7: Social investment	6.8.9

Figure 1: Schematic overview of ISO 26000

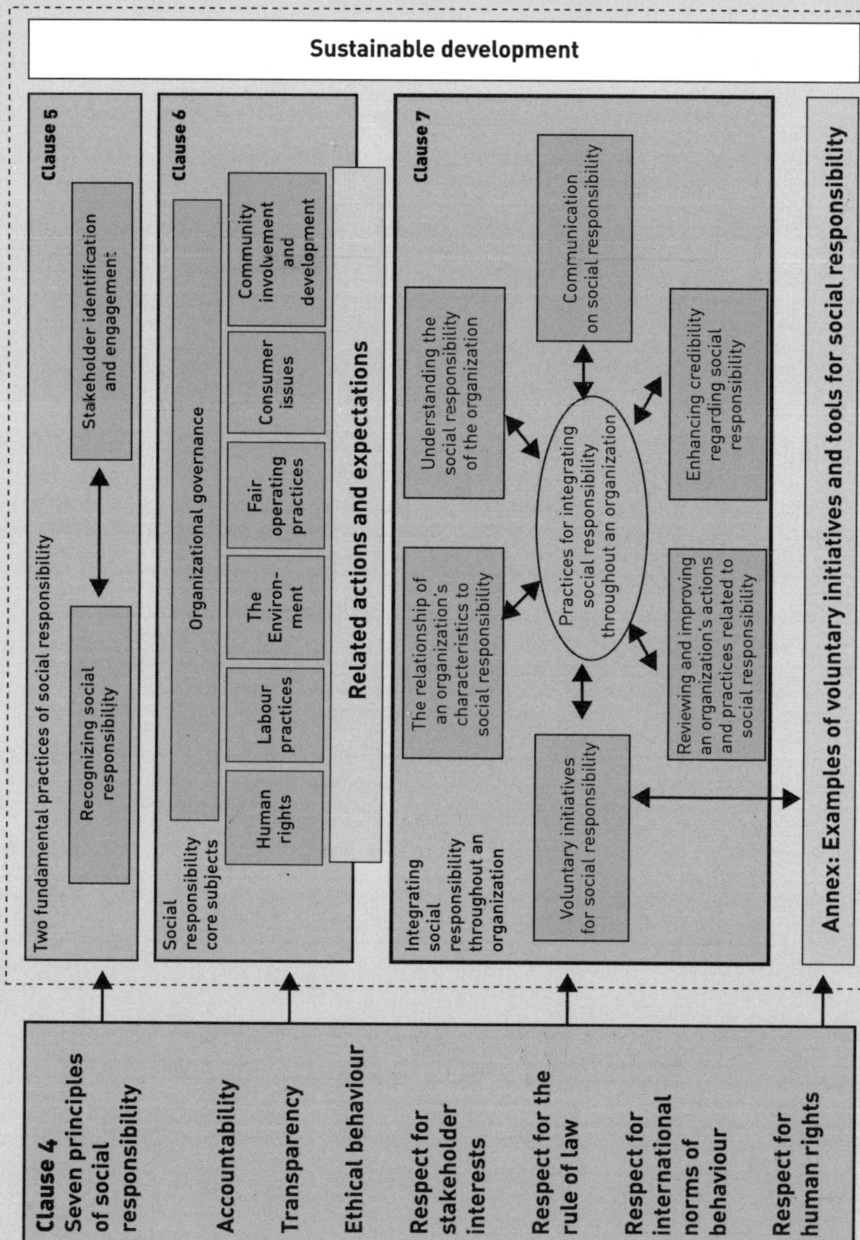

International Finance Corporation's Performance Standards on Social and Environmental Sustainability

PERFORMANCE STANDARDS ON SOCIAL AND ENVIRONMENTAL SUSTAINABILITY

Introduction

1. International Finance Corporation (IFC) applies the Performance Standards to manage social and environmental risks and impacts and to enhance development opportunities in its private sector financing in its member countries eligible for financing.[1] The Performance Standards may also be applied by other financial institutions electing to apply them to projects in emerging markets. Together, the eight Performance Standards establish standards that the client[2] is to meet throughout the life of an investment by IFC or other relevant financial institution:

Performance Standard 1:	Social and Environmental Assessment and Management System
Performance Standard 2:	Labor and Working Conditions
Performance Standard 3:	Pollution Prevention and Abatement
Performance Standard 4:	Community Health, Safety and Security
Performance Standard 5:	Land Acquisition and Involuntary Resettlement
Performance Standard 6:	Biodiversity Conservation and Sustainable Natural Resource Management

1 IFC will apply the Performance Standards to projects it finances, consistent with the provisions in the accompanying IFC's Policy on Social and Environmental Sustainability. IFC's institutional disclosure of information will be pursuant to IFC's Policy on Disclosure of Information.

2 The term "client" is used throughout the Performance Standards broadly to refer to the party responsible for implementing and operating the project that is being financed, or the recipient of the financing, depending on the project structure and type of financing. The term "project" is defined in Performance Standard 1.

Performance Standard 7: Indigenous Peoples

Performance Standard 8: Cultural Heritage

2. Performance Standard 1 establishes the importance of: (i) integrated assessment to identify the social and environmental impacts, risks, and opportunities of projects; (ii) effective community engagement through disclosure of project-related information and consultation with local communities on matters that directly affect them; and (iii) the client's management of social and environmental performance throughout the life of the project. Performance Standards 2 through 8 establish requirements to avoid, reduce, mitigate or compensate for impacts on people and the environment, and to improve conditions where appropriate. While all relevant social and environmental risks and potential impacts should be considered as part of the assessment, Performance Standards 2 through 8 describe potential social and environmental impacts that require particular attention in emerging markets. Where social or environmental impacts are anticipated, the client is required to manage them through its Social and Environmental Management System consistent with Performance Standard 1.

3. In addition to meeting the requirements under the Performance Standards, clients must comply with applicable national laws, including those laws implementing host country obligations under international law.

4. A set of Guidance Notes, corresponding to the Performance Standards, offers helpful guidance on the requirements contained in the Performance Standards, including reference materials, and on good sustainability practices to help clients improve project performance.

PERFORMANCE STANDARD 1
SOCIAL AND ENVIRONMENTAL ASSESSMENT AND MANAGEMENT SYSTEMS

Introduction

1. Performance Standard 1 underscores the importance of managing social and environmental performance throughout the life of a project (any business activity that is subject to assessment and management). An effective social and environmental management system is a dynamic, continuous process initiated by management and involving communication between the client, its workers, and the local communities directly affected by the project (the affected communities). Drawing on the elements of the established business management process of "plan, implement, check, and act," the system entails the thorough assessment of potential social and environmental impacts and risks from the early stages of project development, and provides order and consistency for mitigating and managing these on an ongoing basis. A good management system appropriate to the size and nature of a project promotes sound and sustainable social and environmental performance, and can lead to improved financial, social and environmental project outcomes.

Objectives

- To identify and assess social and environment impacts, both adverse and beneficial, in the project's area of influence
- To avoid, or where avoidance is not possible, minimize, mitigate, or compensate for adverse impacts on workers, affected communities, and the environment
- To ensure that affected communities are appropriately engaged on issues that could potentially affect them
- To promote improved social and environment performance of companies through the effective use of management systems

Scope of Application

2. This Performance Standard applies to projects with social or environmental risks and impacts that should be managed, in the early stages of project development, and on an ongoing basis.

Requirements

Social and Environmental Management System

3. The client will establish and maintain a Social and Environmental Management System appropriate to the nature and scale of the project and commensurate with the level of social and environmental risks and impacts. The Management System will incorporate the following elements: (i) Social and Environmental Assessment; (ii) management program; (iii) organizational capacity; (iv) training; (v) community engagement; (vi) monitoring; and (vii) reporting.

Social and Environmental Assessment

4. The client will conduct a process of Social and Environmental Assessment that will consider in an integrated manner the potential social and environmental (including labor, health, and safety) risks and impacts of the project. The Assessment process will be based on current information, including an accurate project description, and appropriate social and environmental baseline data. The Assessment will consider all relevant social and environmental risks and impacts of the project, including the issues identified in Performance Standards 2 through 8, and those who will be affected by such risks and impacts. Applicable laws and regulations of the jurisdictions in which the project operates that pertain to social and environmental matters, including those laws implementing host country obligations under international law, will also be taken into account.

5. Risks and impacts will be analyzed in the context of the project's area of influence. This area of influence encompasses, as appropriate: (i) the primary project site(s) and related facilities that the client (including its contractors) develops or controls, such as power transmission corridors, pipelines, canals, tunnels, relocation and access roads, borrow and disposal areas, construction camps; (ii) associated facilities that are not funded as part of the project (funding may be provided separately by the client or by third parties including the government), and whose viability and existence depend exclusively on the project and whose goods or services are essential for the successful operation of the project; (iii) areas potentially impacted by cumulative impacts from further planned development of the project, any existing project or condition, and other project-related developments that are realistically defined at the time the Social and Environmental Assessment is undertaken; and (iv) areas potentially affected by impacts from unplanned but predictable developments caused by the project that may occur later or at a different location. The area of influence does not include potential impacts that would occur without the project or independently of the project.

6. Risks and impacts will also be analyzed for the key stages of the project cycle, including pre-construction, construction, operations, and decommissioning or closure. Where relevant, the Assessment will also consider the role and capacity of third parties (such as local and national governments, contractors and suppliers), to the extent that they pose a risk to the project, recognizing that the client should address these risks and impacts commensurate to the client's control and influence over the third party actions. The impacts associated with supply chains will be considered where the resource utilized by the project is ecologically sensitive, or in cases where low labor cost is a factor in the competitiveness of the item supplied. The Assessment will also consider potential transboundary effects, such as pollution of air, or use or pollution of international waterways, as well as global impacts, such as the emission of greenhouse gasses.

7. The Assessment will be an adequate, accurate, and objective evaluation and presentation of the issues, prepared by qualified and experienced persons. In projects with significant adverse impacts or where technically complex issues are involved, clients may be required to retain external experts to assist in the Assessment process.

8. Depending on the type of project and the nature and magnitude of its risks and impacts, the Assessment may comprise a full-scale social and environmental impact assessment, a limited or focused environmental or social assessment, or straightforward application of environmental siting, pollution standards, design criteria, or construction standards. When the project involves existing business activities, social and/or environmental audits may need to be performed to determine any areas of concern. The types of issues, risks and impacts to be assessed, and the scope of the community engagement (see paragraphs 19 through 23 below) can also vary considerably, depending on the nature of the project, and its size, location, and stage of development.

9. Projects with potential significant adverse impacts that are diverse, irreversible, or unprecedented will have comprehensive social and environmental impact assessments. This assessment will include an examination of technically and financially feasible[1] alternatives to the source of such impacts, and documentation of the rationale for selecting the particular course of action proposed. In exceptional circumstances, a regional, sectoral or strategic assessment may be required.

10. Narrower scopes of Assessments may be conducted for projects with limited impacts that are few in number, generally site-specific, largely reversible, and readily addressed through mitigation measures.

11. Projects with minimal or no adverse impacts will not be subject to further assessment beyond their identification as such.

12. As part of the Assessment, the client will identify individuals and groups that may be differentially or disproportionately affected by the project because of their disadvantaged or vulnerable status.[2] Where groups are identified as disadvantaged or vulnerable, the client will propose and implement differentiated measures so that adverse impacts do not fall disproportionately on them and they are not disadvantaged in sharing development benefits and opportunities.

Management Program

13. Taking into account the relevant findings of the Social and Environmental Assessment and the result of consultation with affected communities, the client will establish and manage a program of mitigation and performance improvement measures and actions that address the identified social and environmental risks and impacts (the management program).

14. Management programs consist of a combination of operational policies, procedures and practices. The program may apply broadly across the client's organization, or to specific sites, facilities, or activities. The measures and actions to address identified impacts and risks will favor the avoidance and prevention of impacts over minimization, mitigation, or compensation, wherever technically and financially feasible. Where risks and impacts cannot be avoided or prevented, mitigation measures and actions will be identified so that the project operates in compliance with applicable laws and regulations, and meets the requirements of Performance Standards 1 through 8 (see paragraph 16 below). The level of detail and complexity of this

1 "Technical feasibility" is based on whether the proposed measures and actions can be implemented with commercially available skills, equipment and materials, taking into consideration prevailing local factors such as climate, geography, demography, infrastructure, security, governance, capacity and operational reliability. "Financial feasibility" is based on commercial considerations, including the relative magnitude of the incremental cost of adopting such measures and actions compared to the project's investment, operating and maintenance costs and whether this incremental cost could make the project nonviable to the client.

2 This status may stem from an individual's or group's race, color, sex, language, religion, political or other opinion, national or social origin, property, birth or other status. The client should also consider factors such as gender, ethnicity, culture, sickness, physical or mental disability, poverty or economic disadvantage, and dependence on unique natural resources.

program and the priority of the identified measures and actions will be commensurate with the project's risks and impacts.

15. The program will define desired outcomes as measurable events to the extent possible, with elements such as performance indicators, targets, or acceptance criteria that can be tracked over defined time periods, and with estimates of the resources and responsibilities for implementation. Recognizing the dynamic nature of the project development and implementation process, the program will be responsive to changes in project circumstances, unforeseen events, and the results of monitoring (see paragraph 24 below).

Action Plan

16. Where the client identifies specific mitigation measures and actions necessary for the project to comply with applicable laws and regulations and to meet the requirements of Performance Standards 1 through 8, the client will prepare an Action Plan. These measures and actions will reflect the outcomes of consultation on social and environmental risks and adverse impacts and the proposed measures and actions to address these, consistent with the requirements under paragraph 21. The Action Plan may range from a brief description of routine mitigation measures to a series of specific plans.[3] The Action Plan will: (i) describe the actions necessary to implement the various sets of mitigation measures or corrective actions to be undertaken; (ii) prioritize these actions; (iii) include the time-line for their implementation; (iv) be disclosed to the affected communities (see paragraph 26); and (v) describe the schedule and mechanism for external reporting on the client's implementation of the Action Plan.

Organizational Capacity

17. The client will establish, maintain, and strengthen as necessary an organizational structure that defines roles, responsibilities, and authority to implement the management program, including the Action Plan. Specific personnel, including management representative(s), with clear lines of responsibility and authority should be designated. Key social and environmental responsibilities should be well defined and communicated to the relevant personnel and to the rest of the organization. Sufficient management sponsorship and human and financial resources will be provided on an ongoing basis to achieve effective and continuous social and environmental performance.

Training

18. The client will train employees and contractors with direct responsibility for activities relevant to the project's social and environmental performance so that they have the knowledge and skills necessary to perform their work, including current

3 For example, Resettlement Action Plans, Biodiversity Action Plans, Hazardous Materials Management Plans, Emergency Preparedness and Response Plans, Community Health and Safety Plans, and Indigenous Peoples Development Plans.

knowledge of the host country's regulatory requirements and the applicable requirements of Performance Standards 1 through 8. Training will also address the specific measures and actions required under the management program, including the Action Plan, and the methods required to perform the action items in a competent and efficient manner.

Community Engagement

19. Community engagement is an on-going process involving the client's disclosure of information. When local communities may be affected by risks or adverse impacts from a project, the engagement process will include consultation with them. The purpose of community engagement is to build and maintain over time a constructive relationship with these communities. The nature and frequency of community engagement will reflect the project's risks to and adverse impacts on the affected communities. Community engagement will be free of external manipulation, interference, or coercion, and intimidation, and conducted on the basis of timely, relevant, understandable and accessible information.

Disclosure

20. Disclosure of relevant project information helps affected communities understand the risks, impacts and opportunities of the project. Where the client has undertaken a process of Social and Environmental Assessment, the client will publicly disclose the Assessment document. If communities may be affected by risks or adverse impacts from the project, the client will provide such communities with access to information on the purpose, nature and scale of the project, the duration of proposed project activities, and any risks to and potential impacts on such communities. For projects with adverse social or environmental impacts, disclosure should occur early in the Social and Environmental Assessment process and in any event before the project construction commences, and on an ongoing basis (see paragraph 26 below).

Consultation

21. If affected communities may be subject to risks or adverse impacts from a project, the client will undertake a process of consultation in a manner that provides the affected communities with opportunities to express their views on project risks, impacts, and mitigation measures, and allows the client to consider and respond to them. Effective consultation: (i) should be based on the prior disclosure of relevant and adequate information, including draft documents and plans; (ii) should begin early in the Social and Environmental Assessment process; (iii) will focus on the social and environmental risks and adverse impacts, and the proposed measures and actions to address these; and (iv) will be carried out on an ongoing basis as risks and impacts arise. The consultation process will be undertaken in a manner that is inclusive and culturally appropriate. The client will tailor its consultation process to the language preferences of the affected communities, their decision-making process, and the needs of disadvantaged or vulnerable groups.

22. For projects with significant adverse impacts on affected communities, the consultation process will ensure their free, prior and informed consultation and facilitate their informed participation. Informed participation involves organized and iterative consultation, leading to the client's incorporating into their decision-making process the views of the affected communities on matters that affect them directly, such as proposed mitigation measures, the sharing of development benefits and opportunities, and implementation issues. The client will document the process, in particular the measures taken to avoid or minimize risks to and adverse impacts on the affected communities.

Grievance Mechanism

23. The client will respond to communities' concerns related to the project. If the client anticipates ongoing risks to or adverse impacts on affected communities, the client will establish a grievance mechanism to receive and facilitate resolution of the affected communities' concerns and grievances about the client's environmental and social performance. The grievance mechanism should be scaled to the risks and adverse impacts of the project. It should address concerns promptly, using an understandable and transparent process that is culturally appropriate and readily accessible to all segments of the affected communities, and at no cost and without retribution. The mechanism should not impede access to judicial or administrative remedies. The client will inform the affected communities about the mechanism in the course of its community engagement process.

Monitoring

24. As an element of its Management System, the client will establish procedures to monitor and measure the effectiveness of the management program. In addition to recording information to track performance and establishing relevant operational controls, the client should use dynamic mechanisms, such as inspections and audits, where relevant, to verify compliance and progress toward the desired outcomes. For projects with significant impacts that are diverse, irreversible, or unprecedented, the client will retain qualified and experienced external experts to verify its monitoring information. The extent of monitoring should be commensurate with the project's risks and impacts and with the project's compliance requirements. Monitoring should be adjusted according to performance experience and feedback. The client will document monitoring results, and identify and reflect the necessary corrective and preventive actions in the amended management program. The client will implement these corrective and preventive actions, and follow up on these actions to ensure their effectiveness.

Reporting

Internal Reporting

25. Senior management in the client organization will receive periodic assessments of the effectiveness of the management program, based on systematic data collection and analysis. The scope and frequency of such reporting will depend upon the nature and scope of the activities identified and undertaken in accordance with the client's management program and other applicable project requirements.

External Reporting on Action Plans

26. The client will disclose the Action Plan to the affected communities. In addition, the client will provide periodic reports that describe progress with implementation of the Action Plan on issues that involve ongoing risk to or impacts on affected communities, and on issues that the consultation process or grievance mechanism has identified as of concern to those communities. If the management program results in material changes in, or additions to, the mitigation measures or actions described in the Action Plan on issues of concern to the affected communities, the updated mitigation measures or actions will also be disclosed. These reports will be in a format accessible to the affected communities. The frequency of these reports will be proportionate to the concerns of affected communities but not less than annually.

PERFORMANCE STANDARD 2
LABOR AND WORKING CONDITIONS

Introduction

1. Performance Standard 2 recognizes that the pursuit of economic growth through employment creation and income generation should be balanced with protection for basic rights of workers. For any business, the workforce is a valuable asset, and a sound worker-management relationship is a key ingredient to the sustainability of the enterprise. Failure to establish and foster a sound worker–management relationship can undermine worker commitment and retention, and can jeopardize a project. Conversely, through a constructive worker–management relationship, and by treating the workers fairly and providing them with safe and healthy working conditions, clients may create tangible benefits, such as enhancement of the efficiency and productivity of their operations.

2. The requirements set out in this Performance Standard have been in part guided by a number of international conventions negotiated through the International Labour Organization (ILO) and the United Nations (UN).[1]

1 These conventions are:

ILO Convention 87 on Freedom of Association and Protection of the Right to Organize
ILO Convention 98 on the Right to Organize and Collective Bargaining
ILO Convention 29 on Forced Labor
ILO Convention 105 on the Abolition of Forced Labor
ILO Convention 138 on Minimum Age (of Employment)
ILO Convention 182 on the Worst Forms of Child Labor
ILO Convention 100 on Equal Remuneration
ILO Convention 111 on Discrimination (Employment and Occupation)
United Nations Convention on the Rights of the Child, Article 32.1

Objectives

- To establish, maintain and improve the worker-management relationship
- To promote the fair treatment, non-discrimination and equal opportunity of workers, and compliance with national labor and employment laws
- To protect the workforce by addressing child labor and forced labor
- To promote safe and healthy working conditions, and to protect and promote the health of workers

Scope of Application

3. The applicability of this Performance Standard is established during the Social and Environmental Assessment process, while implementation of the actions necessary to meet the requirements of this Performance Standard is managed through the client's Social and Environmental Management System. The assessment and management system requirements are outlined in Performance Standard 1.

4. Throughout this Performance Standard, the term "workers" is used to refer to employees of the client, as well as to certain types of non-employee workers described in paragraph 17. The application of this Performance Standard will vary depending on the type of workers, as follows:

- **Employees:** All the requirements of this Performance Standard, except for the requirements under paragraphs 17 and 18, apply
- **Non-Employee Workers:** The requirements of paragraph 17 apply

5. Supply chain[2] issues are addressed in paragraph 18.

Requirements

Working Conditions and Management of Worker Relationship

Human Resources Policy

6. The client will adopt a human resources policy appropriate to its size and workforce that sets out its approach to managing employees consistent with the requirements of this Performance Standard. Under the policy, the client will provide employees with information regarding their rights under national labor and employment law, including their rights related to wages and benefits. This policy will be clear and understandable to employees and will be explained or made accessible to each employee upon taking employment.

2 Supply chain refers to both labor and material inputs for the life-cycle of a good or service.

Working Relationship

7. The client will document and communicate to all employees and workers directly contracted by the client their working conditions and terms of employment, including their entitlement to wages and any benefits.

Working Conditions and Terms of Employment

8. Where the client is a party to a collective bargaining agreement with a workers' organization, such agreement will be respected. Where such agreements do not exist, or do not address working conditions and terms of employment (such as wages and benefits, hours of work, overtime arrangements and overtime compensation, and leave for illness, maternity, vacation or holiday) the client will provide reasonable working conditions and terms of employment that, at a minimum, comply with national law.

Workers' Organizations

9. In countries where national law recognizes workers' rights to form and to join workers' organizations of their choosing without interference and to bargain collectively, the client will comply with national law. Where national law substantially restricts workers' organizations, the client will enable alternative means for workers to express their grievances and protect their rights regarding working conditions and terms of employment.

10. In either case described in paragraph 9, and where national law is silent, the client will not discourage workers from forming or joining workers' organizations of their choosing or from bargaining collectively, and will not discriminate or retaliate against workers who participate, or seek to participate, in such organizations and bargain collectively. Clients will engage with such worker representatives. Worker organizations are expected to fairly represent the workers in the workforce.

Non-Discrimination and Equal Opportunity

11. The client will not make employment decisions on the basis of personal characteristics unrelated to inherent job requirements. The client will base the employment relationship on the principle of equal opportunity and fair treatment, and will not discriminate with respect to aspects of the employment relationship, including recruitment and hiring, compensation (including wages and benefits), working conditions and terms of employment, access to training, promotion, termination of employment or retirement, and discipline. In countries where national law provides for nondiscrimination in employment, the client will comply with national law. When national laws are silent on non-discrimination in employment, the client will meet this Performance Standard. Special measures of protection or assistance to remedy past discrimination or selection for a particular job based on the inherent requirements of the job will not be deemed discrimination.

Retrenchment

12. The client will develop a plan to mitigate the adverse impacts of retrenchment on employees, if it anticipates the elimination of a significant number of jobs or a layoff of a significant number of employees. The plan will be based on the principle of non-discrimination and will reflect the client's consultation with employees, their organizations and, where appropriate, the government.

Grievance Mechanism

13. The client will provide a grievance mechanism for workers (and their organizations, where they exist) to raise reasonable workplace concerns. The client will inform the workers of the grievance mechanism at the time of hire, and make it easily accessible to them. The mechanism should involve an appropriate level of management and address concerns promptly, using an understandable and transparent process that provides feedback to those concerned, without any retribution. The mechanism should not impede access to other judicial or administrative remedies that might be available under law or through existing arbitration procedures, or substitute for grievance mechanisms provided through collective agreements.

Protecting the Work Force

Child Labor

14. The client will not employ children in a manner that is economically exploitative, or is likely to be hazardous or to interfere with the child's education, or to be harmful to the child's health or physical, mental, spiritual, moral, or social development. Where national laws have provisions for the employment of minors, the client will follow those laws applicable to the client. Children below the age of 18 years will not be employed in dangerous work.

Forced Labor

15. The client will not employ forced labor, which consists of any work or service not voluntarily performed that is exacted from an individual under threat of force or penalty. This covers any kind of involuntary or compulsory labor, such as indentured labor, bonded labor or similar labor-contracting arrangements.

Occupational Health and Safety

16. The client will provide the workers with a safe and healthy work environment, taking into account inherent risks in its particular sector and specific classes of hazards in the client's work areas, including physical, chemical, biological, and radiological hazards. The client will take steps to prevent accidents, injury, and disease arising from, associated with, or occurring in the course of work by minimizing, so far as reasonably practicable, the causes of hazards. In a manner consistent with good international industry practice,[3] the client will address areas, including: the identification of potential hazards to workers, particularly those that may be life-threat-

---

3 Defined as the exercise of professional skill, diligence, prudence and foresight that would reasonably be expected from skilled and experienced professionals engaged in the same type of undertaking under the same or similar circumstances globally.

ening; provision of preventive and protective measures, including modification, substitution, or elimination of hazardous conditions or substances; training of workers; documentation and reporting of occupational accidents, diseases, and incidents; and emergency prevention, preparedness and response arrangements.

Non-Employee Workers

17. For purpose of this Performance Standard, "non-employee workers" refers to workers who are: (i) directly contracted by the client, or contracted through contractors or other intermediaries; and (ii) performing work directly related to core functions essential to the client's products or services for a substantial duration. When the client contracts non-employee workers directly, the client will use commercially reasonable efforts to apply the requirements of this Performance Standard, except for paragraphs 6, 12, and 18. With respect to contractors or other intermediaries procuring non- employee workers, the client will use commercially reasonable efforts to: (i) ascertain that these contractors or intermediaries are reputable and legitimate enterprises; and (ii) require that these contractors or intermediaries apply the requirements of this Performance Standard, except for paragraphs 6, 12, and 13.

Supply Chain

18. The adverse impacts associated with supply chains will be considered where low labor cost is a factor in the competitiveness of the item supplied. The client will inquire about and address child labor and forced labor in its supply chain, consistent with paragraphs 14 and 15 above.

PERFORMANCE STANDARD 3
POLLUTION PREVENTION AND ABATEMENT

Introduction

1. Performance Standard 3 recognizes that increased industrial activity and urbanization often generate increased levels of pollution to air, water, and land that may threaten people and the environment at the local, regional, and global level.[1] On the other hand, along with international trade, pollution prevention and control technologies and practices have become more accessible and achievable in virtually all parts of the world. This Performance Standard outlines a project approach to pollution prevention and abatement in line with these internationally disseminated technologies and practices. In addition, this Performance Standard promotes the private

1 For the purposes of this performance standard, the term "pollution" is used to refer to both hazardous and nonhazardous pollutants in the solid, liquid, or gaseous forms, and is intended to include other forms such as nuisance odors, noise, vibration, radiation, electromagnetic energy, and the creation of potential visual impacts including light.

sector's ability to integrate such technologies and practices as far as their use is technically and financially feasible and cost-effective in the context of a project that relies on commercially available skills and resources.

Objectives

- To avoid or minimize adverse impacts on human health and the environment by avoiding or minimizing pollution from project activities
- To promote the reduction of emissions that contribute to climate change

Scope of Application

2. The applicability of this Performance Standard is established during the Social and Environmental Assessment process, while implementation of the actions necessary to meet the requirements of this Performance Standard is managed through the client's Social and Environmental Management System. The assessment and management system requirements are outlined in Performance Standard 1.

Requirements

General Requirements

3. During the design, construction, operation and decommissioning of the project (the project life-cycle) the client will consider ambient conditions and apply pollution prevention and control technologies and practices (techniques) that are best suited to avoid or, where avoidance is not feasible, minimize or reduce adverse impacts on human health and the environment while remaining technically and financially feasible and cost-effective.[2] The project-specific pollution prevention and control techniques applied during the project life-cycle will be tailored to the hazards and risks associated with project emissions and consistent with good international industry practice,[3] as reflected in various internationally recognized sources, including IFC's Environmental, Health and Safety Guidelines (the EHS Guidelines).

2 "Technical feasibility" and "financial feasibility" are defined in Performance Standard 1. "Cost-effectiveness" is based on the effectiveness of reducing emissions relative to the additional cost required to do so.

3 Defined as the exercise of professional skill, diligence, prudence and foresight that would reasonably be expected from skilled and experienced professionals engaged in the same type of undertaking under the same or similar circumstances globally. The circumstances that skilled and experienced professionals may find when evaluating the range of pollution prevention and control techniques available to a project may include, but are not limited to, varying levels of environmental degradation and environmental assimilative capacity as well as varying levels of financial and technical feasibility.

Pollution Prevention, Resource Conservation and Energy Efficiency

4. The client will avoid the release of pollutants or, when avoidance is not feasible, minimize or control the intensity or load of their release. This applies to the release of pollutants due to routine, non-routine or accidental circumstances with the potential for local, regional, and transboundary impacts.[4] In addition, the client should examine and incorporate in its operations resource conservation and energy efficiency measures, consistent with the principles of cleaner production.

Wastes

5. The client will avoid or minimize the generation of hazardous and non-hazardous waste materials as far as practicable. Where waste generation cannot be avoided but has been minimized, the client will recover and reuse waste; where waste can not be recovered or reused, the client will treat, destroy, and dispose of it in an environmentally sound manner. If the generated waste is considered hazardous,[5] the client will explore commercially reasonable alternatives for its environmentally sound disposal considering the limitations applicable to its transboundary movement.[6] When waste disposal is conducted by third parties, the client will use contractors that are reputable and legitimate enterprises licensed by the relevant regulatory agencies.

Hazardous Materials

6. The client will avoid or, when avoidance is not feasible, minimize or control the release of hazardous materials resulting from their production, transportation, handling, storage and use for project activities. The client will avoid the manufacture, trade, and use of chemicals and hazardous materials subject to international bans or phase-outs due to their high toxicity to living organisms, environmental persistence, potential for bioaccumulation, or potential for depletion of the ozone layer,[7] and consider the use of less hazardous substitutes for such chemicals and materials.

Emergency Preparedness and Response

7. The client will be prepared to respond to process upset, accidental, and emergency situations in a manner appropriate to the operational risks and the need to prevent their potential negative consequences. This preparation will include a plan that addresses the training, resources, responsibilities, communication, procedures, and other aspects required to effectively respond to emergencies associated with project hazards. Additional requirements on emergency preparedness and response are found in paragraph 12 of Performance Standard 4.

---

4 In reference to transboundary pollutants, including those covered under the Convention on Long-range Transboundary Air Pollution.

5 As defined by local legislation or international conventions.

6 Consistent with the objectives of the Basel Convention on the Control of Transboundary Movements of Hazardous Wastes.

7 Consistent with the objectives of the Stockholm Convention on Persistent Organic Pollutants and the Montreal Protocol on Substances that Deplete the Ozone Layer. Similar considerations will apply to certain World Health Organization (WHO) classes of pesticides.

Technical Guidance

8. The client will refer to the current version of the EHS Guidelines when evaluating and selecting pollution prevention and control techniques for the project. These Guidelines contain the performance levels and measures that are normally acceptable and applicable to projects. When host country regulations differ from the levels and measures presented in the EHS Guidelines, clients will achieve whichever is more stringent. If less stringent levels or measures are appropriate in view of specific project circumstances, the client will provide full and detailed justification for any proposed alternatives. This justification will demonstrate that the choice for any alternate performance levels is consistent with the overall requirements of this Performance Standard.

Ambient Considerations

9. To address adverse project impacts on existing ambient conditions,[8] the client will: (i) consider a number of factors, including the finite assimilative capacity[9] of the environment, existing and future land use, existing ambient conditions, the project's proximity to ecologically sensitive or protected areas, and the potential for cumulative impacts with uncertain and irreversible consequences; and (ii) promote strategies that avoid or, where avoidance is not feasible, minimize or reduce the release of pollutants, including strategies that contribute to the improvement of ambient conditions when the project has the potential to constitute a significant source of emissions in an already degraded area. These strategies include, but are not limited to, evaluation of project location alternatives and emissions offsets.

Greenhouse Gas Emissions

10. The client will promote the reduction of project-related greenhouse gas (GHG) emissions in a manner appropriate to the nature and scale of project operations and impacts.

11. During the development or operation of projects that are expected to or currently produce significant quantities of GHGs,[10] the client will quantify direct emissions from the facilities owned or controlled within the physical project boundary and indirect emissions associated with the off-site production of power used by the project. Quantification and monitoring of GHG emissions will be conducted annually in accor-

---

8 Such as air, surface and groundwater, and soils.

9 The capacity of the environment for absorbing an incremental load of pollutants while remaining below a threshold of unacceptable risk to human health and the environment.

10 The significance of a project's contribution to GHG emissions varies between industry sectors. The threshold for this Performance Standard is 100,000 tons CO_2 equivalent per year for the aggregate emissions of direct sources and indirect sources associated with purchased electricity for own consumption. This or similar thresholds will apply to such industry sectors or activities as energy, transport; heavy industry, agriculture, forestry, and waste management in order to help promote awareness and reduction of emissions.

dance with internationally recognized methodologies.[11] In addition, the client will evaluate technically and financially feasible and cost-effective options to reduce or offset project-related GHG emissions during the design and operation of the project. These options may include, but are not limited to, carbon financing, energy efficiency improvement, the use of renewable energy sources, alterations of project design, emissions offsets, and the adoption of other mitigation measures such as the reduction of fugitive emissions and the reduction of gas flaring.

Pesticide Use and Management

12. The client will formulate and implement an integrated pest management (IPM) and/or integrated vector management (IVM) approach for pest management activities. The client's IPM and IVM program will entail coordinated use of pest and environmental information along with available pest control methods, including cultural practices, biological, genetic and, as a last resort, chemical means to prevent unacceptable levels of pest damage.

13. When pest management activities include the use of pesticides, the client will select pesticides that are low in human toxicity, known to be effective against the target species, and have minimal effects on non-target species and the environment. When the client selects pesticides, the selection will be based on whether the pesticides are packaged in safe containers, are clearly labeled for safe and proper use, and have been manufactured by an entity currently licensed by relevant regulatory agencies.

14. The client will design its pesticide application regime to minimize damage to natural enemies and prevent the development of resistance in pests. In addition, pesticides will be handled, stored, applied, and disposed of in accordance with the Food and Agriculture Organization's International Code of Conduct on the Distribution and Use of Pesticides or other good international industry practice.

15. The client will not use products that fall in World Health Organization Recommended Classification of Pesticides by Hazard Classes Ia (extremely hazardous) and Ib (highly hazardous); or Class II (moderately hazardous), if the project host country lacks restrictions on distribution and use of these chemicals, or if they are likely to be accessible to personnel without proper training, equipment, and facilities to handle, store, apply, and dispose of these products properly.

11 Estimation methodologies are provided by the Intergovernmental Panel on Climate Change (IPCC), various international organizations, and relevant host country agencies.

PERFORMANCE STANDARD 4
COMMUNITY HEALTH, SAFETY AND SECURITY

Introduction

1. Performance Standard 4 recognizes that project activities, equipment, and infrastructure often bring benefits to communities including employment, services, and opportunities for economic development. However, projects can also increase the potential for community exposure to risks and impacts arising from equipment accidents, structural failures, and releases of hazardous materials. Communities may also be affected by impacts on their natural resources, exposure to diseases, and the use of security personnel. While acknowledging the public authorities' role in promoting the health, safety and security of the public, this Performance Standard addresses the client's responsibility to avoid or minimize the risks and impacts to community health, safety and security that may arise from project activities. The level of risks and impacts described in this Performance Standard may be greater in projects located in conflict and post-conflict areas.

Objectives

- To avoid or minimize risks to and impacts on the health and safety of the local community during the project life cycle from both routine and non-routine circumstances
- To ensure that the safeguarding of personnel and property is carried out in a legitimate manner that avoids or minimizes risks to the community's safety and security

Scope of Application

2. The applicability of this Performance Standard is established during the Social and Environmental Assessment process, while implementation of the actions necessary to meet the requirements of this Performance Standard is managed through the client's Social and Environmental Management System. The assessment and management system requirements are outlined in Performance Standard 1.

3. This Performance Standard addresses potential risks and impacts to the affected community from project activities. Occupational health and safety standards are found in paragraph 16 of Performance Standard 2, and environmental standards to prevent impacts on human health and the environment due to pollution are found in Performance Standard 3.

Requirements

Community Health and Safety Requirements

General Requirements

4. The client will evaluate the risks and impacts to the health and safety of the affected community during the design, construction, operation, and decommissioning of the project and will establish preventive measures to address them in a manner commensurate with the identified risks and impacts. These measures will favor the prevention or avoidance of risks and impacts over minimization and reduction.

5. Where the project poses risks to or adverse impacts on the health and safety of affected communities, the client will disclose the Action Plan and any other relevant project-related information to enable the affected communities and relevant government agencies to understand these risks and impacts, and will engage the affected communities and agencies on an ongoing basis consistent with the requirements of Performance Standard 1.

Infrastructure and Equipment Safety

6. The client will design, construct, and operate and decommission the structural elements or components of the project in accordance with good international industry practice,[1] and will give particular consideration to potential exposure to natural hazards, especially where the structural elements are accessible to members of the affected community or where their failure could result in injury to the community. Structural elements will be designed and constructed by qualified and experienced professionals, and certified or approved by competent authorities or professionals. When structural elements or components, such as dams, tailings dams, or ash ponds, are situated in high-risk locations, and their failure or malfunction may threaten the safety of communities, the client will engage one or more qualified experts with relevant and recognized experience in similar projects, separate from those responsible for the design and construction, to conduct a review as early as possible in project development and throughout the stages of project design, construction, and commissioning. For projects that operate moving equipment on public roads and other forms of infrastructure, the client will seek to prevent the occurrence of incidents and accidents associated with the operation of such equipment.

Hazardous Materials Safety

7. The client will prevent or minimize the potential for community exposure to hazardous materials that may be released by the project. Where there is a potential for the community (including workers and their families) to be exposed to hazards, particularly those that may be life-threatening, the client will exercise special care to avoid or minimize their exposure by modifying, substituting or eliminating the condition or

1 Defined as the exercise of that degree of skill, diligence, prudence and foresight that would reasonably and ordinarily be expected from skilled and experienced professionals engaged in the same type of undertaking under the same or similar circumstances globally.

substance causing the hazards. Where hazardous materials are part of existing project infrastructure or components, the client will exercise special care when conducting decommissioning activities in order to prevent exposure to the community. In addition, the client will exercise commercially reasonable efforts to control the safety of deliveries of raw materials and of transportation and disposal of wastes, and will implement measures to avoid or control community exposure to pesticides in accordance with the requirements outlined in paragraphs 6 and 12 through 15 of Performance Standard 3.

Environmental and Natural Resource Issues

8. The client will avoid or minimize the exacerbation of impacts caused by natural hazards, such as landslides or floods that could arise from land use changes due to project activities.

9. The client will also avoid or minimize adverse impacts due to project activities on soil, water, and other natural resources in use by the affected communities.

Community Exposure to Disease

10. The client will prevent or minimize the potential for community exposure to water-borne, water-based, water-related, vector-borne disease, and other communicable diseases that could result from project activities. Where specific diseases are endemic in communities in the project area of influence, the client is encouraged to explore opportunities during the project life cycle to improve environmental conditions that could help reduce their incidence.

11. The client will prevent or minimize transmission of communicable diseases that may be associated with the influx of temporary or permanent project labor.

Emergency Preparedness and Response

12. The client will assess the potential risks and impacts from project activities and inform affected communities of significant potential hazards in a culturally appropriate manner. The client will also assist and collaborate with the community and the local government agencies in their preparations to respond effectively to emergency situations, especially when their participation and collaboration are necessary to respond to such emergency situations. If local government agencies have little or no capacity to respond effectively, the client will play an active role in preparing for and responding to emergencies associated with the project. The client will document its emergency preparedness and response activities, resources, and responsibilities, and will disclose appropriate information in the Action Plan or other relevant document to affected communities and relevant government agencies.

Security Personnel Requirements

13. When the client directly retains employees or contractors to provide security to safeguard its personnel and property, it will assess risks to those within and outside the project site posed by its security arrangements. In making such arrangements, the client will be guided by the principles of proportionality, good international practices in terms of hiring, rules of conduct, training, equipping and monitoring of such personnel, and applicable law. The client will make reasonable inquiries to satisfy itself that those providing security are not implicated in past abuses, will train them adequately in the use of force (and where applicable, firearms) and appropriate conduct toward workers and the local community, and require them to act within the applicable law. The client will not sanction any use of force except when used for preventive and defensive purposes in proportion to the nature and extent of the threat. A grievance mechanism should allow the affected community to express concerns about the security arrangements and acts of security personnel.

14. If government security personnel are deployed to provide security services for the client, the client will assess risks arising from such use, communicate its intent that the security personnel act in a manner consistent with paragraph 13 above, and encourage the relevant public authorities to disclose the security arrangements for the client's facilities to the public, subject to overriding security concerns.

15. The client will investigate any credible allegations of unlawful or abusive acts of security personnel, take action (or urge appropriate parties to take action) to prevent recurrence, and report unlawful and abusive acts to public authorities when appropriate.

PERFORMANCE STANDARD 5
LAND ACQUISITION AND INVOLUNTARY RESETTLEMENT

Introduction

1. Involuntary resettlement refers both to physical displacement (relocation or loss of shelter) and to economic displacement (loss of assets or access to assets that leads to loss of income sources or means of livelihood) as a result of project-related land acquisition.[1] Resettlement is considered involuntary when affected individuals or communities do not have the right to refuse land acquisition that results in displacement. This occurs in cases of: (i) lawful expropriation or restrictions on land use based on eminent domain;[2] and ii) negotiated settlements in which the buyer can resort to expropriation or impose legal restrictions on land use if negotiations with the seller fail.

2. Unless properly managed, involuntary resettlement may result in long-term hardship and impoverishment for affected persons and communities, as well as environmental damage and social stress in areas to which they have been displaced. For these reasons, involuntary resettlement should be avoided or at least minimized. However, where it is unavoidable, appropriate measures to mitigate adverse impacts

1 Land acquisition includes both outright purchases of property and purchases of access rights, such as rights-of-way.

2 Such restriction may include restrictions of access to legally designated nature conservation areas.

on displaced persons and host communities[3] should be carefully planned and implemented. Experience demonstrates that the direct involvement of the client in resettlement activities can result in cost-effective, efficient, and timely implementation of those activities, as well as innovative approaches to improving the livelihoods of those affected by resettlement.

3. Negotiated settlements help avoid expropriation and eliminate the need to use governmental authority to remove people forcibly. Negotiated settlements can usually be achieved by providing fair and appropriate compensation and other incentives or benefits to affected persons or communities, and by mitigating the risks of asymmetry of information and bargaining power. Clients are encouraged to acquire land rights through negotiated settlements wherever possible, even if they have the legal means to gain access to the land without the seller's consent.

Objectives

- To avoid or at least minimize involuntary resettlement wherever feasible by exploring alternative project designs
- To mitigate adverse social and economic impacts from land acquisition or restrictions on affected persons' use of land by: (i) providing compensation for loss of assets at replacement cost; and (ii) ensuring that resettlement activities are implemented with appropriate disclosure of information, consultation, and the informed participation of those affected
- To improve or at least restore the livelihoods and standards of living of displaced persons
- To improve living conditions among displaced persons through provision of adequate housing with security of tenure[4] at resettlement sites

Scope of Application

4. The applicability of this Performance Standard is established during the Social and Environmental Assessment process, while implementation of the actions necessary to meet the requirements of this Performance Standard is managed through the client's Social and Environmental Management System. The assessment and management system requirements are outlined in Performance Standard 1.

5. This Performance Standard applies to physical or economic displacement resulting from the following types of land transactions:

---

3 A host community is any community receiving displaced persons.

4 A resettlement site offers security of tenure if it protects the resettled persons from forced evictions.

- Type I: Land rights for a private sector project acquired through expropriation or other compulsory procedures
- Type II: Land rights for a private sector project acquired through negotiated settlements with property owners or those with legal rights to land, including customary or traditional rights recognized or recognizable under the laws of the country, if expropriation or other compulsory process would have resulted upon the failure of negotiation[5]

Paragraph 18 and part of paragraph 20 below apply to displaced persons with no recognizable legal right or claim to the land they occupy.

6. This Performance Standard does not apply to resettlement resulting from voluntary land transactions (i.e., market transactions in which the seller is not obliged to sell and the buyer cannot resort to expropriation or other compulsory procedures if negotiations fail). In the event of adverse economic, social, or environmental impacts from project activities other than land acquisition (e.g., loss of access to assets or resources or restrictions on land use), such impacts will be avoided, minimized, mitigated or compensated for through the process of Social and Environmental Assessment under Performance Standard 1. If these impacts become significantly adverse at any stage of the project, the client should consider applying the requirements of Performance Standard 5, even where no initial land acquisition was involved.

Requirements

General Requirements

Project Design

7. The client will consider feasible alternative project designs to avoid or at least minimize physical or economic displacement, while balancing environmental, social, and financial costs and benefits.

Compensation and Benefits for Displaced Persons

8. When displacement cannot be avoided, the client will offer displaced persons and communities compensation for loss of assets at full replacement cost and other assistance[6] to help them improve or at least restore their standards of living or livelihoods, as provided in this Performance Standard. Standards for compensation will be transparent and consistent within the project. Where livelihoods of displaced persons are land-based, or where land is collectively owned, the client will offer land-based compensation, where feasible.[7] The client will provide opportunities to dis-

5 These negotiations can be carried out by the private sector company acquiring the land or by an agent of the company. In the case of private sector projects in which land rights are acquired by the government, the negotiations may be carried out by the government or by the private company as an agent of the government.

6 As described in paragraphs 18 and 20.

7 See also footnote 9.

placed persons and communities to derive appropriate development benefits from the project.

Consultation

9. Following disclosure of all relevant information, the client will consult with and facilitate the informed participation of affected persons and communities, including host communities, in decision-making processes related to resettlement. Consultation will continue during the implementation, monitoring, and evaluation of compensation payment and resettlement to achieve outcomes that are consistent with the objectives of this Performance Standard.

Grievance Mechanism

10. The client will establish a grievance mechanism consistent with Performance Standard 1 to receive and address specific concerns about compensation and relocation that are raised by displaced persons or members of host communities, including a recourse mechanism designed to resolve disputes in an impartial manner.

Resettlement Planning and Implementation

11. Where involuntary resettlement is unavoidable, the client will carry out a census with appropriate socio-economic baseline data to identify the persons who will be displaced by the project, to determine who will be eligible for compensation and assistance, and to discourage inflow of people who are ineligible for these benefits. In the absence of host government procedures, the client will establish a cut-off date for eligibility. Information regarding the cut-off date will be well documented and disseminated throughout the project area.

12. In the case of Type I transactions (acquisition of land rights through the exercise of eminent domain) or Type II transactions (negotiated settlements) that involve the physical displacement of people, the client will develop a resettlement action plan or a resettlement framework based on a Social and Environmental Assessment that covers, at a minimum, the applicable requirements of this Performance Standard regardless of the number of people affected. The plan or framework will be designed to mitigate the negative impacts of displacement, identify development opportunities, and establish the entitlements of all categories of affected persons (including host communities), with particular attention paid to the needs of the poor and the vulnerable (see Performance Standard 1, paragraph 12). The client will document all transactions to acquire land rights, as well as compensation measures and relocation activities. The client will also establish procedures to monitor and evaluate the implementation of resettlement plans and take corrective action as necessary. A resettlement will be considered complete when the adverse impacts of resettlement have been addressed in a manner that is consistent with the objectives stated in the resettlement plan or framework as well as the objectives of this Performance Standard.

13. In the case of Type II transactions (negotiated settlements) involving economic (but not physical) displacement of people, the client will develop procedures to offer to the affected persons and communities compensation and other assistance that meet the objectives of this Performance Standard. The procedures will establish the entitlements of affected persons or communities and will ensure that these are provided in a transparent, consistent, and equitable manner. The implementation of the procedures will be considered complete when affected persons or communities have received compensation and other assistance according to the requirements of this Performance Standard. In cases where affected persons reject compensation offers that meet the requirements of this Performance Standard and, as a result, expropriation or other legal procedures are initiated, the client will explore opportunities to collaborate with the responsible government agency, and if permitted by the agency, play an active role in the resettlement planning, implementation, and monitoring.

Displacement

14. Displaced persons may be classified as persons: (i) who have formal legal rights to the land they occupy; (ii) who do not have formal legal rights to land, but have a claim to land that is recognized or recognizable under the national laws[8]; or (iii) who have no recognizable legal right or claim to the land they occupy.[9] The census will establish the status of the displaced persons.

15. Land acquisition for the project may result in the physical displacement of people as well as their economic displacement. As a result, requirements for both physical displacement and economic displacement may apply.

Physical Displacement

16. If people living in the project area must move to another location, the client will: (i) offer displaced persons choices among feasible resettlement options, including adequate replacement housing or cash compensation where appropriate; and (ii) provide relocation assistance suited to the needs of each group of displaced persons, with particular attention paid to the needs of the poor and the vulnerable. Alternative housing and/or cash compensation will be made available prior to relocation. New resettlement sites built for displaced persons will offer improved living conditions.

17. In the case of physically displaced persons under paragraph 14 (i) or (ii), the client will offer the choice of replacement property of equal or higher value, equivalent or better characteristics and advantages of location, or cash compensation at full replacement value where appropriate.[10]

---

8 Such claims could be derived from adverse possession or from customary or traditional law.

9 Such as opportunistic squatters and recently arrived economic migrants who occupy land prior to the cut-off date.

10 Payment of cash compensation for lost assets may be appropriate where: (a) livelihoods are not land-based; (b) livelihoods are land-based but the land taken for the project is a small fraction of the affected asset and the residual land is economically viable; or (c) active markets for land, housing, and labor exist, displaced persons use such markets, and there is sufficient supply of land and housing. Cash compensation levels should be sufficient to replace the lost land and other assets at full replacement cost in local markets.

18. In the case of physically displaced persons under paragraph 14 (iii), the client will offer them a choice of options for adequate housing with security of tenure so that they can resettle legally without having to face the risk of forced eviction. Where these displaced persons own and occupy structures, the client will compensate them for the loss of assets other than land, such as dwellings and other improvements to the land, at full replacement cost, provided that these people occupy the project area prior to the cut-off date for eligibility. Compensation in kind will be offered in lieu of cash compensation where feasible. Based on consultation with such displaced persons, the client will provide relocation assistance sufficient for them to restore their standards of living at an adequate alternative site.[11] The client is not required to compensate or assist those who encroach on the project area after the cut-off date.

19. Where communities of Indigenous Peoples are to be physically displaced from their communally held traditional or customary lands under use, the client will meet the applicable requirements of this Performance Standard, as well as those of Performance Standard 7 (in particular paragraph 14).

Economic Displacement

20. If land acquisition for the project causes loss of income or livelihood, regardless of whether or not the affected people are physically displaced, the client will meet the following requirements:

- Promptly compensate economically displaced persons for loss of assets or access to assets at full replacement cost
- In cases where land acquisition affects commercial structures, compensate the affected business owner for the cost of reestablishing commercial activities elsewhere, for lost net income during the period of transition, and for the costs of the transfer and reinstallation of the plant, machinery or other equipment
- Provide replacement property (e.g., agricultural or commercial sites) of equal or greater value, or cash compensation at full replacement cost where appropriate, to persons with legal rights or claims to land which are recognized or recognizable under the national laws (see paragraph 14 (i) and (ii))
- Compensate economically displaced persons who are without legally recognizable claims to land (see paragraph 14 (iii)) for lost assets (such as crops, irrigation infrastructure and other improvements made to the land) other than land, at full replacement cost. The client is not required to compensate or assist opportunistic settlers who encroach on the project area after the cut-off date
- Provide additional targeted assistance (e.g., credit facilities, training, or job opportunities) and opportunities to improve or at least restore their income-earning capacity, production levels, and standards of living to economically displaced persons whose livelihoods or income levels are adversely affected

11 Relocation of informal settlers in urban areas often has trade-offs. For example, the relocated families may gain security of tenure, but they may lose advantages of location.

- Provide transitional support to economically displaced persons, as necessary, based on a reasonable estimate of the time required to restore their income-earning capacity, production levels, and standards of living

21. Where communities of Indigenous Peoples are economically displaced (but not relocated) as a result of project-related land acquisition, the client will meet the applicable requirements of this Performance Standard, as well as those of Performance Standard 7 (in particular paragraphs 12 and 13).

Private Sector Responsibilities under Government-Managed Resettlement

22. Where land acquisition and resettlement are the responsibility of the host government, the client will collaborate with the responsible government agency, to the extent permitted by the agency, to achieve outcomes that are consistent with the objectives of this Performance Standard. In addition, where government capacity is limited, the client will play an active role during resettlement planning, implementation and monitoring, as described below in paragraphs 23 through 25.

23. In the case of Type I transactions (acquisition of land rights through expropriation or other legal procedures) involving physical or economic displacement, and Type II transactions (negotiated settlements) involving physical displacement, the client will prepare a plan (or a framework) that, together with the documents prepared by the responsible government agency, will address the relevant requirements of this Performance Standard (the General Requirements, except for paragraph 13, and requirements for Physical Displacement and Economic Displacement above). The client may need to include in its plan: (i) a description of the entitlements of displaced persons provided under applicable laws and regulations; (ii) the measures proposed to bridge any gaps between such entitlements and the requirements of this Performance Standard; and (iii) the financial and implementation responsibilities of the government agency and/or the client.

24. In the case of Type II transactions (negotiated settlements) involving economic (but not physical) displacement, the client will identify and describe the procedures that the responsible government agency plans to use to compensate affected persons and communities. If these procedures do not meet the relevant requirements of this Performance Standard (the General Requirements, except for paragraph 12, and requirements for Economic Displacement above), the client will develop its own procedures to supplement government action.

25. If permitted by the responsible government agency, the client will, in collaboration with such agency: (i) implement its plan or procedures established in accordance with paragraph 23 or 24 above; and (ii) monitor resettlement activity that is undertaken by the government agency until such activity has been completed.

PERFORMANCE STANDARD 6
BIODIVERSITY CONSERVATION AND SUSTAINABLE NATURAL RESOURCE MANAGEMENT

Introduction

1. Performance Standard 6 recognizes that protecting and conserving biodiversity — the variety of life in all its forms, including genetic, species and ecosystem diversity — and its ability to change and evolve, is fundamental to sustainable development. The components of biodiversity, as defined in the Convention on Biological Diversity, include ecosystems and habitats, species and communities, and genes and genomes, all of which have social, economic, cultural and scientific importance. This Performance Standard reflects the objectives of the Convention on Biological Diversity to conserve biological diversity and promote use of renewable natural resources in a sustainable manner. This Performance Standard addresses how clients can avoid or mitigate threats to biodiversity arising from their operations as well as sustainably manage renewable natural resources.

Objectives

- To protect and conserve biodiversity
- To promote the sustainable management and use of natural resources through the adoption of practices that integrate conservation needs and development priorities

Scope of Application

2. The applicability of this Performance Standard is established during the Social and Environmental Assessment process, while implementation of the actions necessary to meet the requirements of this Performance Standard is managed through the client's Social and Environmental Management System. The assessment and management system requirements are outlined in Performance Standard 1.

3. Based on the Assessment of risks and impacts and the vulnerability of the biodiversity and the natural resources present, the requirements of this Performance Standard are applied to projects in all habitats, whether or not those habitats have been previously disturbed and whether or not they are legally protected.

Requirements

Protection and Conservation of Biodiversity

4. In order to avoid or minimize adverse impacts to biodiversity in the project's area of influence (see Performance Standard 1, paragraph 5), the client will assess the significance of project impacts on all levels of biodiversity as an integral part of the Social and Environmental Assessment process. The Assessment will take into account the differing values attached to biodiversity by specific stakeholders, as well as identify impacts on ecosystem services. The Assessment will focus on the major threats to biodiversity, which include habitat destruction and invasive alien species. When requirements of paragraphs 9, 10, or 11 apply, the client will retain qualified and experienced external experts to assist in conducting the Assessment.

Habitat

5. Habitat destruction is recognized as the major threat to the maintenance of biodiversity. Habitats can be divided into natural habitats (which are land and water areas where the biological communities are formed largely by native plant and animal species, and where human activity has not essentially modified the area's primary ecological functions) and modified habitats (where there has been apparent alteration of the natural habitat, often with the introduction of alien species of plants and animals, such as agricultural areas). Both types of habitat can support important biodiversity at all levels, including endemic or threatened species.

Modified Habitat

6. In areas of modified habitat, the client will exercise care to minimize any conversion or degradation of such habitat, and will, depending on the nature and scale of the project, identify opportunities to enhance habitat and protect and conserve biodiversity as part of their operations.

Natural Habitat

7. In areas of natural habitat, the client will not significantly convert or degrade[1] such habitat, unless the following conditions are met:

- There are no technically and financially feasible alternatives
- The overall benefits of the project outweigh the costs, including those to the environment and biodiversity
- Any conversion or degradation is appropriately mitigated

1 Significant conversion or degradation is: (i) the elimination or severe diminution of the integrity of a habitat caused by a major, long-term change in land or water use; or (ii) modification of a habitat that substantially reduces the habitat's ability to maintain viable population of its native species.

8. Mitigation measures will be designed to achieve no net loss of biodiversity where feasible, and may include a combination of actions, such as:

- Post-operation restoration of habitats
- Offset of losses through the creation of ecologically comparable area(s) that is managed for biodiversity[2]
- Compensation to direct users of biodiversity

Critical Habitat

9. Critical habitat is a subset of both natural and modified habitat that deserves particular attention. Critical habitat includes areas with high biodiversity value,[3] including habitat required for the survival of critically endangered or endangered species;[4] areas having special significance for endemic or restricted-range species; sites that are critical for the survival of migratory species; areas supporting globally significant concentrations or numbers of individuals of congregatory species; areas with unique assemblages of species or which are associated with key evolutionary processes or provide key ecosystem services; and areas having biodiversity of significant social, economic or cultural importance to local communities.

10. In areas of critical habitat, the client will not implement any project activities unless the following requirements are met:

- There are no measurable adverse impacts on the ability of the critical habitat to support the established population of species described in paragraph 9 or the functions of the critical habitat described in paragraph 9
- There is no reduction in the population of any recognized critically endangered or endangered species[5]
- Any lesser impacts are mitigated in accordance with paragraph 8

Legally Protected Areas

11. In circumstances where a proposed project is located within a legally protected area,[6] the client, in addition to the applicable requirements of paragraph 10 above, will meet the following requirements:

- Act in a manner consistent with defined protected area management plans
- Consult protected area sponsors and managers, local communities, and other key stakeholders on the proposed project

---

2 Clients will respect the ongoing usage of such biodiversity by Indigenous Peoples or traditional communities.

3 Such as areas that meet the criteria of the World Conservation Union (IUCN) classification.

4 As defined by the IUCN Red List of Threatened Species or as defined in any national legislation.

5 As defined by the IUCN Red List of Threatened Species or as defined in any national legislation.

6 An area may be designated as legally protected for different purposes. This Performance Standard refers to areas legally designated for the protection or conservation of biodiversity, including areas proposed by governments for such designation.

- Implement additional programs, as appropriate, to promote and enhance the conservation aims of the protected area

Invasive Alien Species

12. Intentional or accidental introduction of alien, or non-native, species of flora and fauna into areas where they are not normally found can be a significant threat to biodiversity, since some alien species can become invasive, spreading rapidly and outcompeting native species.

13. The client will not intentionally introduce any new alien species (not currently established in the country or region of the project) unless this is carried out in accordance with the existing regulatory framework for such introduction, if such framework is present, or is subject to a risk assessment (as part of the client's Social and Environmental Assessment) to determine the potential for invasive behavior. The client will not deliberately introduce any alien species with a high risk of invasive behavior or any known invasive species, and will exercise diligence to prevent accidental or unintended introductions.

Management and Use of Renewable Natural Resources

14. The client will manage renewable natural resources in a sustainable manner.[7] Where possible, the client will demonstrate the sustainable management of the resources through an appropriate system of independent certification.[8]

15. In particular, forests and aquatic systems are principal providers of natural resources, and need to be managed as specified below.

Natural and Plantation Forests

16. Clients involved in natural forest harvesting or plantation development will not cause any conversion or degradation of critical habitat. Where feasible, the client will locate plantation projects on unforested land or land already converted (excluding land that is converted in anticipation of the project). In addition, the client will ensure that all natural forests and plantations over which they have management control are independently certified as meeting performance standards compatible with internationally accepted principles and criteria for sustainable forest management.[9] Where a pre-assessment determines that the operation does not yet meet the requirements of

7 Sustainable resource management is the management of the use, development and protection of resources in a way, or at a rate, which enables people and communities, including Indigenous Peoples, to provide for their present social, economic and cultural well-being while also sustaining the potential of those resources to meet the reasonably foreseeable needs of future generations and safeguarding the life-supporting capacity of air, water and soil ecosystems.

8 An appropriate certification system would be one which is independent, cost-effective, based on objective and measurable performance standards and developed through consultation with relevant stakeholders, such as local people and communities, indigenous peoples, civil society organizations representing consumer, producer, and conservation interests. Such a system has fair, transparent, independent decision-making procedures that avoid conflicts of interest.

9 See footnote 7.

such an independent forest certification system, the client will develop and adhere to a time-bound, phased action plan for achieving such certification.

Freshwater and Marine Systems

17. Clients involved in the production and harvesting of fish populations or other aquatic species must demonstrate that their activities are being undertaken in a sustainable manner, through application of an internationally accepted system of independent certification, if available, or through appropriate studies carried out in conjunction with the Social and Environmental Assessment process.

PERFORMANCE STANDARD 7
INDIGENOUS PEOPLES

Introduction

1. Performance Standard 7 recognizes that Indigenous Peoples, as social groups with identities that are distinct from dominant groups in national societies, are often among the most marginalized and vulnerable segments of the population. Their economic, social and legal status often limits their capacity to defend their interests in, and rights to, lands and natural and cultural resources, and may restrict their ability to participate in and benefit from development. They are particularly vulnerable if their lands and resources are transformed, encroached upon by outsiders, or significantly degraded. Their languages, cultures, religions, spiritual beliefs, and institutions may also be under threat. These characteristics expose Indigenous Peoples to different types of risks and severity of impacts, including loss of identity, culture, and natural resource-based livelihoods, as well as exposure to impoverishment and disease.

2. Private sector projects may create opportunities for Indigenous Peoples to participate in, and benefit from, project-related activities that may help them fulfill their aspiration for economic and social development. In addition, this Performance Standard recognizes that Indigenous Peoples may play a role in sustainable development by promoting and managing activities and enterprises as partners in development.

Objectives

- To ensure that the development process fosters full respect for the dignity, human rights, aspirations, cultures and natural resource-based livelihoods of Indigenous Peoples
- To avoid adverse impacts of projects on communities of Indigenous Peoples, or when avoidance is not feasible, to minimize, mitigate, or compensate for such impacts, and to provide opportunities for development benefits, in a culturally appropriate manner

- To establish and maintain an ongoing relationship with the Indigenous Peoples affected by a project throughout the life of the project
- To foster good faith negotiation with and informed participation of Indigenous Peoples when projects are to be located on traditional or customary lands under use by the Indigenous Peoples
- To respect and preserve the culture, knowledge and practices of Indigenous Peoples

Scope of Application

3. The applicability of this Performance Standard is established during the Social and Environmental Assessment process, while implementation of the actions necessary to meet the requirements of this Performance Standard is managed through the client's Social and Environmental Management System. The assessment and management system requirements are outlined in Performance Standard 1.

4. There is no universally accepted definition of "Indigenous Peoples". Indigenous Peoples may be referred to in different countries by such terms as "Indigenous ethnic minorities," "aboriginals," "hill tribes," "minority nationalities," "scheduled tribes," "first nations," or "tribal groups."

5. In this Performance Standard, the term "Indigenous Peoples" is used in a generic sense to refer to a distinct social and cultural group possessing the following characteristics in varying degrees:

- Self-identification as members of a distinct indigenous cultural group and recognition of this identity by others
- Collective attachment to geographically distinct habitats or ancestral territories in the project area and to the natural resources in these habitats and territories
- Customary cultural, economic, social, or political institutions that are separate from those of the dominant society or culture
- An indigenous language, often different from the official language of the country or region

6. Ascertaining whether a particular group is considered as Indigenous Peoples for the purpose of this Performance Standard may require technical judgment.

Requirements

General Requirements

Avoidance of Adverse Impacts

7. The client will identify through a process of Social and Environmental Assessment all communities of Indigenous Peoples who may be affected by the project within the project's area of influence, as well as the nature and degree of the expected social, cultural (including cultural heritage[1]), and environmental impacts on them, and avoid adverse impacts whenever feasible.

8. When avoidance is not feasible, the client will minimize, mitigate or compensate for these impacts in a culturally appropriate manner. The client's proposed action will be developed with the informed participation of affected Indigenous Peoples and contained in a time-bound plan, such as an Indigenous Peoples Development Plan, or a broader community development plan with separate components for Indigenous Peoples consistent with the requirements of paragraph 9.[2]

Information Disclosure, Consultation and Informed Participation

9. The client will establish an ongoing relationship with the affected communities of Indigenous Peoples from as early as possible in the project planning and throughout the life of the project. In projects with adverse impacts on affected communities of Indigenous Peoples, the consultation process will ensure their free, prior, and informed consultation and facilitate their informed participation on matters that affect them directly, such as proposed mitigation measures, the sharing of development benefits and opportunities, and implementation issues. The process of community engagement will be culturally appropriate and commensurate with the risks and potential impacts to the Indigenous Peoples. In particular, the process will include the following steps:

- Involve Indigenous Peoples' representative bodies (for example, councils of elders or village councils, among others)
- Be inclusive of both women and men and of various age groups in a culturally appropriate manner
- Provide sufficient time for Indigenous Peoples' collective decision-making processes
- Facilitate the Indigenous Peoples' expression of their views, concerns, and proposals in the language of their choice, without external manipulation, interference, or coercion, and without intimidation
- Ensure that the grievance mechanism established for the project, as described in Performance Standard 1, paragraph 23, is culturally appropriate and accessible for Indigenous Peoples

Development Benefits

10. The client will seek to identify, through the process of free, prior, and informed consultation with and the informed participation of the affected communities of

1 Additional client requirements on protection of cultural heritage are set out in Performance Standard 8.

2 The determination of the appropriate plan will require technical judgment. A community development plan may be appropriate when Indigenous Peoples are integrated into larger affected communities.

Indigenous Peoples, opportunities for culturally appropriate development benefits. Such opportunities should be commensurate with the degree of project impacts, with the aim of improving their standard of living and livelihoods in a culturally appropriate manner, and to fostering the long-term sustainability of the natural resource on which they depend. The client will document identified development benefits consistent with the requirements of paragraphs 8 and 9 above, and provide them in a timely and equitable manner.

Special Requirements

11. Because Indigenous Peoples may be particularly vulnerable to the project circumstances described below, the following requirements will also apply, in the circumstances indicated, in addition to the General Requirements above. When any of these Special Requirements apply, the client will retain qualified and experienced external experts to assist in conducting the Assessment.

Impacts on Traditional or Customary Lands under Use

12. Indigenous Peoples are often closely tied to their traditional or customary lands and natural resources on these lands. While these lands may not be under legal ownership pursuant to national law, use of these lands, including seasonal or cyclical use, by communities of Indigenous Peoples for their livelihoods, or cultural, ceremonial, or spiritual purposes that define their identity and community, can often be substantiated and documented. Paragraphs 13 and 14 below specify the requirements that the client will follow when traditional or customary lands are under use in a manner described in this paragraph.

13. If the client proposes to locate the project on, or commercially develop natural resources located within, traditional or customary lands under use, and adverse impacts[3] can be expected on the livelihoods, or cultural, ceremonial, or spiritual use that define the identity and community of the Indigenous Peoples, the client will respect their use by taking the following steps:

- The client will document its efforts to avoid or at least minimize the size of land proposed for the project
- The Indigenous Peoples' land use will be documented by experts in collaboration with the affected communities of Indigenous Peoples without prejudicing any Indigenous Peoples' land claim[4]
- The affected communities of Indigenous People will be informed of their rights with respect to these lands under national laws, including any national law recognizing customary rights or use

3 Such adverse impacts may include impacts from loss of access to assets or resources, or restrictions on land use, resulting from project activities.

4 While this Performance Standard requires substantiation and documentation of the use of such land, clients should also be aware that the land may already be under alternative use, as designated by the host government.

- The client will offer affected communities of Indigenous Peoples at least compensation and due process available to those with full legal title to land in the case of commercial development of their land under national laws, together with culturally appropriate development opportunities; land-based compensation or compensation-in-kind will be offered in lieu of cash compensation where feasible
- The client will enter into good faith negotiation with the affected communities of Indigenous Peoples, and document their informed participation and the successful outcome of the negotiation

Relocation of Indigenous Peoples from Traditional or Customary Lands

14. The client will consider feasible alternative project designs to avoid the relocation of Indigenous Peoples from their communally held[5] traditional or customary lands under use. If such relocation is unavoidable, the client will not proceed with the project unless it enters into a good faith negotiation with the affected communities of Indigenous Peoples, and documents their informed participation and the successful outcome of the negotiation. Any relocation of Indigenous Peoples will be consistent with the Resettlement Planning and Implementation requirements of Performance Standard 5. Where feasible, the relocated Indigenous Peoples should be able to return to their traditional or customary lands, should the reason for their relocation cease to exist.

Cultural Resources

15. Where a project proposes to use the cultural resources, knowledge, innovations, or practices of Indigenous Peoples for commercial purposes, the client will inform the Indigenous Peoples of: (i) their rights under national law; (ii) the scope and nature of the proposed commercial development; and (iii) the potential consequences of such development. The client will not proceed with such commercialization unless it: (i) enters into a good faith negotiation with the affected communities of Indigenous People; (ii) documents their informed participation and the successful outcome of the negotiation; and (iii) provides for fair and equitable sharing of benefits from commercialization of such knowledge, innovation, or practice, consistent with their customs and traditions.

5 Where members of the affected communities of Indigenous Peoples individually hold legal title, or where the relevant national law recognizes customary rights for individuals, the requirements of Performance Standard 5 will apply, rather than the requirements under this heading.

PERFORMANCE STANDARD 8
CULTURAL HERITAGE

Introduction

1. Performance Standard 8 recognizes the importance of cultural heritage for current and future generations. Consistent with the Convention Concerning the Protection of the World Cultural and Natural Heritage, this Performance Standard aims to protect irreplaceable cultural heritage and to guide clients on protecting cultural heritage in the course of their business operations. In addition, the requirements of this Performance Standard on a project's use of cultural heritage are based in part on standards set by the Convention on Biological Diversity.

Objectives

- To protect cultural heritage from the adverse impacts of project activities and support its preservation
- To promote the equitable sharing of benefits from the use of cultural heritage in business activities

Scope of Application

2. The applicability of this Performance Standard is established during the Social and Environmental Assessment process, while implementation of the actions necessary to meet the requirements of this Performance Standard is managed through the client's Social and Environmental Management System. The assessment and management system requirements are outlined in Performance Standard 1.

3. For the purposes of this Performance Standard, cultural heritage refers to tangible forms of cultural heritage, such as tangible property and sites having archaeological (prehistoric), paleontological, historical, cultural, artistic, and religious values, as well as unique natural environmental features that embody cultural values, such as sacred groves. However, for the purpose of paragraph 11 below, intangible forms of culture, such as cultural knowledge, innovations and practices of communities embodying traditional lifestyles, are also included. The requirements of this Performance Standard apply to cultural heritage regardless of whether or not it has been legally protected or previously disturbed.

Requirements

Protection of Cultural Heritage in Project Design and Execution

Internationally Recognized Practices

4. In addition to complying with relevant national law on the protection of cultural heritage, including national law implementing the host country's obligations under the Convention Concerning the Protection of the World Cultural and Natural Heritage and other relevant international law, the client will protect and support cultural heritage by undertaking internationally recognized practices for the protection, field-based study, and documentation of cultural heritage. If the requirements of paragraphs 7, 8, 9, 10 or 11 apply, the client will retain qualified and experienced experts to assist in the Assessment.

Chance Find Procedures

5. The client is responsible for siting and designing a project to avoid significant damage to cultural heritage. When the proposed location of a project is in areas where cultural heritage is expected to be found, either during construction or operations, the client will implement chance find procedures established through the Social and Environmental Assessment. The client will not disturb any chance finds further until an Assessment by a competent specialist is made and actions consistent with the requirements of this Performance Standard are identified.

Consultation

6. Where a project may affect cultural heritage, the client will consult with affected communities within the host country who use, or have used within living memory, the cultural heritage for long-standing cultural purposes to identify cultural heritage of importance, and to incorporate into the client's decision-making process the views of the affected communities on such cultural heritage. Consultation will also involve the relevant national or local regulatory agencies that are entrusted with the protection of cultural heritage.

Removal of Cultural Heritage

7. Most cultural heritage is best protected by preservation in its place, since removal is likely to result in irreparable damage or destruction of the cultural heritage. The client will not remove any cultural heritage, unless the following conditions are met:

- There are no technically or financially feasible alternatives to removal
- The overall benefits of the project outweigh the anticipated cultural heritage loss from removal
- Any removal of cultural heritage is conducted by the best available technique Critical Cultural Heritage

8. Critical cultural heritage consists of (i) the internationally recognized heritage of communities who use, or have used within living memory the cultural heritage for long-standing cultural purposes; and (ii) legally protected cultural heritage areas, including those proposed by host governments for such designation.

9. The client will not significantly alter, damage, or remove any critical cultural heritage. In exceptional circumstances, where a project may significantly damage critical cultural heritage, and its damage or loss may endanger the cultural or economic survival of communities within the host country who use the cultural heritage for long-standing cultural purposes, the client will: (i) meet the requirements of Paragraph 6 above; and (ii) conduct a good faith negotiation with and document the informed participation of the affected communities and the successful outcome of the negotiation. In addition, any other impacts on critical cultural heritage must be appropriately mitigated with the informed participation of the affected communities.

10. Legally protected cultural heritage areas are important for the protection and conservation of cultural heritage, and additional measures are needed for any projects that would be permitted under the applicable national laws in these areas. In circumstances where a proposed project is located within a legally protected area or a legally defined buffer zone, the client, in addition to the requirements for critical cultural heritage cited above in Paragraph 9, will meet the following requirements:

- Comply with defined national or local cultural heritage regulations or the protected area management plans
- Consult the protected area sponsors and managers, local communities and other key stakeholders on the proposed project
- Implement additional programs, as appropriate, to promote and enhance the conservation aims of the protected area

Project's Use of Cultural Heritage

11. Where a project proposes to use the cultural resources, knowledge, innovations, or practices of local communities embodying traditional lifestyles for commercial purposes, the client will inform these communities of: (i) their rights under national law; (ii) the scope and nature of the proposed commercial development; and (iii) the potential consequences of such development. The client will not proceed with such commercialization unless it: (i) enters into a good faith negotiation with the affected local communities embodying traditional lifestyles; (ii) documents their informed participation and the successful outcome of the negotiation; and (iii) provides for fair and equitable sharing of benefits from commercialization of such knowledge, innovation, or practice, consistent with their customs and traditions.

Part II Human rights

> **Where, after all, do universal human rights begin? In small places, close to home—so close and so small that they cannot be seen on any maps of the world. Yet they are the world of the individual person; the neighbourhood he lives in; the school or college he attends; the factory, farm or office where he works. Such are the places where every man, woman and child seeks equal justice, equal opportunity, equal dignity without discrimination. Unless these rights have meaning there, they have little meaning anywhere. Without concerned citizen action to uphold them close to home, we shall look in vain for progress in the larger world.**
>
> *Eleanor Roosevelt*[1]

Human rights are those rights enshrined in the Universal Declaration of Human Rights. As used in this book, the term 'human rights' conveys the broadest scope of that term to include political, social, economic, cultural and civil (previously known as civic) rights.

There are various types of human rights. Civil and political rights include freedom of religion, freedom of association and protection from torture, slavery and discrimination. Economic, cultural and social rights include the right to

1 At the presentation of 'In Your Hands: A Guide for Community Action for the Tenth Anniversary of the Universal Declaration of Human Rights', 27 March 1958, United Nations, New York (www.udhr.org/history/inyour.htm).

education, the right to adequate working conditions and the right to participate in cultural activities. In addition, over the past few years consideration of solidarity rights has been emerging to include issues that require international co-operation, such as environmental protection and the right to development (for more information, see Novib 1997).

The beginning of any discussion on human rights is the Universal Declaration of Human Rights (UDHR). Drafted in 1948, the Universal Declaration has been endorsed by all member countries of the United Nations. The Declaration is addressed to 'every individual and every organ of society'—and so business is urged to comply with the Universal Declaration, or as Goran Lindahl, former president and chief executive officer (CEO) of ABB, has stated, businesses 'must now act as co-guarantors of human rights' (quoted in Frankental and House 2001: 5).

Part II of this book includes the texts of two key documents in the field of human rights:[2]

- Universal Declaration of Human Rights
- Voluntary Principles on Security and Human Rights

References

Frankental, P., and F. House (2001) *Human Rights: Is it Any of Your Business?* (London: Amnesty International, and Prince of Wales Business Leaders' Forum, April 2001).

Novib (1997) *Human Rights and Development: Novib's Challenges in the Field of Human Rights* (The Hague: Novib, December 1997).

2 The fundamental labour conventions of the International Labour Organisation (ILO) are discussed in Chapter 7, in Part III on labour rights.

5
The Universal Declaration of Human Rights

> The Universal Declaration of Human Rights is the first comprehensive international proclamation of the basic rights of the individual. It ranks with the Magna Carta, the French Declaration of the Rights of Man and of the Citizen, and the American Declaration of Independence as a milestone in mankind's struggle for freedom and human dignity.
>
> *Thomas Buergenthal, Judge, International Court of Justice*[1]

> The Universal Declaration is the internationally accepted framework for human rights created by the United Nations . . . This framework should form the basis of a company's human rights policy . . . Business should comply within the company's full chain of operation with each particular right.
>
> *International Business Leaders' Forum*[2]

Type Foundation initiative

Strength Its legitimacy

Keywords United Nations • Human rights • Foundation standard • Slavery • Freedom of opinion • Freedom of expression

1 Buergenthal 1998: 91.

2 IBLF 2003.

5.1 Background

The Universal Declaration of Human Rights (UDHR) is one of the most significant documents ever drafted. It enshrines the concept of human rights broadly, to include not only political rights but also social and economic rights. Universally accepted, the UDHR has formed the basis of many constitutions around the world. Moreover, the UDHR is cited in many of the corporate responsibility (CR) codes and principles contained in this book as a foundation standard.

Adopted by the UN General Assembly in 1948, the UDHR was unanimously adopted by the then 48 member states of the United Nations. In 1993, 171 governments adopted the Vienna Declaration,[3] which reaffirms support for the Universal Declaration. The UDHR is not legally binding but is accepted as customary law. The UDHR is elaborated on in two UN international covenants—one on civil and political rights,[4] and one on social, economic and cultural rights.[5] These two covenants are binding for states that decide to become a party to these treaties.

5.2 Strengths and weaknesses

One of the greatest strengths of the UDHR is its acceptance around the world as a cornerstone of human rights. The clarity of its composition is also a great strength. Despite the fact that it is already over half a century old, it remains as relevant in 2003 as it was in 1948.

The drafters of the UDHR were predominantly of Western background, leading some critics to argue that the concept of human rights is a 'Western' notion. To refute this argument, it is worth noting that very few governments have filed significant reservations on any of the human rights treaties (which are based on the UDHR) they have ratified, despite being allowed to do so under international law (for more information on this debate, see Avery 1997). The UDHR has also been criticised for its lack of focus on minorities and indigenous peoples. However, subsequent UN documents have compensated for the oversight (van Boven 1998: 78). According to Gemma Crijns of Nyenrode University, formerly with Amnesty International, approximately 80 conventions, declarations and resolutions have been developed from the UDHR on a variety of human rights issues.[6]

According to Geoffrey Chandler (2001):

3 www.unhchr.ch/huridocda/huridoca.nsf/%28symbol%29/A.CONF.157.23.En?OpenDocument

4 International Covenant on Civil and Political Rights (1966): www2.ohchr.org/english/law/ccpr.htm.

5 International Covenant on Economic, Social and Cultural Rights (1966): www2.ohchr.org/english/law/cescr.htm.

6 Personal communication with Gemma Crijns, Nyenrode University, Breukelen, The Netherlands, 2003.

> The Universal Declaration on its own, however, is not easily translatable into immediate corporate action which is why [Amnesty International asks] companies to support it explicitly as a starting point, so expressing a commitment in principle to human rights, but then apply its relevant sections to their own operations.

5.3 Companies to which the Universal Declaration of Human Rights applies

The UDHR calls on 'every organ of society' to follow its underlying principles. Hence, business is included in the UDHR, along with individuals and states. A growing number of multinational companies refer to the Declaration on their websites and within their own statements of principles, including Aviva, BP, British Telecommunications (BT), Shell and Vodafone. Others, such as Novo Nordisk (www.novonordisk.com), have conducted a review of their operations against the Declaration and redefined their focus. For example, Novo Nordisk has realised that it needs to do more to promote the right to health, especially with regard to diabetes care, as well as enhance its work to promote diversity.[7]

5.4 Questions posed and answered

The UDHR poses and answers a fundamental question: What are human rights?

5.5 The challenge and the promise

One of the challenges in the human rights field is to translate the UDHR into business principles. Social and economic rights are being translated into business codes, but civil and political rights are rarely included in business principles. The Danish Centre on Human Rights (www.humanrightsbusiness.org) is working to translate the articles of the UDHR into business principles, with the support of companies and stakeholders. It currently uses approximately 1,400 indicators; however, indicators are selected according to each user, based on the company type and area of operations. As a result, a small company operating with only a handful of employees in Denmark may receive around 20 indicators; and a large global

7 See www.novonordisk.com/sustainability/positions/human_rights.asp.

company with thousands of employees around the world may receive close to a thousand indicators.[8]

References

Avery, C. (1997) 'Business and Human Rights: Five Common Misconceptions', http://198.170.85.29/Misconceptions.htm, accessed 2010.

Buergenthal, T. (1998) 'Centerpiece of the Human Rights Revolution', in B. van der Heijden and B. Tahzib-Lie (eds.), *Reflections on the Universal Declaration of Human Rights: A Fiftieth Anniversary Anthology* (Dordrecht, Netherlands: Martinius Nijhoff): 91-94.

Chandler, G. (2001) 'Companies and Human Rights: Recent Developments', 5 April 2001, http://208.55.16.210/Chandler-UN-Guidelines.htm, accessed 2003.

IBLF (International Business Leaders' Forum) (2003) 'Business and Human Rights', www.iblf.org, accessed 2003.

Van Boven, T. (1998) 'A Universal Declaration of Human Responsibilities?', in B. van der Heijden and B. Tahzib-Lie (eds.), *Reflections on the Universal Declaration of Human Rights: A Fiftieth Anniversary Anthology* (Dordrecht, Netherlands: Martinius Nijhoff): 73-79.

Additional resources

Websites

Business and Human Rights Resource Centre: www.business-humanrights.org
Human Rights and Business Project of the Danish Institute for Human Rights: www.humanrightsbusiness.org
Universal Declaration of Human Rights: www.udhr.org

8 E-mail to author from Margaret Jungk, Danish Centre for Human Rights, 8 October 2003.

The Universal Declaration of Human Rights

PREAMBLE

Whereas recognition of the inherent dignity and of the equal and inalienable rights of all members of the human family is the foundation of freedom, justice and peace in the world,

Whereas disregard and contempt for human rights have resulted in barbarous acts which have outraged the conscience of mankind, and the advent of a world in which human beings shall enjoy freedom of speech and belief and freedom from fear and want has been proclaimed as the highest aspiration of the common people,

Whereas it is essential, if man is not to be compelled to have recourse, as a last resort, to rebellion against tyranny and oppression, that human rights should be protected by the rule of law,

Whereas it is essential to promote the development of friendly relations between nations,

Whereas the peoples of the United Nations have in the Charter reaffirmed their faith in fundamental human rights, in the dignity and worth of the human person and in the equal rights of men and women and have determined to promote social progress and better standards of life in larger freedom,

Whereas Member States have pledged themselves to achieve, in co-operation with the United Nations, the promotion of universal respect for and observance of human rights and fundamental freedoms,

Whereas a common understanding of these rights and freedoms is of the greatest importance for the full realization of this pledge,

Now, Therefore THE GENERAL ASSEMBLY proclaims THIS UNIVERSAL DECLARATION OF HUMAN RIGHTS as a common standard of achievement for all peoples and all nations, to the end that every individual and every organ of society, keeping this Declaration constantly in mind, shall strive by teaching and education to promote respect for these rights and freedoms and by progressive measures, national and international, to secure their universal and effective recognition and observance, both among the peoples of Member States themselves and among the peoples of territories under their jurisdiction.

Article 1.

All human beings are born free and equal in dignity and rights. They are endowed with reason and conscience and should act towards one another in a spirit of brotherhood.

Article 2.

Everyone is entitled to all the rights and freedoms set forth in this Declaration, without distinction of any kind, such as race, colour, sex, language, religion, political or other opinion, national or social origin, property, birth or other status. Furthermore, no distinction shall be made on the basis of the political, jurisdictional or international status of the country or territory to which a person belongs, whether it be independent, trust, non-self-governing or under any other limitation of sovereignty.

Article 3.

Everyone has the right to life, liberty and security of person.

Article 4.

No one shall be held in slavery or servitude; slavery and the slave trade shall be prohibited in all their forms.

Article 5.

No one shall be subjected to torture or to cruel, inhuman or degrading treatment or punishment.

Article 6.

Everyone has the right to recognition everywhere as a person before the law.

Article 7.

All are equal before the law and are entitled without any discrimination to equal protection of the law. All are entitled to equal protection against any discrimination in violation of this Declaration and against any incitement to such discrimination.

Article 8.

Everyone has the right to an effective remedy by the competent national tribunals for acts violating the fundamental rights granted him by the constitution or by law.

Article 9.

No one shall be subjected to arbitrary arrest, detention or exile.

Article 10.

Everyone is entitled in full equality to a fair and public hearing by an independent and impartial tribunal, in the determination of his rights and obligations and of any criminal charge against him.

Article 11.

(1) Everyone charged with a penal offence has the right to be presumed innocent until proved guilty according to law in a public trial at which he has had all the guarantees necessary for his defence.

(2) No one shall be held guilty of any penal offence on account of any act or omission which did not constitute a penal offence, under national or international law, at the time when it was committed. Nor shall a heavier penalty be imposed than the one that was applicable at the time the penal offence was committed.

Article 12.

No one shall be subjected to arbitrary interference with his privacy, family, home or correspondence, nor to attacks upon his honour and reputation. Everyone has the right to the protection of the law against such interference or attacks.

Article 13.

(1) Everyone has the right to freedom of movement and residence within the borders of each state.

(2) Everyone has the right to leave any country, including his own, and to return to his country.

Article 14.

(1) Everyone has the right to seek and to enjoy in other countries asylum from persecution.

(2) This right may not be invoked in the case of prosecutions genuinely arising from non-political crimes or from acts contrary to the purposes and principles of the United Nations.

Article 15.

(1) Everyone has the right to a nationality.

(2) No one shall be arbitrarily deprived of his nationality nor denied the right to change his nationality.

Article 16.

(1) Men and women of full age, without any limitation due to race, nationality or religion, have the right to marry and to found a family. They are entitled to equal rights as to marriage, during marriage and at its dissolution.

(2) Marriage shall be entered into only with the free and full consent of the intending spouses.

(3) The family is the natural and fundamental group unit of society and is entitled to protection by society and the State.

Article 17.

(1) Everyone has the right to own property alone as well as in association with others.

(2) No one shall be arbitrarily deprived of his property.

Article 18.

Everyone has the right to freedom of thought, conscience and religion; this right includes freedom to change his religion or belief, and freedom, either alone or in community with others and in public or private, to manifest his religion or belief in teaching, practice, worship and observance.

Article 19.

Everyone has the right to freedom of opinion and expression; this right includes freedom to hold opinions without interference and to seek, receive and impart information and ideas through any media and regardless of frontiers.

Article 20.

(1) Everyone has the right to freedom of peaceful assembly and association.

(2) No one may be compelled to belong to an association.

Article 21.

(1) Everyone has the right to take part in the government of his country, directly or through freely chosen representatives.

(2) Everyone has the right of equal access to public service in his country.

(3) The will of the people shall be the basis of the authority of government; this will shall be expressed in periodic and genuine elections which shall be by universal and equal suffrage and shall be held by secret vote or by equivalent free voting procedures.

Article 22.

Everyone, as a member of society, has the right to social security and is entitled to realization, through national effort and international co-operation and in accordance with the organization and resources of each State, of the economic, social and cultural rights indispensable for his dignity and the free development of his personality.

Article 23.

(1) Everyone has the right to work, to free choice of employment, to just and favourable conditions of work and to protection against unemployment.

(2) Everyone, without any discrimination, has the right to equal pay for equal work.

(3) Everyone who works has the right to just and favourable remuneration ensuring for himself and his family an existence worthy of human dignity, and supplemented, if necessary, by other means of social protection.

(4) Everyone has the right to form and to join trade unions for the protection of his interests.

Article 24.

Everyone has the right to rest and leisure, including reasonable limitation of working hours and periodic holidays with pay.

Article 25.

(1) Everyone has the right to a standard of living adequate for the health and well-being of himself and of his family, including food, clothing, housing and medical care and necessary social services, and the right to security in the event of unemployment, sickness, disability, widowhood, old age or other lack of livelihood in circumstances beyond his control.

(2) Motherhood and childhood are entitled to special care and assistance. All children, whether born in or out of wedlock, shall enjoy the same social protection.

Article 26.

(1) Everyone has the right to education. Education shall be free, at least in the elementary and fundamental stages. Elementary education shall be compulsory. Technical and professional education shall be made generally available and higher education shall be equally accessible to all on the basis of merit.

(2) Education shall be directed to the full development of the human personality and to the strengthening of respect for human rights and fundamental freedoms. It shall promote understanding, tolerance and friendship among all nations, racial or religious groups, and shall further the activities of the United Nations for the maintenance of peace.

(3) Parents have a prior right to choose the kind of education that shall be given to their children.

Article 27.

(1) Everyone has the right freely to participate in the cultural life of the community, to enjoy the arts and to share in scientific advancement and its benefits.

(2) Everyone has the right to the protection of the moral and material interests resulting from any scientific, literary or artistic production of which he is the author.

Article 28.

Everyone is entitled to a social and international order in which the rights and freedoms set forth in this Declaration can be fully realized.

Article 29.

(1) Everyone has duties to the community in which alone the free and full development of his personality is possible.

(2) In the exercise of his rights and freedoms, everyone shall be subject only to such limitations as are determined by law solely for the purpose of securing due recognition and respect for the rights and freedoms of others and of meeting the just requirements of morality, public order and the general welfare in a democratic society.

(3) These rights and freedoms may in no case be exercised contrary to the purposes and principles of the United Nations.

Article 30.

Nothing in this Declaration may be interpreted as implying for any State, group or person any right to engage in any activity or to perform any act aimed at the destruction of any of the rights and freedoms set forth herein.

6
The Voluntary Principles on Security and Human Rights

> **In an area where no standards exist, we see the development of some guiding principles as a positive first step. But this is only the beginning of the process. The business, human rights and government communities all still have a lot of talking to do.**
>
> ***Kenneth Roth, Human Rights Watch*[1]**

> **The Voluntary Principles are a very creative effort by governments, non-governmental organisations and extractive industry companies working in remote areas of developing nations to establish practical standards and best practices for providing security while supporting the universally recognised human rights of local residents. While the issues remain complex, the initiative is already clarifying and improving relationships and practices for subscribing companies and their neighbours, and it is hoped this will lead to more such agreements to enhance the benefits and minimise the negatives of globalisation.**
>
> ***Judge Gabrielle Kirk McDonald*[2]**

Type Performance-oriented principles, sectoral

Strength The ability to institutionalise dialogue

Keywords Governments • Extractive sector • Private security forces • Non-governmental organisations • Human rights

1 Human Rights Watch, 'Human Rights Principles for Oil and Mining Companies Welcomed', New York, www.hrw.org/en/news/2000/12/20/human-rights-principles-oil-and-mining-companies-welcomed, 21 December 2000.

2 E-mail to author from Judge McDonald, 7 May 2003. Judge McDonald represented Freeport McMoran in the negotiations of the Voluntary Principles.

6.1 Background

The Voluntary Principles represent an unprecedented step in the field of corporate responsibility. Convened by the US and UK governments, non-governmental organisations (NGOs), companies and a trade union reached a consensus on principles in the difficult area of human rights and security for the extractive sector (i.e. mining and petroleum). The agreement sets an important precedent for other sectoral discussions. First released in December of 2000, the agreement is noteworthy because it was convened by governments and included key stakeholders.

The participants include:

- **Governments**: the US and UK governments (the Dutch, Norwegian and Canadian governments have joined subsequently)
- **Companies**: The list of companies signed onto the Voluntary Principles has grown to 18 (see Box 6.1)
- **NGOs**: Amnesty International, Business for Social Responsibility, the Council on Economic Priorities, Fund for Peace, Human Rights Watch, International Alert, International Federation of Chemical, Energy, Mine, and General Workers' Unions, Lawyers Committee for Human Rights and the International Business Leaders' Forum

The Voluntary Principles address the issue of security forces, including:

- The criteria companies need to consider in assessing the risk to human rights in forming security agreements

Corporate participants

- Amerada Hess Corporation
- Anglo American
- AngloGold Ashanti
- BG Group
- BHP Billiton
- BP
- Chevron
- ConocoPhillips
- ExxonMobil
- Freeport McMoRan Copper and Gold
- Hydro
- Marathon Oil
- Newmont Mining Corporation
- Occidental Petroleum Corporation
- Rio Tinto
- Shell
- Statoil Hydro
- Talisman Energy

NGO participants

- Amnesty International
- The Fund for Peace
- Human Rights Watch
- Human Rights First
- International Alert
- IKV Pax Christi
- Oxfam
- Pact, Inc.

Government participants

- Canada
- The Netherlands
- Norway
- United States of America
- United Kingdom

Box 6.1 **Participants in the Voluntary Principles**

- The relationship between a company's security and state security, such as the army or police
- The relationship between the company's security force and private armies

By narrowing the debate to include only security arrangements, the negotiations bypassed more difficult areas of debate that could have polarised the process, such as whether or not to conduct business in countries with severe human rights violations.

The Voluntary Principles are based, in part, on the UN Code of Conduct for Law Enforcement Officials[3] and the UN Basic Principles on the Use of Force and Firearms by Law Enforcement Officials.[4]

6.2 Strengths and weaknesses

The role of governments as convenors is an emerging trend in corporate citizenship. The US and UK governments are concerned with the reputation of their companies abroad and with the security of their citizens abroad.[5] According to Bennett Freeman, one of the architects of the Voluntary Principles:

> One key to success was the willingness of the two governments to use their convening authority and diplomatic capacity not only to facilitate the dialogue between companies and NGOs, but to draft and announce a standard that would advance the interests of the companies, NGOs and governments alike (Freeman 2001: 6).

Like all ground-breaking agreements, the Principles have been criticised. One of the criticisms is that the Principles are voluntary—a similar criticism is made of the UN Global Compact (see Chapter 3), the OECD Principles (Chapter 19) and SA8000 (Chapter 8). There is widespread agreement that the companies would not have been able to commit to binding principles for fear of litigation. A second criticism levelled at the Principles is the absence of involvement of other key governments affected by this issue, especially governments in the South. After all, the governments of Ecuador, Colombia and Nigeria are but a few of those that have a significant interest with regard to the extractive industries. The US and UK governments opted to broker an agreement and then work with other governments to gain their approval. The goal of the initiative was to reach an agreement within a one-year time-period, which would have been difficult had more governments been involved.

3 Adopted by the General Assembly, 17 December 1979: www2.ohchr.org/english/law/codeofconduct.htm.

4 Adopted by the UN Congress on the Prevention of Crime and Treatment of Offenders, 7 September 1990: www2.ohchr.org/english/law/firearms.htm.

5 For an excellent overview of US interests in promoting human rights and corporate social responsibility, see Freeman 2001.

6.3 Companies to which the Voluntary Principles on Security and Human Rights apply

The Principles specifically apply to the extractive sector, including mining and petroleum. However, as crime and terrorism are on the rise, the Principles could apply to companies who need to hire guards to ensure the safety of their staff.

6.4 Questions posed and answered

What criteria should 'companies take into account as they assess the risk to human rights in their security arrangements?' What are the optimal forms for the 'relationships between companies and security forces, both military and police?' (Freeman 2002: 2).

6.5 The challenge and the promise

The challenge for companies involved will be to operationalise the Principles. Another important challenge is to bring additional governments, especially from the South, into the discussion.

References

Freeman, B. (2001) 'Corporate Responsibility and Human Rights', transcript of speech available at www.lse.ac.uk/collections/globalDimensions/seminars/humanRightsAndCorporateResponsibility/freemanTranscript.htm.

—— (2002) 'Finding Common Ground: The Voluntary Principles on Security and Human Rights', text of a draft speech provided to the author in Oslo.

The Voluntary Principles on Security and Human Rights

The Governments of the United States and the United Kingdom, companies in the extractive and energy sectors ("Companies"), and non-governmental organizations, all with an interest in human rights and corporate social responsibility, have engaged in a dialogue on security and human rights.

The participants recognize the importance of the promotion and protection of human rights throughout the world and the constructive role business and civil society—including non-governmental organizations, labor/trade unions, and local communities—can play in advancing these goals. Through this dialogue, the participants have developed the following set of voluntary principles to guide Companies in maintaining the safety and security of their operations within an operating framework that ensures respect for human rights and fundamental freedoms. Mindful of these goals, the participants agree to the importance of continuing this dialogue and keeping under review these principles to ensure their continuing relevance and efficacy.

Acknowledging that security is a fundamental need, shared by individuals, communities, businesses, and governments alike, and acknowledging the difficult security issues faced by Companies operating globally, we recognize that security and respect for human rights can and should be consistent;

Understanding that governments have the primary responsibility to promote and protect human rights and that all parties to a conflict are obliged to observe applicable international humanitarian law, we recognize that we share the common goal of promoting respect for human rights, particularly those set forth in the Universal Declaration of Human Rights, and international humanitarian law;

Emphasizing the importance of safeguarding the integrity of company personnel and property, Companies recognize a commitment to act in a manner consistent with the laws of the countries within which they are present, to be mindful of the highest applicable international standards, and to promote the observance of applicable international law enforcement principles (e.g., the UN Code of Conduct for Law Enforcement Officials and the UN Basic Principles on the Use of Force and Firearms by Law Enforcement Officials), particularly with regard to the use of force;

Taking note of the effect that Companies' activities may have on local communities, we recognize the value of engaging with civil society and host and home governments to contribute to the welfare of the local community while mitigating any potential for conflict where possible;

Understanding that useful, credible information is a vital component of security and human rights, we recognize the importance of sharing and understanding our respective experiences regarding, *inter alia*, best security practices and procedures, country human rights situations, and public and private security, subject to confidentiality constraints;

Acknowledging that home governments and multilateral institutions may, on occasion, assist host governments with security sector reform, developing institutional capacities and strengthening the rule of law, we recognize the important role Companies and civil society can play in supporting these efforts;

We hereby express our support for the following voluntary principles regarding security and human rights in the extractive sector, which fall into three categories, risk assessment, relations with public security, and relations with private security:

RISK ASSESSMENT

The ability to assess accurately risks present in a Company's operating environment is critical to the security of personnel, local communities and assets; the success of the Company's short and long-term operations; and to the promotion and protection of human rights. In some circumstances, this is relatively simple; in others, it is important to obtain extensive background information from different sources; monitoring and adapting to changing, complex political, economic, law enforcement, military and social situations; and maintaining productive relations with local communities and government officials.

The quality of complicated risk assessments is largely dependent on the assembling of regularly updated, credible information from a broad range of perspectives—local and national governments, security firms, other companies, home governments, multilateral institutions, and civil society knowledgeable about local conditions. This information may be most effective when shared to the fullest extent possible (bearing in mind confidentiality considerations) between Companies, concerned civil society, and governments.

Bearing in mind these general principles, we recognize that accurate, effective risk assessments should consider the following factors:

- **Identification of security risks.** Security risks can result from political, economic, civil or social factors. Moreover, certain personnel and assets may be at greater risk than others. Identification of security risks allows a Company to take measures to minimize risk and to assess whether Company actions may heighten risk.
- **Potential for violence.** Depending on the environment, violence can be widespread or limited to particular regions, and it can develop with little or no warning. Civil society, home and host government representatives, and other sources should be consulted to identify risks presented by the potential for violence. Risk

assessments should examine patterns of violence in areas of Company operations for educational, predictive, and preventative purposes.

- **Human rights records.** Risk assessments should consider the available human rights records of public security forces, paramilitaries, local and national law enforcement, as well as the reputation of private security. Awareness of past abuses and allegations can help Companies to avoid recurrences as well as to promote accountability. Also, identification of the capability of the above entities to respond to situations of violence in a lawful manner (i.e., consistent with applicable international standards) allows Companies to develop appropriate measures in operating environments.
- **Rule of law.** Risk assessments should consider the local prosecuting authority and judiciary's capacity to hold accountable those responsible for human rights abuses and for those responsible for violations of international humanitarian law in a manner that respects the rights of the accused.
- **Conflict analysis.** Identification of and understanding the root causes and nature of local conflicts, as well as the level of adherence to human rights and international humanitarian law standards by key actors, can be instructive for the development of strategies for managing relations between the Company, local communities, Company employees and their unions, and host governments. Risk assessments should also consider the potential for future conflicts.
- **Equipment transfers.** Where Companies provide equipment (including lethal and non-lethal equipment) to public or private security, they should consider the risk of such transfers, any relevant export licensing requirements, and the feasibility of measures to mitigate foreseeable negative consequences, including adequate controls to prevent misappropriation or diversion of equipment which may lead to human rights abuses. In making risk assessments, companies should consider any relevant past incidents involving previous equipment transfers.

INTERACTIONS BETWEEN COMPANIES AND PUBLIC SECURITY

Although governments have the primary role of maintaining law and order, security and respect for human rights, Companies have an interest in ensuring that actions taken by governments, particularly the actions of public security providers, are consistent with the protection and promotion of human rights. In cases where there is a need to supplement security provided by host governments, Companies may be required or expected to contribute to, or otherwise reimburse, the costs of protecting Company facilities and personnel borne by public security. While public security is expected to act in a manner consistent with local and national laws as well as with human rights standards and international humanitarian law, within this context abuses may nevertheless occur.

In an effort to reduce the risk of such abuses and to promote respect for human rights generally, we have identified the following voluntary principles to guide relationships between Companies and public security regarding security provided to Companies:

Security Arrangements

- Companies should consult regularly with host governments and local communities about the impact of their security arrangements on those communities.
- Companies should communicate their policies regarding ethical conduct and human rights to public security providers, and express their desire that security be provided in a manner consistent with those policies by personnel with adequate and effective training.
- Companies should encourage host governments to permit making security arrangements transparent and accessible to the public, subject to any overriding safety and security concerns.

Deployment and Conduct

- The primary role of public security should be to maintain the rule of law, including safeguarding human rights and deterring acts that threaten Company personnel and facilities. The type and number of public security forces deployed should be competent, appropriate and proportional to the threat.
- Equipment imports and exports should comply with all applicable law and regulations. Companies that provide equipment to public security should take all appropriate and lawful measures to mitigate any foreseeable negative consequences, including human rights abuses and violations of international humanitarian law.
- Companies should use their influence to promote the following principles with public security: (a) individuals credibly implicated in human rights abuses should not provide security services for Companies; (b) force should be used only when strictly necessary and to an extent proportional to the threat; and (c) the rights of individuals should not be violated while exercising the right to exercise freedom of association and peaceful assembly, the right to engage in collective bargaining, or other related rights of Company employees as recognized by the Universal Declaration of Human Rights and the ILO Declaration on Fundamental Principles and Rights at Work.
- In cases where physical force is used by public security, such incidents should be reported to the appropriate authorities and to the Company. Where force is used, medical aid should be provided to injured persons, including to offenders.

Consultation and Advice

- Companies should hold structured meetings with public security on a regular basis to discuss security, human rights and related work-place safety issues. Companies should also consult regularly with other Companies, host and home governments, and civil society to discuss security and human rights. Where Companies operating in the same region have common concerns, they should consider collectively raising those concerns with the host and home governments.

- In their consultations with host governments, Companies should take all appropriate measures to promote observance of applicable international law enforcement principles, particularly those reflected in the UN Code of Conduct for Law Enforcement Officials and the UN Basic Principles on the Use of Force and Firearms.
- Companies should support efforts by governments, civil society and multilateral institutions to provide human rights training and education for public security as well as their efforts to strengthen state institutions to ensure accountability and respect for human rights.

Responses to Human Rights Abuses

- Companies should record and report any credible allegations of human rights abuses by public security in their areas of operation to appropriate host government authorities. Where appropriate, Companies should urge investigation and that action be taken to prevent any recurrence.
- Companies should actively monitor the status of investigations and press for their proper resolution.
- Companies should, to the extent reasonable, monitor the use of equipment provided by the Company and to investigate properly situations in which such equipment is used in an inappropriate manner.
- Every effort should be made to ensure that information used as the basis for allegations of human rights abuses is credible and based on reliable evidence. The security and safety of sources should be protected. Additional or more accurate information that may alter previous allegations should be made available as appropriate to concerned parties.

INTERACTIONS BETWEEN COMPANIES AND PRIVATE SECURITY

Where host governments are unable or unwilling to provide adequate security to protect a Company's personnel or assets, it may be necessary to engage private security providers as a complement to public security. In this context, private security may have to coordinate with state forces, (law enforcement, in particular) to carry weapons and to consider the defensive local use of force. Given the risks associated with such activities, we recognize the following voluntary principles to guide private security conduct:

- Private security should observe the policies of the contracting Company regarding ethical conduct and human rights; the law and professional standards of the country in which they operate; emerging best practices developed by industry, civil society, and governments; and promote the observance of international humanitarian law.
- Private security should maintain high levels of technical and professional proficiency, particularly with regard to the local use of force and firearms.

- Private security should act in a lawful manner. They should exercise restraint and caution in a manner consistent with applicable international guidelines regarding the local use of force, including the UN Principles on the Use of Force and Firearms by Law Enforcement Officials and the UN Code of Conduct for Law Enforcement Officials, as well as with emerging best practices developed by Companies, civil society, and governments.
- Private security should have policies regarding appropriate conduct and the local use of force (e.g., rules of engagement). Practice under these policies should be capable of being monitored by Companies or, where appropriate, by independent third parties. Such monitoring should encompass detailed investigations into allegations of abusive or unlawful acts; the availability of disciplinary measures sufficient to prevent and deter; and procedures for reporting allegations to relevant local law enforcement authorities when appropriate.
- All allegations of human rights abuses by private security should be recorded. Credible allegations should be properly investigated. In those cases where allegations against private security providers are forwarded to the relevant law enforcement authorities, Companies should actively monitor the status of investigations and press for their proper resolution.
- Consistent with their function, private security should provide only preventative and defensive services and should not engage in activities exclusively the responsibility of state military or law enforcement authorities. Companies should designate services, technology and equipment capable of offensive and defensive purposes as being for defensive use only.
- Private security should (a) not employ individuals credibly implicated in human rights abuses to provide security services; (b) use force only when strictly necessary and to an extent proportional to the threat; and (c) not violate the rights of individuals while exercising the right to exercise freedom of association and peaceful assembly, to engage in collective bargaining, or other related rights of Company employees as recognized by the Universal Declaration of Human Rights and the ILO Declaration on Fundamental Principles and Rights at Work.
- In cases where physical force is used, private security should properly investigate and report the incident to the Company. Private security should refer the matter to local authorities and/or take disciplinary action where appropriate. Where force is used, medical aid should be provided to injured persons, including to offenders.
- Private security should maintain the confidentiality of information obtained as a result of its position as security provider, except where to do so would jeopardize the principles contained herein.

To minimize the risk that private security exceed their authority as providers of security, and to promote respect for human rights generally, we have developed the following additional voluntary principles and guidelines:

- Where appropriate, Companies should include the principles outlined above as contractual provisions in agreements with private security providers and ensure that private security personnel are adequately trained to respect the rights of employees and the local community. To the extent practicable, agreements between Companies and private security should require investigation of unlawful or abusive behavior and appropriate disciplinary action. Agreements should also permit termination of the relationship by Companies where there is credible evidence of unlawful or abusive behavior by private security personnel.

- Companies should consult and monitor private security providers to ensure they fulfil their obligation to provide security in a manner consistent with the principles outlined above. Where appropriate, Companies should seek to employ private security providers that are representative of the local population.
- Companies should review the background of private security they intend to employ, particularly with regard to the use of excessive force. Such reviews should include an assessment of previous services provided to the host government and whether these services raise concern about the private security firm's dual role as a private security provider and government contractor.
- Companies should consult with other Companies, home country officials, host country officials, and civil society regarding experiences with private security. Where appropriate and lawful, Companies should facilitate the exchange of information about unlawful activity and abuses committed by private security providers.

Part III
Labour rights

The International Labour Organisation (ILO, www.ilo.org) provides a key starting point for understanding initiatives in the field of workers' rights. Established in 1919, the ILO promotes social justice and internationally recognised human and labour rights. The ILO is the only agency of the United Nations to have a tripartite structure, in which three parties—governments, trade unions and employer organisations—play an equal role. The tripartite nature of the ILO ensures that a wide range of perspectives is taken into account.

The ILO formulates labour standards by developing conventions and recommendations on minimum standards. These conventions are international treaties which governments decide whether or not to sign and ratify. Once a country has ratified a convention, the convention becomes legally binding in that country. Recommendations are not legally binding.

To date, the ILO has adopted more than 180 conventions and 185 recommendations. Of these conventions, there are four 'core conventions' (ILO 1998: 7):

- Freedom of association and the effective recognition of the right to collective bargaining
- The elimination of all form of forced and compulsory labour
- The effective abolition of child labour
- The elimination of discrimination with respect to employment and occupation

These core conventions are an integral part of many standards and, as such, are foundation standards. The ILO conventions are ratified by countries that commit themselves to ensuring that their domestic legislation conforms to their obligations under the conventions.

The ILO Declaration on Fundamental Principles and Rights at Work is an important landmark for workers' rights. Adopted in 1998, the Principles require all member states of the ILO to respect the fundamental (core) conventions listed above, *even if those countries have not ratified the conventions.*

Although it is states that commit to the conventions, many of the countries with the worst records for protecting workers' rights are unable to guarantee those rights because of a lack of inspectors and because of the forces of globalisation that cause countries to compete with one another to offer low wages.

Part III contains the text of the following principles, codes and standards on labour rights:

- ILO Tripartite Declaration of Principles Concerning Multinational Enterprises and Social Policy
- Social Accountability 8000
- Workplace Code of Conduct of the Fair Labor Association
- Base Code of the Ethical Trading Initiative

There is also a brief chapter (Chapter 11) listing other major initiatives in the field of labour rights in the clothing industry.

A note on the challenges and problems of multi-sectoral approaches

The late 1990s saw the rise of new types of initiatives to promote workers' rights, including multi-stakeholder initiatives convened by non-governmental organisations (NGOs), often with the financial support of governments. Among these initiatives are those discussed in this part: Social Accountability 8000, the Ethical Trading Initiative and the Fair Labor Association. These labour initiatives share several points of convergence:

- They are based on ILO conventions and are thus quite similar; it is the implementation and monitoring systems that differ and the frameworks and models that underpin the codes.
- They utilise management systems, such as training, job descriptions and review processes, to embed new policies within the organisation(s).
- They all have benefited from multi-stakeholder discussions and/or partnerships.

- Most approaches apply the highest standard in cases where there are conflicting standards, such as the use of international rather than national codes of conduct.

Human rights include positive and negative rights—positive rights are the 'dos'; negative rights are the 'don'ts'. The multi-stakeholder standards discussed in this part include positive and negative rights, prohibiting child labour, forced labour and discrimination, while promoting wages that support basic needs. According to research conducted by Shareen Hertel of the Human Rights Programme at Columbia University, grass-roots leaders in Mexico and Bangladesh favour a greater inclusion of positive rights in codes of conduct, rather than just prohibitions.[1]

The key divergences between initiatives address the following issues:

- Is the initiative regional or global?
- Is the initiative sectoral or multi-sectoral?
- Where does the ultimate accountability lie—at the factory or retailer or branding company?
- Who carries out the audits—NGOs, professional auditors or focus groups?
- What type of monitoring is involved—internal and/or external?
- Is a living wage required?
- Is there systematic surveillance and implementation of corrective actions?
- Are site visits to workplaces announced or unannounced?

The key initiatives are those presented in Part III. In 2003, the multi-stakeholder organisations involved in the initiatives covered in Part III—together with the Fair Wear Foundation and the Worker Rights Consortium—decided to work together on a trial project 'to evaluate the effective implementation of a common approach to observing the provisions of voluntary codes of labour practice'.[2] Collaboration between initiatives is a positive development that can promote clarity and cohesion in a splintered field.

The challenges and promises of these initiatives are quite similar, so in this part of the book the section on challenges and initiatives consists of an explanation of the key points of divergence from (or convergence with) the other initiatives discussed in this part. The type of approach taken for each of the initiatives covered in this part may be summarised as follows:

- Social Accountability 8000: accreditation and certification standard
- Workplace Code of Conduct of the Fair Labor Association: accreditation and certification standard

1 Correspondence between Deborah Leipziger and Shareen Hertel, 25 November 2002.

2 'Multistakeholder Organisations Decide on Trial Collaboration', joint communiqué issued from the meeting on 24 February 2003; document shared by Dan Rees of the Ethical Trading Initiative.

- Base Code of the Ethical Trading Initiative: membership and learning network

Reference

ILO (International Labour Organisation) (1998) *ILO Declaration on Fundamental Principles and Rights at Work and its Follow-up* (Geneva: ILO).

7
International Labour Organisation: Tripartite Declaration of Principles concerning Multinational Enterprises and Social Policy

The ILO Tripartite Declaration on MNEs is the only global tripartite instrument related to CSR.

International Labour Organization[1]

Type Performance-oriented foundation standard

Strength Integrates key ILO conventions and recommendations

Keywords Labour rights • Development • Training • ILO • ILO conventions

7.1 Background

Launched in 1977, the Tripartite Declaration of Principles concerning Multinational Enterprises and Social Policy (hereafter referred to as the Declaration) is directed towards companies, governments, trade unions and employer organisations. The Declaration is often cited, but it is not as relevant today as many other standards. However, it remains an important precursor in the field of corporate responsibility (CR) codes and standards.

1 International Labour Organisation, 'The ILO and CSR: Why Responsible Business Matters', slide presentation, www.unescap.org/tid/projects/csr_mons1_ilo.pdf, accessed 2010.

One way in which standards can be understood is to view them on a time-line, in which the early codes of the 1970s, such as the OECD Guidelines for Multinational Enterprises (Chapter 2) and the Declaration, are precursors of the more recent standards such as the UN Global Compact (Chapter 3). The Declaration is significant for several reasons. First, the Declaration refers to 28 ILO conventions, and as many recommendations, that were negotiated within a multilateral framework. Second, the Declaration includes procedures for examining disputes[2] that arise in the implementation of the Declaration. A government or trade union can seek to establish whether or not the behaviour of a company is in accordance with the Declaration. To cite an example, Belgium has brought a case to the ILO Committee on Multinational Enterprises concerning a closure of a Michelin plant in which workers were not given adequate warning. The Committee concluded that multinational companies should not close factories without consulting workers (Gallin 1997). Like the OECD Guidelines (Chapter 2), procedures exist for challenging company behaviour but are rarely used.

7.2 Strengths and weaknesses

Like the OECD Guidelines (Chapter 2), which influenced the Declaration, companies are encouraged to observe standards comparable to the host country in which they operate. For many parts of the developing world, the observance of local norms could still involve poor working conditions.

The Declaration is very much a product of its era—a time when multinational corporations were heavily criticised for their political activities in Chile and elsewhere (Vernon 1977). As such, it is a bit dated.

The key strength of the ILO Declaration is that it defines the obligations of governments as well as companies in promoting social and economic development.

7.3 Companies to which the Tripartite Declaration of Principles concerning Multinational Enterprises and Social Policy applies

The Declaration focuses on multinational enterprises. However, the Declaration is very clear that

> the principles laid down in this Declaration do not aim at introducing or maintaining inequalities of treatment between multinational and national enterprises. They reflect good practice for all (ILO 2001: 4; see also page 171).

2 See http://training.itcilo.it/ils/foa/library/tridecl/procedure_en.htm

7.4 Questions posed and answered

The Declaration asks:

- How can multinational enterprises promote development and the needs of developing countries?
- What are the obligations of governments in promoting training? Equal opportunity? And other frameworks to promote social and environmental development?

7.5 The promise and the challenge

On the promises and challenges of this and the other initiatives discussed in Part III on labour rights, see the introductory text (pages 161-64).

With its focus on development, the Declaration is a precursor to the Global Compact (Chapter 3).

References

Gallin, D. (1997) 'The Tripartite Declaration on Multinational Enterprises', a comment in answer to a request for interpretation on the 20th anniversary of the Global Labour Institute, www.global-labour.org/tripartite_declaration_ilo.htm, accessed 2003.

ILO (International Labour Organisation) (2001) *Tripartite Declaration of Principles concerning Multinational Enterprises and Social Policy* (Geneva: ILO).

Vernon, R. (1977) *Storm over the Multinationals: The Real Issues* (Cambridge, MA: Harvard University Press, June 1977).

Tripartite Declaration of Principles concerning Multinational Enterprises and Social Policy*

including

- *List of international labour Conventions and Recommendations referred to in the Tripartite Declaration of Principles concerning Multinational Enterprises and Social Policy, and*
- *Addendum to the Tripartite Declaration of Principles concerning Multinational Enterprises and Social Policy*

(Declaration adopted by the Governing Body of the International Labour Office at its 204th Session (Geneva, November 1977)).

The Governing Body of the International Labour Office:

Recalling that the International Labour Organization for many years has been involved with certain social issues related to the activities of multinational enterprises;

Noting in particular that various Industrial Committees, Regional Conferences, and the International Labour Conference since the mid-1960s have requested appropriate action by the Governing Body in the field of multinational enterprises and social policy;

Having been informed of the activities of other international bodies, in particular the UN Commission on Transnational Corporations and the Organization for Economic Cooperation and Development (OECD);

Considering that the ILO, with its unique tripartite structure, its competence, and its long-standing experience in the social field, has an essential role to play in evolving principles for the guidance of governments, workers' and employers' organizations, and multinational enterprises themselves;

Recalling that it convened a Tripartite Meeting of Experts on the Relationship between Multinational Enterprises and Social Policy in 1972, which recommended an ILO programme of research and study, and a Tripartite Advisory Meeting on the Relationship of Multinational Enterprises and Social Policy in 1976 for the purpose of reviewing the ILO programme of research and suggesting appropriate ILO action in the social and labour field;

* Reprinted with permission from the *Tripartite Declaration of Principles Concerning Multinational Enterprises and Social Policy*, © International Labour Organization, 2002.

Bearing in mind the deliberations of the World Employment Conference;

Having thereafter decided to establish a tripartite group to prepare a Draft Tripartite Declaration of Principles covering all of the areas of ILO concern which relate to the social aspects of the activities of multinational enterprises, including employment creation in the developing countries, all the while bearing in mind the recommendations made by the Tripartite Advisory Meeting held in 1976;

Having also decided to reconvene the Tripartite Advisory Meeting to consider the Draft Declaration of Principles as prepared by the tripartite group;

Having considered the Report and the Draft Declaration of Principles submitted to it by the reconvened Tripartite Advisory Meeting;

Hereby approves the following Declaration which may be cited as the Tripartite Declaration of Principles concerning Multinational Enterprises and Social Policy, adopted by the Governing Body of the International Labour Office, and invites governments of States Members of the ILO, the employers' and workers' organizations concerned and the multinational enterprises operating in their territories to observe the principles embodied therein.

1. Multinational enterprises play an important part in the economies of most countries and in international economic relations. This is of increasing interest to governments as well as to employers and workers and their respective organizations. Through international direct investment and other means such enterprises can bring substantial benefits to home and host countries by contributing to the more efficient utilization of capital, technology and labour. Within the framework of development policies established by governments, they can also make an important contribution to the promotion of economic and social welfare; to the improvement of living standards and the satisfaction of basic needs; to the creation of employment opportunities, both directly and indirectly; and to the enjoyment of basic human rights, including freedom of association, throughout the world. On the other hand, the advances made by multinational enterprises in organizing their operations beyond the national framework may lead to abuse of concentrations of economic power and to conflicts with national policy objectives and with the interest of the workers. In addition, the complexity of multinational enterprises and the difficulty of clearly perceiving their diverse structures, operations and policies sometimes give rise to concern either in the home or in the host countries, or in both.

2. The aim of this Tripartite Declaration of Principles is to encourage the positive contribution which multinational enterprises can make to economic and social progress and to minimize and resolve the difficulties to which their various operations may give rise, taking into account the United Nations resolutions advocating the Establishment of a New International Economic Order.

3. This aim will be furthered by appropriate laws and policies, measures and actions adopted by the governments and by cooperation among the governments and the employers' and workers' organizations of all countries.

4. The principles set out in this Declaration are commended to the governments, the employers' and workers' organizations of home and host countries and to the multinational enterprises themselves.

5. These principles are intended to guide the governments, the employers' and workers' organizations and the multinational enterprises in taking such measures and actions and adopting such social policies, including those based on the principles laid down in the Constitution and the relevant Conventions and Recommendations of the ILO, as would further social progress.

6. To serve its purpose this Declaration does not require a precise legal definition of multinational enterprises; this paragraph is designed to facilitate the understanding of the Declaration and not to provide such a definition. Multinational enterprises include enterprises, whether they are of public, mixed or private ownership, which own or control production, distribution, services or other facilities outside the country in which they are based. The degree of autonomy of entities within multinational enterprises in relation to each other varies widely from one such enterprise to another, depending on the nature of the links between such entities and their fields of activity and having regard to the great diversity in the form of ownership, in the size, in the nature and location of the operations of the enterprises concerned. Unless otherwise specified, the term "multinational enterprise" is used in this Declaration to designate the various entities (parent companies or local entities or both or the organization as a whole) according to the distribution of responsibilities among them, in the expectation that they will cooperate and provide assistance to one another as necessary to facilitate observance of the principles laid down in the Declaration.

7. This Declaration sets out principles in the fields of employment, training, conditions of work and life and industrial relations which governments, employers' and workers' organizations and multinational enterprises are recommended to observe on a voluntary basis; its provisions shall not limit or otherwise affect obligations arising out of ratification of any ILO Convention.

General policies

8. All the parties concerned by this Declaration should respect the sovereign rights of States, obey the national laws and regulations, give due consideration to local practices and respect relevant international standards. They should respect the Universal Declaration of Human Rights and the corresponding International Covenants adopted by the General Assembly of the United Nations as well as the Constitution of the International Labour Organization and its principles according to which freedom of expression and association are essential to sustained progress. They should also honour commitments which they have freely entered into, in conformity with the national law and accepted international obligations.

9. Governments which have not yet ratified Conventions Nos. 87, 98, 111 and 122 are urged to do so and in any event to apply, to the greatest extent possible, through their national policies, the principles embodied therein and in Recommendations Nos. 111, 119 and 122[1]. Without prejudice to the obligation of governments to ensure compliance with Conventions they have ratified, in countries in which the Conventions and Recommendations cited in this paragraph are not complied with, all parties should refer to them for guidance in their social policy.

10. Multinational enterprises should take fully into account established general policy objectives of the countries in which they operate. Their activities should be in harmony with the development priorities and social aims and structure of the country in which they operate. To this effect, consultations should be held between multinational enterprises, the government and, wherever appropriate, the national employers' and workers' organizations concerned.

11. The principles laid down in this Declaration do not aim at introducing or maintaining inequalities of treatment between multinational and national enterprises. They reflect good practice for all. Multinational and national enterprises, wherever the principles of this Declaration are relevant to both, should be subject to the same expectations in respect of their conduct in general and their social practices in particular.

12. Governments of home countries should promote good social practice in accordance with this Declaration of Principles, having regard to the social and labour law, regulations and practices in host countries as well as to relevant international standards. Both host and home country governments should be prepared to have consultations with each other, whenever the need arises, on the initiative of either.

Employment promotion

13. With a view to stimulating economic growth and development, raising living standards, meeting manpower requirements and overcoming unemployment and underemployment, governments should declare and pursue, as a major goal, an active policy designed to promote full, productive and freely chosen employment[2].

14. This is particularly important in the case of host country governments in developing areas of the world where the problems of unemployment and underemployment are at their most serious. In this connection, the general conclusions adopted by the Tripartite World Conference on Employment, Income Distribution and Social Progress and the International Division of Labour (Geneva, June 1976) should be kept in mind[3].

15. Paragraphs 13 and 14 above establish the framework within which due attention should be paid, in both home and host countries, to the employment impact of multinational enterprises.

16. Multinational enterprises, particularly when operating in developing countries, should endeavour to increase employment opportunities and standards, taking into account the employment policies and objectives of the governments, as well as security of employment and the long-term development of the enterprise.

17. Before starting operations, multinational enterprises should, wherever appropriate, consult the competent authorities and the national employers' and workers' organizations in order to keep their manpower plans, as far as practicable, in harmony with national social development policies. Such consultation, as in the case of national enterprises, should continue between the multinational enterprises and all parties concerned, including the workers' organizations.

18. Multinational enterprises should give priority to the employment, occupational development, promotion and advancement of nationals of the host country at all levels in cooperation, as appropriate, with representatives of the workers employed by them or of the organizations of these workers and governmental authorities.

19. Multinational enterprises, when investing in developing countries, should have regard to the importance of using technologies which generate employment, both directly and indirectly. To the extent permitted by the nature of the process and the conditions prevailing in the economic sector concerned, they should adapt technologies to the needs and characteristics of the host countries. They should also, where possible, take part in the development of appropriate technology in host countries.

20. To promote employment in developing countries, in the context of an expanding world economy, multinational enterprises, wherever practicable, should give consideration to the conclusion of contracts with national enterprises for the manufacture of parts and equipment, to the use of local raw materials and to the progressive promotion of the local processing of raw materials. Such arrangements should not be used by multinational enterprises to avoid the responsibilities embodied in the principles of this Declaration.

Equality of opportunity and treatment

21. All governments should pursue policies designed to promote equality of opportunity and treatment in employment, with a view to eliminating any discrimination based on race, colour, sex, religion, political opinion, national extraction or social origin[4].

22. Multinational enterprises should be guided by this general principle throughout their operations without prejudice to the measures envisaged in paragraph 18 or to government policies designed to correct historical patterns of discrimination and thereby to extend equality of opportunity and treatment in employment. Multinational enterprises should accordingly make qualifications, skill and experience the basis for the recruitment, placement, training and advancement of their staff at all levels.

23. Governments should never require or encourage multinational enterprises to discriminate on any of the grounds mentioned in paragraph 21, and continuing guidance from governments, where appropriate, on the avoidance of such discrimination in employment is encouraged.

Security of employment

24. Governments should carefully study the impact of multinational enterprises on employment in different industrial sectors. Governments, as well as multinational enterprises themselves, in all countries should take suitable measures to deal with the employment and labour market impacts of the operations of multinational enterprises.

25. Multinational enterprises equally with national enterprises, through active manpower planning, should endeavour to provide stable employment for their employees and should observe freely negotiated obligations concerning employment stability and social security. In view of the flexibility which multinational enterprises may have, they should strive to assume a leading role in promoting security of employment, particularly in countries where the discontinuation of operations is likely to accentuate long-term unemployment.

26. In considering changes in operations (including those resulting from mergers, take-overs or transfers of production) which would have major employment effects, multinational enterprises should provide reasonable notice of such changes to the appropriate government authorities and representatives of the workers in their employment and their organizations so that the implications may be examined jointly in order to mitigate adverse effects to the greatest possible extent. This is particularly important in the case of the closure of an entity involving collective lay-offs or dismissals.

27. Arbitrary dismissal procedures should be avoided[5].

28. Governments, in cooperation with multinational as well as national enterprises, should provide some form of income protection for workers whose employment has been terminated[6].

Training

29. Governments, in cooperation with all the parties concerned, should develop national policies for vocational training and guidance, closely linked with employment[7]. This is the framework within which multinational enterprises should pursue their training policies.

30. In their operations, multinational enterprises should ensure that relevant training is provided for all levels of their employees in the host country, as appropriate, to meet the needs of the enterprise as well as the development policies of the country. Such training should, to the extent possible, develop generally useful skills and promote career opportunities. This responsibility should be carried out, where appropriate, in cooperation with the authorities of the country, employers' and workers' organizations and the competent local, national or international institutions.

31. Multinational enterprises operating in developing countries should participate, along with national enterprises, in programmes, including special funds, encouraged by host governments and supported by employers' and workers' organizations. These programmes should have the aim of encouraging skill formation and development as well as providing vocational guidance, and should be jointly administered by the parties which support them. Wherever practicable, multinational enterprises should make the services of skilled resource personnel available to help in training programmes organized by governments as part of a contribution to national development.

32. Multinational enterprises, with the cooperation of governments and to the extent consistent with the efficient operation of the enterprise, should afford opportunities within the enterprise as a whole to broaden the experience of local management in suitable fields such as industrial relations.

Conditions of work and life

Wages, benefits and conditions of work

33. Wages, benefits and conditions of work offered by multinational enterprises should be not less favourable to the workers than those offered by comparable employers in the country concerned.

34. When multinational enterprises operate in developing countries, where comparable employers may not exist, they should provide the best possible wages, benefits and conditions of work, within the framework of government policies[8]. These should be related to the economic position of the enterprise, but should be at least adequate to satisfy basic needs of the workers and their families. Where they provide workers with basic amenities such as housing, medical care or food, these amenities should be of a good standard[9].

35. Governments, especially in developing countries, should endeavour to adopt suitable measures to ensure that lower income groups and less developed areas benefit as much as possible from the activities of multinational enterprises.

Safety and health

36. Governments should ensure that both multinational and national enterprises provide adequate safety and health standards for their employees. Those governments which have not yet ratified the ILO Conventions on Guarding of Machinery (No. 119), Ionizing Radiation (No. 115), Benzene (No. 136) and Occupational Cancer (No. 139) are urged nevertheless to apply to the greatest extent possible the principles embodied in these Conventions and in their related Recommendations (Nos. 118, 114, 144 and 147). The Codes of Practice and Guides in the current list of ILO publications on Occupational Safety and Health should also be taken into account[10].

37. Multinational enterprises should maintain the highest standards of safety and health, in conformity with national requirements, bearing in mind their relevant experience within the enterprise as a whole, including any knowledge of special hazards. They should also make available to the representatives of the workers in the enterprise, and upon request, to the competent authorities and the workers' and employers' organizations in all countries in which they operate, information on the safety and health standards relevant to their local operations, which they observe in other countries. In particular, they should make known to those concerned any special hazards and related protective measures associated with new products and processes. They, like comparable domestic enterprises, should be expected to play a leading role in the examination of causes of industrial safety and health hazards and in the application of resulting improvements within the enterprise as a whole.

38. Multinational enterprises should cooperate in the work of international organizations concerned with the preparation and adoption of international safety and health standards.

39. In accordance with national practice, multinational enterprises should cooperate fully with the competent safety and health authorities, the representatives of the workers and their organizations, and established safety and health organizations. Where appropriate, matters relating to safety and health should be incorporated in agreements with the representatives of the workers and their organizations.

Industrial relations

40. Multinational enterprises should observe standards of industrial relations not less favourable than those observed by comparable employers in the country concerned.

Freedom of association and the right to organize

41. Workers employed by multinational enterprises as well as those employed by national enterprises should, without distinction whatsoever, have the right to establish and, subject only to the rules of the organization concerned, to join organizations of their own choosing without previous authorisation[11]. They should also enjoy adequate protection against acts of anti-union discrimination in respect of their employment[12].

42. Organizations representing multinational enterprises or the workers in their employment should enjoy adequate protection against any acts of interference by each other or each other's agents or members in their establishment, functioning or administration[13].

43. Where appropriate, in the local circumstances, multinational enterprises should support representative employers' organizations.

44. Governments, where they do not already do so, are urged to apply the principles of Convention No. 87, Article 5, in view of the importance, in relation to multinational enterprises, of permitting organizations representing such enterprises or the workers in their employment to affiliate with international organizations of employers and workers of their own choosing.

45. Where governments of host countries offer special incentives to attract foreign investment, these incentives should not include any limitation of the workers' freedom of association or the right to organize and bargain collectively.

46. Representatives of the workers in multinational enterprises should not be hindered from meeting for consultation and exchange of views among themselves, provided that the functioning of the operations of the enterprise and the normal procedures which govern relationships with representatives of the workers and their organizations are not thereby prejudiced.

47. Governments should not restrict the entry of representatives of employers' and workers' organizations who come from other countries at the invitation of the local or national organizations concerned for the purpose of consultation on matters of mutual concern, solely on the grounds that they seek entry in that capacity.

Collective bargaining

48. Workers employed by multinational enterprises should have the right, in accordance with national law and practice, to have representative organizations of their own choosing recognized for the purpose of collective bargaining.

49. Measures appropriate to national conditions should be taken, where necessary, to encourage and promote the full development and utilization of machinery for voluntary negotiation between employers or employers' organizations and workers' organizations, with a view to the regulation of terms and conditions of employment by means of collective agreements[14].

50. Multinational enterprises, as well as national enterprises, should provide workers' representatives with such facilities as may be necessary to assist in the development of effective collective agreements[15].

51. Multinational enterprises should enable duly authorized representatives of the workers in their employment in each of the countries in which they operate to conduct negotiations with representatives of management who are authorized to take decisions on the matters under negotiation.

52. Multinational enterprises, in the context of bona fide negotiations with the workers' representatives on conditions of employment, or while workers are exercising the right to organize, should not threaten to utilize a capacity to transfer the whole or part of an operating unit from the country concerned in order to influence unfairly those negotiations or to hinder the exercise of the right to organize; nor should they transfer workers from affiliates in foreign countries with a view to undermining bona fide negotiations with the workers' representatives or the workers' exercise of their right to organize.

53. Collective agreements should include provisions for the settlement of disputes arising over their interpretation and application and for ensuring mutually respected rights and responsibilities.

54. Multinational enterprises should provide workers' representatives with information required for meaningful negotiations with the entity involved and, where this accords with local law and practices, should also provide information to enable them to obtain a true and fair view of the performance of the entity or, where appropriate, of the enterprise as a whole[16].

55. Governments should supply to the representatives of workers' organizations on request, where law and practice so permit, information on the industries in which the enterprise operates, which would help in laying down objective criteria in the collective bargaining process. In this context, multinational as well as national enterprises should respond constructively to requests by governments for relevant information on their operations.

Consultation

56. In multinational as well as in national enterprises, systems devised by mutual agreement between employers and workers and their representatives should provide, in accordance with national law and practice, for regular consultation on matters of mutual concern. Such consultation should not be a substitute for collective bargaining[17].

Examination of grievances

57. Multinational as well as national enterprises should respect the right of the workers whom they employ to have all their grievances processed in a manner consistent with the following provision: any worker who, acting individually or jointly with other workers, considers that he has grounds for a grievance should have the right to submit such grievance without suffering any prejudice whatsoever as a result, and to have such grievance examined pursuant to an appropriate procedure[18]. This is particularly important whenever the multinational enterprises operate in countries which do not abide by the principles of ILO Conventions pertaining to freedom of association, to the right to organize and bargain collectively and to forced labour[19].

Settlement of industrial disputes

58. Multinational as well as national enterprises jointly with the representatives and organizations of the workers whom they employ should seek to establish voluntary conciliation machinery, appropriate to national conditions, which may include provisions for voluntary arbitration, to assist in the prevention and settlement of industrial disputes between employers and workers. The voluntary conciliation machinery should include equal representation of employers and workers[20].

List of international labour Conventions and Recommendations referred to in the Tripartite Declaration of Principles concerning Multinational Enterprises and Social Policy

(adopted by the Governing Body of the International Labour Office at its 204th Session (Geneva, November 1977))[21]

Conventions

- Convention (No. 29) concerning Forced or Compulsory Labour, 1930.
- Convention (No. 87) concerning Freedom of Association and Protection of the Right to Organize, 1948.
- Convention (No. 98) concerning the Application of the Principles of the Right to Organize and to Bargain Collectively, 1949.
- Convention (No. 100) concerning Equal Remuneration for Men and Women Workers for Work of Equal Value, 1951.
- Convention (No. 105) concerning the Abolition of Forced Labour, 1957.

- Convention (No. 110) concerning Conditions of Employment of Plantation Workers, 1958.
- Convention (No. 111) concerning Discrimination in Respect of Employment and Occupation, 1958.
- Convention (No. 115) concerning the Protection of Workers against Ionizing Radiations, 1960.
- Convention (No. 119) concerning the Guarding of Machinery, 1963.
- Convention (No. 122) concerning Employment Policy, 1964.
- Convention (No. 130) concerning Medical Care and Sickness Benefits, 1969.
- Convention (No. 135) concerning Protection and Facilities to be Afforded to Workers' Representatives in the Undertaking, 1971.
- Convention (No. 136) concerning Protection against Hazards of Poisoning arising from Benzene, 1971.
- Convention (No. 139) concerning Prevention and Control of Occupational Hazards caused by Carcinogenic Substances and Agents, 1974.
- Convention (No. 142) concerning Vocational Guidance and Vocational Training in the Development of Human Resources, 1975.

Recommendations

- Recommendation (No. 35) concerning Indirect Compulsion to Labour, 1930.
- Recommendation (No. 69) concerning Medical Care, 1944.
- Recommendation (No. 90) concerning Equal Remuneration for Men and Women Workers for Work of Equal Value, 1951.
- Recommendation (No. 92) concerning Voluntary Conciliation and Arbitration, 1951.
- Recommendation (No. 94) concerning Consultation and Cooperation between Employers and Workers at the Level of the Undertaking, 1952.
- Recommendation (No. 110) concerning Conditions of Employment of Plantation Workers, 1958.
- Recommendation (No. 111) concerning Discrimination in Respect of Employment and Occupation, 1958.
- Recommendation (No. 114) concerning the Protection of Workers against Ionizing Radiations, 1960.
- Recommendation (No. 115) concerning Workers' Housing, 1961.
- Recommendation (No. 116) concerning Reduction of Hours of Work, 1962.
- Recommendation (No. 118) concerning the Guarding of Machinery, 1963.

- Recommendation (No. 119) concerning Termination of Employment at the Initiative of the Employer, 1963.
- Recommendation (No. 122) concerning Employment Policy, 1964.
- Recommendation (No. 129) concerning Communications between Management and Workers within the Undertaking, 1967.
- Recommendation (No. 130) concerning the Examination of Grievances within the Undertaking with a View to their Settlement, 1967.
- Recommendation (No. 134) concerning Medical Care and Sickness Benefits, 1969.
- Recommendation (No. 144) concerning Protection against Hazards of Poisoning arising from Benzene, 1971.
- Recommendation (No. 147) concerning Prevention and Control of Occupational Hazards caused by Carcinogenic Substances and Agents, 1974.
- Recommendation (No. 150) concerning Vocational Guidance and Vocational Training in the Development of Human Resources, 1975.

Addendum to the Tripartite Declaration of Principles concerning Multinational Enterprises and Social Policy

(adopted by the Governing Body of the International Labour Office at its 238th Session (Geneva, November 1987) and 264th Session (November 1995))

References to Conventions and Recommendations in the Tripartite Declaration of Principles concerning Multinational Enterprises and Social Policy

A number of international labour Conventions and Recommendations containing provisions relevant to the Declaration are referred to in footnotes in the Declaration as well as in an annex. These footnotes do not affect the meaning of the provisions of the Declaration to which they refer. They should be considered as references to relevant instruments adopted by the International Labour Organization in the corresponding subject areas, which have helped shape the provisions of the Declaration.

Since the adoption of the Declaration by the Governing Body on 16 November 1977, new Conventions and Recommendations have been adopted by the International Labour Conference. This makes it necessary to include a new list of Conventions and Recommendations adopted since 1977 (including those adopted in June 1977), containing provisions relevant to the Declaration, and this list is set out below. Like the footnotes included in the Declaration at the time of its adoption, the new references do not affect the meaning of the provisions of the Declaration.

In keeping with the voluntary nature of the Declaration all of its provisions, whether derived from ILO Conventions and Recommendations or other sources, are recommendatory, except of course for provisions in Conventions which are binding on the member States which have ratified them.

List of Conventions and Recommendations adopted since 1977 (inclusive) which contain provisions relevant to the Declaration

Number and title of Convention and Recommendation	Relevant paragraphs
Conventions	
No. 148 concerning the Protection of Workers against Occupational Hazards in the Working Environment Due to Air Pollution, Noise and Vibration, 1977	36
No. 154 concerning the Promotion of Collective Bargaining, 1981	9, 49
No. 155 concerning Occupational Safety and Health and the Working Environment, 1981	36
No. 156 concerning Equal Opportunities and Equal Treatment for Men and Women Workers: Workers with Family Responsibilities, 1981	21
No. 158 concerning Termination of Employment at the Initiative of the Employer, 1982	9, 26, 27, 28
No. 161 concerning Occupational Health Services, 1985	36
No. 162 concerning Safety in the Use of Asbestos, 1986	36
No. 167 concerning Safety and Health in Construction, 1988	36
No. 168 concerning Employment Promotion and Protection against Unemployment, 1988	13
No. 170 concerning Safety in the Use of Chemicals at Work, 1990	36
No. 173 concerning the Protection of Workers' Claims in the Event of the Insolvency of their Employer, 1992	28
No. 174 concerning the Prevention of Major Industrial Accidents, 1993	36
No. 176 concerning Safety and Health in Mines, 1995	36
Recommendations	
No. 156 concerning the Protection of Workers against Occupational Hazards in the Working Environment Due to Air Pollution, Noise and Vibration, 1977	36
No. 163 concerning the Promotion of Collective Bargaining, 1981	51, 54, 55
No. 164 concerning Occupational Safety and Health and the Working Environment, 1981	36
No. 165 concerning Equal Opportunities and Equal Treatment for Men and Women Workers: Workers With Family Responsibilities, 1981	21
No. 166 concerning Termination of Employment at the Initiative of the Employer	9, 26, 27, 28
No. 169 concerning Employment Policy, 1984	9, 13
No. 171 concerning Occupational Health Services, 1985	36
No. 172 concerning Safety in the Use of Asbestos, 1986	36

Number and title of Convention and Recommendation	Relevant paragraphs
Recommendations	
No. 175 concerning Safety and Health in Construction, 1988	36
No. 176 concerning Employment Promotion and Protection against Unemployment, 1988	13
No. 177 concerning Safety in the Use of Chemicals at Work, 1990	36
No. 180 concerning the Protection of Workers' Claims in the event of the Insolvency of their Employer, 1992	28
No. 181 concerning the Prevention of Major Industrial Accidents, 1993	36
No. 183 concerning Safety and Health in Mines, 1995	36

Notes:

1 Convention (No. 87) concerning Freedom of Association and Protection of the Right to Organize; Convention (No. 98) concerning the Application of the Principles of the Right to Organize and to Bargain Collectively; Convention (No. 111) concerning Discrimination in Respect of Employment and Occupation; Convention (No. 122) concerning Employment Policy; Recommendation (No. 111) concerning Discrimination in Respect of Employment and Occupation; Recommendation (No. 119) concerning Termination of Employment at the Initiative of the Employer; Recommendation (No. 122) concerning Employment Policy.

2 Convention (No. 122) and Recommendation (No. 122) concerning Employment Policy.

3 ILO, World Employment Conference, Geneva, 4-17 June 1976.

4 Convention (No. 111) and Recommendation (No. 111) concerning Discrimination in Respect of Employment and Occupation; Convention (No. 100) and Recommendation (No. 90) concerning Equal Remuneration for Men and Women Workers for Work of Equal Value.

5 Recommendation (No. 119) concerning Termination of Employment at the Initiative of the Employer.

6 Recommendation (No. 119) concerning Termination of Employment at the Initiative of the Employer.

7 Convention (No. 142) and Recommendation (No. 150) concerning Vocational Guidance and Vocational Training in the Development of Human Resources.

8 Recommendation (No. 116) concerning Reduction of Hours of Work.

9 Convention (No. 110) and Recommendation (No. 110) concerning Conditions of Employment of Plantation Workers; Recommendation (No. 115) concerning Workers' Housing; Recommendation (No. 69) concerning Medical Care; Convention (No. 130) and Recommendation (No. 134) concerning Medical Care and Sickness.

10 The ILO Conventions and Recommendations referred to are listed in "Publications on Occupational Safety and Health", ILO, Geneva, 1976, pp. 1-3. An up-to-date list of Codes of Practice and Guides can be found in the latest edition.

11 Convention No. 87, Article 2.

[12] Convention No. 98, Article 1(1).

[13] Convention No. 98, Article 2(1).

[14] Convention No. 98, Article 4.

[15] Convention (No. 135) concerning Protection and Facilities to be Afforded to Workers' Representatives in the Undertaking.

[16] Recommendation (No. 129) concerning Communications between Management and Workers within Undertakings.

[17] Recommendation (No. 94) concerning Consultation and Cooperation between Employers and Workers of the Level of Undertaking; Recommendation (No. 129) concerning Communications within the Undertaking.

[18] Recommendation (No. 130) concerning the Examination of Grievances within the Undertaking with a view to their Settlement.

[19] Convention (No. 29) concerning Forced or Compulsory Labour; Convention (No. 105) concerning the Abolition of Forced Labour; Recommendation (No. 35) concerning Indirect Compulsion to Labour.

[20] Recommendation (No. 92) concerning Voluntary Conciliation and Arbitration.

[21] It was proposed that the Office make available, on request, offprints of the international labour Conventions and Recommendations referred to in the Tripartite Declaration. ILO: Report of the Reconvened Tripartite Advisory Meeting on the Relationship of Multinational Enterprises and Social Policy, Geneva, 4-7 April 1977, GB.204/4/2, 204th Session, Geneva, 15-18 November 1977, p. 2.

8
Social Accountability 8000

SA8000, a truly global standard, is today the best management tool available to ensure social accountability.

Neil Kearney, General Secretary, International Textile, Garment and Leather Workers' Federation[1]

Social Accountability 8000 (SA8000) is the current benchmark in the field of corporate social accountability.'

Morton Winston, Amnesty International, USA[2]

I was very impressed and pleased with the Gap Analysis and then with the Audit because both processes transformed even the most skeptical of our employees into supporters of the SA8000, having realised that it is a useful instrument for both people and company to bring about positive results and better understanding. It is in this spirit that we will apply the improvements and welcome future audits.

Lorenzo Bertolli, Chief Executive, Cirio Del Monte Kenya Limited[3]

Type Performance-oriented standard, process-oriented standard, certification standard

Strength Its inclusion of management systems

Keywords Labour rights • Accreditation • Certification • Management systems • Multi-sectoral • Multi-stakeholder

1 Quoted in SAI 2001.
2 Quoted in SAI 2001.
3 E-mail from Lorenzo Bertolli, Chief Executive, Cirio Del Monte Kenya Limited, to Alice Tepper Marlin, President and CEO, Social Accountability International, 20 March 2003.

8.1 Background

Social Accountability 8000 (SA8000[4]) is a global and verifiable standard designed to make workplaces more humane. The standard combines key elements of the ILO conventions with the management systems of the International Organisation for Standardisation (ISO). SA8000 is a certification standard developed, overseen and updated through multi-stakeholder dialogue with trade unions, companies, non-governmental organisations (NGOs) and academics.[5]

SA8000's management systems differentiate the standard from most codes of conduct and statements of intent. Its requirement of the creation of management systems ensures that social issues are integrated into all aspects of company policy and day-to-day operations. Management systems include the need for: training programmes, communications, elected representatives, management representatives, clear lines of authority, management reviews, control of suppliers, and planning and policies. Such management systems guarantee that social policies are still in effect long after an auditor leaves the facility. The management systems of SA8000 also ensure that there will be continuous improvement to the social conditions of the workplace.

8.2 Strengths and weaknesses

SA8000 is both a process and a performance standard in a field dominated by standards that are generally one or the other. Its management systems represent an important point of differentiation. The management standards embed the standard into daily practice. Also, SA8000 certification is gaining recognition in the developing world, with factories seeking certification even without pressure from their customers.

SA8000 applies to companies around the world and across industries, serving as a common benchmark to ensure that basic rights are respected within the supply chains of those companies and industries. As of 31 December 2009, there are 2,103 SA8000-certified facilities in 63 countries and 66 sectors affecting 1,213,796 workers worldwide. The global nature of SA8000 allows companies selecting suppliers to use a common system across their operations. The past decade has seen the rise of many national and sectoral standards; although such standards are useful for galvanising an industry into action, they can lead to duplication and multiple audits of the same facilities.

SA8000 has developed extensive training programmes to promote worker rights. Training is very important in helping to promote the awareness necessary for

4 SA8000 is a registered trademark.

5 For more information on the implementation of SA8000 and other labour standards, see Leipziger 2001, 2009.

sustainable improvements to be achieved. There are many types of training being offered and developed: for workers on how to use SA8000 as a tool; for managers on how to follow the requirements; for supply chain managers on how to communicate the requirements and partner with suppliers to enable compliance; and for auditors.[6]

One of the key elements of a certification standard is that, if companies can be certified, they can subsequently lose that certification if they fail to live up to SA8000. Under SA8000, any individual or organisation has the right to complain that a certification is improper, triggering an investigation. Thus, certified facilities can lose their certification and accredited bodies can lose their standing to conduct SA8000 audits.

SA8000 promotes corrective action. During an SA8000 audit, the auditor alerts the facility that it needs to take corrective action in one or more areas before it can gain the SA8000 certificate. This process is critical for guaranteeing continuous improvement.

SA8000 leads to business benefits. Social Accountability International (SAI) has sent questionnaires to all certified facilities to test whether some benefits assumed to occur are in fact being realised, such as the generation of new sales, fewer days lost to injury, the creation of higher-quality products and services, productivity increases and greater retention of workers. The results were positive: over half the respondents reported benefits in each of the above-listed categories. SAI has also surveyed certified facilities regarding the perceived costs and benefits of earning certification.

Since its inception, researchers have studied and written about the use of SA8000 certification in action in India, South Africa, the Philippines, Thailand, the USA and Kenya, providing examples of the problems met and solutions found in use of the SA8000 standard as a tool for workplace improvement (see Leipziger and Kaufman 2003).

Criticism of SA8000 varies and sometimes appears contradictory. For example, some criticise SA8000 for being very rigorous, whereas others regard it as being too lenient. For some, it is a strength that SA8000 requires investment, whereas others regard SA8000 as 'expensive'.

Many of the criticisms made of SA8000 may also be made regarding other major workplace standards. For example, all management standards are biased in favour of companies that have established management systems and that are certified to other management standards, such as ISO 14001 (Chapter 29). As such, it is easier for large companies to implement SA8000 than it is for smaller companies. More research needs to be done on how small and medium-sized enterprises can overcome these barriers, perhaps with technical assistance from governments.

In addition, a study from the Friedrich Ebert Foundation has criticised SA8000 for not requiring the multinational companies that source from certified suppliers to cover the cost of the SA8000 audit and related improvements (Wick 2003: 37). As with ISO standards, the facility being audited bears the costs of the audit under

6 Social Accountability International and the International Garment, Textile and Leather Workers' Federation (ITGLWF) have conducted training in 12 countries to make codes of conduct more useful to workers (Wick 2003).

SA8000. However, a significant number of multinational companies, including Toys'R'Us (Leipziger 2001: 14) and Otto Versand (Leipziger 2001: 31), have provided assistance, such as training and advice, to suppliers. In many cases, SA8000-certified companies are given priority over non-certified companies and granted longer-term contracts.

8.3 Companies to which Social Accountability 8000 applies

Although SA8000 is suited to all companies, the majority of the companies seeking certification are those where labour conditions are known to be problematic, including those in the textiles, garments, shoes, toys and agriculture sectors. Pressure from US and European buyers is generally an important factor in companies seeking certification. As it is based on the management systems of ISO, SA8000 is well suited to companies that have implemented strong management systems, especially those that have already attained ISO 14001 or ISO 9000 certification.

8.4 Questions posed and answered

SA8000 answers the following questions:

- What are the minimum standards for creating a humane work place?
- What management systems can assist in the implementation of humane working conditions?

It encourages company owners and managers to ask (Leipziger 2001: 111):

- How can I ensure that my company and members of its supply chain are respecting workers' rights?

8.5 The promise and the challenge

On the promises and challenges of this and the other initiatives discussed in Part III on labour rights, see the introductory text (pages 161-64).

8.5.1 Points of convergence

8.5.1.1 Training

Training is essential to the success of SA8000. In order to promote compliance, it is necessary to build awareness and capacity, and training has a role to play in this process. In addition, training of managers, workers, NGO staff and auditors is critical to fostering dialogue between stakeholders.

8.5.1.2 Auditing

One of the problems facing suppliers is that they undergo many different audits—for quality, environment and social issues. SA8000, which has been modelled on ISO management systems (Leipziger 2001: 139), can be combined with other types of audits, thus reducing costs and streamlining systems. Although use of combined audits is still in its infancy, this is an important trend, which will require investment in terms of training.

8.5.1.3 Achieving a critical mass and convergence of standards

As with other standards, one of the key challenges is to create a critical mass of certified suppliers. Another key challenge is convergence with other initiatives, which SA8000 is fostering through several initiatives,[7] including worker and manager training in China and Vietnam.

8.6 Update

In 2008, SA8000 launched a third edition of the standard, known as SA8000:2008. After a two-year process of consultation, nearly every provision of the standard was revised in some manner, although in many cases the changes were largely editorial.

Some of the significant changes include:

- A provision was added to SA8000 to prohibit human trafficking, clarifying that human trafficking is included as a form of forced labour.
- The new version introduces types of discrimination which must be banned, including 'social origin, birth, family responsibilities, and marital status'.
- SA8000:2008 prohibits companies from testing women for pregnancy or virginity.

7 'Multistakeholder Organisations Decide on Trial Collaboration', joint communiqué issued from the meeting on 24 February 2003; document shared by Dan Rees of the Ethical Trading Initiative.

- The 2008 standard clarifies that companies need to allow workers the ability to exercise the right to freedom of association and collective bargaining even in countries where these rights are not protected. The phrase requiring companies to 'facilitate parallel means' has been deleted.
- In order to conform to ILO Convention 138, the definition of a child is now anyone less than 15 years old, without any exemptions for developing countries.

For a complete list of all of the changes, it is useful to review the Drafters' Notes (SAI 2008).

References

Leipziger, D. (2001) *SA8000: The Definitive Guide to the New Social Standard* (London: FT Prentice Hall).

—— (ed.) (2009) *SA8000: The First Decade: Implementation, Influence, and Impact* (Sheffield, UK: Greenleaf Publishing).

——, and E. Kaufman (2003) 'SA8000: Human Rights in the Workplace', in R. Sullivan (ed.), *Business and Human Rights: Dilemmas and Solutions* (Sheffield, UK: Greenleaf Publishing): 197-206.

SAI (Social Accountability International) (2001) 'Setting Standards for a Just World' (brochure; New York: SAI).

—— (2008) 'SA8000: 2008 Drafters' Notes' (Prepared in consultation with the Standard Revision Committee of the SAI Board; www.sa-intl.org/_data/n_0001/resources/live/SA8000.2008DraftersNotes.pdf).

Wick, I. (2003) *Workers' Tool or PR Ploy? A Guide to Codes of International Labour Practice* (Bonn/Siegburg: Friedrich Ebert Foundation and Südwind Institut für Ökonomie und Ökumene, 3rd rev. edn, www.fes.de).

Additional resource

Further reading

Smith, D. (2002) *Demonstrating Corporate Values: Which Standard for your Company?* (London: IBE).

Social Accountability 8000 (SA8000:2008)*

I. PURPOSE AND SCOPE

The intent of SA8000 is to provide a standard based on international human rights norms and national labour laws that will protect and empower all personnel within a company's scope of control and influence, who produce products or provide services for that company, including personnel employed by the company itself, as well as by its suppliers/subcontractors, sub-suppliers, and home workers.

SA8000 is verifiable through an evidenced-based process. Its requirements apply universally, regardless of a company's size, geographic location, or industry sector. Complying with the requirements for social accountability of this standard will enable a company to:

a) Develop, maintain, and enforce policies and procedures in order to manage those issues which it can control or influence;

b) Credibly demonstrate to interested parties that existing company policies, procedures, and practices conform to the requirements of this standard.

II. NORMATIVE ELEMENTS AND THEIR INTERPRETATION

The company shall comply with national and all other applicable laws, prevailing industry standards, other requirements to which the company subscribes, and this standard. When such national and other applicable laws, prevailing industry standards, other requirements to which the company subscribes, and this standard address the same issue, the provision most favourable to workers shall apply.

The company shall also respect the principles of the following international instruments:

- ILO Convention 1 (Hours of Work – Industry) and Recommendation 116 (Reduction of Hours of Work)
- ILO Conventions 29 (Forced Labour) and 105 (Abolition of Forced Labour)

- ILO Convention 87 (Freedom of Association)
- ILO Convention 98 (Right to Organise and Collective Bargaining)
- ILO Conventions 100 (Equal Remuneration) and 111 (Discrimination – Employment and Occupation)
- ILO Convention 102 (Social Security – Minimum Standards)
- ILO Convention 131 (Minimum Wage Fixing)
- ILO Convention 135 (Workers' Representatives)
- ILO Convention 138 and Recommendation 146 (Minimum Age)
- ILO Convention 155 and Recommendation 164 (Occupational Safety and Health)
- ILO Convention 159 (Vocational Rehabilitation and Employment – Disabled Persons)
- ILO Convention 169 (Indigenous and Tribal Peoples)
- ILO Convention 177 (Home Work)
- ILO Convention 182 (Worst Forms of Child Labour)
- ILO Convention 183 (Maternity Protection)
- ILO Code of Practice on HIV/AIDS and the World of Work
- Universal Declaration of Human Rights
- The International Covenant on Economic, Social and Cultural Rights
- The International Covenant on Civil and Political Rights
- The United Nations Convention on the Rights of the Child
- The United Nations Convention on the Elimination of All Forms of Discrimination Against Women
- The United Nations Convention on the Elimination of All Forms of Racial Discrimination

III. DEFINITIONS

1. ***Definition of company:*** The entirety of any organisation or business entity responsible for implementing the requirements of this standard, including all personnel employed by the company.
2. ***Definition of personnel:*** All individual men and women directly employed or contracted by a company, including directors, executives, managers, supervisors, and workers.
3. ***Definition of worker:*** All non-management personnel.

4. ***Definition of supplier/subcontractor:*** An organisation which provides the company with goods and/or services integral to and utilised in or for the production of the company's goods and/or services.

5. ***Definition of sub-supplier:*** A business entity in the supply chain which, directly or indirectly, provides the supplier with goods and/or services integral to and utilised in or for the production of the supplier's and/or the company's goods and/or services.

6. ***Definition of corrective and preventive action:*** an immediate and continuing remedy to a non-conformance to the SA8000 standard.

7. ***Definition of interested party:*** An individual or group concerned with or affected by the social performance of the company.

8. ***Definition of child:*** Any person less than 15 years of age, unless the minimum age for work or mandatory schooling is stipulated as being higher by local law, in which case the stipulated higher age applies in that locality.

9. ***Definition of young worker:*** Any worker over the age of a child, as defined above, and under the age of 18.

10. ***Definition of child labour:*** Any work performed by a child younger than the age(s) specified in the above definition of a child, except as provided for by ILO Recommendation 146.

11. ***Definition of forced and compulsory labour:*** All work or service that a person has not offered to do voluntarily and is made to do under the threat of punishment or retaliation, or is demanded as a means of repayment of debt.

12. ***Definition of human trafficking:*** The recruitment, transfer, harbouring or receipt of persons, by means of the use of threat, force, other forms of coercion, or deception for the purpose of exploitation.

13. ***Definition of remediation of children:*** All support and actions necessary to ensure the safety, health, education, and development of children who have been subjected to child labour, as defined above, and have been subsequently dismissed.

14. ***Definition of home worker:*** A person who is contracted by the company or by a supplier, sub-supplier or subcontractor, but does not work on their premises.

15. ***Definition of SA8000 worker representative:*** A worker chosen to facilitate communication with senior management on matters related to SA8000, undertaken by the recognized trade union(s) in unionised facilities and, elsewhere, by a worker elected by non-management personnel for that purpose.

16. ***Management representative:*** A member of senior management personnel appointed by the company to ensure that the requirements of the standard are met.

17. ***Worker organisation:*** A voluntary association of workers organised on a continuing basis for the purpose of maintaining and improving their terms of employment and workplace conditions.

18. ***Collective bargaining agreement:*** A contract for labour negotiated between an employer or group of employers and one or more worker organisations, which specifies the terms and conditions of employment.

IV. SOCIAL ACCOUNTABILITY REQUIREMENTS

1. CHILD LABOUR

Criteria:

1.1 The company shall not engage in or support the use of child labour as defined above.

1.2 The company shall establish, document, maintain, and effectively communicate to personnel and other interested parties, policies and written procedures for remediation of children found to be working in situations which fit the definition of child labour above, and shall provide adequate financial and other support to enable such children to attend and remain in school until no longer a child as defined above.

1.3 The company may employ young workers, but where such young workers are subject to compulsory education laws, they may work only outside of school hours. Under no circumstances shall any young worker's school, work, and transportation time exceed a combined total of 10 hours per day, and in no case shall young workers work more than 8 hours a day. Young workers may not work during night hours.

1.4 The company shall not expose children or young workers to any situations – in or outside of the workplace – that are hazardous or unsafe to their physical and mental health and development.

2. FORCED AND COMPULSORY LABOUR

Criteria:

2.1 The company shall not engage in or support the use of forced or compulsory labour as defined in ILO Convention 29, nor shall personnel be required to pay 'deposits' or lodge identification papers with the company upon commencing employment.

2.2 Neither the company nor any entity supplying labour to the company shall withhold any part of any personnel's salary, benefits, property, or documents in order to force such personnel to continue working for the company.

2.3 Personnel shall have the right to leave the workplace premises after completing the standard workday, and be free to terminate their employment provided that they give reasonable notice to their employer.

2.4 Neither the company nor any entity supplying labour to the company shall engage in or support trafficking in human beings.

3. HEALTH AND SAFETY

Criteria:

3.1 The company shall provide a safe and healthy workplace environment and shall take effective steps to prevent potential accidents and injury to workers' health arising out of, associated with, or occurring in the course of work, by minimising, so far as is reasonably practicable, the causes of hazards inherent in the workplace environment, and bearing in mind the prevailing knowledge of the industry and of any specific hazards.

3.2 The company shall appoint a senior management representative to be responsible for ensuring a safe and healthy workplace environment for all personnel, and for implementing the Health and Safety elements of this standard.

3.3 The company shall provide to personnel on a regular basis effective health and safety instructions, including on-site instruction and, where needed, job-specific instructions. Such instructions shall be repeated for new and reassigned personnel and in cases where accidents have occurred.

3.4 The company shall establish systems to detect, avoid, or respond to potential threats to the health and safety of personnel. The company shall maintain written records of all accidents that occur in the workplace and in company-controlled residences and property.

3.5 The company shall provide at its expense appropriate personal protective equipment to personnel. In the event of a work related injury the company shall provide first aid and assist the worker in obtaining follow-up medical treatment.

3.6 The company shall undertake to assess all the risks to new and expectant mothers arising out of their work activity and to ensure that all reasonable steps are taken to remove or reduce any risks to their health and safety.

3.7 The company shall provide, for use by all personnel, access to clean toilet facilities, access to potable water, and, where applicable, sanitary facilities for food storage.

3.8 The company shall ensure that any dormitory facilities provided for personnel are clean, safe, and meet the basic needs of the personnel.

3.9 All personnel shall have the right to remove themselves from imminent serious danger without seeking permission from the company.

4. FREEDOM OF ASSOCIATION & RIGHT TO COLLECTIVE BARGAINING

Criteria:

4.1 All personnel shall have the right to form, join, and organise trade unions of their choice and to bargain collectively on their behalf with the company. The company shall respect this right, and shall effectively inform personnel that they are free to join an organisation of their choosing and that their doing so will not result in any negative consequences to them, or retaliation, from the company. The company shall not in any way interfere with the establishment, functioning, or administration of such workers' organisations or collective bargaining.

4.2 In situations where the right to freedom of association and collective bargaining are restricted under law, the company shall allow workers to freely elect their own representatives.

4.3 The company shall ensure that representatives of workers and any personnel engaged in organising workers are not subjected to discrimination, harassment, intimidation, or retaliation for reason of their being members of a union or participating in trade union activities, and that such representatives have access to their members in the workplace.

5. DISCRIMINATION

Criteria:

5.1 The company shall not engage in or support discrimination in hiring, remuneration, access to training, promotion, termination, or retirement based on race, national or social origin, caste, birth, religion, disability, gender, sexual orientation, family responsibilities, marital status, union membership, political opinions, age, or any other condition that could give rise to discrimination.

5.2 The company shall not interfere with the exercise of personnel's rights to observe tenets or practices, or to meet needs relating to race, national or social origin, religion, disability, gender, sexual orientation, family responsibilities, union membership, political opinions, or any other condition that could give rise to discrimination.

5.3 The company shall not allow any behaviour that is threatening, abusive, exploitative, or sexually coercive, including gestures, language, and physical contact, in the workplace and, where applicable, in residences and other facilities provided by the company for use by personnel.

5.4 The company shall not subject personnel to pregnancy or virginity tests under any circumstances.

6. DISCIPLINARY PRACTICES

Criterion:

6.1 The company shall treat all personnel with dignity and respect. The company shall not engage in or tolerate the use of corporal punishment, mental or physical coercion, or verbal abuse of personnel. No harsh or inhumane treatment is allowed.

7. WORKING HOURS

Criteria:

7.1 The company shall comply with applicable laws and industry standards on working hours and public holidays. The normal work week, not including overtime, shall be defined by law but shall not exceed 48 hours.

7.2 Personnel shall be provided with at least one day off following every six consecutive days of working. Exceptions to this rule apply only where both of the following conditions exist:

a) National law allows work time exceeding this limit; and

b) A freely negotiated collective bargaining agreement is in force that allows work time averaging, including adequate rest periods.

7.3 All overtime work shall be voluntary, except as provided in 7.4 below, shall not exceed 12 hours per week, nor be requested on a regular basis.

7.4 In cases where overtime work is needed in order to meet short-term business demand and the company is party to a collective bargaining agreement freely negotiated with worker organisations (as defined above) representing a significant portion of its workforce, the company may require such overtime work in accordance with such agreements. Any such agreement must comply with the requirements above.

8. REMUNERATION

Criteria:

8.1 The company shall respect the right of personnel to a living wage and ensure that wages paid for a normal work week shall always meet at least legal or industry minimum standards and shall be sufficient to meet the basic needs of personnel and to provide some discretionary income.

8.2 The company shall ensure that deductions from wages are not made for disciplinary purposes. Exceptions to this rule apply only when both of the following conditions exist:

a) Deductions from wages for disciplinary purposes are permitted by national law; and

b) A freely negotiated collective bargaining agreement is in force.

8.3 The company shall ensure that personnel's wages and benefits composition are detailed clearly and regularly in writing for them for each pay period. The company shall also ensure that wages and benefits are rendered in full compliance with all applicable laws and that remuneration is rendered either in cash or check form, in a manner convenient to workers.

8.4 All overtime shall be reimbursed at a premium rate as defined by national law. In countries where a premium rate for overtime is not regulated by law or a collective bargaining agreement, personnel shall be compensated for overtime at a premium rate or equal to prevailing industry standards, whichever is more favourable to workers' interests.

8.5 The company shall not use labour-only contracting arrangements, consecutive short-term contracts, and/or false apprenticeship schemes to avoid fulfilling its obligations to personnel under applicable laws pertaining to labour and social security legislation and regulations.

9. MANAGEMENT SYSTEMS

Criteria:

Policy

9.1 Top management shall define in writing, in workers' own language, the company's policy for social accountability and labour conditions, and display this policy and the SA8000 standard in a prominent, easily viewable place on the company's premises, to inform personnel that it has voluntarily chosen to comply with the requirements of the SA8000 standard. Such policy shall clearly include the following commitments:

a) To conform to all requirements of this standard;

b) To comply with national and other applicable laws and other requirements to which the company subscribes, and to respect the international instruments and their interpretation (as listed in Section II above);

c) To review its policy regularly in order to continually improve, taking into consideration changes in legislation, in its own code-of-conduct requirements, and any other company requirements;

d) To see that its policy is effectively documented, implemented, maintained, communicated, and made accessible in a comprehensible form to all personnel, including directors, executives, management, supervisors, and staff, whether directly employed by, contracted with, or otherwise representing the company;

e) To make its policy publicly available in an effective form and manner to interested parties, upon request.

Management Representative

9.2 The company shall appoint a senior management representative who, irrespective of other responsibilities, shall ensure that the requirements of this standard are met.

SA8000 Worker Representative

9.3 The company shall recognize that workplace dialogue is a key component of social accountability and ensure that all workers have the right to representation to facilitate communication with senior management in matters relating to SA8000. In unionised facilities, such representation shall be undertaken by recognized trade union(s). Elsewhere, workers may elect a SA8000 worker representative from among themselves for this purpose. In no circumstances, shall the SA8000 worker representative be seen as a substitute for trade union representation.

Management Review

9.4 Top management shall periodically review the adequacy, suitability, and continuing effectiveness of the company's policy, procedures, and performance results vis-à-vis the requirements of this standard and other requirements to which the company subscribes. Where appropriate, system amendments and improvements shall be implemented. The worker representative shall participate in this review.

Planning and Implementation

9.5 The company shall ensure that the requirements of this standard are understood and implemented at all levels of the organisation. Methods shall include, but are not limited to:

a) Clear definition of all parties' roles, responsibilities, and authority;

b) Training of new, reassigned, and/or temporary personnel upon hiring;

c) Periodic instruction, training, and awareness programs for existing personnel;

d) Continuous monitoring of activities and results to demonstrate the effectiveness of systems implemented to meet the company's policy and the requirements of this standard.

9.6 The company is required to consult the SA8000 Guidance Document for interpretative guidance with respect to this standard.

Control of Suppliers/Subcontractors and Sub-Suppliers

9.7 The company shall maintain appropriate records of suppliers/subcontractors' (and, where appropriate, sub-suppliers') commitments to social accountability, including, but not limited to, contractual agreements and/or the written commitment of those organisations to:

a) Conform to all requirements of this standard and to require the same of sub-suppliers;

b) Participate in monitoring activities as requested by the company;

c) Identify the root cause and promptly implement corrective and preventive action to resolve any identified non-conformance to the requirements of this standard;

d) Promptly and completely inform the company of any and all relevant business relationship(s) with other suppliers/subcontractors and sub-suppliers.

9.8 The company shall establish, maintain, and document in writing appropriate procedures to evaluate and select suppliers/subcontractors (and, where appropriate, sub-suppliers) taking into account their performance and commitment to meet the requirements of this standard.

9.9 The company shall make a reasonable effort to ensure that the requirements of this standard are being met by suppliers and subcontractors within their sphere of control and influence.

9.10 In addition to the requirements of Sections 9.7 through 9.9 above, where the company receives, handles, or promotes goods and/or services from suppliers/subcontractors or sub-suppliers who are classified as home workers, the company shall take special steps to ensure that such home workers are afforded a level of protection similar to that afforded to directly employed personnel under the requirements of this standard. Such special steps shall include, but not be limited to:

a) Establishing legally binding, written purchasing contracts requiring conformance to minimum criteria in accordance with the requirements of this standard;

b) Ensuring that the requirements of the written purchasing contract are understood and implemented by home workers and all other parties involved in the purchasing contract;

c) Maintaining, on the company premises, comprehensive records detailing the identities of home workers, the quantities of goods produced, services provided, and/or hours worked by each home worker;

d) Frequent announced and unannounced monitoring activities to verify compliance with the terms of the written purchasing contract.

Addressing Concerns and Taking Corrective Action

9.11 The company shall provide a confidential means for all personnel to report non-conformances with this standard to the company management, and the worker representative. The company shall investigate, address, and respond to the concerns of personnel and other interested parties with regard to conformance/non-conformance with the company's policies and/or the requirements of this standard. The company shall refrain from disciplining, dismissing, or otherwise discriminating against any personnel for providing information concerning observance of the standard.

9.12 The company shall identify the root cause, promptly implement corrective and preventive action, and allocate adequate resources appropriate to the nature and severity of any identified non-conformance with the company's policy and/or the standard.

Outside Communication and Stakeholder Engagement

9.13 The company shall establish and maintain procedures to communicate regularly to all interested parties data and other information regarding compliance with the requirements of this document, including, but not limited to, the results of management reviews and monitoring activities.

9.14 The company shall demonstrate its willingness to participate in dialogues with all interested stakeholders, including, but not limited to: workers, trade unions, suppliers, subcontractors, sub-suppliers, buyers, nongovernmental organisations, and local and national government officials, aimed at attaining sustainable compliance with this standard.

Access for Verification

9.15 In the case of announced and unannounced audits of the company for the purpose of certifying its compliance with the requirements of this standard, the company shall ensure access to its premises and to reasonable information required by the auditor.

Records

9.16 The company shall maintain appropriate records to demonstrate conformance to the requirements of this standard.

9
Fair Labor Association: Workplace Code of Conduct

> **We've always believed that industry-wide action is essential to achieving real and lasting changes in working conditions . . . The FLA's programme . . . has the potential to make a real difference in the lives of workers across the industry and around the globe.**
>
> ***Susheela Jayapal, General Counsel Adidas America*** [1]

Type Process-oriented standard, performance-oriented standard, certification standard

Strength Operates at brand level

Keywords Labour rights • Brands • Independent monitoring • Verification

9.1 Background

The Fair Labor Association (FLA) is a network of companies, human rights and labour organisations and colleges and universities seeking to improve working conditions. The FLA accredits independent monitors to inspect factories.

The FLA works with companies to improve internal monitoring systems. Companies are expected to implement systems to ensure that the FLA Code of Conduct is upheld throughout their supply chains. The FLA accredits, selects, hires and pays monitors to conduct independent and external monitoring visits in 5% of participating-company factories. This sample is selected through a weighted process that focuses on countries with the highest risk of labour problems.

1 Quoted by Rutgers (1999).

Participating companies must remediate problems found through internal and external monitoring visits (for more details, see van Heerden and Shubash 2003). These findings are posted on the website of the FLA (www.fairlabor.org) within 60 days of the monitoring visit. This system of verification through independent monitoring is reinforced through the third-party complaint system, through which trade unions, non-governmental organisations (NGOs) and companies can notify the FLA of non-compliance in any facilities producing for an FLA member company.

In 1996, US President Clinton convened the Apparel Industry Partnership to address the issue of workers' rights. The result of the negotiations was the Fair Labor Association—a non-profit organisation that accredits independent monitors to inspect factories. FLA members include Nike, Reebok, Philips–Van Heusen, Liz Clairborne, adidas group, Puma, Patagonia and Tumi, among others.[2] Although NGOs and trade unions participated in the drafting of the FLA Code of Conduct, trade unions and the Interfaith Center on Corporate Responsibility (ICCR, www.iccr.org) have since withdrawn their support because of the absence of a living-wage requirement in the FLA Code of Conduct. The FLA also plans to deal with complaints from interested parties.

The FLA model combines both internal monitoring by the participating company in the USA, in addition to independent, external monitoring by groups accredited by the FLA. Under the FLA system, at least 30% of all contractors must undergo independent, external monitoring, with the selection of which contractors will undergo external auditing to be made on the basis of risk analysis by the FLA. At the end of three years, the participating company should have monitored each of its relevant facilities. FLA companies must:[3]

1. Adopt and communicate a code
2. Train internal compliance staff
3. Provide employees with confidential reporting channels
4. Conduct internal monitoring
5. Submit to Independent External Monitoring
6. Collect and manage compliance information
7. Remediate in a timely manner
8. Take all steps necessary to prevent persistent forms of noncompliance
9. Consult with civil society
10. Pay dues and meets its other procedural requirements

Once 30% of all contractors have been independently monitored by FLA-accredited monitors, the company can use the FLA 'service mark' in its advertising, within its stores or on its products. The FLA staff evaluates the company perfor-

2 See www.fairlabor.org/fla_affiliates_a1.html, accessed May 2010.

3 See www.fairlabor.org/images/FLAAffiliates/obligations%20of%20companies.pdf, accessed May 2010.

mance in fulfilling each of its obligations (see above). Independent, external monitoring is one means by which internal compliance systems are evaluated. The FLA staff also can use their discretion to perform independent verification through a visit to a factory to confirm that remediation efforts have been undertaken and have been effective. In addition, companies report to the FLA on a quarterly and annual basis, and these reports are verified by yearly visits to headquarters and/or field offices to review information.

The FLA has accredited a range of organisations to conduct external monitoring against various components of its code. These organisations include large companies, such as Société Générale de Surveillance (SGS), and small NGOs, such as Phulki, based in Bangladesh.

The FLA is also working with more than 200 colleges and universities participating in its programmes. Together, these universities have 1,000 collegiate licensees that manufacture goods on their behalf, such as shirts with a university 'brand', key-rings and yearbooks.

9.2 Strengths and weaknesses

Trade unions have failed to support the FLA because of its lack of commitment to introducing a living-wage requirement (see Greenhouse 1998). The FLA responds to this criticism by stating that too little is known about a living wage to include it as a standard. According to Anne Lally of the FLA, 'the logic is that if this standard cannot always be implemented, and brands take commitments seriously, how can they commit to it?'[4] The FLA held a stakeholder forum to address wages in 2009 which explored practical ways to address this complex issue.[5]

9.3 Companies to which the Workplace Code of Conduct of the Fair Labor Association applies

The Workplace Code of Conduct applies to all companies, but is most applicable to companies that produce branded goods for the US market.

4 Personal communication from Anne Lally, 27 June 2003.

5 To review the findings, go to https://www.fairlabor.org/images/WhatWeDo/CurrentIssues/fairwagereport_oct2009.pdf, accessed 11 June 2010.

9.4 Questions posed and answered

Under what conditions should products be manufactured so as to ensure that workers' rights are being respected?

9.5 The promise and the challenge

On the promises and challenges of this and the other initiatives discussed in Part III on labour rights, see the introductory text (pages 161-64).

9.5.1 Points of divergence

9.5.1.1 Geographical target

The FLA works primarily with US companies and their contractors all over the world; it also works with some companies with European headquarters, such as Adidas (www.adidas.com). In contrast, SA8000 (Chapter 8) works with companies from around the world, and the Ethical Trading Initiative (ETI, Chapter 10) works primarily with companies producing consumer goods sold within the United Kingdom.

9.5.1.2 Sectoral target

The FLA is focused primarily on the apparel and footwear industries, with licensees producing electronic and paper goods. SA8000 is not industry-specific or sector-specific, with participating companies producing toys, agriculture and a wide range of other goods and services.[6]

9.5.1.3 Wages

The FLA Workplace Code of Conduct requires companies to pay the prevailing wage rather than a 'living wage'.[7]

6 On 23 October 2001, the Board of Directors of the FLA expanded the scope of the FLA beyond the apparel and footwear industries by admitting licensees that have a line of goods that manufacture rings, yearbooks, hosiery and other items generally sold in university shops (www.fairlabor.org).

7 The FLA has called for further research on wages (www.fairlabor.org).

9.5.1.4 Right to organise

Although both the FLA Code and SA8000 guarantee the right of workers to organise, only SA8000 sets a requirement for countries in which the right to organise is restricted by law. In these countries, companies shall facilitate parallel means of organising under SA8000. The FLA system allows for the board of the FLA to provide guidance in this area. The FLA requires that participating companies take 'steps to ensure that employees have the ability to exercise these rights without fear of discrimination or punishment' (FLA 2001: 20).

9.5.1.5 Monitoring

The FLA, like the ETI, relies on both internal and external monitoring. The FLA will determine which factories should be monitored, based on risk analysis and company recommendation. As a result, 85% of applicable facilities will not be monitored in a given year (ILRF 1999). Internal monitoring for some companies covers 100% of the supply chain. External monitoring is simply a verification that such systems are working.

Factory visits are exclusively unannounced. This is a point of divergence with SA8000, which requires that the contractor prepare a significant amount of documentation in preparation for the audit, similar to the ISO model.

References

FLA (Fair Labor Association) (2001) Fair Labor Association Charter Document, as amended October 2009, www.fairlabor.org/images/AboutUs/flacharter_october2009.pdf, accessed May 2010.

Greenhouse, G. (1998) 'Plan to Curtail Sweatshops Rejected by Union', *New York Times*, 5 November 1998 (www.sweatsoap.org/resources/ccc/corporate-accountability/code-implementation-a-verification/479).

ILRF (International Labour Rights Fund) (1999) *Assessment of Fair Labor Association Agreement of November 2, 1998* (Washington, DC: ILRF, 1 January 1999).

Leipziger, D. (2001) *SA8000: The Definitive Guide to the New Social Standard* (London: FT Prentice Hall).

Rutgers (1999) 'Adidas-Salomon Joins Fair Labor Association', 7 July 1999, http://ur.rutgers.edu/news/ACLA/adidas.htm, accessed 2003.

Van Heerden, A., and J.S. Shubash II (2003) 'Labor Relations and International Labor Rights: The Role of Private Labor Rights Initiatives', in *The Permanent Court of Arbitration/Peace Palace Papers*. XI. *Internationalization of Labor Dispute Settlement* (ed. International Bureau of the Permanent Court of Arbitration; Dordrecht, Netherlands: Kluwer Law International).

Additional resources

Further reading

Wick, I. (2003) *Workers' Tool or PR Ploy? A Guide to Codes of International Labour Practice* (Bonn/Siegburg: Friedrich Ebert Foundation and Südwind Institut für Ökonomie und Ökumene, 3rd rev. edn, www.fes.de).

Website

Fair Labor Association: www.fairlabor.org

Workplace Code of Conduct*

The Apparel Industry Partnership has addressed issues related to the eradication of sweatshops in the United States and abroad. On the basis of this examination, the Partnership has formulated the following set of standards defining decent and humane working conditions. The Partnership believes that consumers can have confidence that products that are manufactured in compliance with these standards are not produced under exploitative or inhumane conditions.

Forced Labor. There shall not be any use of forced labor, whether in the form of prison labor, indentured labor, bonded labor or otherwise.

Child Labor. No person shall be employed at an age younger than 15 (or 14 where the law of the country of manufacture[8] allows) or younger than the age for completing compulsory education in the country of manufacture where such age is higher than 15.

Harassment or Abuse. Every employee shall be treated with respect and dignity. No employee shall be subject to any physical, sexual, psychological or verbal harassment or abuse.

Nondiscrimination. No person shall be subject to any discrimination in employment, including hiring, salary, benefits, advancement, discipline, termination or retirement, on the basis of gender, race, religion, age, disability, sexual orientation, nationality, political opinion, or social or ethnic origin.

Health and Safety. Employers shall provide a safe and healthy working environment to prevent accidents and injury to health arising out of, linked with, or occurring in the course of work or as a result of the operation of employer facilities.

Freedom of Association and Collective Bargaining. Employers shall recognize and respect the right of employees to freedom of association and collective bargaining.

Wages and Benefits. Employers recognize that wages are essential to meeting employees' basic needs. Employers shall pay employees, as a floor, at least the mini-

* Reproduced with the permission of the Fair Labor Association.

mum wage required by local law or the prevailing industry wage, whichever is higher, and shall provide legally mandated benefits.

Hours of Work. Except in extraordinary business circumstances, employees shall (i) not be required to work more than the lesser of (a) 48 hours per week and 12 hours overtime or (b) the limits on regular and overtime hours allowed by the law of the country of manufacture or, where the laws of such country do not limit the hours of work, the regular work week in such country plus 12 hours overtime and (ii) be entitled to at least one day off in every seven day period.

Overtime Compensation. In addition to their compensation for regular hours of work, employees shall be compensated for overtime hours at such premium rate as is legally required in the country of manufacture or, in those countries where such laws do not exist, at a rate at least equal to their regular hourly compensation rate.

Any Company that determines to adopt the Workplace Code of Conduct shall, in addition to complying with all applicable laws of the country of manufacture, comply with and support the Workplace Code of Conduct in accordance with the attached Principles of Monitoring and shall apply the higher standard in cases of differences or conflicts. Any Company that determines to adopt the Workplace Code of Conduct also shall require its licensees and contractors and, in the case of a retailer, its suppliers to comply with applicable local laws and with this Code in accordance with the attached Principles of Monitoring and to apply the higher standard in cases of differences or conflicts.

Note:

[8] All references to local law throughout this Code shall include regulations implemented in accordance with applicable local law.

10
Ethical Trading Initiative: Base Code

> **I think the Ethical Trading Initiative is an enormously important and impressive initiative . . . we are at a new point in our potential capacity to pull together the real interests of NGOs, the trade union movement and the business community, with the business community not being involved simply to do a bit of 'charitable extra' but in the mainstream of their business interests.**
>
> ***Claire Short, UK Member of Parliament, former Secretary of State for International Development***[1]

Type Performance-oriented initiative, process-oriented initiative

Strength Promotion of learning and good practice

Keywords Labour rights • Tripartite • Good practice • Development

10.1 Background

The Ethical Trading Initiative (ETI) seeks to improve the lives of workers in global supply chains by creating a forum to identify and promote good practice in the implementation of codes of conduct. The ETI is tripartite, consisting of membership groups from three sectors: companies, non-governmental organisations (NGOs) and trade unions. It is funded by the UK government's Department for International Development and its members, which include NGOs and companies, which pay dues.

1 Short 1998.

In pursuit of its aims, the ETI conducts experimental projects into aspects of code implementation, hosts seminars, events and conferences and has a research and publications programme. The ETI is interested in sharing the lessons learned from various different approaches to monitoring, verification and other aspects of code implementation. ETI members include over 50 corporations including: Marks & Spencer, Sainsbury's, Gap and Inditex, along with NGOs such as Save the Children, the FairTrade Foundation and the international trade union movement.[2]

Members of the ETI provide a progress report to the ETI each year. Company members must demonstrate continued progress and improvements towards implementing the ETI Base Code in order to remain a member.

10.2 Strengths and weaknesses

The ETI has produced valuable research from its pilot studies in China, South Africa, Zimbabwe, Costa Rica and Sri Lanka. According to Dan Rees, manager of the ETI secretariat, through its pilot in Zimbabwe ETI learned that 'combining international audit firms with an aid agency approach' was key (interview with Rees, quoted in Cowe 2001).

Another major lesson learned concerns the degree of complexity and ambiguity within the field. As the pilot studies replicate the ETI tripartite model they are forging important alliances. However, working within the tripartite structure can be time-consuming[3] and expensive.

Company members report that the ETI provides a valuable forum in which to engage trade unions and NGOs. In addition, the ETI catalyses learning by sharing good practice and networking while providing a peer review of corporate progress and co-operation rather than competition.

10.3 Companies to which the Base Code of the Ethical Trading Initiative applies

The ETI and the best practices it disseminates are relevant to all companies seeking to promote better working conditions in global supply chains.

2 www.ethicaltrade.org/about-eti/our-members, accessed May 2010

3 Interview with Sumithra Dhanarajan, Policy Adviser, Private Sector, Oxfam United Kingdom, 8 April 2003.

10.4 Questions posed and answered

What constitutes best practice in ethical supply chains? What types of alliance can be developed to promote ethical supply chains?

10.5 The promise and the challenge

On the promises and challenges of this and the other initiatives discussed in Part III on labour rights, see the introductory text (pages 161-64).

10.5.1 Points of divergence

10.5.1.1 Commitment to providing regular employment

The ETI Base Code of conduct is very similar to the other codes discussed in Part III, with one significant exception: ETI companies make a commitment to provide 'regular employment'. To quote the Base Code: 'To every extent possible work performed must be on the basis of recognised employment relationship established through national law and practice' (see page 214).

10.5.1.2 Verification

Unlike SA8000 (Chapter 8) and the Fair Labor Association (FLA, Chapter 9), the ETI does not verify brands or suppliers; rather, it focuses on the identification of good practice.

10.5.1.3 Approach

ETI promotes a comparative analysis of different approaches to promoting workers' rights, whereas SA8000 is an operational system for accredited certification.

10.5.1.4 Consultation

Like the FLA, both ETI and the creators of SA8000 have consulted with a wide range of NGOs and unions around the world.

10.5.1.5 Focus

ETI has a strong focus on the context within which companies operate. According to its website, 'ETI will, where appropriate, consider the broader impact of its members' activities on human rights, environment and development issues within the wider community in which they operate' (ETI 1998: 2).

10.5.1.6 Partnership approach

The forging of new partnerships is also an important priority for the ETI and it works in partnership with industry stakeholders in all its experimental work. For example, in the Western Cape of Africa, the ETI has helped to establish the Ethical Trading Forum, which brings together producers, trade unions, NGOs and government to promote better working conditions within the field of agriculture.

References

Cowe, R. (2001) 'Hard Labour to Put Code into Practice', *Financial Times*, 12 June 2001: 12.

ETI (Ethical Trade Initiative) (1998) 'Base Code', www.ethicaltrade.org/eti-base-code.

Short, C. (1998) Speech by the Right Honourable Clare Short, MP, First Annual Conference of the Ethical Trading Initiative, 2 December 1998, www.dfid.gov.uk/News/Speeches/files/sp2dec.html.

Additional resources

Further reading

Wick, I. (2003) *Workers' Tool or PR Ploy? A Guide to Codes of International Labour Practice* (Bonn/Siegburg: Friedrich Ebert Foundation and Südwind Institut für Ökonomie und Ökumene, 3rd rev. edn, www.fes.de).

Website

Ethical Trade Initiative: www.ethicaltrade.org

The Base Code
Ethical Trading Initiative*

1. EMPLOYMENT IS FREELY CHOSEN

1.1 There is no forced, bonded or involuntary prison labour.

1.2 Workers are not required to lodge "deposits" or their identity papers with their employer and are free to leave their employer after reasonable notice.

2. FREEDOM OF ASSOCIATION AND THE RIGHT TO COLLECTIVE BARGAINING ARE RESPECTED

2.1 Workers, without distinction, have the right to join or form trade unions of their own choosing and to bargain collectively.

2.2 The employer adopts an open attitude towards the activities of trade unions and their organisational activities.

2.3 Workers' representatives are not discriminated against and have access to carry out their representative functions in the workplace.

2.4 Where the right to freedom of association and collective bargaining is restricted under law, the employer facilitates, and does not hinder, the development of parallel means for independent and free association and bargaining.

3. WORKING CONDITIONS ARE SAFE AND HYGIENIC

3.1 A safe and hygienic working environment shall be provided, bearing in mind the prevailing knowledge of the industry and of any specific hazards. Adequate steps shall be taken to prevent accidents and injury to health arising out of, associated with, or occurring in the course of work, by minimising, so far as is reasonably practicable, the causes of hazards inherent in the working environment.

3.2 Workers shall receive regular and recorded health and safety training, and such training shall be repeated for new or reassigned workers.

---

* Reproduced with the permission of the Ethical Trading Initiative.

3.3 Access to clean toilet facilities and to potable water, and, if appropriate, sanitary facilities for food storage shall be provided.

3.4 Accommodation, where provided, shall be clean, safe, and meet the basic needs of the workers.

3.5 The company observing the code shall assign responsibility for health and safety to a senior management representative.

4. CHILD LABOUR SHALL NOT BE USED

4.1 There shall be no new recruitment of child labour.

4.2 Companies shall develop or participate in and contribute to policies and programmes which provide for the transition of any child found to be performing child labour to enable her or him to attend and remain in quality education until no longer a child; "child" and "child labour" being defined in the appendices.

4.3 Children and young persons under 18 shall not be employed at night or in hazardous conditions.

4.4 These policies and procedures shall conform to the provisions of the relevant ILO standards.

5. LIVING WAGES ARE PAID

5.1 Wages and benefits paid for a standard working week meet, at a minimum, national legal standards or industry benchmark standards, whichever is higher. In any event wages should always be enough to meet basic needs and to provide some discretionary income.

5.2 All workers shall be provided with written and understandable information about their employment conditions in respect to wages before they enter employment and about the particulars of their wages for the pay period concerned each time that they are paid.

5.3 Deductions from wages as a disciplinary measure shall not be permitted nor shall any deductions from wages not provided for by national law be permitted without the expressed permission of the worker concerned. All disciplinary measures should be recorded.

6. WORKING HOURS ARE NOT EXCESSIVE

6.1 Working hours comply with national laws and benchmark industry standards, whichever affords greater protection.

6.2 In any event, workers shall not on a regular basis be required to work in excess of 48 hours per week and shall be provided with at least one day off for every 7 day period on average. Overtime shall be voluntary, shall not exceed

12 hours per week, shall not be demanded on a regular basis and shall always be compensated at a premium rate.

7. NO DISCRIMINATION IS PRACTISED

7.1 There is no discrimination in hiring, compensation, access to training, promotion, termination or retirement based on race, caste, national origin, religion, age, disability, gender, marital status, sexual orientation, union membership or political affiliation.

8. REGULAR EMPLOYMENT IS PROVIDED

8.1 To every extent possible work performed must be on the basis of recognised employment relationship established through national law and practice.

8.2 Obligations to employees under labour or social security laws and regulations arising from the regular employment relationship shall not be avoided through the use of labour-only contracting, sub-contracting, or home-working arrangements, or through apprenticeship schemes where there is no real intent to impart skills or provide regular employment, nor shall any such obligations be avoided through the excessive use of fixed-term contracts of employment.

9. NO HARSH OR INHUMANE TREATMENT IS ALLOWED

9.1 Physical abuse or discipline, the threat of physical abuse, sexual or other harassment and verbal abuse or other forms of intimidation shall be prohibited.

The provisions of this code constitute minimum and not maximum standards, and this code should not be used to prevent companies from exceeding these standards. Companies applying this code are expected to comply with national and other applicable law and, where the provisions of law and this Base Code address the same subject, to apply that provision which affords the greater protection.

11 Other major initiatives in the clothing industry

Other major initiatives in the field of labour rights include the following.

11.1 The Fair Wear Foundation

The Fair Wear Foundation (FWF, http://fairwear.org) is a Dutch initiative to promote humane working conditions in the garment industry around the world. Business associations in the garment sector, non-governmental organisations (NGOs) and trade unions launched the FWF in May 2002. The Foundation has developed the Fair Wear Code of Labour Practice. Member companies implement the Code at each of their supplier locations, and the FWF verifies compliance with the Code.

11.2 Worldwide Responsible Accredited Production

Worldwide Responsible Accredited Production (WRAP, www.wrapcompliance.org, formerly 'Worldwide Responsible Apparel Production') is a certification system that has developed the WRAP Principles. These Principles have been endorsed by the organisation representing apparel manufacturers in 18 countries. In addition to labour issues, WRAP also addresses the environment, customs compliance and drug interdiction.

11.3 The Worker Rights Consortium

The Worker Rights Consortium (WRC, www.workersrights.org) was established by US colleges and universities—along with students and labour rights experts—to assist colleges and universities in implementing codes of conduct. Currently, 186 colleges and universities support the WRC. Affiliates adopt a manufacturing code of conduct to guarantee workers' rights. The code is integrated into contracts with lisensees.

Additional resources

Further reading

ILO (International Labour Organisation) (2001) *Tripartite Declaration of Principles concerning Multinational Enterprises and Social Policy* (Geneva: ILO).

Wick, I. (2003) *Workers' Tool or PR Ploy? A Guide to Codes of International Labour Practice* (Bonn/Siegburg: Friedrich Ebert Foundation and Südwind Institut für Ökonomie und Ökumene, 3rd rev. edn, www.fes.de).

Websites

International Labour Office: www.ilo.org
Worldwide Responsible Accredited Production (WRAP): www.wrapcompliance.org
Worker Rights Consortium (WRC): www.workersrights.org

Part IV
Health issues

12
ILO Code of Practice on HIV/AIDS and the World of Work

> **AIDS and HIV affect people at all levels of society, but it has a profound impact on workers and their families, enterprises, employers, and national economies. As it affects the most economically active members of society, it reduces earnings, productivity, skills and experience while imposing huge costs on enterprises, labour and governments. Thus, AIDS is not only a workplace issue, but a challenge to development worldwide.**
>
> *Juan Somavía, (former) Director General of the International Labour Organisation*[1]

Type Tripartite

Strength Addresses informal as well as formal sector

Keywords Tripartite • HIV/AIDS • Discrimination • Gender

12.1 Overview

The ILO Code of Practice on HIV/AIDS and the World of Work is a useful tool for companies, governments and trade unions. It represents an important contribution to the field of health and CR, a field that is poised to grow.

The ILO Code of Practice was launched in 2001, under the leadership of the visionary Director General of the ILO, Juan Somavía, who also chaired the UN

1 'ILO to launch new Code of Practice on HIV/AIDS and the world of work', press release, International Labour Organisation, 22 June 2001.

Social Summit in Copenhagen in 1995. The Code was developed in partnership between the tripartite bodies of the ILO: employers, employers' organisations and governments. The Code provides guidance to these diverse groups to allow for coherent and integrated implementation.

The key principles include:

- Recognising that HIV/AIDS is a workplace issue
- Non-discrimination in employment
- Gender equality
- Screening and confidentiality
- Social dialogue
- Prevention and care and support

The ILO Code of Practice seeks to:

- Manage and mitigate the impact of HIV/AIDS on the world of work
- Prevent the spread of HIV/AIDS
- Allow for the care and support of workers infected and affected by HIV/AIDS
- Eliminate the stigma and discrimination on the basis of real or perceived HIV status

The Code of Practice describes how the AIDS epidemic has become a business issue, as it affects the most productive segment of the workforce, can decrease productivity and loss of skills and experience.

The ILO has laid out an ambitious and comprehensive agenda in its Code of Practice, and references two other important codes in the field:

- The Code of Practice on the Protection of Workers' Personal Data
- The Universal Precautions, which deal with procedures for handling blood by healthcare workers

The latter was developed by the US Centers for Disease Control in 1985.

As with many codes and guidelines, the success of the initiative can be measured by its commitment to and investment in training. The Code specifies various groups who should be given training:

> Testing for HIV should not be carried out at the workplace except as specified in this code. It is unnecessary and imperils the human rights and dignity of workers: test results may be revealed and misused and the informed consent of workers may not always be fully free or based on an appreciation of all of the facts and implications of testing.

Box 12.1 **Key messages for companies**

- Manager, supervisors and personnel officers
- Peer educators
- Workers' representatives
- Health and safety officers
- Factory and labour inspectors
- Workers who come into contact with human blood and other bodily fluids

12.2 Strengths and weaknesses

One of the strengths of the ILO Code of Practice is that it also addresses the informal sector, which is rare in the field of CR codes and standards: this is something that other codes and standards can learn from the ILO Code model. The Code of Practice also addresses the special needs of vulnerable groups, including women and children.

The definitions included in the Code are helpful, especially the term 'reasonable accommodation'. The Code also addresses the needs of affected persons: persons whose lives are changed due to HIV/AIDS.

The Code is to be commended for encouraging culturally appropriate and culturally sensitive content in the training.

The Code encourages all actors to include people with HIV/AIDS in the development of policies, procedures and training.

One weakness is how little attention it pays to following up how companies are using and implementing the Code. It would be useful to have statistics on companies offering training, for example, with a focus on lessons learned.

12.3 Opportunities and challenges

The ILO Code of Practice is one of the least well-known codes in the CR field, despite the importance of its subject matter. But its importance and relevance will continue to grow, as health risks in the workplace grow.

Many aspects of the Code of Practice are useful to others working on code development, especially as regards the role of governments in creating and enabling environments that support human rights.

An ILO Code of Practice on HIV/AIDS and the World of Work*

1. OBJECTIVE

The objective of this code is to provide a set of guidelines to address the HIV/AIDS epidemic in the world of work and within the framework of the promotion of decent work. The guidelines cover the following key areas of action:

(a) prevention of HIV/AIDS;

(b) management and mitigation of the impact of HIV/AIDS on the world of work;

(c) care and support of workers infected and affected by HIV/AIDS;

(d) elimination of stigma and discrimination on the basis of real or perceived HIV status.

2. USE

This code should be used to:

(a) develop concrete responses at enterprise, community, regional, sectoral, national and international levels;

(b) promote processes of dialogue, consultations, negotiations and all forms of cooperation between governments, employers and workers and their representatives, occupational health personnel, specialists in HIV/AIDS issues, and all relevant stakeholders (which may include community-based and non-governmental organizations [NGOs]);

(c) give effect to its contents in consultation with the social partners:
- in national laws, policies and programmes of action,
- in workplace/enterprise agreements, and
- in workplace policies and plans of action.

3. SCOPE AND TERMS USED IN THE CODE

3.1. *Scope*

This code applies to:

(a) all employers and workers (including applicants for work) in the public and private sectors; and

(b) all aspects of work, formal and informal.

3.2. *Terms used in the code*

HIV: the Human Immunodeficiency Virus, a virus that weakens the body's immune system, ultimately causing AIDS.

Affected persons: persons whose lives are changed in any way by HIV/AIDS duc to the broader impact of this epidemic.

AIDS: the Acquired Immune Deficiency Syndrome, a cluster of medical conditions, often referred to as opportunistic infections and cancers and for which, to date, there is no cure.

Discrimination is used in this code in accordance with the definition given in the Discrimination (Employment and Occupation) Convention, 1958 (No. 111), to include HIV status. It also includes discrimination on the basis of a worker's perceived HIV status, including discrimination on the ground of sexual orientation.

Persons with disabilities is used in this code in accordance with the definition given in the Vocational Rehabilitation and Employment (Disabled Persons) Convention, 1983 (No. 159), namely individuals whose prospects of securing, retaining and advancing in suitable employment are substantially reduced as a result of a duly recognized physical or mental impairment.

Employer: a person or organization employing workers under a written or verbal contract of employment which establishes the rights and duties of both parties, in accordance with national law and practice. Governments, public authorities, private enterprises and individuals may be employers.

Occupational health services (OHS) is used in this code in accordance with the description given in the Occupational Health Services Convention, 1985 (No. 161), namely health services which have an essentially preventative function and which are responsible for advising the employer, as well as workers and their representatives, on the requirements for establishing and maintaining a safe and healthy working environment and work methods to facilitate optimal physical and mental health in relation to work. The OHS also provide advice on the adaptation of work to the capabilities of workers in the light of their physical and mental health.

Reasonable accommodation: any modification or adjustment to a job or to the workplace that is reasonably practicable and will enable a person living with HIV or AIDS to have access to or participate or advance in employment.

Screening: measures whether direct (HIV testing), indirect (assessment of risk-taking behaviour) or asking questions about tests already taken or about medication.

Sex and gender: there are both biological and social differences between men and women. The term "sex" refers to biologically determined differences, while the term "gender" refers to differences in social roles and relations between men and women. Gender roles are learned through socialization and vary widely within and between cultures. Gender roles are affected by age, class, race, ethnicity and religion, and by the geographical, economic and political environment.

STI: sexually transmitted infection, which includes, among others, syphilis, chancroid, chlamydia, gonorrhoea. It also includes conditions commonly known as sexually transmitted diseases (STDs).

Termination of employment has the meaning attributed in the Termination of Employment Convention, 1982 (No. 158), namely dismissal at the initiative of the employer.

Universal Precautions are a simple standard of infection control practice to be used to minimize the risk of blood-borne pathogens.

Workers in informal activities (also known as informal sector): this term is described in Appendix I.*

Workers' representatives, in accordance with the Workers' Representatives Convention, 1971 (No. 135), are persons recognized as such by national law or practice whether they are:

(a) trade union representatives, namely, representatives designated or elected by trade unions or by members of such unions; or

(b) elected representatives, namely, representatives who are freely elected by the workers of the undertaking in accordance with provisions of national laws or regulations or of collective agreements and whose functions do not include activities which are recognized as the exclusive prerogative of trade unions in the country concerned.

Vulnerability refers to socio-economic disempowerment and cultural context, work situations that make workers more susceptible to the risk of infection and situations which put children at greater risk of being involved in child labour.

4. KEY PRINCIPLES

4.1. *Recognition of HIV/AIDS as a workplace issue*

HIV/AIDS is a workplace issue, and should be treated like any other serious illness/condition in the workplace. This is necessary not only because it affects the workforce, but also because the workplace, being part of the local community, has a role to play in the wider struggle to limit the spread and effects of the epidemic.

* Not reproduced here.

4.2. *Non-discrimination*

In the spirit of decent work and respect for the human rights and dignity of persons infected or affected by HIV/AIDS, there should be no discrimination against workers on the basis of real or perceived HIV status. Discrimination and stigmatization of people living with HIV/AIDS inhibits efforts aimed at promoting HIV/AIDS prevention.

4.3. *Gender equality*

The gender dimensions of HIV/AIDS should be recognized. Women are more likely to become infected and are more often adversely affected by the HIV/AIDS epidemic than men due to biological, socio-cultural and economic reasons. The greater the gender discrimination in societies and the lower the position of women, the more negatively they are affected by HIV. Therefore, more equal gender relations and the empowerment of women are vital to successfully prevent the spread of HIV infection and enable women to cope with HIV/AIDS.

4.4. *Healthy work environment*

The work environment should be healthy and safe, so far as is practicable, for all concerned parties, in order to prevent transmission of HIV, in accordance with the provisions of the Occupational Safety and Health Convention, 1981 (No. 155).

A healthy work environment facilitates optimal physical and mental health in relation to work and adaptation of work to the capabilities of workers in light of their state of physical and mental health.

4.5. *Social dialogue*

The successful implementation of an HIV/AIDS policy and programme requires cooperation and trust between employers, workers and their representatives and government, where appropriate, with the active involvement of workers infected and affected by HIV/AIDS.

4.6. *Screening for purposes of exclusion from employment or work processes*

HIV/AIDS screening should not be required of job applicants or persons in employment.

4.7. *Confidentiality*

There is no justification for asking job applicants or workers to disclose HIV-related personal information. Nor should co-workers be obliged to reveal such personal information about fellow workers. Access to personal data relating to a worker's HIV status should be bound by the rules of confidentiality consistent with the ILO's code of practice on the protection of workers' personal data, 1997.

4.8. *Continuation of employment relationship*

HIV infection is not a cause for termination of employment. As with many other conditions, persons with HIV-related illnesses should be able to work for as long as medically fit in available, appropriate work.

4.9. *Prevention*

HIV infection is preventable. Prevention of all means of transmission can be achieved through a variety of strategies which are appropriately targeted to national conditions and which are culturally sensitive.

Prevention can be furthered through changes in behaviour, knowledge, treatment and the creation of a non-discriminatory environment.

The social partners are in a unique position to promote prevention efforts particularly in relation to changing attitudes and behaviours through the provision of information and education, and in addressing socio-economic factors.

4.10. *Care and support*

Solidarity, care and support should guide the response to HIV/AIDS in the world of work. All workers, including workers with HIV, are entitled to affordable health services. There should be no discrimination against them and their dependants in access to and receipt of benefits from statutory social security programmes and occupational schemes.

5. GENERAL RIGHTS AND RESPONSIBILITIES

5.1. *Governments and their competent authorities*

(a) *Coherence.* Governments should ensure coherence in national HIV/AIDS strategy and programmes, recognizing the importance of including the world of work in national plans, for example by ensuring that the composition of national AIDS councils includes representatives of employers, workers, people living with HIV/AIDS and of ministries responsible for labour and social matters.

(b) *Multi-sectoral participation.* The competent authorities should mobilize and support broad partnerships for protection and prevention, including public agencies, the private sector, workers' and employers' organizations, and all relevant stakeholders so that the greatest number of partners in the world of work are involved.

(c) *Coordination.* Governments should facilitate and coordinate all interventions at the national level that provide an enabling environment for world of work interventions and capitalize on the presence of the social partners and all relevant stakeholders. Coordination should build on measures and support services already in place.

(d) *Prevention and health promotion.* The competent authorities should instigate and work in partnership with other social partners to promote awareness and prevention programmes, particularly in the workplace.

(e) *Clinical guidelines.* In countries where employers assume a primary responsibility for providing direct health-care services to workers, governments should offer guidelines to assist employers in the care and clinical management of HIV/AIDS. These guidelines should take account of existing services.

(f) *Social protection.* Governments should ensure that benefits under national laws and regulations apply to workers with HIV/AIDS no less favourably than to workers with other serious illnesses. In designing and implementing social security programmes, governments should take into account the progressive and intermittent nature of the disease and tailor schemes accordingly, for example by making benefits available as and when needed and by the expeditious treatment of claims.

(g) *Research.* In order to achieve coherence with national AIDS plans, to mobilize the social partners, to evaluate the costs of the epidemic on workplaces, for the social security system and for the economy, and to facilitate planning to mitigate its socio-economic impact, the competent authorities should encourage, support, carry out and publish the findings of demographic projections, incidence and prevalence studies and case studies of best practice. Governments should endeavour to provide the institutional and regulatory framework to achieve this. The research should include gender-sensitive analyses that make use of research and data from employers and their organizations and workers' organizations. Data collection should, to the extent possible, be sector-specific and disaggregated by sex, race, sexual orientation, age, employment and occupational status and be done in a culturally sensitive manner. Where possible, permanent impact assessment mechanisms should exist.

(h) *Financial resourcing.* Governments, where possible, in consultation with the social partners and other stakeholders, should estimate the financial implications of HIV/AIDS and seek to mobilize funding locally and internationally for their national AIDS strategic plans including, where relevant, for their social security systems.

(i) *Legislation.* In order to eliminate workplace discrimination and ensure workplace prevention and social protection, governments, in consultation with the social partners and experts in the field of HIV/AIDS, should provide the relevant regulatory framework and, where necessary, revise labour laws and other legislation.

(j) *Conditionalities for government support.* When governments provide start-up funding and incentives for national and international enterprises, they should require recipients to adhere to national laws and encourage recipients to adhere to this code, and policies or codes that give effect to the provisions of this code.

(k) *Enforcement.* The competent authorities should supply technical information and advice to employers and workers concerning the most effective way of complying with legislation and regulations applicable to HIV/AIDS and the world of work. They should strengthen enforcement structures and procedures, such as factory/labour inspectorates and labour courts and tribunals.

(l) *Workers in informal activities (also known as informal sector).* Governments should extend and adapt their HIV/AIDS prevention programmes to such workers including income generation and social protection. Governments should also design and develop new approaches using local communities where appropriate.

(m) *Mitigation.* Governments should promote care and support through public health-care programmes, social security systems and/or other relevant government initiatives. Governments should also strive to ensure access to treatment and, where appropriate, to work in partnership with employers and workers' organizations.

(n) *Children and young persons.* In programmes to eliminate child labour, governments should ensure that attention is paid to the impact of the epidemic on children and young persons whose parent or parents are ill or have died as a result of HIV/AIDS.

(o) *Regional and international collaboration.* Governments should promote and support collaboration at regional and international levels, and through intergovernmental agencies and all relevant stakeholders, so as to focus international attention on HIV/AIDS and on the related needs of the world of work.

(p) *International assistance.* Governments should enlist international assistance where appropriate in support of national programmes. They should encourage initiatives aimed at supporting international campaigns to reduce the cost of, and improve access to, antiretroviral drugs.

(q) *Vulnerability.* Governments should take measures to identify groups of workers who are vulnerable to infection, and adopt strategies to overcome the factors that make these workers susceptible. Governments should also endeavour to ensure that appropriate prevention programmes are in place for these workers.

5.2. *Employers and their organizations*

(a) *Workplace policy.* Employers should consult with workers and their representatives to develop and implement an appropriate policy for their workplace, designed to prevent the spread of the infection and protect all workers from discrimination related to HIV/AIDS.

(b) *National, sectoral and workplace/enterprise agreements.* Employers should adhere to national law and practice in relation to negotiating terms and conditions of employment about HIV/AIDS issues with workers and their representatives, and endeavour to include provisions on HIV/AIDS protection and prevention in national, sectoral and workplace/enterprise agreements.

(c) *Education and training.* Employers and their organizations, in consultation with workers and their representatives, should initiate and support programmes at their workplaces to inform, educate and train workers about HIV/AIDS prevention, care and support and the enterprise's policy on HIV/AIDS, including measures to reduce discrimination against people infected or affected by HIV/AIDS and specific staff benefits and entitlements.

(d) *Economic impact.* Employers, workers and their organizations, should work together to develop appropriate strategies to assess and appropriately respond to the economic impact of HIV/AIDS on their particular workplace and sector.

(e) *Personnel policies.* Employers should not engage in nor permit any personnel policy or practice that discriminates against workers infected with or affected by HIV/AIDS. In particular, employers should:

- not require HIV/AIDS screening or testing unless otherwise specified in section 8 of this code;
- ensure that work is performed free of discrimination or stigmatization based on perceived or real HIV status;
- encourage persons with HIV and AIDS-related illnesses to work as long as medically fit for appropriate work; and
- provide that, where a worker with an AIDS-related condition is too ill to continue to work and where alternative working arrangements including extended sick leave have been exhausted, the employment relationship may cease in accordance with anti-discrimination and labour laws and respect for general procedures and full benefits.

(f) *Grievance and disciplinary procedures.* Employers should have procedures that can be used by workers and their representatives for work-related grievances. These procedures should specify under what circumstances disciplinary proceedings can be commenced against any employee who discriminates on the grounds of real or perceived HIV status or who violates the workplace policy on HIV/AIDS.

(g) *Confidentiality.* HIV/AIDS-related information of workers should be kept strictly confidential and kept only on medical files, whereby access to information complies with the Occupational Health Services Recommendation, 1985 (No. 171), and national laws and practices. Access to such information should be strictly limited to medical personnel and such information may only be disclosed if legally required or with the consent of the person concerned.

(h) *Risk reduction and management.* Employers should ensure a safe and healthy working environment, including the application of Universal Precautions and measures such as the provision and maintenance of protective equipment and first aid. To support behavioural change by individuals, employers should also make available, where appropriate, male and female condoms, counselling, care, support and referral services. Where size and cost considerations make this difficult, employers and/or their organizations should seek support from government and other relevant institutions.

(i) *Workplaces where workers come into regular contact with human blood and body fluids.* In such workplaces, employers need to take additional measures to ensure that all workers are trained in Universal Precautions, that they are knowledgeable about procedures to be followed in the event of an occupational incident and that Universal Precautions are always observed. Facilities should be provided for these measures.

(j) *Reasonable accommodation.* Employers, in consultation with the worker(s) and their representatives, should take measures to reasonably accommodate the worker(s) with AIDS-related illnesses. These could include rearrangement of working time, special equipment, opportunities for rest breaks, time off for medical appointments, flexible sick leave, part-time work and return-to-work arrangements.

(k) *Advocacy.* In the spirit of good corporate citizenship, employers and their organizations should, where appropriate, encourage fellow employers to contribute to the prevention and management of HIV/AIDS in the workplace, and encourage governments to take all necessary action to stop the spread of HIV/AIDS and mitigate its effects. Other partnerships can support this process such as joint business/trade union councils on HIV/AIDS.

(l) *Support for confidential voluntary HIV counselling and testing.* Employers, workers and their representatives should encourage support for, and access to, confidential voluntary counselling and testing that is provided by qualified health services.

(m) *Workers in informal activities (also known as informal sector).* Employers of workers in informal activities should investigate and, where appropriate, develop prevention and care programmes for these workers.

(n) *International partnerships.* Employers and their organizations should contribute, where appropriate, to international partnerships in the fight against HIV/AIDS.

5.3. *Workers and their organizations*

(a) *Workplace policy.* Workers and their representatives should consult with their employers on the implementation of an appropriate policy for their workplace, designed to prevent the spread of the infection and protect all workers from discrimination related to HIV/AIDS.

(b) *National, sectoral and workplace/enterprise agreements.* Workers and their organizations should adhere to national law and practice when negotiating terms and conditions of employment relating to HIV/AIDS issues, and endeavour to include provisions on HIV/AIDS protection and prevention in national, sectoral and workplace/enterprise agreements.

(c) *Information and education.* Workers and their organizations should use existing union structures and other structures and facilities to provide information on HIV/AIDS in the workplace, and develop educational materials and activities appropriate for workers and their families, including regularly updated information on workers' rights and benefits.

(d) *Economic impact.* Workers and their organizations should work together with employers to develop appropriate strategies to assess and appropriately respond to the economic impact of HIV/AIDS in their particular workplace and sector.

(e) *Advocacy.* Workers and their organizations should work with employers, their organizations and governments to raise awareness of HIV/AIDS prevention and management.

(f) *Personnel policies.* Workers and their representatives should support and encourage employers in creating and implementing personnel policy and practices that do not discriminate against workers with HIV/AIDS.

(g) *Monitoring of compliance.* Workers' representatives have the right to take up issues at their workplaces through grievance and disciplinary procedures and/or should report all discrimination on the basis of HIV/AIDS to the appropriate legal authorities.

(h) *Training.* Workers' organizations should develop and carry out training courses for their representatives on workplace issues raised by the epidemic, on appropriate responses, and on the general needs of people living with HIV/AIDS and their carers.

(i) *Risk reduction and management.* Workers and their organizations should advocate for, and cooperate with, employers to maintain a safe and healthy working environment, including the correct application and maintenance of protective equipment and first aid. Workers and their organizations should assess the vulnerability of the working environment and promote tailored programmes for workers as appropriate.

(j) *Confidentiality.* Workers have the right to access their own personal and medical files. Workers' organizations should not have access to personnel data relating to a worker's HIV status. In all cases, when carrying out trade union responsibilities and functions, the rules of confidentiality and the requirement for the concerned person's consent set out in the Occupational Health Services Recommendation, 1985 (No. 171), should apply.

(k) *Workers in informal activities (also known as informal sector).* Workers and their organizations should extend their activities to these workers in partnership with all other relevant stakeholders, where appropriate, and support new initiatives which help both prevent the spread of HIV/AIDS and mitigate its impact.

(l) *Vulnerability.* Workers and their organizations should ensure that factors that increase the risk of infection for certain groups of workers are addressed in consultation with employers.

(m) *Support for confidential voluntary HIV counselling and testing.* Workers and their organizations should work with employers to encourage and support access to confidential voluntary counselling and testing.

(n) *International partnerships.* Workers' organizations should build solidarity across national borders by using sectoral, regional and international groupings to highlight HIV/AIDS and the world of work, and to include it in workers' rights campaigns.

6. PREVENTION THROUGH INFORMATION AND EDUCATION

Workplace information and education programmes are essential to combat the spread of the epidemic and to foster greater tolerance for workers with HIV/AIDS. Effective education can contribute to the capacity of workers to protect themselves against HIV infection. It can significantly reduce HIV-related anxiety and stigmatization, minimize disruption in the workplace, and bring about attitudinal and behavioural change. Programmes should be developed through consultations between governments, employers and workers and their representatives to ensure support at the highest levels and the fullest participation of all concerned. Information and education should be provided in a variety of forms, not relying exclusively on the written word and including distance learning where necessary. Programmes should be targeted and tailored to the age, gender, sexual orientation, sectoral characteristics and behavioural risk factors of the workforce and its cultural context. They should be delivered by trusted and respected individuals. Peer education has been found to be particularly effective, as has the involvement of people living with HIV/AIDS in the design and implementation of programmes.

6.1. *Information and awareness-raising campaigns*

(a) Information programmes should, where possible, be linked to broader HIV/AIDS campaigns within the local community, sector, region or country. The programmes should be based on correct and up-to-date information about how HIV is and is not transmitted, dispel the myths surrounding HIV/AIDS, how HIV can be prevented, medical aspects of the disease, the impact of AIDS on individuals, and the possibilities for care, support and treatment.

(b) As far as is practicable, information programmes, courses and campaigns should be integrated into existing education and human resource policies and programmes as well as occupational safety and health and anti-discrimination strategies.

6.2. *Educational programmes*

(a) Educational strategies should be based on consultation between employers and workers, and their representatives and, where appropriate, government and other relevant stakeholders with expertise in HIV/AIDS education, counselling and care. The methods should be as interactive and participatory as possible.

(b) Consideration should be given to educational programmes taking place during paid working hours and developing educational materials to be used by workers outside workplaces. Where courses are offered, attendance should be considered as part of work obligations.

(c) Where practical and appropriate, programmes should:

- include activities to help individuals assess the risks that face them personally (both as individuals and as members of a group) and reduce these risks through decision-making, negotiation and communication skills, as well as educational, preventative and counselling programmes;
- give special emphasis to high-risk behaviour and other risk factors such as occupational mobility that expose certain groups of workers to increased risk of HIV infection;
- provide information about transmission of HIV through drug injection and information about how to reduce the risk of such transmission;
- enhance dialogue among governments and employers' and workers' organizations from neighbouring countries and at regional level;
- promote HIV/AIDS awareness in vocational training programmes carried out by governments and enterprises, in collaboration with workers' organizations;
- promote campaigns targeted at young workers and women;

- give special emphasis to the vulnerability of women to HIV and prevention strategies that can lessen this vulnerability (see section 6.3);
- emphasize that HIV cannot be contracted through casual contact, and that people who are HIV-positive do not need to be avoided or stigmatized, but rather should be supported and accommodated in the workplace;
- explain the debilitating effects of the virus and the need for all workers to be empathetic and non-discriminatory towards workers with HIV/AIDS;
- give workers the opportunity to express and discuss their reactions and emotions caused by HIV/AIDS;
- instruct workers (especially health-care workers) on the use of Universal Precautions and inform them of procedures to be followed in case of exposure;
- provide education about the prevention and management of STIs and tuberculosis, not only because of the associated risk of HIV infection but also because these conditions are treatable, thus improving the workers' general health and immunity;
- promote hygiene and proper nutrition;
- promote safer sex practices, including instructions on the use of male and female condoms;
- encourage peer education and informal education activities;
- be regularly monitored, evaluated, reviewed and revised where necessary.

6.3. *Gender-specific programmes*

(a) All programmes should be gender-sensitive, as well as sensitive to race and sexual orientation. This includes targeting both women and men explicitly, or addressing either women or men in separate programmes, in recognition of the different types and degrees of risk for men and women workers.

(b) Information for women needs to alert them to, and explain their higher risk of, infection, in particular the special vulnerability of young women.

(c) Education should help both women and men to understand and act upon the unequal power relations between them in employment and personal situations; harassment and violence should be addressed specifically.

(d) Programmes should help women to understand their rights, both within the workplace and outside it, and empower them to protect themselves.

(e) Education for men should include awareness-raising, risk assessment and strategies to promote men's responsibilities regarding HIV/AIDS prevention.

(f) Appropriately targeted prevention programmes should be developed for homosexually active men in consultation with these workers and their representatives.

6.4. *Linkage to health promotion programmes*

Educational programmes should be linked, where feasible, to health promotion programmes dealing with issues such as substance abuse, stress and reproductive health at the workplace. Existing work councils or health and safety committees provide an entry point to HIV/AIDS awareness campaigns and educational programmes. This linkage should highlight the increased risk of infection in the use of contaminated needles in intravenous drug-injection. It should also highlight that intoxication due to alcohol and drugs could lead to behaviour which increases the risk of HIV infection.

6.5. *Practical measures to support behavioural change*

(a) Workers should be provided with sensitive, accurate and up-to-date education about risk reduction strategies, and, where appropriate, male and female condoms should be made available.

(b) Early and effective STI and tuberculosis diagnosis, treatment and management, as well as a sterile needle and syringe-exchange programmes, should also be made available, where appropriate, or information provided on where they can be obtained.

(c) For women workers in financial need, education should include strategies to supplement low incomes, for example, by supplying information on income-generating activities, tax relief and wage support.

6.6. *Community outreach programmes*

Employers, workers and their representatives should encourage and promote information and education programmes on prevention and management of HIV/AIDS within the local community, especially in schools. Participation in outreach programmes should be encouraged in order to provide an opportunity for people to express their views and enhance the welfare of workers with HIV/AIDS by reducing their isolation and ostracism. Such programmes should be run in partnership with appropriate national or local bodies.

7. TRAINING

Training should be targeted at, and adapted to, the different groups being trained: managers, supervisors and personnel officers; workers and their representatives; trainers of trainers (both male and female); peer educators; occupational health and safety officers; and factory/labour inspectors. Innovative approaches should be sought to defray costs. For example, enterprises can seek external support from national AIDS programmes or other relevant stakeholders by borrowing instructors or having their own trained. Training materials can vary enormously, according to available resources. They can be adapted to local customs and to the different circumstances of women and men. Trainers should also be trained to deal with prejudices against minorities, especially in relation to ethnic origin or sexual orientation. They should draw on case studies and available good practice materials. The best trainers are often staff themselves and peer education is therefore recommended at all levels. It should become part of a workplace's annual training plan, which should be developed in consultation with workers' representatives.

7.1. *Training for managers, supervisors and personnel officers*

In addition to participating in information and education programmes that are directed at all workers, supervisory and managerial personnel should receive training to:

- enable them to explain and respond to questions about the workplace's HIV/AIDS policy;
- be well informed about HIV/AIDS so as to help other workers overcome misconceptions about the spread of HIV/AIDS at the workplace;
- explain reasonable accommodation options to workers with HIV/AIDS so as to enable them to continue to work as long as possible;
- identify and manage workplace behaviour, conduct or practices which discriminate against or alienate workers with HIV/AIDS;
- enable them to advise about the health services and social benefits which are available.

7.2. *Training for peer educators*

Peer educators should receive specialized training so as to:

- be sufficiently knowledgeable about the content and methods of HIV/AIDS prevention so that they can deliver, in whole or in part, the information and education programme to the workforce;
- be sensitive to race, sexual orientation, gender and culture in developing and delivering their training;
- link into and draw from other existing workplace policies, such as those on sexual harassment or for persons with disabilities in the workplace;
- enable their co-workers to identify factors in their lives that lead to increased risk of infection;
- be able to counsel workers living with HIV/AIDS about coping with their condition and its implications.

7.3. *Training for workers' representatives*

Workers' representatives should, during paid working hours, receive training so as to:

- enable them to explain and respond to questions about the workplace HIV/AIDS policy;
- enable them to train other workers in trainer education programmes;

- identify individual workplace behaviour, conduct or practices which discriminate or alienate workers with HIV/AIDS, in order to effectively combat such conduct;
- help and represent workers with AIDS-related illnesses to access reasonable accommodation when so requested;
- be able to counsel workers to identify and reduce risk factors in their personal lives;
- be well instructed about HIV/AIDS in order to inform workers about the spread of HIV/AIDS;
- ensure that any information that they acquire about workers with HIV/AIDS in the course of performing their representative functions is kept confidential.

7.4. *Training for health and safety officers*

In addition to becoming familiar with the information and education programmes that are directed at all workers, health and safety officers should receive specialized training in order to:

- be sufficiently knowledgeable about the content and methods of HIV/AIDS prevention so that they can deliver information and education programmes to workers;
- be able to assess the working environment and identify working methods or conditions which could be changed or improved in order to lessen the vulnerability of workers with HIV/AIDS;
- verify whether the employer provides and maintains a healthy and safe working environment and processes for the workers, including safe first-aid procedures;
- ensure that HIV/AIDS-related information, if any, is maintained under conditions of strict confidentiality as with other medical data pertinent to workers and disclosed only in accordance with the ILO's code of practice on the protection of workers' personal data;
- be able to counsel workers to identify and reduce risk factors in their personal lives;
- be able to refer workers to in-house medical services or those outside the workplace which can effectively respond to their needs.

7.5. *Training for factory/labour inspectors*

The competent authority should ensure that factory and labour inspectors have sufficient means at their disposal to fulfil their supervisory, enforcement and advisory functions, in particular regarding HIV/AIDS prevention in enterprises. To achieve this, they should receive specialized training on HIV/AIDS prevention and protection strategies at the workplace. This training should include:

- information on relevant international labour standards, especially the Discrimination (Employment and Occupation) Convention, 1958 (No. 111), and national laws and regulations;
- how to provide awareness about HIV/AIDS to workers and management;
- how to incorporate HIV/AIDS topics into their regular occupational safety and health briefings and workplace training;
- how to assist workers to access available benefits (such as how to complete benefit forms) and to exercise other legal rights;
- how to identify violations, or the lack of implementation of, workers' rights in respect of HIV status;
- skills to collect and analyse data relating to HIV/AIDS in workplaces when this is for epidemiological or social impact studies and in conformity with this code.

7.6. *Training for workers who come into contact with human blood and other body fluids*

All workers should receive training about infection control procedures in the context of workplace accidents and first aid. The programmes should provide training:

- in the provision of first aid;
- about Universal Precautions to reduce the risk of exposure to human blood and other body fluids;
- in the use of protective equipment;
- in the correct procedures to be followed in the event of exposure to human blood or body fluids;
- rights to compensation in the event of an occupational incident, and emphasize that the taking of precautions is not necessarily related to the perceived or actual HIV status of individuals.

8. TESTING

Testing for HIV should not be carried out at the workplace except as specified in this code. It is unnecessary and imperils the human rights and dignity of workers: test results may be revealed and misused, and the informed consent of workers may not always be fully free or based on an appreciation of all the facts and implications of testing. Even outside the workplace, confidential testing for HIV should be the consequence of voluntary informed consent and performed by suitably qualified personnel only, in conditions of the strictest confidentiality.

8.1. *Prohibition in recruitment and employment*

HIV testing should not be required at the time of recruitment or as a condition of continued employment. Any routine medical testing, such as testing for fitness carried out prior to the commencement of employment or on a regular basis for workers, should not include mandatory HIV testing.

8.2. *Prohibition for insurance purposes*

(a) HIV testing should not be required as a condition of eligibility for national social security schemes, general insurance policies, occupational schemes and health insurance.

(b) Insurance companies should not require HIV testing before agreeing to provide coverage for a given workplace. They may base their cost and revenue estimates and their actuarial calculations on available epidemiological data for the general population.

(c) Employers should not facilitate any testing for insurance purposes and all information that they already have should remain confidential.

8.3. *Epidemiological surveillance*

Anonymous, unlinked surveillance or epidemiological HIV testing in the workplace may occur provided it is undertaken in accordance with the ethical principles of scientific research, professional ethics and the protection of individual rights and confidentiality. Where such research is done, workers and employers should be consulted and informed that it is occurring. The information obtained may not be used to discriminate against individuals or groups of persons. Testing will not be considered anonymous if there is a reasonable possibility that a person's HIV status can be deduced from the results.

8.4. *Voluntary testing*

There may be situations where workers wish at their own initiative to be tested including as part of voluntary testing programmes. Voluntary testing should normally be carried out by the community health services and not at the workplace. Where adequate medical services exist, voluntary testing may be undertaken at the request and with the written informed consent of a worker, with advice from the workers' representative if so requested. It should be performed by suitably qualified personnel with adherence to strict confidentiality and disclosure requirements. Gender-sensitive pre- and post-test counselling, which facilitates an understanding of the nature and purpose of the HIV tests, the advantages and disadvantages of the tests and the effect of the result upon the worker, should form an essential part of any testing procedure.

8.5. *Tests and treatment after occupational exposure*

(a) Where there is a risk of exposure to human blood, body fluids or tissues, the workplace should have procedures in place to manage the risk of such exposure and occupational incidents.

(b) Following risk of exposure to potentially infected material (human blood, body fluids, tissue) at the workplace, the worker should be immediately counselled to cope with the incident, about the medical consequences, the desirability of testing for HIV and the availability of post-exposure prophylaxis, and referred to appropriate medical facilities. Following the conclusion of a risk assessment, further guidance as to the worker's legal rights, including eligibility and required procedures for workers' compensation, should be given.

9. CARE AND SUPPORT

Solidarity, care and support are critical elements that should guide a workplace in responding to HIV/AIDS. Mechanisms should be created to encourage openness, acceptance and support for those workers who disclose their HIV status, and ensure that they are not discriminated against nor stigmatized. To mitigate the impact of the HIV/AIDS epidemic in the workplace, workplaces should endeavour to provide counselling and other forms of social support to workers infected and affected by HIV/AIDS. Where health-care services exist at the workplace, appropriate treatment should be provided. Where these services are not possible, workers should be informed about the location of available outside services. Linkages such as this have the advantage of reaching beyond the workers to cover their families, in particular their children. Partnership between governments, employers, workers and their organizations and other relevant stakeholders also ensures effective delivery of services and saves costs.

9.1. *Parity with other serious illnesses*

(a) HIV infection and clinical AIDS should be managed in the workplace no less favourably than any other serious illness or condition.

(b) Workers with HIV/AIDS should be treated no less favourably than workers with other serious illnesses in terms of benefits, workers' compensation and reasonable accommodation.

(c) As long as workers are medically fit for appropriate employment, they should enjoy normal job security and opportunities for transfer and advancement.

9.2. *Counselling*

(a) Employers should encourage workers with HIV/AIDS to use expertise and assistance outside the enterprise for counselling or, where available, its own occupational safety and health unit or other workplace programme, if specialized and confidential counselling is offered.

(b) To give effect to this, employers should consider the following actions:

- identify professionals, self-help groups and services within the local community or region which specialize in HIV/AIDS-related counselling and the treatment of HIV/AIDS;
- identify community-based organizations, both of a medical and non-medical character, that may be useful to workers with HIV/AIDS;
- suggest that the worker contact his or her doctor or qualified health-care providers for initial assessment and treatment if not already being treated, or help the worker locate a qualified health-care provider if he or she does not have one.

(c) Employers should provide workers with HIV/AIDS with reasonable time off for counselling and treatment in conformity with minimum national requirements.

(d) Counselling support should be made accessible at no cost to the workers and adapted to the different needs and circumstances of women and men. It may be appropriate to liaise with government, workers and their organizations and other relevant stakeholders in establishing and providing such support.

(e) Workers' representatives should, if requested, assist a worker with HIV/AIDS to obtain professional counselling.

(f) Counselling services should inform all workers of their rights and benefits in relation to statutory social security programmes and occupational schemes and any life-skills programmes which may help workers cope with HIV/AIDS.

(g) In the event of occupational exposure to HIV, employers should provide workers with reasonable paid time off for counselling purposes.

9.3. *Occupational and other health services*

(a) Some employers may be in a position to assist their workers with access to antiretroviral drugs. Where health services exist at the workplace these should offer, in cooperation with government and all other stakeholders, the broadest range of health services possible to prevent and manage HIV/AIDS and assist workers living with HIV/AIDS.

(b) These services could include the provision of antiretroviral drugs, treatment for the relief of HIV-related symptoms, nutritional counselling and supplements, stress reduction and treatment for the more common opportunistic infections including STIs and tuberculosis.

9.4. *Linkages with self-help and community-based groups*

Where appropriate, employers, workers' organizations and occupational health personnel should facilitate the establishment of self-help groups within the enterprise or the referral of workers affected by HIV/AIDS to self-help groups and support organizations in the local community.

9.5. *Benefits*

(a) Governments, in consultation with the social partners, should ensure that benefits under national laws and regulations apply to workers with HIV/AIDS no less favourably than to workers with other serious illnesses. They should also explore the sustainability of new benefits specifically addressing the progressive and intermittent nature of HIV/AIDS.

(b) Employers and employers' and workers' organizations should pursue with governments the adaptation of existing benefit mechanisms to the needs of workers with HIV/AIDS, including wage subsidy schemes.

9.6. *Social security coverage*

(a) Governments, employers and workers' organizations should take all steps necessary to ensure that workers with HIV/AIDS and their families are not excluded from the full protection and benefits of social security programmes and occupational schemes. This should also apply to workers and their families from occupational and social groups perceived to be at risk of HIV/AIDS.

(b) These programmes and schemes should provide similar benefits for workers with HIV/AIDS as those for workers with other serious illnesses.

9.7. *Privacy and confidentiality*

(a) Governments, private insurance companies and employers should ensure that information relating to counselling, care, treatment and receipt of benefits is kept confidential, as with medical data pertinent to workers, and accessed only in accordance with the Occupational Health Services Recommendation, 1985 (No. 171).

(b) Third parties, such as trustees and administrators of social security programmes and occupational schemes, should keep all HIV/AIDS-related information confidential, as with medical data pertinent to workers, in accordance with the ILO's code of practice on the protection of workers' personal data.

9.8. *Employee and family assistance programmes*

(a) In the light of the nature of the epidemic, employee assistance programmes may need to be established or extended appropriately to include a range of services for workers as members of families, and to support their family members. This should be done in consultation with workers and their representatives, and can be done in collaboration with government and other relevant stakeholders in accordance with resources and needs.

(b) Such programmes should recognize that women normally undertake the major part of caring for those with AIDS-related illnesses. They should also recognize the particular needs of pregnant women. They should respond to the needs of children who have lost one or both parents to AIDS, and who may then drop out of school, be forced to work, and become increasingly vulnerable to sexual exploitation. The programmes may be in-house, or enterprises could support such programmes collectively or contract out for such services from an independent enterprise.

(c) The family assistance programme may include:

- compassionate leave;
- invitations to participate in information and education programmes;
- referrals to support groups, including self-help groups;
- assistance to families of workers to obtain alternative employment for the worker or family members provided that the work does not interfere with schooling;
- specific measures, such as support for formal education, vocational training and apprenticeships, to meet the needs of children and young persons who have lost one or both parents to AIDS;
- coordination with all relevant stakeholders and community-based organizations including the schools attended by the workers' children;
- direct or indirect financial assistance;
- managing financial issues relating to sickness and the needs of dependants;
- legal information, advice and assistance;
- assistance in relation to understanding the legal processes of illness and death such as managing financial issues relating to sickness, preparation of wills and succession plans;
- helping families to deal with social security programmes and occupational schemes;
- provision of advanced payments due to the worker;
- directing families to the relevant legal and health authorities or providing a list of recommended authorities.

Part V
From environment to sustainability

Companies are in the midst of a transition from environmental management to the broader concept of sustainability. Part V traces this journey by introducing the key tools in each area.

It is useful to begin by distinguishing the two concepts:

- Environmental management focuses on how an organisation addresses its physical surroundings at the local and global level. For example, environmental management addresses issues of energy consumption, biodiversity, recycling, packaging and so on.
- Sustainability is a much broader concept, encompassing the environmental issues covered by environmental management but also addressing social and economic issues. Sustainable development was described in the Brundtland Report as 'development that meets the needs of the present without compromising the ability of future generations to meet their needs' (WCED 1987). Although this provides a useful starting point for discussion, and is often quoted in company environmental reports, it raises as many questions as it answers. According to Professor Thomas Gladwin of New York University (1997), sustainability transcends this definition to include 'equity, justice, alleviation of poverty and redistribution of opportunity' (quoted in Elkington 1997: 6).

Although there are more than 100 definitions of sustainability, none would be complete without a discussion of the triple bottom line:

> Sustainable development involves the simultaneous pursuit of economic prosperity, environmental quality and social equity. Companies aiming for sustainability need to perform not against a single financial bottom line but against the triple bottom line (Elkington 1997: 397).

For many companies, the triple bottom line remains a 'Holy Grail'—a remote and distant theory. The tools in this part of the book will assist companies in defining their own triple bottom line. However, just as the companies of the future must be integrationist, readers will also need to integrate this part with Part X, on implementation.

The environment–sustainability continuum

A full description of each of the key environmental and sustainability standards would require an entire volume. Among the key principles and guidelines available (and the chapters in which they are discussed in this book) are:

- Environment
  - Rio Declaration on Environment and Development (Chapter 13)
  - Responsible Care® (Chapter 23, Section 23.6.2 and page 424)
  - Coalition for Environmentally Responsible Economies (Ceres; Chapter 14)
  - Business Charter for Sustainable Development (reproduced at the end of this section, page 246)
  - ISO 14001 (Chapter 29)
  - Eco-Management and Audit Scheme (EMAS) of the European Union (reproduced at the end of this section, page 251)
- Sustainability
  - The Natural Step (Chapter 15)
  - Global Reporting Initiative (Chapter 28)
  - The Bellagio Principles[2]

2 www.iisd.org/measure/principles/progress/bellagio.asp

References

Elkington, J. (1997) *Cannibals with Forks: The Triple Bottom Line of 21st Century Business* (Oxford, UK: Capstone Publishing).

Gladwin, T. (1997) 'Sustainable Development: Is It Industry's Business?', *Business and the Environment*, February 1997.

WCED (World Commission on Environment and Development) (1987) *Our Common Future* (Brundtland Report; Oxford, UK: Oxford University Press).

The Business Charter for Sustainable Development

Principles for Environmental Management*

Foreword

There is widespread recognition today that environmental protection must be among the highest priorities of every business.

In its milestone 1987 report, "Our Common Future," the World Commission on Environment and Development (Brundtland Commission) emphasised the importance of environmental protection to the pursuit of sustainable development.

To help business around the world improve its environmental performance, the International Chamber of Commerce created this Business Charter for Sustainable Development. It comprises sixteen Principles for environmental management which, for business, is a vitally important aspect of sustainable development.

This Charter assists enterprises in fulfilling their commitment to environmental stewardship in a comprehensive fashion, in line with national and international guidelines and standards for environmental management. It was formally launched in April 1991 at the Second World Industry Conference on Environmental Management in Rotterdam, and continues to be widely applied and recognised around the world.

Introduction

Sustainable development involves meeting the needs of the present without compromising the ability of future generations to meet their own needs. Economic growth provides the conditions in which protection of the environment can best be achieved, and environmental protection, in balance with other human goals, is necessary to achieve growth that is sustainable.

In turn, versatile, dynamic, responsive and profitable businesses are required as the driving force for sustainable economic development and for providing the managerial,

* Reprinted with permission by ICC.

technical and financial resources to contribute to the resolution of environmental challenges. Market economies, characterised by entrepreneurial initiatives, are essential to achieve this.

Business thus shares the view that there should be a common goal, not a conflict, between economic development and environmental protection, both now and for future generations.

Making market forces work in this way to protect and improve the quality of the environment—with the help of standards such as ISO 14000, and judicious use of economic instruments in a harmonious regulatory framework—is an on-going challenge that the world faces in entering the 21st century.

This challenge was recognised by the nations of the world at the 1992 United Nations Conference on Environment and Development, which called on the co-operation of business in tackling it. To this end, business leaders have launched initiatives in their individual enterprises as well as through sectoral and cross-sectoral associations.

In order that more businesses join this effort and that their environmental performance continues to improve, the International Chamber of Commerce continues to call upon enterprises and their associations to use the following Principles as a basis for pursuing such improvement and to express publicly their support for them.

Individual programmes to implement these Principles will reflect the wide diversity among enterprises in size and function.

The objective remains that the widest range of enterprises commit themselves to improving their environmental performance in accordance with these Principles, to having in place management practices to effect such improvement, to measuring their progress, and to reporting this progress as appropriate internally and externally.

Note: The term environment as used in this document also refers to environmentally related aspects of health, safety and product stewardship.

Principles

1. Corporate priority

To recognise environmental management as among the highest corporate priorities and as a key determinant to sustainable development; to establish policies, programmes and practices for conducting operations in an environmentally sound manner.

2. Integrated management

To integrate these policies, programmes and practices fully into each business as an essential element of management in all its functions.

3. Process of improvement

To continue to improve corporate policies, programmes and environmental performance, taking into account technical developments, scientific understanding, consumer needs and community expectations, with legal regulations as a starting point; and to apply the same environmental criteria internationally.

4. Employee education

To educate, train and motivate employees to conduct their activities in an environmentally responsible manner.

5. Prior assessment

To assess environmental impacts before starting a new activity or project and before decommissioning a facility or leaving a site.

6. Products and services

To develop and provide products or services that have no undue environmental impact and are safe in their intended use, that are efficient in their consumption of energy and natural resources, and that can be recycled, reused, or disposed of safely.

7. Customer advice

To advise, and where relevant educate, customers, distributors and the public in the safe use, transportation, storage and disposal of products provided; and to apply similar considerations to the provision of services.

8. Facilities and operations

To develop, design and operate facilities and conduct activities taking into consideration the efficient use of energy and materials, the sustainable use of renewable resources, the minimisation of adverse environmental impact and waste generation, and the safe and responsible disposal of residual wastes.

9. Research

To conduct or support research on the environmental impacts of raw materials, products, processes, emissions and wastes associated with the enterprise and on the means of minimizing such adverse impacts.

10. Precautionary approach

To modify the manufacture, marketing or use of products or services or the conduct of activities, consistent with scientific and technical understanding, to prevent serious or irreversible environmental degradation.

11. Contractors and suppliers

To promote the adoption of these principles by contractors acting on behalf of the enterprise, encouraging and, where appropriate, requiring improvements in their practices to make them consistent with those of the enterprise; and to encourage the wider adoption of these principles by suppliers.

12. Emergency preparedness

To develop and maintain, where significant hazards exist, emergency preparedness plans in conjunction with the emergency services, relevant authorities and the local community, recognizing potential transboundary impacts.

13. Transfer of technology

To contribute to the transfer of environmentally sound technology and management methods throughout the industrial and public sectors.

14. Contributing to the common effort

To contribute to the development of public policy and to business, governmental and intergovernmental programmes and educational initiatives that will enhance environmental awareness and protection.

15. Openness to concerns

To foster openness and dialogue with employees and the public, anticipating and responding to their concerns about the potential hazards and impacts of operations, products, wastes or services, including those of transboundary or global significance.

16. Compliance and reporting

To measure environmental performance; to conduct regular environmental audits and assessments of compliance with company requirements, legal requirements and these principles; and periodically to provide appropriate information to the Board of Directors, shareholders, employees, the authorities and the public.

Support for the Charter

The ICC undertakes to encourage member companies and others to express their support and implement the Charter and its Principles.

A list of these companies can be obtained from ICC Headquarters. The ICC also publishes regularly a Charter bulletin which provides more specific information on the Charter's Principles and different interpretations possible—an attribute of the Charter that has been widely commended.

The first edition of Business Charter for Sustainable Development was adopted by the ICC Executive Board on 27 November 1990, and first published in April 1991.

It was prepared and revised by the ICC Working Party for Sustainable Development.

Chair Peter Scupholme (British Petroleum) **Vice-Chair** W. Ross Stevens III (Du Pont)

The ICC is indebted to numerous companies and business organisations for their input in preparing and revising the Charter.

The Business Charter for Sustainable Development provides a basic framework of reference for action by individual corporations and business organisations throughout the world. It has been recognised as a complement to environmental management systems. To this end, the ICC, the United Nations Environment Programme (UNEP) and the International Federation of Consulting Engineers (FIDIC) have developed a kit to help enterprises integrate environmental management systems in the daily management practices, a step consistent with the objectives set out in this Charter.

The Business Charter has been published in over 20 languages, including all the official languages of the United Nations.

Regulation (EC) No 761/2001 of the European Parliament and of the Council of 19 March 2001 allowing voluntary participation by organisations in a Community eco-management and audit scheme (EMAS)

THE EUROPEAN PARLIAMENT AND THE COUNCIL OF THE EUROPEAN UNION,

Having regard to the Treaty establishing the European Community, and in particular Article 175(1) thereof,

Having regard to the proposal from the Commission[1],

Having regard to the Opinion of the Economic and Social Committee[2],

After consulting the Committee of the Regions,

Acting in accordance with the procedure laid down in Article 251 of the Treaty[3], in the light of the joint text approved by the Conciliation Committee on 20 December 2000,

Whereas:

(1) Article 2 of the Treaty stipulates that the Community shall have among its tasks to promote throughout the Community sustainable growth and the Resolution of 1 February 1993[4] stresses the importance of such sustainable growth.

(2) The programme 'Towards Sustainability', presented by the Commission and approved as to its general approach by the Resolution of 1 February 1993, underlines the role and responsibilities of organisations, both to reinforce the economy and to protect the environment throughout the Community.

[1] OJ C 400, 22.12.1998, p. 7 and OJ C 212 E, 25.7.2000, p. 1.

[2] OJ C 209, 22.7.1999, p. 43.

[3] Opinion of the European Parliament of 15 April 1999 (OJ C 219, 30.7.1999, p. 385), confirmed on 6 May 1999 (OJ C 279, 1.10.1999, p. 253), Council Common Position of 28 February 2000 (OJ C 128, 8.5.2000, p. 1) and Decision of the European Parliament of 6 July 2000 (not yet published in the Official Journal). Decision of the European Parliament of 14 February 2001 and Decision of the Council of 12 February 2001.

[4] Resolution of the Council and the Representatives of the Governments of the Member States, meeting within the Council of 1 February 1993 on a Community programme of policy and action in relation to the environment and sustainable development (OJ C 138, 17.5.1993, p. 1).

(3) The programme 'Towards Sustainability' calls for broadening the range of instruments in the field of environmental protection and for using market-mechanisms to commit organisations to adopt a pro-active approach in this field beyond compliance with all relevant regulatory requirements regarding the environment.

(4) The Commission should promote a coherent approach between the legislative instruments developed at Community level in the field of environmental protection.

(5) Council Regulation (EEC) No 1836/93 of 29 June 1993 allowing voluntary participation by companies in the industrial sector in a Community eco-management and audit scheme[5] demonstrated its effectiveness in promoting improvements of the environmental performance of industry.

(6) The experience gathered from the implementation of Regulation (EEC) No 1836/93 should be used to enhance the ability of the Community eco-management and audit scheme (EMAS) to bring about an improvement in the overall environmental performance of organisations.

(7) EMAS should be made available to all organisations having environmental impacts, providing a means for them to manage these impacts and to improve their overall environmental performance.

(8) In accordance with the principles of subsidiarity and proportionality referred to in Article 5 of the Treaty, the effectiveness of EMAS in contributing to improved environmental performance of European organisations can be better achieved at Community level. This Regulation limits itself to ensuring an equal implementation of EMAS throughout the Community by providing for common rules, procedures and essential requirements regarding EMAS whilst the measures that can be adequately performed at national level are left to the Member States.

(9) Organisations should be encouraged to participate in EMAS on a voluntary basis and may gain added value in terms of regulatory control, cost savings and public image.

(10) It is important that small and medium-sized enterprises participate in EMAS and that their participation should be promoted by facilitating access to information, to existing support funds and to public institutions and by establishing or promoting technical assistance measures.

(11) The information provided by Member States should be used by the Commission to assess the need for developing specific measures aimed at greater participation in EMAS by organisations, in particular small and medium-sized enterprises.

(12) The transparency and credibility of organisations implementing environmental management systems are enhanced when their management system, audit programme and environmental statement are examined to verify that they meet

[5] OJ L 168, 10.7.1993, p. 1.

the relevant requirements of this Regulation and when the environmental statement and its subsequent updates are validated by accredited environmental verifiers.

(13) It is therefore necessary to ensure and steadily improve the competence of the environmental verifiers by providing for an independent and neutral accreditation system, retraining and an appropriate supervision of their activities in order to ensure the overall credibility of EMAS. Close cooperation between the national accreditation bodies should accordingly be set up.

(14) Organisations should be encouraged to produce and make publicly available periodic environmental statements providing the public and other interested parties with information on their environmental performance.

(15) The Member States could create incentives to encourage organisations to participate in EMAS.

(16) The Commission should provide technical support to accession candidate countries in the setting up of the necessary structures for the application of EMAS.

(17) In addition to the general requirements of the environmental management system EMAS places special significance on the following elements: legal compliance, improvement of environmental performance and also external communication and employee involvement.

(18) The Commission should adapt the Annexes to this Regulation, with the exception of Annex V, recognise European and international standards for environmental issues of relevance to EMAS and establish guidelines in partnership with EMAS interested parties for the purpose of ensuring consistent implementation of the EMAS requirements across Member States. In drafting such guidelines, the Commission should take account of Community policy on the environment and in particular Community legislation as well as international commitments where relevant.

(19) The measures necessary for the implementation of this Regulation should be adopted in accordance with Council Decision 1999/468/EC of 28 June 1999 laying down the procedures for the exercise of implementing powers conferred on the Commission[1].

(20) This Regulation should be revised, if appropriate, in the light of experience gained after a certain period of operation.

(21) The European institutions should endeavour to adopt the principles laid down in this Regulation.

(22) This Regulation takes over and replaces Regulation (EEC) 1836/93 which should therefore be repealed,

[1] OJ L 184, 17.7.1999, p. 23.

HAVE ADOPTED THIS REGULATION:

Article 1

The eco-management and audit scheme and its objectives

1. A Community eco-management and audit scheme allowing voluntary participation by organisations, hereafter referred to as 'EMAS', is hereby established for the evaluation and improvement of the environmental performance of organisations and the provision of relevant information to the public and other interested parties.

2. The objective of EMAS shall be to promote continual improvements in the environmental performance of organisations by:

(a) the establishment and implementation of environmental management systems by organisations as described in Annex I;

(b) the systematic, objective and periodic evaluation of the performance of such systems as described in Annex I;

(c) the provision of information on environmental performance and an open dialogue with the public and other interested parties;

(d) the active involvement of employees in the organisation and appropriate initial and advanced training that makes active participation in the tasks referred to under (a) possible. Where they so request, any employee representatives shall also be involved.

Article 2

Definitions

For the purposes of this Regulation:

(a) 'environmental policy' shall mean an organisation's overall aims and principles of action with respect to the environment including compliance with all relevant regulatory requirements regarding the environment and also a commitment to continual improvement of environmental performance; the environmental policy provides the framework for setting and reviewing environmental objectives and targets;

(b) 'continual improvement of environmental performance' shall mean the process of enhancing, year by year, the measurable results of the environmental management system related to an organisation's management of its significant environmental aspects, based on its environmental policy, objectives and targets; the enhancing of the results need not take place in all spheres of activity simultaneously;

(c) 'environmental performance' shall mean the results of an organisation's management of its environmental aspects;

(d) 'prevention of pollution' shall mean use of processes, practices, materials or products that avoid, reduce or control pollution, which may include recycling, treatment, process changes, control mechanisms, efficient use of resources and material substitution;

(e) 'environmental review' shall mean an initial comprehensive analysis of the environmental issues, impact and performance related to activities of an organisation, (Annex VII);

(f) 'environmental aspect' shall mean an element of an organisation's activities, products or services that can interact with the environment, (Annex VI); a significant environmental aspect is an environmental aspect that has or can have a significant environmental impact;

(g) 'environmental impact' shall mean any change to the environment, whether adverse or beneficial, wholly or partially resulting from an organisation's activities, products or services;

(h) 'environmental programme' shall mean a description of the measures (responsibilities and means) taken or envisaged to achieve environmental objectives and targets and the deadlines for achieving the environmental objectives and targets;

(i) 'environmental objective' shall mean an overall environ mental goal, arising from the environmental policy, that an organisation sets itself to achieve, and which is quantified where practicable;

(j) 'environmental target' shall mean a detailed performance requirement, quantified where practicable, applicable to the organisation or parts thereof, that arises from the environmental objectives and that needs to be set and met in order to achieve those objectives;

(k) 'environmental management system' shall mean the part of the overall management system that includes the organisational structure, planning activities, responsibilities, practices, procedures, processes and resources for developing, implementing, achieving, reviewing and maintaining the environmental policy;

(l) 'environmental audit' shall mean a management tool comprising a systematic, documented, periodic and objective evaluation of the performance of the organisation, management system and processes designed to protect the environment with the aim of:

(i) facilitating management control of practices which may have an impact on the environment;

(ii) assessing compliance with the environmental policy, including environmental objectives and targets of the organisation (Annex II);

(m) 'audit cycle' shall mean the period of time in which all the activities in an organisation are audited, (Annex II);

(n) 'auditor' shall mean an individual or a team, belonging to the organisation personnel or external to the organisation, acting on behalf of the organisation's top management, possessing, individually or collectively, the competences referred to in Annex II, point 2.4 and being sufficiently independent of the activities they audit to make an objective judgment;

(o) 'environmental statement' shall mean the information detailed in Annex III point 3.2 ((a) to (g));

(p) 'interested party' shall mean an individual or group, including authorities, concerned with or affected by the environmental performance of an organisation;

(q) 'environmental verifier' shall mean any person or organisation independent of the organisation being verified, who has obtained accreditation, in accordance with the conditions and procedures referred to in Article 4;

(r) 'accreditation system' shall mean a system for the accreditation and supervision of environmental verifiers operated by an impartial institution or organisation designated or created by the Member State (accreditation body), with sufficient resources and competency and having appropriate procedures for performing the functions defined by this Regulation for such a system;

(s) 'organisation' shall mean a company, corporation, firm, enterprise, authority or institution, or part or combination thereof, whether incorporated or not, public or private, that has its own functions and administrations. The entity to be registered as an organisation under EMAS shall be agreed with the environmental verifier and, where appropriate, the competent bodies, taking account of Commission guidance, established in accordance with the procedure laid down in Article 14(2), but shall not exceed the boundaries of one Member State. The smallest entity to be considered shall be a site. Under exceptional circumstances identified by the Commission in accordance with the procedure laid down in Article 14(2), the entity to be considered for registration under EMAS may be smaller than a site, such as a sub-division with its own functions.

(t) 'site' shall mean all land at a distinct geographic location under the management control of an organisation covering activities, products and services. This includes all infrastructure, equipment and materials;

(u) 'competent bodies' shall mean the bodies designated by Member States, whether national, regional or local, in accordance with Article 5, to perform the tasks specified in this Regulation.

Article 3

Participation in EMAS

1. EMAS shall be open to the participation of any organisation dedicated to improving its overall environmental performance.

2. In order for an organisation to be registered under EMAS it shall:

(a) Conduct an environmental review of its activities, products and services in accordance with Annex VII addressing the issues contained in Annex VI and, in the light of the results of that review, implement an environmental management system covering all the requirements referred to in Annex I, in particular the compliance with the relevant environmental legislation.

However, organisations which have a certified environmental management system, recognised according to the requirements of Article 9, do not need to conduct a formal environmental review when moving on to EMAS implementation, if the necessary information for the identification and evaluation of the environmental aspects set out in Annex VI is provided by the certified environ mental management system.

(b) carry out, or cause to be carried out, environmental auditing in accordance with the requirements set out in Annex II. The audits shall be designed to assess the environmental performance of the organisation;

(c) prepare, in accordance with Annex III, point 3.2, an environmental statement. The statement shall pay particular attention to the results achieved by an organisation against its environmental objectives and targets and the requirement of continuing to improve its environmental performance, and shall consider the information needs of relevant interested parties;

(d) have the environmental review, if appropriate, management system, audit procedure and environmental statement examined to verify that they meet the relevant requirements of this Regulation and have the environmental statement validated by the environmental verifier to ensure it meets the requirements of Annex III;

(e) forward the validated environmental statement to the competent body of the Member State in which the organisation seeking registration is located and, after registration, make it publicly available.

3. In order for an organisation to maintain registration to EMAS it shall:

(a) have the environmental management system and audit programme verified in accordance with the requirements of Annex V, point 5.6;

(b) forward the yearly necessary validated updates of its environmental statement to the competent body and make them publicly available. Deviations from the frequency with which updates shall be performed can be made under circumstances laid down in Commission guidance adopted in accordance with the procedure laid down in Article 14(2), in particular for small organisations and small enterprises according to Commission Recommendation 96/280/EC[1] and when there is no operational change in the environmental management system.

Article 4
Accreditation system

1. Member States shall establish a system for the accreditation of independent environmental verifiers and for the supervision of their activities. To this end, Member States may either use existing accreditation institutions or the competent bodies referred to in Article 5 or designate or set up any other body with an appropriate status.

[1] OJ L 107, 30.4.1996, p. 4.

Member States shall ensure that the composition of these systems is such as to guarantee their independence and neutrality in the execution of their tasks.

2. Member States shall ensure that these systems are fully operational within 12 months following the date of entry into force of this Regulation.

3. Member States shall ensure appropriate consultation of parties involved, in setting up and directing the accreditation systems.

4. The accreditation of environmental verifiers and supervision of their activities shall be in accordance with the requirements of Annex V.

5. Environmental verifiers accredited in one Member State may perform verification activities in any other Member State in accordance with the requirements laid down in Annex V. The start of the verification activity shall be notified to the Member State in which it is being performed and the activity shall be subject to supervision by the latter's accreditation system.

6. Member States shall inform the Commission of the measures taken pursuant to this Article and communicate relevant changes in the structure and procedures of the accreditation systems.

7. The Commission shall, in accordance with the procedure laid down in Article 14(2), promote collaboration between Member States in order, in particular, to avoid inconsistency between Annex V and the criteria, conditions and procedures which the national accreditation bodies apply for the accreditation and supervision of environmental verifiers to ensure a consistent quality of environmental verifiers.

8. A forum, constituted of all accreditation bodies, shall be set up by the accreditation bodies with the aim of providing the Commission with the elements and means to fulfil its obligation under paragraph (7). It shall meet at least once per year in the presence of a representative of the Commission.

The forum shall as appropriate develop guidance on issues in the field of accreditation, competence and supervision of environmental verifiers. Guidance documents produced shall be submitted to the procedure laid down in Article 14(2).

In order to ensure a harmonised development of the functioning of accreditation bodies and the verification process in all the Member States, the forum shall develop procedures for a peer review process. The aim of the peer review shall be to ensure that the accreditation systems of Member States meet the requirements of this Regulation. A report of the peer review activities shall be transmitted to the Commission which shall forward it for information to the Committee referred to in Article 14(1) and make it publicly available.

Article 5
Competent bodies

1. Within 3 months of the entry into force of this Regulation, each Member State shall designate the competent body responsible for carrying out the tasks provided for in this Regulation, in particular in Articles 6 and 7 and shall inform the Commission thereof.

2. Member States shall ensure that the composition of the competent bodies is such as to guarantee their independence and neutrality and that the competent bodies apply the provisions of this Regulation in a consistent manner.

3. Member States shall have guidelines for suspension and deletion of the registration of organisations, for the use of competent bodies. Competent bodies shall, in particular, have procedures for:

- considering observations from interested parties concerning registered organisations, and
- refusal of registration, deletion or suspension of organisations from registration.

4. The competent body shall be responsible for the registration of organisations under EMAS. It shall therefore control the entry and maintenance of organisations on the register.

5. Competent bodies from all Member States shall meet, at least once per year in the presence of a representative of the Commission. The objective of these meetings is to ensure the consistency of procedures relating to the registration of organisations under EMAS, including suspension and deletion of registration. A peer review process shall be put in place by the competent bodies for the purpose of developing a common understanding of their practical approach towards registration. A report of the peer review activities shall be transmitted to the Commission which shall forward it for information to the Committee referred to in Article 14(1), and make it publicly available.

Article 6

Registration of organisations

Registration of organisations shall be dealt with by competent bodies on the basis of the following cases:

1. If a competent body
   - has received a validated environmental statement and
   - has received a completed form, which includes at least the minimum information set out in Annex VIII, from the organisation and
   - has received any registration fee that may be payable under Article 16 and
   - is satisfied, on the basis of evidence received, and in particular through inquiries made at the competent enforcement authority regarding the compliance of the organisation with the relevant environmental legislation, that the organisation meets all the requirements of this Regulation,

it shall register the applicant organisation and give it a registration number. The competent body shall inform the organisation's management that the organisation appears on the register.

2. If a competent body receives a supervision report from the accreditation body which gives evidence that the activities of the environmental verifier were not performed adequately enough to ensure that the requirements of this Regulation are met by the applicant organisation, registration shall be refused or suspended as appropriate until assurance of the organisation's compliance with EMAS is obtained.

3. If an organisation fails to submit to a competent body, within three months of being required to do so,

- the yearly validated updates of the environmental statement, or
- a completed form, which includes at least the minimum information set out in Annex VIII from the organisation, or
- any relevant registration fees,

the organisation shall be suspended or deleted from the register, as appropriate, depending on the nature and scope of the failure. The competent body shall inform the organisation's management of the reasons for the measures taken.

4. If, at any time, a competent body concludes, on the basis of evidence received, that the organisation is no longer complying with one or more of the conditions of this Regulation, the organisation shall be suspended or deleted from the register, as appropriate, depending on the nature and scope of the failure.

If a competent body is informed by the competent enforcement authority of a breach by the organisation of relevant regulatory requirements regarding environmental protection, it shall refuse registration of that organisation or suspend it from the register as appropriate.

5. Refusal of registration, suspension or deletion of organisations from the register shall require the consultation of the appropriate interested parties, in order to provide the competent body with the necessary elements of evidence for taking its decision. The competent body shall inform the organisation's management of the reasons for the measures taken and of the process of discussion with the competent enforcement authority.

6. Refusal or suspension shall be lifted if the competent body has received satisfactory information that the organisation is in compliance with the requirements of EMAS or if it has received satisfactory information from the competent enforcement authority that the breach has been rectified and that the organisation has made satisfactory arrangements with the aim of ensuring that it does not recur.

Article 7

List of registered organisations and environmental verifiers

1. The accreditation body shall establish, revise and update a list of environmental verifiers and their scope of accreditation in their Member State and shall directly, or via the national authorities as decided by the Member State concerned, communicate changes in this list each month to the Commission and to the competent body.

2. The competent bodies shall establish and maintain a list of registered organisations in their Member State and update this list on a monthly basis. The competent bodies shall directly, or via the national authorities as decided by the Member State concerned, communicate changes in this list each month to the Commission and may organise a system of information exchanges by economic sector and area of competence in the network of delegated local bodies.

3. The register of environmental verifiers and EMAS registered organisations shall be maintained by the Commission which shall make it publicly available.

Article 8
Logo

1. Organisations participating in EMAS may use the logo set out in Annex IV only if they have a current EMAS registration. Technical specifications regarding the reproduction of the logo shall be adopted in accordance with the procedure laid down in Article 14(2) and published by the Commission.

2. The EMAS logo may be used by organisations in the following cases:

(a) on validated information as described in Annex III, point 3.5, under circumstances defined in Commission guidance adopted under the procedure laid down in Article 14(2) which shall ensure that there is no confusion with environmental product labels (version 2 of the logo, as given in Annex IV, shall be used in this case);

(b) on validated environmental statements (version 2 of the logo, as given in Annex IV, shall be used in this case);

(c) on registered organisations' letterheads (version 1 of the logo, as given in Annex IV, shall be used in this case);

(d) on information advertising an organisation's participation in EMAS (version 1 of the logo, as given in Annex IV, shall be used in this case);

(e) on or in adverts for products, activities and services, only under circumstances defined in Commission guidance adopted in accordance with Article 14(2) which shall ensure that there is no confusion with environmental product labels.

3. The logo shall not be used in the following cases:

(a) on products or their packaging,

(b) in conjunction with comparative claims concerning other products, activities and services.

The Commission shall however, as a part of the evaluation provided for in Article 15(3), consider under which exceptional circumstances the logo may be used and, for these cases, shall adopt rules in accordance with the procedure laid down in Article 14(2) which shall ensure that there is no confusion with environmental product labels.

Article 9

Relationship with European and international standards

1. Organisations implementing European or international standards for environmental issues relevant to EMAS and certified, according to appropriate certification procedures, as complying with those standards shall be considered as meeting the corresponding requirements of this Regulation, provided that:

(a) the standards are recognised by the Commission acting in accordance with the procedure laid down in Article 14(2);

(b) the accreditation requirements for the certification bodies are recognised by the Commission acting in accordance with the procedure laid down in Article 14(2).

The references of the recognised standards (including the relevant sections of EMAS to which they apply) and recognised accreditation requirements shall be published in the *Official Journal of the European Communities*.

2. To enable organisations referred to in paragraph 1 to be registered under EMAS, the organisations concerned shall demonstrate to the environmental verifier compliance with requirements not covered by the recognised standards.

Article 10

Relationship with other environmental legislation in the Community

1. EMAS shall be without prejudice to:

(a) Community law, or

(b) national laws or technical standards not governed by Community law and

(c) the duties of organisations under those laws and standards regarding environmental controls.

2. Member States should consider how registration under EMAS in accordance with this Regulation may be taken into account in the implementation and enforcement of environmental legislation in order to avoid unnecessary duplication of effort by both organisations and competent enforcement authorities.

Member States shall inform the Commission of the measures taken in this regard. The Commission shall transmit the information received from Member States to the European Parliament and to the Council as soon as available and at least on a three-yearly basis.

Article 11

Promotion of organisations' participation, in particular of small and medium-sized enterprises

1. Member States shall promote organisations' participation in EMAS and shall, in particular, consider the need to ensure the participation of small and medium-sized enterprises (SMEs) by

- facilitating access to information, support funds, public institutions and public procurement, without prejudice to the Community rules governing public procurement,
- establishing or promoting technical assistance measures, especially in conjunction with initiatives from appropriate professional or local points of contact (e.g. local authorities, chambers of commerce, trade or craft associations),
- ensuring that reasonable registration fees encourage higher participation.

In order to promote participation of SMEs, including those concentrated in well defined geographical areas, local authorities, in participation with industrial associations, chambers of commerce and interested parties may provide assistance in the identification of significant environmental impacts. SMEs may then use this in defining their environmental programme and setting the objectives and targets of their EMAS management system. In addition, programmes designed to encourage the participation of SMEs, such as a step by step approach which will eventually lead to EMAS registration, may be developed at regional or national level. The system shall operate with the objective of avoiding unnecessary administrative burden for participants, in particular small organisations.

2. In order to encourage organisations' participation in EMAS the Commission and other institutions of the Community as well as other public authorities at national level should consider, without prejudice to Community law, how registration under EMAS may be taken into account when setting criteria for their procurement policies.

3. Member States shall inform the Commission of the measures taken under this Article. The Commission shall transmit the information received from Member States to the European Parliament and to the Council as soon as available and at least on a three-yearly basis.

Article 12
Information

1. Each Member State shall take appropriate measures to ensure that:

(a) organisations are informed of the content of this Regulation;

(b) the public is informed of the objectives and principal components of EMAS.

Member States shall, where appropriate, in cooperation with, amongst others, industrial associations, consumer organisations, environmental organisations, trade unions and local institutions, in particular use professional publications, local journals, promotion campaigns or any other functional means to promote general awareness of EMAS.

2. Member States shall inform the Commission of the measures taken under this Article.

3. The Commission shall be responsible for promoting EMAS at Community level. It shall, in particular, examine in consultation with the members of the Committee referred to in Article 14(1) the possibility of disseminating best practice by appropriate ways and means.

Article 13
Infringements

Member States shall take appropriate legal or administrative measures in case of non-compliance with the provisions of this Regulation and communicate these measures to the Commission.

Article 14
Committee

1. The Commission shall be assisted by a committee.

2. Where reference is made to this paragraph, Articles 5 and 7 of Decision 1999/468/EC shall apply, having regard to the provisions of Article 8 thereof.

The period referred to in Article 5(6) of Decision 1999/468/EC shall be set at three months.

3. The Committee shall adopt its rules of procedure.

Article 15
Revision

1. The Commission shall review EMAS in the light of the experience gained during its operation and international developments no later than five years after the entry into force of this Regulation, and shall, if necessary, propose to the European Parliament and Council the appropriate amendments.

2. All the Annexes to this Regulation, with the exception of Annex V, shall be adapted by the Commission, acting in accordance with the procedure laid down in Article 14(2) in the light of experience gained in the operation of EMAS and in response to identified needs for guidance on EMAS requirements.

3. The Commission shall in particular evaluate, in cooperation with the Member States, no later than 5 years after the entry into force of this Regulation, the use, recognition and interpretation, especially by the public and other interested parties, of the EMAS logo and assess whether there is a need to revise the logo and the requirements for its use.

Article 16
Costs and fees

1. A system of fees in accordance with arrangements established by Member States may be set up for the administrative costs incurred in connection with the registration procedures for organisations and the accreditation and supervision of environmental verifiers and other related costs of EMAS.

2. Member States shall inform the Commission of the measures taken under this Article.

Article 17

Repeal of Regulation (EEC) No 1836/93

1. Regulation (EEC) No 1836/93 shall be repealed as from the date of entry into force of this Regulation, subject to paragraphs 2 to 5 of this Article.

2. National accreditation systems and competent bodies set up pursuant to Regulation (EEC) No 1836/93 shall remain in force. Member States shall modify the procedures followed by accreditation systems and competent bodies under the corresponding provisions of this Regulation. Member States shall ensure that these systems are fully operational within 12 months following the date of entry into force of this Regulation.

3. Environmental verifiers accredited in accordance with Regulation (EEC) No 1836/93 may continue to perform their activities in accordance with the requirements established by this Regulation.

4. Sites registered in accordance with Regulation (EEC) No 1836/93 will remain on the EMAS register. The new requirements of this Regulation shall be checked at the time of the next verification of a site. If the next verification is to be carried out sooner than 6 months after entry into force of this Regulation, the date of the next verification may be extended by 6 months in agreement with the environmental verifier and the competent bodies.

5. Paragraphs 3 and 4 shall also apply to environmental verifiers accredited and sites registered in accordance with Article 14 of Regulation (EEC) No 1836/93, provided that the responsible accreditation bodies and competent bodies have agreed that the environmental verifiers and registered sites comply with all the requirements of Regulation (EEC) No 1836/93 and notify this to the Commission.

Article 18

Entry into force

This Regulation shall enter into force on the third day following that of its publication in the *Official Journal of the European Communities*.

This Regulation shall be binding in its entirety and directly applicable in all Member States.

Done at Brussels, 19 March 2001.

The European Parliament	*For the Council*
The President	*The President*
N. FONTAINE	A. LINDH

ANNEX I

A. ENVIRONMENTAL MANAGEMENT SYSTEM REQUIREMENTS

The environmental Management system shall be implemented according to the requirements given below (section 4 of EN ISO 14001:1996)*:

I-A Environmental Management System Requirements

I-A.1. *General requirements*

The organisation shall establish and maintain an environmental management system, the requirements of which are described in this annex.

I-A.2. *Environmental policy*

Top management shall define the organisation's environmental policy and ensure that it

(a) is appropriate to the nature, scale and environmental impacts of its activities, products and services;

(b) includes a commitment to continual improvement and prevention of pollution;

(c) includes a commitment to comply with relevant environmental legislation and regulations, and with other requirements to which the organisation subscribes;

(d) provides the framework for setting and reviewing environmental objectives and targets;

(e) is documented, implemented and maintained and communicated to all employees;

(f) is available to the public.

I-A.3. *Planning*

I-A.3.1. *Environmental aspects*

The organisation shall establish and maintain (a) procedure(s) to identify the environmental aspects of its activities, products or services that it can control and over which it can be expected to have an influence, in order to determine those which have or can have significant impacts on the environment. The organisation shall ensure that the aspects related to these significant impacts are considered in setting its environmental objectives.

The organisation shall keep this information up-to-date.

* The use of the text of the national standard reproduced in this Annex is made with the permission of CEN. The full text of the national standard can be purchased from the national standard bodies the list of which is given in this Annex.

I-A.3.2. *Legal and other requirements*

The organisation shall establish and maintain a procedure to identify and have access to legal and other requirements to which the organisation subscribes, that are applicable to the environmental aspects of its activities, products or services.

I-A.3.3. *Objectives and targets*

The organisation shall establish and maintain documented environmental objectives and targets, at each relevant function and level within the organisation.

When establishing and reviewing its objectives, an organisation shall consider the legal and other requirements, its significant environmental aspects, its technological options and its financial, operational and business requirements, and the views of interested parties.

The objectives and targets shall be consistent with the environmental policy, including the commitment to prevention of pollution.

I-A.3.4. *Environmental management programme(s)*

The organisation shall establish and maintain (a) programme(s) for achieving its objectives and targets. It shall include

(a) designation of responsibility for achieving objectives and targets at each relevant function and level of the organisation;

(b) the means and timeframe by which they are to be achieved.

If a project relates to new developments and new or modified activities, products or services, programme(s) shall be amended where relevant to ensure that environmental management applies to such projects.

I-A.4. *Implementation and operation*

I-A.4.1. *Structure and responsibility*

Roles, responsibility and authorities shall be defined, documented and communicated in order to facilitate effective environmental management.

Management shall provide resources essential to the implementation and control of the environmental management system. Resources include human resources and specialised skills, technology and financial resources.

The organisation's top management shall appoint (a) specific management representative(s) who, irrespective of other responsibilities, shall have defined roles, responsibilities and authority for

(a) ensuring that environmental management system requirements are established, implemented and maintained in accordance with this International Standard;

(b) reporting on the performance of the environmental management system to top management for review and as a basis for improvement of the environmental management system.

I-A.4.2. *Training, awareness and competence*

The organisation shall identify training needs. It shall require that all personnel whose work may create a significant impact upon the environment, have received appropriate training.

It shall establish and maintain procedures to make its employees or members at each relevant function and level aware of

(a) the importance of conformance with the environmental policy and procedures and with the requirements of the environmental management system;

(b) the significant environmental impacts, actual or potential, of their work activities and the environmental benefits of improved personal performance;

(c) their roles and responsibilities in achieving conformance with the environmental policy and procedures and with the requirements of the environmental management system, including emergency preparedness and response requirements;

(d) the potential consequences of departure from specified operating procedures.

Personnel performing the tasks which can cause significant environmental impacts shall be competent on the basis of appropriate education, training and/or experience.

I-A.4.3. *Communication*

With regard to its environmental aspects and environmental management system, the organisation shall establish and maintain procedures for

(a) internal communication between the various levels and functions of the organisation;

(b) receiving, documenting and responding to relevant communication from external interested parties.

The organisation shall consider processes for external communication on its significant environmental aspects and record its decision.

I-A.4.4. *Environmental management system documentation*

The organisation shall establish and maintain information, in paper or electronic form, to

(a) describe the core elements of the management system and their interaction;

(b) provide direction to related documentation.

I-A.4.5. *Document control*

The organisation shall establish and maintain procedures for controlling all documents required by this International Standard to ensure that

(a) they can be located;

(b) they are periodically reviewed, revised as necessary and approved for adequacy by authorised personnel;

(c) the current versions of relevant documents are available at all locations where operations essential to the effective functioning of the environmental management system are performed;

(d) obsolete documents are promptly removed from all points of issue and points of use, or otherwise assured against unintended use;

(e) any obsolete documents retained for legal and/or knowledge preservation purposes are suitably identified.

Documentation shall be legible, dated (with dates of revision) and readily identifiable, maintained in an orderly manner and retained for a specified period. Procedures and responsibilities shall be established and maintained concerning the creation and modification of the various types of document.

I-A.4.6. *Operational control*

The organisation shall identify those operations and activities that are associated with the identified significant environmental aspects in line with its policy, objectives and targets. The organisation shall plan these activities, including maintenance, in order to ensure that they are carried out under specified conditions by

(a) establishing and maintaining documented procedures to cover situations where their absence could lead to deviations from the environmental policy and the objectives and targets;

(b) stipulating operating criteria in the procedures;

(c) establishing and maintaining procedures related to the identifiable significant environmental aspects of goods and services used by the organisation and communicating relevant procedures and requirements to suppliers and contractors.

I-A.4.7. *Emergency preparedness and response*

The organisation shall establish and maintain procedures to identify potential for and respond to accidents and emergency situations, and for preventing and mitigating the environmental impacts that may be associated with them.

The organisation shall review and revise, where necessary, its emergency preparedness and response procedures, in particular, after the occurrence of accidents or emergency situations.

The organisation shall also periodically test such procedures where practicable.

I-A.5. *Checking and corrective action*

I-A.5.1. *Monitoring and measurement*

The organisation shall establish and maintain documented procedures to monitor and measure, on a regular basis, the key characteristics of its operations and activities that can have a significant impact on the environment. This shall include the recording of information to track performance, relevant operational controls and conformance with the organisation's environmental objectives and targets. Monitoring equipment shall be calibrated and maintained and records of this process shall be retained according to the organisation's procedures.

The organisation shall establish and maintain a documented procedure for periodically evaluating compliance with relevant environmental legislation and regulations.

I-A.5.2. *Nonconformance and corrective and preventive action*

The organisation shall establish and maintain procedures for defining responsibility and authority for handling and investigating nonconformance, taking action to mitigate any impacts caused and for initiating and completing corrective and preventive action.

Any corrective or preventive action taken to eliminate the causes of actual and potential nonconformances shall be appropriate to the magnitude of problems and commensurate with the environmental impact encountered.

The organisation shall implement and record any changes in the documented procedures resulting from corrective and preventive action.

I-A.5.3. *Records*

The organisation shall establish and maintain procedures for the identification, maintenance and disposition of environmental records. These records shall include training records and the results of audits and reviews.

Environmental records shall be legible, identifiable and traceable to the activity, product or service involved. Environmental records shall be stored and maintained in such a way that they are readily retrievable and protected against damage, deterioration or loss. Their retention times shall be established and recorded.

Records shall be maintained, as appropriate to the system and to the organisation, to demonstrate conformance to the requirements of this International Standard.

I-A.5.4. *Environmental management system audit*

The organisation shall establish and maintain (a) programme(s) and procedures for periodic environmental management system audits to be carried out, in order to

(a) determine whether or not the environmental management system

  (1) conforms to planned arrangements for environmental management including the requirements of this International Standard; and

  (2) has been properly implemented and maintained; and

(b) provide information on the results of audits to management

The organisation's audit programme, including any schedule, shall be based on the environmental importance of the activity concerned and the results of previous audits. In order to be comprehensive, the audit procedures shall cover the audit scope, frequency and methodologies, as well as the responsibilities and requirements for conducting audits and reporting results.

I-A.6. *Management review*

The organisation's top management shall, at intervals that it determines, review the environmental management system, to ensure its continuing suitability, adequacy and effectiveness. The management review process shall ensure that the necessary information is collected to allow management to carry out this evaluation. This review shall be documented.

The management review shall address the possible need for changes to policy, objectives and other elements of the environmental management system, in the light of environmental management system audit results, changing circumstances and the commitment to continual improvement.

List of national standard bodies

B: IBN/BIN (Institut Belge de Normalisation/Belgisch Instituut voor Normalisatie)
DK: DS (Dansk Standard)
D: DIN (Deutsches Institut für Normung e.V.)
EL: ELOT (Ελληνικός οργανισμός τυποποίησης)
E: AENOR (Asociación Española de Normalización y Certificación)
F: AFNOR (Association Française de Normalisation)
IRL: NSAI (National Standards Authority of Ireland)
I: UNI (Ente Nazionale Italiano di Unificazione)
L: EE (Service de l'Energie de l'Etat) (Luxembourg)
NL: NEN (Nederlands Normalisatie-Instituut)
A: ON (Österreichisches Normungsinstitut)
P: IPQ (Instituto Português da Qualidade)
FIN: SFS (Suomen Standardisoimisliitto r.y)
S: SIS (Standardiseringen i Sverige)
UK: BSI (British Standards Institution).

B. ISSUES TO BE ADDRESSED BY ORGANISATIONS IMPLEMENTING EMAS

1. Legal compliance

Organisations shall be able to demonstrate that they:

(a) have identified, and know the implications to the organisation of, all relevant environmental legislation;

(b) provide for legal compliance with environmental legislation; and

(c) have procedures in place that enable the organisation to meet these requirements on an ongoing basis.

2. Performance

Organisations shall be able to demonstrate that the management system and the audit procedures address the actual environmental performance of the organisation with respect to the aspects identified from Annex VI. The performance of the organisation against its objectives and targets shall be evaluated as part of the management review process. The organisation shall also commit itself to the continual improvement of its environmental performance. In doing so, the organisation may base its action on local, regional and national environmental programmes.

The means to achieve the objectives and targets cannot be environmental objectives. If the organisation comprises one or more sites, each of the sites to which EMAS applies shall comply with all the requirements of EMAS including the continual improvement of environmental performance as defined in Article 2(b).

3. External communication and relations

Organisations shall be able to demonstrate an open dialogue with the public and other interested parties including local communities and customers with regard to the environmental impact of their activities, products and services in order to identify the public's and other interested parties' concerns.

4. Employee involvement

In addition to the requirements in Annex I—Section A employees shall be involved in the process aimed at continually improving the organisation's environmental performance. Appropriate forms of participation such as the suggestion-book system or project-based group works or environmental committees should be used for this purpose. Organisations shall take note of Commission guidance on best practice in this field. Where they so request, any employee representatives shall also be involved.

ANNEX II

REQUIREMENTS CONCERNING INTERNAL ENVIRONMENTAL AUDITING

2.1. General requirements

Internal audits ensure that the activities carried out by an organisation are being conducted in accordance with established procedures. The audit may also identify any problems with those established procedures or any opportunities for improving those procedures. The scope of audits carried out within an organisation may vary from the audit of a simple procedure to the audit of complex activities. Over a period of time all activities in a particular organisation shall be subject to an audit. The period of time taken to complete audits of all activities is known as the audit cycle. For small non-complex organisations, it may be possible to audit all activities at one time. For these organisations the audit cycle is the interval between these audits.

Internal audits shall be carried out by persons sufficiently independent of the activity being audited to ensure an impartial view. They may be carried out by employees of the organisation or by external parties (employees from other organisations, employees from other parts of the same organisation or consultants).

2.2. Objectives

The organisation's environmental auditing programme shall define in writing the objectives of each audit or audit cycle including the audit frequency for each activity.

The objectives shall include, in particular, assessing the management systems in place, and determining conformity with the organisation's policy and programme, which shall include compliance with relevant environmental regulatory requirements.

2.3. Scope

The overall scope of the individual audits, or of each stage of an audit cycle where appropriate, shall be clearly defined and shall explicitly specify the:

1. subject areas covered;
2. activities to be audited;
3. environmental criteria to be considered;
4. period covered by the audit.

Environmental audit includes assessment of the factual data necessary to evaluate performance.

2.4. Organisation and resources

Environmental audits shall be performed by persons or groups of persons with appropriate knowledge of the sectors and fields audited, including knowledge and experience on the relevant environmental, management, technical and regulatory issues, and sufficient training and proficiency in the specific skills of auditing to achieve the stated objectives. The resources and time allocated to the audit shall be commensurate with the scope and objectives of the audit.

The top organisation management shall support the auditing.

The auditors shall be sufficiently independent of the activities they audit to make an objective and impartial judgment.

2.5. Planning and preparation for an audit

Each audit shall be planned and prepared with the objectives, in particular, of:

- ensuring the appropriate resources are allocated,
- ensuring that each individual involved in the audit process (including auditors, management, and staff) understands his or her role and responsibilities.

Preparation shall include familiarisation with activities of the organisation and with the environmental management system established there and review of the findings and conclusions of previous audits.

2.6. Audit activities

Audit activities shall include discussions with personnel, inspection of operating conditions and equipment and reviewing of records, written procedures and other relevant documentation, with the objective of evaluating the environmental performance of the activity being audited to determine whether it meets the applicable standards, regulations or objectives and targets set and whether the system in place to manage environmental responsibilities is effective and appropriate. Inter alia, spot-checking of compliance with these criteria should be used to determine the effectiveness of the entire management system.

The following steps, in particular, shall be included in the audit process:

(a) understanding of the management systems;

(b) assessing strengths and weaknesses of the management systems;

(c) gathering relevant evidence;

(d) evaluating audit findings;

(e) preparing audit conclusions;

(f) reporting audit findings and conclusions.

2.7. Reporting audit findings and conclusions

1. A written audit report of the appropriate form and content shall be prepared by the auditors to ensure full, formal submission of the findings and conclusions of the audit, at the end of each audit and audit cycle.

The findings and conclusions of the audit shall be formally communicated to the top organisation management.

2. The fundamental objectives of a written audit report are:

(a) to document the scope of the audit;

(b) to provide management with information on the state of compliance with the organisations' environmental policy and the environmental progress at the organisation;

(c) to provide management with information on the effectiveness and reliability of the arrangements for monitoring environmental impacts of the organisation;

(d) to demonstrate the need for corrective action, where appropriate.

2.8. Audit follow-up

The audit process shall culminate in the preparation and implementation of a plan of appropriate corrective action.

Appropriate mechanisms shall be in place and in operation to ensure that the audit results are followed up.

2.9. Audit frequency

The audit or audit cycle shall be completed, as appropriate, at intervals no longer than 3 years. The frequency with which any activity is audited will vary depending upon the

(a) nature, scale and complexity of the activities;

(b) significance of associated environmental impacts;

(c) importance and urgency of the problems detected by previous audits;

(d) history of environmental problems.

More complex activities with a more significant environmental impact shall be audited more frequently.

An organisation shall define its own audit programme and audit frequency taking account of Commission guidance adopted in accordance with the procedure laid down in Article 14(2).

ANNEX III

ENVIRONMENTAL STATEMENT

3.1. Introduction

The aim of the environmental statement is to provide environmental information to the public and other interested parties regarding the environmental impact and performance and the continual improvement of environmental performance of the organisation. It is also a vehicle to address the concerns of interested parties identified as a result of Annex I—Section B.3 and considered as significant by the organisation (Annex VI, point 6.4). Environmental information shall be presented in a clear and coherent manner in printed form for those who have no other means of obtaining this information. Upon its first registration and every three years thereafter, the organisation is required to make available the information detailed under point 3.2 in a consolidated printed version.

The Commission shall adopt guidance about the environmental statement in accordance with the procedure laid down in Article 14(2).

3.2. Environmental statement

Upon its first registration an organisation shall produce environmental information, taking into account the criteria of point 3.5 to be referred to as the environmental statement, to be validated by the environmental verifier. This information shall be submitted to the competent body following validation, and then be made publicly available. The environmental statement is a tool for communication and dialogue with the public and other interested parties regarding environmental performance. The organisation shall consider the information needs of the public and other interested parties when writing and designing the environmental statement.

The minimum requirements for this information shall be as follows:

(a) a clear and unambiguous description of the organisation registering under EMAS and a summary of its activities, products and services and its relationship to any parent organisations as appropriate;

(b) the environmental policy and a brief description of the environmental management system of the organisation;

(c) a description of all the significant direct and indirect environmental aspects which result in significant environmental impacts of the organisation and an explanation of the nature of the impacts as related to these aspects (Annex VI);

(d) a description of the environmental objectives and targets in relation to the significant environmental aspects and impacts;

(e) a summary of the data available on the performance of the organisation against its environmental objectives and targets with respect to its significant environmental impacts. The summary may include figures on pollutant emissions, waste generation, consumption of raw material, energy and water, noise as well as other aspects indicated in Annex VI. The data should allow for year-by-year comparison to assess the development of the environmental performance of the organisation;

(f) other factors regarding environmental performance including performance against legal provisions with respect to their significant environmental impacts;

(g) the name and accreditation number of the environmental verifier and the date of validation.

3.3. Criteria for environmental performance reporting

The raw data generated by an environmental management system will be used in a number of different ways to show the environmental performance of an organisation. For this purpose organisations may use relevant existing environmental performance indicators, making sure that the indicators chosen:

(a) give an accurate appraisal of the organisation's performance;

(b) are understandable and unambiguous;

(c) allow for year on year comparison to assess the development of the environmental performance of the organisation;

(d) allow for comparison with sector, national or regional benchmarks as appropriate;

(e) allow for comparison with regulatory requirements as appropriate.

3.4. Maintenance of publicly available information

The organisation shall update the information detailed in point 3.2 and shall have any changes validated by an environmental verifier, on a yearly basis. Deviations from the frequency with which updates shall be performed may be made under circumstances laid down in Commission guidance adopted in accordance with the procedure laid down in Article 14(2). After validation changes shall also be submitted to the competent body and be made publicly available.

3.5. Publication of information

Organisations may wish to address different audiences or interested parties with the information generated by its environmental management system and use only selected information from the environmental statement. Any environmental information published by an organisation may bear the EMAS logo provided it has been validated by an environmental verifier as being:

(a) accurate and non deceptive;

(b) substantiated and verifiable;

(c) relevant and used in an appropriate context or setting;

(d) representative of the overall environmental performance of the organisation;

(e) unlikely to result in misinterpretation;

(f) significant in relation to the overall environmental impact,

and makes reference to the organisation's latest environmental statement from which it was drawn.

3.6. Public availability

The information generated in point 3.2(a) to (g) which forms the environmental statement for an organisation and the updated information specified in point 3.4 shall be available to the public and other interested parties. The environmental statement shall be made accessible to the public. To this end, organisations are encouraged to use all methods available (electronic publication, libraries etc.) The organisation shall be able to demonstrate to the environmental verifier that anybody interested in the organisation's environmental performance can easily and freely be given access to the information required in point 3.2(a) to (g) and point 3.4.

3.7. Local accountability

Organisations registering under EMAS may wish to produce one corporate environmental statement covering a number of different geographic locations. The intention of EMAS is to ensure local accountability and thus organisations shall ensure that the significant environmental impacts of each site are clearly identified and reported within the corporate statement.

ANNEX V

ACCREDITATION, SUPERVISION AND FUNCTION OF THE ENVIRONMENTAL VERIFIERS

5.1. General

The accreditation of environmental verifiers shall be based on the general principles of competence set out in this Annex. Accreditation bodies may choose to accredit individuals, organisations or both, as environmental verifiers. The procedural requirements and detailed criteria for accrediting environmental verifiers are defined pursuant to Article 4 by national accreditation systems in accordance with these principles. Conformity with these principles shall be ensured through the peer review process established by Article 4.

5.2. Requirements for the accreditation of environmental verifiers

5.2.1. *The following competence constitutes the minimum requirements with which an environmental verifier, individual or organisation, shall comply:*

(a) knowledge and understanding of the Regulation, the general functioning of environmental management systems, relevant standards and guidance issued by the Commission, under Article 4 and 14(2), for the use of this Regulation;

(b) knowledge and understanding of the legislative, regulatory and administrative requirements relevant to the activity subject to verification;

(c) knowledge and understanding of environmental issues, including the environmental dimension of sustainable development;

(d) knowledge and understanding of the technical aspects, relevant to environmental issues, of the activity subject to verification;

(e) understanding of the general functioning of the activity subject to verification in order to assess the appropriateness of the management system;

(f) knowledge and understanding of environmental auditing requirements and methodology;

(g) knowledge of information audit (Environmental Statement).

Appropriate evidence of the verifier's knowledge and of his/her/its relevant experience and technical capacities in the abovementioned fields should be provided to the accreditation body to which the candidate verifier has applied for accreditation

In addition, the environmental verifier shall be independent, in particular of the organisation's auditor or consultant, impartial and objective in performing his or her activities.

The individual environmental verifier or verification organisation shall ensure that he or she or the organisation and its staff is free of any commercial, financial or other pressures which might influence their judgment or endanger trust in their independence of judgment and integrity in relation to their activities, and that they comply with any rules applicable in this respect.

The environmental verifier shall have documented methodologies and procedures, including quality control mechanisms and confidentiality provisions, for the verification requirements of this Regulation. In case the environmental verifier is an organisation, the environmental verifier shall have and make available on request an organisation chart detailing structures and responsibilities within the organisation and a statement of legal status, ownership and funding sources.

5.2.2. *Scope of accreditation*

The scope of accreditation of environmental verifiers shall be defined according to the classification of economic activities (NACE codes) as established by Council Regulation (EEC) 3037/90[1]. The scope of accreditation shall be limited by the competence of the environmental verifier. The scope of accreditation shall also take into account the size and complexity of the activity, where appropriate; this will be assured through supervision.

5.2.3. *Additional requirements for the accreditation of individual environmental verifiers performing verifications on their own*

Individual environmental verifiers performing verification on their own, in addition to complying with the requirements of point 5.2.1 and 5.2.2 shall have:

- all the necessary competence to perform verifications, in their accredited fields,
- a limited scope of accreditation dependant on their personal competence.

Compliance with these requirements shall be ensured through the assessment carried out prior to the accreditation and through the supervisory role of the accreditation body.

5.3. Supervision of environmental verifiers

5.3.1. *Supervision of environmental verifiers carried out by the accreditation body which granted their accreditation*

The environmental verifier shall immediately inform the accreditation body of all changes which have a bearing on the accreditation or its scope.

Provision shall be made, at regular intervals not exceeding 24 months, to ensure that the environmental verifier continues to comply with the accreditation requirements and to monitor the quality of the verifications undertaken. Supervision may consist of office audit, witnessing in organisations, questionnaires, review of environmental statements validated by the environmental verifiers and review of verification report. It should be proportionate with the activity undertaken by the environmental verifier.

Any decision taken by the accreditation body to terminate or suspend accreditation or curtail the scope of accreditation shall be taken only after the environmental verifier has had the possibility of a hearing.

5.3.2. *Supervision of environmental verifiers performing verification activities in a Member State other than that where their accreditation was granted*

An environmental verifier accredited in one Member State, before performing verification activities in another Member State, shall provide to the accreditation body of the latter Member State, at least four weeks in advance, notification of:

- his or her accreditation details, competences and team composition if appropriate,

[1] OJ L 293, 24.10.1990, p. 1. Regulation as amended by Regulation (EEC) No 761/93 (OJ L 83, 3.4.1993, p. 1).

- when and where the verification will occur: address and contact details of the organisation, measures taken to deal with legal and language knowledge if necessary.

The accreditation body may request further clarification of the necessary legal and language knowledge as detailed above.

This notification shall be communicated before each new verification.

The accreditation body shall not require other conditions which would prejudice the right of the environmental verifier to provide services in a Member State other than the one where accreditation was granted. In particular, discriminatory fees for notification shall not be charged. The accreditation body shall also not use the notification procedure to delay the arrival of the environmental verifier. Any difficulty to supervise the environmental verifier on the date communicated shall be adequately justified. If costs for supervision arise, the accreditation body is allowed to charge appropriate fees.

If the supervising accreditation body is not satisfied with the quality of the work done by the environmental verifier, the supervision report shall be transmitted to the environmental verifier concerned, the accreditation body which granted the accreditation, to the competent body where the organisation being verified is located and, in case of any further dispute, to the forum of accreditation body.

Organisations may not refuse the right of accreditation bodies to supervise the environmental verifier through witnessed assessments during the verification process.

5.4. The function of environmental verifiers

5.4.1. ***The function of the environmental verifier is to check, without prejudice to the enforcement powers of Member States in respect of regulatory requirements:***

(a) compliance with all the requirements of this Regulation: initial environmental review if appropriate, environmental management system, environmental audit and its results and the environmental statement;

(b) the reliability, credibility and correctness of the data and information in:

- the environmental statement (Annex III, point 3.2 and point 3.3),
- environmental information to be validated (Annex III, point 3.4).

The environmental verifier shall, in particular, investigate in a sound professional manner, the technical validity of the initial environmental review, if appropriate, or audit or other procedures carried out by the organisation, without unnecessarily duplicating those procedures. Inter alia, the environmental verifier should use spot-checks to determine whether the results of the internal audit are reliable.

5.4.2. ***At the time of the first verification, the environmental verifier shall, in particular, check that the following requirements are met by the organisation:***

(a) a fully operational environmental management system in accordance with Annex I;

(b) a fully planned audit programme, which had already begun in accordance with Annex II so that at least areas with the most significant environmental impact have been covered;

(c) completion of one management review;

(d) the preparation of an environmental statement in accordance with Annex III, point 3.2.

5.4.3. *Legal compliance*

The environmental verifier shall ensure that an organisation has procedures in place to control those aspects of its operations subject to relevant Community or national laws and that these procedures are capable of delivering compliance. The checks of the audit, shall in particular, provide for evidence of the capability of the procedures in place to deliver legal compliance.

The environmental verifier shall not validate the environmental statement, if during the verification process he observes, for example through spot-checks, that the organisation is not in legal compliance.

5.4.4. *Organisation definition*

When verifying the environmental management system and validating the environmental statement, the environmental verifier shall ensure that the components of the organisation are unambiguously defined and corresponds to a real division of the activities. The content of the statement shall clearly cover the different parts of the organisation to which EMAS applies.

5.5. Conditions for the environmental verifier to perform his/her activities

5.5.1. The environmental verifier shall operate within his/her scope of accreditation, on the basis of a written agreement with the organisation which defines the scope of the work, enables the environmental verifier to operate in an independent professional manner and commits the organisation to providing the necessary cooperation.

5.5.2. The verification shall involve examination of documentation, a visit to the organisation including, in particular, interviews with personnel, preparation of a report to the organisations' management and the organisations' solution of the issues raised by the report.

5.5.3. The documentation to be examined in advance of the visit shall include basic information about the organisation and activities there, the environmental policy and programme, the description of the environmental management system in operation in the organisation, details of the environmental review or audit carried out, the report on that review or audit and on any corrective action taken afterwards, and the draft environmental statement.

5.5.4. The environmental verifier shall prepare a report for the organisation's management. This report shall specify:

(a) all issues relevant to the work carried out by the environmental verifier;

(b) the starting point of the organisation towards implementation of an environmental management system;

(c) in general, cases of nonconformity with the provisions of this Regulation, and in particular:

- technical defects in the environmental review, or audit method, or environmental management system, or any other relevant process,
- points of disagreement with the draft environmental statement, together with details of the amendments or additions that should be made to the environmental statement,

(d) the comparison with the previous statements and the performance assessment of the organisation.

5.6. Verification frequency

In consultation with the organisation the environmental verifier shall design a programme to ensure that all elements required for registration with EMAS are verified in a period not exceeding 36 months. In addition the environmental verifier shall at intervals not exceeding 12 months validate any updated information in the environmental statement. Deviations from the frequency with which updates shall be performed may be made under circumstances laid down in Commission guidance adopted in accordance with the procedure laid down in Article 14(2).

ANNEX VI

ENVIRONMENTAL ASPECTS

6.1. General

An organisation shall consider all environmental aspects of its activities, products and services and decide, on the basis of criteria taking into account the Community legislation, which of its environmental aspects have a significant impact, as a basis for setting its environmental objectives and targets. These criteria shall be publicly available.

An organisation shall consider both direct and indirect environmental aspects of its activities, products and services.

6.2. Direct environmental aspects

These cover the activities of an organisation over which it has management control and may include, but is not limited to:

(a) emissions to air;

(b) releases to water;

(c) avoidance, recycling, reuse, transportation and disposal of solid and other wastes, particularly hazardous wastes;

(d) use and contamination of land;

(e) use of natural resources and raw materials (including energy);

(f) local issues (noise, vibration, odour, dust, visual appearance, etc.);

(g) transport issues (both for goods and services and employees);

(h) risks of environmental accidents and impacts arising, or likely to arise, as consequences of incidents, accidents and potential emergency situations;

(i) effects on biodiversity.

6.3. Indirect environmental aspects

As a result of the activities, products and services of an organisation there may be significant environmental aspects over which it may not have full management control.

These may include, but are not limited to:

(a) product related issues (design, development, packaging, transportation, use and waste recovery/disposal);

(b) capital investments, granting loans and insurance services;

(c) new markets;

(d) choice and composition of services (e.g. transport or the catering trade);

(e) administrative and planning decisions;

(f) product range compositions;

(g) the environmental performance and practices of contractors, subcontractors and suppliers.

Organisations must be able to demonstrate that the significant environmental aspects associated with their procurement procedures have been identified and that significant impacts associated with these aspects are addressed within the management system. The organisation should endeavour to ensure that the suppliers and those acting on the organisation's behalf comply with the organisation's environmental policy within the remit of the activities carried out for the contract.

In the case of these indirect environmental aspects, an organisation shall consider how much influence it can have over these aspects, and what measures can be taken to reduce the impact.

6.4. Significance

It is the responsibility of the organisation to define criteria for assessing the significance of the environmental aspects of its activities, products and services, to determine which have a significant environmental impact. The criteria developed by an organisation shall be comprehensive, capable of independent checking, reproducible and made publicly available.

Considerations in establishing the criteria for assessing the significance of an organisation's environmental aspects may include, but are not limited to:

(a) information about the condition of the environment to identify activities, products and services of the organisation that may have an environmental impact;

(b) the organisation's existing data on material and energy inputs, discharges, wastes and emissions in terms of risk;

(c) views of interested parties;

(d) environmental activities of the organisation that are regulated;

(e) procurement activities;

(f) design, development, manufacturing, distribution, servicing, use, re-use, recycling and disposal of the organisation's products;

(g) those activities of the organisation with the most significant environmental costs, and environmental benefits.

In assessing the significance of the environmental impacts of the organisation's activities the organisation shall think not only of normal operating conditions but also of start-up and shutdown conditions and of reasonably foreseeable emergency conditions. Account shall be taken of past, present and planned activities.

ANNEX VII

ENVIRONMENTAL REVIEW

7.1. General

An organisation that has not supplied the necessary information needed to identify and assess the significant environmental aspects according to Annex VI must establish its current position with regard to the environment by means of a review. The aim should be to consider all environmental aspects of the organisation as a basis for establishing the environmental management system.

7.2. Requirements

The review should cover five key areas:

(a) legislative, regulatory and other requirements to which the organisation subscribes;

(b) an identification of all environmental aspects with a significant environmental impact in accordance with Annex VI, qualified and quantified as appropriate, and compiling a register of those identified as significant;

(c) a description of the criteria for assessing the significance of the environmental impact in accordance with Annex VI, point 6.4;

(d) an examination of all existing environmental management practices and procedures;

(e) an evaluation of feedback from the investigation of previous incidents.

13 The Rio Declaration on Environment and Development

> [The Rio Declaration] . . . contains 27 norms for state and inter-state behaviour, many of which have never been universally accepted before . . . To be practical, they need to be applied in a way which reflects the cultural, political and economic nature of the country and the different communities within it. They work best when applied together . . .
>
> *Luc Hens, Vrije Universiteit Brussel*[1]

Type Performance-oriented treaty

Strength Provides definitions of key concepts and principles in environment and development

Keywords Sustainable development • Poverty • Sovereignty • Technology transfer • Compensation • Precautionary approach • Precautionary principle • Environmental impact assessment • Women • Youth • Indigenous people

13.1 Background

In 1992 the UN Conference on Environment and Development (UNCED) signalled a major turning point in environmental issues. It was at UNCED that environmental issues entered the mainstream. Also known as the Earth Summit, the UNCED serves as a critical marker, a pivotal point in history that divided those events before and after so that one can refer to events and issues before and after

1 Source: 'The Rio Conference and Thereafter', p. 8, www.vub.ac.be, accessed 2003.

UNCED. UNCED produced several key documents, including the Rio Declaration on Environment and Development and Agenda 21, a plan of action for organisations of all sizes.

Although the Rio Declaration is addressed to nation-states, it introduced key concepts that are echoed in many of the tools presented in this book, including the Global Compact (Chapter 3).

The Rio Declaration defined two key principles—the precautionary principle and the polluter-pays principle—that are key elements of many environmental standards.

13.2 Strengths and weaknesses

The Rio Conference 'provides an important basis for environmental principles in international law',[2] enshrining many key concepts and definitions.

13.3 Companies to which the Rio Declaration on Environment and Development applies

The Rio Declaration is addressed to states, not companies. However, concepts such as the precautionary principle described in the Rio Declaration also apply to companies.

13.4 Questions posed and answered

What is the role of states in promoting environment and development?

13.5 The promise and the challenge

The Rio Declaration emphasises the importance of addressing the needs of women, youth and indigenous peoples.

2 *Ibid.*: 10.

Additional resources

Further reading

United Nations (1993) *Rio Declaration: Agenda 21* (New York: United Nations).

Website

Rio Declaration on Environment and Development:
www.un.org/documents/ga/conf151/aconf15126-1annex1.htm

The Rio Declaration on Environment and Development*

The United Nations Conference on Environment and Development,

Having met at Rio de Janeiro from 3 to 14 June 1992,

Reaffirming the Declaration of the United Nations Conference on the Human Environment, adopted at Stockholm on 16 June 1972, and seeking to build upon it,

With the goal of establishing a new and equitable global partnership through the creation of new levels of cooperation among States, key sectors of societies and people,

Working towards international agreements which respect the interests of all and protect the integrity of the global environmental and developmental system,

Recognizing the integral and interdependent nature of the Earth, our home,

Proclaims that:

Principle 1

Human beings are at the centre of concerns for sustainable development. They are entitled to a healthy and productive life in harmony with nature.

Principle 2

States have, in accordance with the Charter of the United Nations and the principles of international law, the sovereign right to exploit their own resources pursuant to their own environmental and developmental policies, and the responsibility to ensure that activities within their jurisdiction or control do not cause damage to the environment of other States or of areas beyond the limits of national jurisdiction.

---

* *Source:* Report of the United Nations Conference on the Human Environment, Stockholm, 5-16 June 1972 (United Nations publication, Sales No. E.73.II.A.14 and corrigendum), chap. I.

This document was posted online by the United Nations Department of Economic and Social Affairs (DESA). Reproduction and dissemination of the document—in electronic and/or printed format—is encouraged, provided acknowledgement is made of the role of the United Nations in making it available.

Date last updated: 12 January, 2000 by DESA/DSD.

Principle 3

The right to development must be fulfilled so as to equitably meet developmental and environmental needs of present and future generations.

Principle 4

In order to achieve sustainable development, environmental protection shall constitute an integral part of the development process and cannot be considered in isolation from it.

Principle 5

All States and all people shall cooperate in the essential task of eradicating poverty as an indispensable requirement for sustainable development, in order to decrease the disparities in standards of living and better meet the needs of the majority of the people of the world.

Principle 6

The special situation and needs of developing countries, particularly the least developed and those most environmentally vulnerable, shall be given special priority. International actions in the field of environment and development should also address the interests and needs of all countries.

Principle 7

States shall cooperate in a spirit of global partnership to conserve, protect and restore the health and integrity of the Earth's ecosystem. In view of the different contributions to global environmental degradation, States have common but differentiated responsibilities. The developed countries acknowledge the responsibility that they bear in the international pursuit of sustainable development in view of the pressures their societies place on the global environment and of the technologies and financial resources they command.

Principle 8

To achieve sustainable development and a higher quality of life for all people, States should reduce and eliminate unsustainable patterns of production and consumption and promote appropriate demographic policies.

Principle 9

States should cooperate to strengthen endogenous capacity-building for sustainable development by improving scientific understanding through exchanges of scientific and technological knowledge, and by enhancing the development, adaptation, diffusion and transfer of technologies, including new and innovative technologies.

Principle 10

Environmental issues are best handled with the participation of all concerned citizens, at the relevant level. At the national level, each individual shall have appropriate access to information concerning the environment that is held by public authorities, including information on hazardous materials and activities in their communities, and the opportunity to participate in decision-making processes. States shall facilitate and encourage public awareness and participation by making information widely available. Effective access to judicial and administrative proceedings, including redress and remedy, shall be provided.

Principle 11

States shall enact effective environmental legislation. Environmental standards, management objectives and priorities should reflect the environmental and developmental context to which they apply. Standards applied by some countries may be inappropriate and of unwarranted economic and social cost to other countries, in particular developing countries.

Principle 12

States should cooperate to promote a supportive and open international economic system that would lead to economic growth and sustainable development in all countries, to better address the problems of environmental degradation. Trade policy measures for environmental purposes should not constitute a means of arbitrary or unjustifiable discrimination or a disguised restriction on international trade. Unilateral actions to deal with environmental challenges outside the jurisdiction of the importing country should be avoided. Environmental measures addressing transboundary or global environmental problems should, as far as possible, be based on an international consensus.

Principle 13

States shall develop national law regarding liability and compensation for the victims of pollution and other environmental damage. States shall also cooperate in an expeditious and more determined manner to develop further international law regarding liability and compensation for adverse effects of environmental damage caused by activities within their jurisdiction or control to areas beyond their jurisdiction.

Principle 14

States should effectively cooperate to discourage or prevent the relocation and transfer to other States of any activities and substances that cause severe environmental degradation or are found to be harmful to human health.

Principle 15

In order to protect the environment, the precautionary approach shall be widely applied by States according to their capabilities. Where there are threats of serious or irreversible damage, lack of full scientific certainty shall not be used as a reason for postponing cost-effective measures to prevent environmental degradation.

Principle 16

National authorities should endeavour to promote the internalization of environmental costs and the use of economic instruments, taking into account the approach that the polluter should, in principle, bear the cost of pollution, with due regard to the public interest and without distorting international trade and investment.

Principle 17

Environmental impact assessment, as a national instrument, shall be undertaken for proposed activities that are likely to have a significant adverse impact on the environment and are subject to a decision of a competent national authority.

Principle 18

States shall immediately notify other States of any natural disasters or other emergencies that are likely to produce sudden harmful effects on the environment of those States. Every effort shall be made by the international community to help States so afflicted.

Principle 19

States shall provide prior and timely notification and relevant information to potentially affected States on activities that may have a significant adverse transboundary environmental effect and shall consult with those States at an early stage and in good faith.

Principle 20

Women have a vital role in environmental management and development. Their full participation is therefore essential to achieve sustainable development.

Principle 21

The creativity, ideals and courage of the youth of the world should be mobilized to forge a global partnership in order to achieve sustainable development and ensure a better future for all.

Principle 22

Indigenous people and their communities and other local communities have a vital role in environmental management and development because of their knowledge and traditional practices. States should recognize and duly support their identity, culture and interests and enable their effective participation in the achievement of sustainable development.

Principle 23

The environment and natural resources of people under oppression, domination and occupation shall be protected.

Principle 24

Warfare is inherently destructive of sustainable development. States shall therefore respect international law providing protection for the environment in times of armed conflict and cooperate in its further development, as necessary.

Principle 25

Peace, development and environmental protection are interdependent and indivisible.

Principle 26

States shall resolve all their environmental disputes peacefully and by appropriate means in accordance with the Charter of the United Nations.

Principle 27

States and people shall cooperate in good faith and in a spirit of partnership in the fulfilment of the principles embodied in this Declaration and in the further development of international law in the field of sustainable development.

14
The Ceres Principles

More and more of the players who shape the global business and financial landscape—large investors, and foundations, environmental and public interest organisations, big corporations and small business—have endorsed the Ceres Principles.

William C. Thompson, Jr, New York City Comptroller[1]

Type Multi-stakeholder, aspirational, reporting requirements; performance- and process-oriented (to a lesser extent)

Strength Engagement with companies

Keywords Multi-stakeholder • Environment • Sustainability • Waste • Energy conservation • Protection of whistle-blowers • Valdez Principles

14.1 Background

Founded in 1989, the Coalition for Environmentally Responsible Economies (Ceres) is a network of more than 80 environmental, investor and advocacy groups promoting sustainability. Ceres is best known for the Ceres Principles, a set of ten principles covering the major environmental concerns facing companies, including energy conservation, reduction and disposal of waste, and risk reduction. The Ceres Principles were originally known as the Valdez Principles, which were launched in 1989 as a response to the environmental disaster of the *Exxon Valdez* oil tanker.

1 Welcoming Remarks at the 2003 Ceres Conference: Advancing Sustainable Governance, New York City, 1 April 2003.

Endorsing companies must commit publicly to the Principles, address issues raised by the Ceres network and other stakeholders and report annually on their progress in meeting the Ceres Principles. Ceres is a coalition of more than 80 companies, with Sunoco being the first *Fortune* 500 signatory, joining in 1993.[2] Coca-Cola, the Ford Motor Company, General Motors and Polaroid are among some of the most well-known companies that have endorsed the Ceres Principles.

14.2 Strengths and weaknesses

One of the greatest strengths of the Ceres Principles is the degree to which Ceres engages with companies in ongoing dialogue. Unlike the case with the majority of the principles and standards profiled in this book, a company cannot unilaterally decide to adopt the Ceres Principles: 'endorsing the Principles is a two-way process—commitment by a company and acceptance by the Ceres Board of Directors'.[3] In its dialogue with a company, the Board raises problems that the Ceres network has identified.

Although the Principles are aspirational in nature, the dialogue between the company and Ceres allows for greater specificity, and during this dialogue companies can interpret how the Principles apply to their own operations.

Another factor that differentiates the Ceres Principles from other key initiatives is that it includes a wide range of investors that can pressure companies to endorse the Principles. The nine investors within the Ceres network represent more than US$300 billion in investments, constituting a powerful lever for endorsers. The reports published by the participating companies provide standardised data for investors and other stakeholders.

The engagement between companies and stakeholders within Ceres is one of the hallmarks of the Ceres Principles, building trust and preventing conflict:

> One of the greatest advantages Ceres offers is that differences are discussed privately and in person rather than through the media or in courtrooms. Such conversations are conducted in the spirit of mutual respect and consensus-building. Ceres participants consider this trust-based approach to conflict resolution to be one of the most valuable contributions of the organisation, along with public disclosure of environment-related data through the Ceres report.[4]

The Ceres Principles are among the few initiatives profiled in this book that include a clause to protect whistle-blowers. This is very important to safeguard those employees who disclose damaging information from suffering retaliation for going public with information. The Principles state that 'we will not take any action against employees for reporting dangerous incidents or conditions to management or to appropriate authorities' (see page 299).

2 For a full list of Ceres companies, see: www.ceres.org/Page.aspx?pid=426#list.
3 www.ceres.org, accessed 2003.
4 'About Us: Frequently Asked Questions', www.ceres.org, accessed 2003.

14.3 Companies to which the Ceres Principles apply

The Ceres Principles operate within a US framework and so are best suited to companies headquartered in the USA. Ceres has developed special reporting requirements for small companies, making it more appealing now to companies of all sizes.

14.4 Questions posed and answered

What measures can companies take to promote sustainability of their products and operations?

14.5 The promise and the challenge

Ceres is a US-based organisation addressing global issues. It would be a challenge for an organisation such as Ceres to expand globally and still maintain its cohesive network and sense of trust. Along with the US Environment Programme (UNEP), Ceres helped to launch the Global Reporting Initiative (GRI, Chapter 28). Ceres asks participating companies to publish a report 'consistent with the core expectations of the . . . Sustainability Reporting Guidelines of the GRI'.[5] Hence, Ceres maintains its US roots and identity, but with a global reporting mechanism.

Additional resource

Website

Coalition for Environmentally Responsible Economies: www.ceres.org

5 *Ibid.*: 5.

The Ceres Principles*

PRINCIPLES

Protection of the Biosphere

We will reduce and make continual progress toward eliminating the release of any substance that may cause environmental damage to the air, water, or the earth or its inhabitants. We will safeguard all habitats affected by our operations and will protect open spaces and wilderness, while preserving biodiversity.

Sustainable Use of Natural Resources

We will make sustainable use of renewable natural resources, such as water, soils and forests. We will conserve non-renewable natural resources through efficient use and careful planning.

Reduction and Disposal of Wastes

We will reduce and where possible eliminate waste through source reduction and recycling. All waste will be handled and disposed of through safe and responsible methods.

Energy Conservation

We will conserve energy and improve the energy efficiency of our internal operations and of the goods and services we sell. We will make every effort to use environmentally safe and sustainable energy sources.

Risk Reduction

We will strive to minimize the environmental, health and safety risks to our employees and the communities in which we operate through safe technologies, facilities and operating procedures, and by being prepared for emergencies.

---

* Reproduced with the permission of the Coalition for Responsible Economies (Ceres).

Safe Products and Services

We will reduce and where possible eliminate the use, manufacture or sale of products and services that cause environmental damage or health or safety hazards. We will inform our customers of the environmental impacts of our products or services and try to correct unsafe use.

Environmental Restoration

We will promptly and responsibly correct conditions we have caused that endanger health, safety or the environment. To the extent feasible, we will redress injuries we have caused to persons or damage we have caused to the environment and will restore the environment.

Informing the Public

We will inform in a timely manner everyone who may be affected by conditions caused by our company that might endanger health, safety or the environment. We will regularly seek advice and counsel through dialogue with persons in communities near our facilities. We will not take any action against employees for reporting dangerous incidents or conditions to management or to appropriate authorities.

Management Commitment

We will implement these Principles and sustain a process that ensures that the Board of Directors and Chief Executive Officer are fully informed about pertinent environmental issues and are fully responsible for environmental policy. In selecting our Board of Directors, we will consider demonstrated environmental commitment as a factor.

Audits and Reports

We will conduct an annual self-evaluation of our progress in implementing these Principles. We will support the timely creation of generally accepted environmental audit procedures. We will annually complete the Ceres Report, which will be made available to the public.

Disclaimer: These Principles establish an environmental ethic with criteria by which investors and others can assess the environmental performance of companies. Companies that endorse these Principles pledge to go voluntarily beyond the requirements of the law. The terms "may" and "might" in Principles one and eight are not meant to encompass every imaginable consequence, no matter how remote. Rather, these Principles obligate endorsers to behave as prudent persons who are not governed by conflicting interests and who possess a strong commitment to environmental excellence and to human health and safety. These Principles are not intended to create new legal liabilities, expand existing rights or obligations, waive legal defenses, or otherwise affect the legal position of any endorsing company, and are not intended to be used against an endorser in any legal proceeding for any purpose.

Endorsing Company Statement

By adopting these Principles, we publicly affirm our belief that corporations have a responsibility for the environment, and must conduct all aspects of their business as responsible stewards of the environment by operating in a manner that protects the Earth. We believe that corporations must not compromise the ability of future generations to sustain themselves.

We will update our practices constantly in light of advances in technology and new understandings in health and environmental science. In collaboration with Ceres, we will promote a dynamic process to ensure that the Principles are interpreted in a way that accommodates changing technologies and environmental realities. We intend to make consistent, measurable progress in implementing these Principles and to apply them to all aspects of our operations throughout the world.

15 The Natural Step

> **The Natural Step provides an elegant framework, a compass, to guide us on the road ahead and is a powerful tool for all seeking a new mental model to move their business into a sustainable future.**
>
> *Maurice Strong, Secretary-General, 1992 UN Earth Summit*[1]

Type General principles; performance-oriented

Strength It requires a new vision, a redesigning of the company's approach to environmental and social issues

Keywords Sustainability • Environment • Human needs • Systems • Redesign • Sweden • Thermodynamics • Vision • Assessment

15.1 Background

Founded in Sweden by Dr Karl-Henrik Robèrt, a leading cancer specialist, The Natural Step (TNS) addresses the systemic causes of environmental problems. Robèrt noticed that the increase in cases of childhood leukaemia was linked to environmental problems. TNS principles were developed by scientists and are based on the laws of thermodynamics (for more background on TNS, see Robèrt 2002). The principles focus on systems, requiring the organisations working with TNS to redefine their relationship to the environment and society.

TNS provides companies with tools for visioning, assessment and a framework for action. The Buckminster Fuller Institute in the UK compares TNS to 'a pair of glasses that allow . . . [a company] to see its manufacturing processes with com-

1 Quoted at www.naturalstep.org, accessed 2003.

pletely new eyes, a new vantage point that highlight[s] the potential towards sustainability'.[2]

With offices in ten countries, TNS has gone from being a Swedish approach to one that is gaining momentum among companies based in the USA, the United Kingdom, Japan, Australia, Israel, New Zealand, South Africa, Canada and Brazil. Nike, Ikea, McDonald's Sweden, Home Depot, Electrolux and Interface are among the most well-known companies that have used the TNS principles and approach.

TNS compares the current environmental reality to a funnel, in which a growing population and consumption patterns demand more and more life-supporting resources, causing a decrease in the amount of resources available, leading to new limitations for companies as the funnel narrows (see Fig. 15.1). Put simply, an ever-greater number of people are competing for essential resources that are being depleted. As companies 'hit the walls' of the funnel, they will face increasing financial pressures.

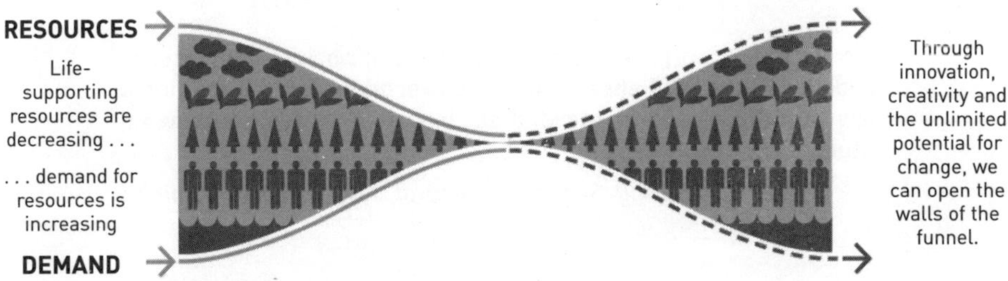

Figure 15.1 **Opening the walls of the funnel**

Source: www.naturalstep.org, accessed 2003; reprinted with permission by The Natural Step

By applying TNS principles and approach, companies can pioneer sustainable solutions and work to restore the Earth's balance. TNS is best understood by providing examples of how companies apply it. Ikea Sweden was one of the first global companies to implement TNS. As a result of working with TNS, Ikea began to 'reconceptualise . . . and redesign the relationship between Ikea and the environment' (TNS 2001). To raise awareness about the environment within the company, Ikea initiated an environmental training programme for 90% of its then 20,000 employees. Specialists were given advanced training. Rather than presenting Ikea with an answer on how to address environmental issues within the company, Ikea staff were asked to develop their own answers and model. Adopting TNS principles and approach required rethinking the Ikea business model. Instead of developing an eco-friendly product line that would have marginalised green issues, Ikea decided to mainstream environmental issues into strategy, investment decisions, transport, product design and specifications, and supply chain management.

2 Buckminster Fuller Institute, www.bfi.org, accessed 2003.

15.2 Strengths and weaknesses

The approach of TNS is both theoretical and practical. Its theoretical underpinnings, based on the laws of thermodynamics, lend it credibility. In addition, TNS principles benefit from being general enough in nature that organisations in different sectors can adopt them and make them their own. In an interview with Michael Toms of New Dimensions World Broadcasting Network, Robèrt, founder of TNS, stated that:

> Instead of telling them what to do, we say, 'How could this be applied to your business or in your world?' That allows them to . . . put the details onto this basic structure which is non-negotiable. This sparks creativity, and recruits enthusiasm into the process instead of defence mechanisms. Any expert in his field of expertise is much more clever than you are. If you give him the overall principles, therefore, and then ask him for advice instead of telling him what to do he finds much smarter solutions than Greenpeace or I or anybody can do (Toms 1994).

The sustainability framework of TNS is absolute; as such it can be audited. It is possible for companies to track their performance with regard to meeting TNS sustainability principles.

According to Forum for the Future, there are business benefits associated with implementing the framework of TNS:

> The Natural Step has assisted many companies and organisations to develop strategic sustainability initiatives. These initiatives have helped them to achieve greater effectiveness, competitive advantage, bottom line results, security, employee satisfaction and public acceptance.[3]

Interface, the first US company to pioneer full-scale application of the approach of TNS, estimates that it has saved US$120 million as a result of implementing the framework.[4]

15.3 Companies to which The Natural Step applies

At the time of writing (September 2003) hundreds of companies, communities and individuals around the world have adopted the framework of TNS. Since the principles are general in nature, they can be adopted in any organisation, large or small.

3 www.forumforthefuture.org.uk, accessed 2003.

4 www.bfi.org, accessed 2003.

15.4 Questions posed and answered

TNS asks:

- How can an organisation view its operations and impact within a systems framework?

15.5 The challenge and the promise

One of the key challenges for TNS, and for many initiatives profiled in this book, is to build capacity and scale up activities, especially in the developing world.

Because of its adaptability and strengths, TNS has influenced a wide range of other initiatives in the field of corporate responsibility. The framework of TNS complements many sustainability tools and resources, such as ISO 14001 (Chapter 29) and the Global Reporting Initiative (Chapter 28).

References

Robèrt, K.-H. (2002) *The Natural Step Story: Seeding a Quiet Revolution* (Gabriola Island, BC, Canada: New Society Publishers).

TNS (The Natural Step) (2001) 'Organizational Case Summary: Ikea', www.naturalstep.org, accessed 2003.

Toms, M. (1994) 'The Natural Step to a Sustainable Future: A Conversation with Karl-Henrik Robèrt MD', www.newdimensions.org, accessed 2003.

Additional resource

Website

The Natural Step: www.naturalstep.org; the text of the principles may be found at www.naturalstep.org/en/usa/principles-sustainability.

The Natural Step Principles*

FOUR SIMPLE PRINCIPLES OF SUSTAINABILITY

Sustainability is fundamentally about maintaining human life on the planet and, thus, addressing human needs is an essential element of creating a sustainable society. Therefore, one of The Natural Step's principles of sustainability is to meet human needs worldwide.

The other three principles focus on interactions between humans and the planet. They are rooted in an understanding that contemporary life is fundamentally supported by natural processes, such as the capturing of energy from the sun by photosynthetic organisms and the purification of air and water. These processes are essential to maintaining human life. However, as a society we are systematically altering the ecosystem structures and functions that provide life-supporting services and resources that we need to survive.

Based on this understanding, The Natural Step sustainability principles are based on science and supported by the analyses that ecosystem functions and processes are altered when:

1. Society mines and disperses materials at a faster rate than they are re-deposited back into the Earth's crust (examples of these materials are oil, coal and metals such as mercury and lead);
2. Society produces substances faster than they can be broken down by natural processes, if they can be broken down at all (examples of such substances include dioxins, DDT and PCBs); and,
3. Society depletes or degrades resources at a faster rate than they are replenished (for example, over-harvesting trees or fish), or by other forms of ecosystem manipulation (for example, paving over fertile land or causing soil erosion).

By considering these three ways in which human life-supporting structures and functions are being altered, The Natural Step has defined three basic principles for maintaining essential ecological processes.

We also recognize that social and economic dynamics fundamentally drive the actions that lead to ecosystem changes. Therefore, the fourth principle focuses on the impor-

* Reproduced with the permission of The Natural Step.

tance of meeting human needs worldwide as an integral and essential part of sustainability.

From this assessment, The Natural Step's sustainability principles, also known as "conditions" that must be met in order to have a sustainable society, are as follows:

In a sustainable society, nature is not subject to systematically increasing:

1. concentrations of substances extracted from the earth's crust;
2. concentrations of substances produced by society;
3. degradation by physical means

   and, in that society . . .

4. human needs are met worldwide.

How can we—company, organization, individual, family, government, school—employ the principles?

1. eliminate our contribution to systematic increases in concentrations of substances from the Earth's crust.
This means substituting certain minerals that are scarce in nature with others that are more abundant, using all mined materials efficiently, and systematically reducing dependence on fossil fuels.

2. eliminate our contribution to systematic increases in concentrations of substances produced by society.
This means systematically substituting certain persistent and unnatural compounds with ones that are normally abundant or break down more easily in nature, and using all substances produced by society efficiently.

3. eliminate our contribution to systematic physical degradation of nature through over-harvesting, depletion, foreign introductions and other forms of modification.
This means drawing resources only from well-managed ecosystems, systematically pursuing the most productive and efficient use both of those resources and land, and exercising caution in all kinds of modification of nature.

4. contribute as much as we can to the goal of meeting human needs in our society and worldwide, going over and above all the substitution and dematerialization measures taken in meeting the first three objectives.
This means using all of our resources efficiently, fairly and responsibly so that the needs of all people on whom we have an impact, and the future needs of people who are not yet born, stand the best chance of being met.

Part VI
Combating corruption

Corruption respects no borders, knows no economic distinctions and infects all forms of government. In the long run, no country can afford the social, political or economic costs that corruption entails.

OECD [1]

There is a significant difference between Part VI and the other parts of this book. Whereas most corporate responsibility (CR) issues are voluntary, violators of anti-corruption norms may face criminal prosecution.[2]

Bribery of public officials may be defined as:

> the promise or giving of any undue payment or other advantages, whether directly or through intermediaries to a public official, for himself [or herself] or for a third party, to influence the official to act or refrain from acting in the performance of his or her official duties in order to obtain or retain business' (CCBIBT 1997; quoted in IMF 2001).

1 OECD 2002.

2 For a thorough background on corruption, see OECD 2002; for more information on business and corruption, see the website of the International Business Leaders' Forum, at www.iblf.org.

Several companies have written into their codes of conduct a no-bribery policy.[3] Among these companies are BP,[4] Shell[5] and Unilever.[6] Anglo-American is unusual in that it does not allow facilitation payments or small bribes often required to gain licences. According to Edward Bickham, a vice-president at Anglo-American, facilitation payments represent a 'chess game that begins to lead to bribery' (*Economist* 2002: 11).

There are a wide range of codes, principles, conventions, laws and rules on corruption. These tools can be seen as a dialogue in which after a series of principles are crafted others emerge as a response to the vacuum left by the previous tools. The following list provides a brief description of the rules, principles and conventions in chronological order to capture this dialogue and sequence:

- **The 1977 Foreign Corrupt Practices Act.** The starting point for understanding codes and standards to prevent bribery is the US Foreign Corrupt Practices Act (FCPA) of 1977.[7] This legislation dramatically altered how US companies conducted their operations, encouraging them to closely monitor their activities. The FCPA placed US firms at a disadvantage relative to multinational companies that were allowed to offer bribes. This disadvantage led the USA to press for a more level playing field, which resulted in the OECD Convention on Combating Bribery of Foreign Public Officials in International Business Transactions, which is described in Chapter 16.
- **The 1977 Rules of Conduct to Combat Extortion and Bribery of the International Chamber of Commerce.** In 1977, the International Chamber of Commerce (ICC) developed the Rules of Conduct to Combat Extortion and Bribery,[8] applicable to governments, the private sector and international organisations. The ICC Rules address both the demand side and the supply side of bribery.
- **The 1999 OECD Convention on Combating Bribery of Foreign Public Officials in International Business Transactions.** In 1999, the OECD Convention on Combating Bribery of Foreign Public Officials in International Business Transactions (Chapter 16) called on members of the OECD and other nations to criminalise bribery of foreign officials. Hence it does not deal with private-to-private bribery, nor with the demand side of bribery.
- **The 2002 Business Principles for Combating Bribery.** In 2002, Transparency International and Social Accountability International launched

3 For information on the development of management systems to combat bribery, see ICC 2000.

4 www.bp.com/liveassets/bp_internet/globalbp/STAGING/global_assets/downloads/C/coc_en_full_document.pdf, accessed May 2010

5 www.shell.com/home/content/aboutshell/who_we_are/our_values/sgbp/sgbp_30032008.html

6 www.unilever.com/aboutus/purposeandprinciples/?WT.GNAV=Purpose_&_principles

7 For more information on the FCPA, see Low 1998.

8 For the latest version (2005), go to www.iccwbo.org/policy/anticorruption/id870/index.html

the Business Principles for Combating Bribery (Chapter 18). The Principles focus on private-to-private bribery and provide a framework for companies on how to develop internal management systems to prevent corrupt practices.

- In 2009, the **UN Convention Against Corruption** was launched to address both public and private sector corruption. The UN Convention commits states parties to the Convention to establish preventative measures to combat corruption, including anti-corruption bodies and codes of conduct for public officials. Public procurement and management of public finances is addressed alongside measures to prevent money laundering.[9]

As with many of the issues described in this book, combating corruption requires the alignment of an array of forces, including governments, civil society and media. In addition, it is not enough to address the supply side of the bribery equation; the demand side of corruption also needs to be addressed. The private sector can influence both the demand side and the supply side. *The Economist* (2002: 11) has called on multinational corporations to encourage governments of countries where bribery is rampant to adequately compensate their civil servants.

This section includes a discussion of two major corporate responsibility tools:

- OECD Convention on Combating Bribery of Foreign Public Officials in International Business Transactions
- Business Principles for Countering Bribery

Other important tools include the Wolfsberg Anti-Money Laundering Principles, consisting of a set of private banking principles agreed on by 11 of the largest international banks (ABN Amro NV; Banco Santander Central Hispano, SA; Bank of Tokyo-Mitsubishi, Ltd; Barclays Bank; Citigroup; Credit Suisse Group; Deutsche Bank AG; Goldman Sachs; HSBC; J.P. Morgan Chase; Société Générale; and UBS AG; see www.wolfsberg-principles.com).

References

CCBIBT (Council on Combating Bribery in International Business Transactions) (1997) 'Annex', in *Revised Recommendation of the Council on Combating Bribery in International Business Transactions* (Paris: CCBIBT, adopted on 23 May 1997).

Economist (2002) 'The Worm That Never Dies', *The Economist*, 2–8 March 2002: 11.

FCPA (Foreign Corrupt Practices Act) (1977) Current through Pub. L 105-366 (November 10, 1998) (Washington, DC: US Government Printing Office).

ICC (International Chamber of Commerce) (2000) *Fighting Bribery: A Corporate Practices Manual* (Paris: ICC).

9 For the text of the Convention, see www.unodc.org/pdf/corruption/publications_unodc_convention-e.pdf (accessed May 2010).

IMF (International Monetary Fund) (2001) *OECD Convention on Combating Bribery of Foreign Public Officials in International Business Transactions* (Policy Development and Review; Washington, DC: IMF, 18 September 2001).

Low, L. (1998) 'Transnational Corruption: New Rules for Old Temptations, New Players to Combat a Perennial Evil', in *Proceedings of the 92nd Annual Meeting: The Challenge of Non-state Actors* (Washington, DC: American Society of International Law, 1–4 April 1998).

OECD (Organisation for Economic Co-operation and Development) (2002) *No Longer Business as Usual: Fighting Bribery and Corruption* (Paris: OECD, October 2002).

16

The OECD Convention on Combating Bribery of Foreign Public Officials in International Business Transactions

> **Since the OECD Convention on Combating Bribery of Foreign Officials . . . entered into force on 15 February 1999, it is no longer business as usual.**
>
> *OECD*[1]

Type Binding performance standard; foundation tool

Strength Its universality

Keywords Bribery • Foreign public officials • Criminalise • Facilitation payments • Functional equivalence

16.1 Background

Launched in 1999, the OECD Convention on Combating Bribery of Foreign Public Officials in International Business Transactions is a landmark agreement, defining key terms and developing a legal framework for addressing bribery. To understand the objectives of the Convention, it is necessary to review the role of the OECD (the Organisation for Economic Co-operation and Development). The OECD promotes policies that contribute to economic growth and development. Founded in 1961, the OECD is a membership organisation for governments from 30 countries (for a

1 OECD website, www.oecd.org.

full list of member countries, see footnote 3, on page 61). The OECD has made a significant contribution to corporate responsibility (CR) by developing several principles relating to corporate responsibility, including the OECD Principles of Corporate Governance (see Chapter 19) and the OECD Guidelines for Multinational Enterprises (see Chapter 2).

The Convention has been ratified by all 30 members of the OECD and by a growing number of non-members as well.[2] The Convention applies to bribery of foreign government officials anywhere, regardless of where the incident takes place. As a result of ratification, the 30 OECD member countries (and some non-members) have agreed to the principle of 'functional equivalence':

> The Convention requires countries to establish the bribery of foreign public officials as a **criminal offence** under their laws; and to ensure that the attempt and conspiracy to bribe foreign public officials shall be criminalised to the same extent as the bribery of national public officials (IMF 2001: 6).

The Convention is intended to serve as a deterrent to bribery.

It is important to note that the Convention criminalises offering and/or paying bribes, but not soliciting and/or accepting bribes. The Convention covers only the bribery of foreign officials and not private-to-private corruption. The Convention allows 'small facilitation payments' to low-ranking officials.

The Convention includes monitoring provisions, based on a peer review system common within the OECD framework. The OECD Working Group on Bribery in International Business Transactions reviews the implementing legislation of all the countries that have ratified the Convention. In a secondary phase, the Working Group examines the structures in place to ensure that the legislation is effective. The OECD welcomes a greater role for non-governmental organisations (NGOs), such as Transparency International, in the monitoring of the Convention.[3]

16.2 Strengths and weaknesses

The OECD works with a wide range of regional programmes to combat bribery, including the programmes of:

- The Council of Europe's Multidisciplinary Group on Corruption[4]
- The Anti-Corruption Network for Transition Economies[5]
- The Stability Pact Anti-Corruption Initiative for South Eastern Europe[6]

2 Argentina, Brazil and Chile have declared their commitment to the Convention but are not OECD members.

3 On the monitoring of the Convention by NGOs, see TICI 1998.

4 www.coe.int/t/dghl/monitoring/greco/general/2.%20historical%20background_EN.asp, accessed May 2010

5 www.anticorruptionnet.org

6 www.stabilitypact.org/anticorruption

- The Inter-American Convention Against Corruption[7]
- The Asian Development Bank/OECD Anti-Corruption Initiative for Asia-Pacific[8]

Despite this widespread co-operation, the corruption of public officials continues. According to Transparency International's Bribe Payers Index, local firms are more likely to bribe government officials than are multinational companies (Stoddard 2002). The Convention does not address bribery of officials by local business.

The Convention has been criticised for failing to capture the full extent of bribery. For example, it does not cover bribery of private-sector employees. Moreover, it fails to address the bribery of political parties and political candidates. The Convention provides no protection for whistle-blowers who uncover corruption, which can lead to reluctance to disclose incidents of bribery.

16.3 Companies to which the OECD Convention on Combating Bribery of Foreign Public Officials in International Business Transactions applies

The OECD Convention applies to all companies.

16.4 Questions posed and answered

The Convention poses and answers the following questions:

- How can bribery be defined?
- Despite differing legal systems, how can governments criminalise the bribery of foreign officials?
- How can adherence to the Convention be monitored?

16.5 The promise and the challenge

See Section 16.2. The OECD Convention applies only to bribery involving government officials, not to bribery of company staff.

7 www.oas.org/juridico/english/treaties/b-58.html
8 www.oecd.org/pages/0,2966,en_34982156_34982385_1_1_1_1_1,00.html

References

IMF (International Monetary Fund) (2001) *OECD Convention on Combating Bribery of Foreign Public Officials in International Business Transactions* (prepared by the Policy Development and Review Department; approved by J. Boorman; Washington, DC: IMF, 18 September 2001).

Stoddard, A. (2002) 'World: Corporate Bribery on the Rise Says Survey', Inter Press Service, 15 May 2002.

TICI (Transparency International Canada Inc.) (1998) 'The Coalition against Corruption in International Business Transactions: Checklist for Monitoring Implementation of OECD Convention', www.transparency.ca, accessed 2003.

Additional resources

Websites

Organisation for Economic Co-operation and Development: www.oecd.org

OECD Convention on Combating Bribery of Foreign Public Officials in International Business Transactions: www.oecd.org/document/21/0,2340,en_2649_34855_2017813_1_1_1_1,00.html

Convention on Combating Bribery of Foreign Public Officials in International Business Transactions*

On 21 November 1997, OECD Member countries and five non-member countries, Argentina, Brazil, Bulgaria, Chile and the Slovak Republic, adopted a Convention on Combating Bribery of Foreign Public Officials in International Business Transactions. Signature of the Convention took place in Paris on 17 December 1997.

PREAMBLE

The Parties,

Considering that bribery is a widespread phenomenon in international business transactions, including trade and investment, which raises serious moral and political concerns, undermines good governance and economic development, and distorts international competitive conditions;

Considering that all countries share a responsibility to combat bribery in international business transactions;

Having regard to the Revised Recommendation on Combating Bribery in International Business Transactions, adopted by the Council of the Organisation for Economic Co-operation and Development (OECD) on 23 May 1997, C(97)123/FINAL, which, inter alia, called for effective measures to deter, prevent and combat the bribery of foreign public officials in connection with international business transactions, in particular the prompt criminalisation of such bribery in an effective and co-ordinated manner and in conformity with the agreed common elements set out in that Recommendation and with the jurisdictional and other basic legal principles of each country;

Welcoming other recent developments which further advance international understanding and co-operation in combating bribery of public officials, including actions of the United Nations, the World Bank, the International Monetary Fund, the World Trade Organisation, the Organisation of American States, the Council of Europe and the European Union;

* The Preamble, 17 Articles and Commentaries reprinted with permission from 'The OECD Convention on Combating Bribery of Foreign Public Officials in International Business Transactions', 17 December 1997. © OECD 1997.

Welcoming the efforts of companies, business organisations and trade unions as well as other non-governmental organisations to combat bribery;

Recognising the role of governments in the prevention of solicitation of bribes from individuals and enterprises in international business transactions;

Recognising that achieving progress in this field requires not only efforts on a national level but also multilateral co-operation, monitoring and follow-up;

Recognising that achieving equivalence among the measures to be taken by the Parties is an essential object and purpose of the Convention, which requires that the Convention be ratified without derogations affecting this equivalence;

Have agreed as follows:

Article 1

The Offence of Bribery of Foreign Public Officials

1. Each Party shall take such measures as may be necessary to establish that it is a criminal offence under its law for any person intentionally to offer, promise or give any undue pecuniary or other advantage, whether directly or through intermediaries, to a foreign public official, for that official or for a third party, in order that the official act or refrain from acting in relation to the performance of official duties, in order to obtain or retain business or other improper advantage in the conduct of international business.

2. Each Party shall take any measures necessary to establish that complicity in, including incitement, aiding and abetting, or authorisation of an act of bribery of a foreign public official shall be a criminal offence. Attempt and conspiracy to bribe a foreign public official shall be criminal offences to the same extent as attempt and conspiracy to bribe a public official of that Party.

3. The offences set out in paragraphs 1 and 2 above are hereinafter referred to as "bribery of a foreign public official".

4. For the purpose of this Convention:

a. "foreign public official" means any person holding a legislative, administrative or judicial office of a foreign country, whether appointed or elected; any person exercising a public function for a foreign country, including for a public agency or public enterprise; and any official or agent of a public international organisation;

b. "foreign country" includes all levels and subdivisions of government, from national to local;

c. "act or refrain from acting in relation to the performance of official duties" includes any use of the public official's position, whether or not within the official's authorised competence.

Article 2
Responsibility of Legal Persons

Each Party shall take such measures as may be necessary, in accordance with its legal principles, to establish the liability of legal persons for the bribery of a foreign public official.

Article 3
Sanctions

1. The bribery of a foreign public official shall be punishable by effective, proportionate and dissuasive criminal penalties. The range of penalties shall be comparable to that applicable to the bribery of the Party's own public officials and shall, in the case of natural persons, include deprivation of liberty sufficient to enable effective mutual legal assistance and extradition.

2. In the event that, under the legal system of a Party, criminal responsibility is not applicable to legal persons, that Party shall ensure that legal persons shall be subject to effective, proportionate and dissuasive non-criminal sanctions, including monetary sanctions, for bribery of foreign public officials.

3. Each Party shall take such measures as may be necessary to provide that the bribe and the proceeds of the bribery of a foreign public official, or property the value of which corresponds to that of such proceeds, are subject to seizure and confiscation or that monetary sanctions of comparable effect are applicable.

4. Each Party shall consider the imposition of additional civil or administrative sanctions upon a person subject to sanctions for the bribery of a foreign public official.

Article 4
Jurisdiction

1. Each Party shall take such measures as may be necessary to establish its jurisdiction over the bribery of a foreign public official when the offence is committed in whole or in part in its territory.

2. Each Party which has jurisdiction to prosecute its nationals for offences committed abroad shall take such measures as may be necessary to establish its jurisdiction to do so in respect of the bribery of a foreign public official, according to the same principles.

3. When more than one Party has jurisdiction over an alleged offence described in this Convention, the Parties involved shall, at the request of one of them, consult with a view to determining the most appropriate jurisdiction for prosecution.

4. Each Party shall review whether its current basis for jurisdiction is effective in the fight against the bribery of foreign public officials and, if it is not, shall take remedial steps.

Article 5
Enforcement

Investigation and prosecution of the bribery of a foreign public official shall be subject to the applicable rules and principles of each Party. They shall not be influenced by considerations of national economic interest, the potential effect upon relations with another State or the identity of the natural or legal persons involved.

Article 6
Statute of Limitations

Any statute of limitations applicable to the offence of bribery of a foreign public official shall allow an adequate period of time for the investigation and prosecution of this offence.

Article 7
Money Laundering

Each Party which has made bribery of its own public official a predicate offence for the purpose of the application of its money laundering legislation shall do so on the same terms for the bribery of a foreign public official, without regard to the place where the bribery occurred.

Article 8
Accounting

1. In order to combat bribery of foreign public officials effectively, each Party shall take such measures as may be necessary, within the framework of its laws and regulations regarding the maintenance of books and records, financial statement disclosures, and accounting and auditing standards, to prohibit the establishment of off-the-books accounts, the making of off-the-books or inadequately identified transactions, the recording of non-existent expenditures, the entry of liabilities with incorrect identification of their object, as well as the use of false documents, by companies subject to those laws and regulations, for the purpose of bribing foreign public officials or of hiding such bribery.

2. Each Party shall provide effective, proportionate and dissuasive civil, administrative or criminal penalties for such omissions and falsifications in respect of the books, records, accounts and financial statements of such companies.

Article 9
Mutual Legal Assistance

1. Each Party shall, to the fullest extent possible under its laws and relevant treaties and arrangements, provide prompt and effective legal assistance to another Party for the purpose of criminal investigations and proceedings brought by a Party concerning offences within the scope of this Convention and for non-criminal proceedings within the scope of this Convention brought by a Party against a legal person. The requested Party shall inform the requesting Party, without delay, of any additional information or documents needed to support the request for assistance and, where requested, of the status and outcome of the request for assistance.

2. Where a Party makes mutual legal assistance conditional upon the existence of dual criminality, dual criminality shall be deemed to exist if the offence for which the assistance is sought is within the scope of this Convention.

3. A Party shall not decline to render mutual legal assistance for criminal matters within the scope of this Convention on the ground of bank secrecy.

Article 10
Extradition

1. Bribery of a foreign public official shall be deemed to be included as an extraditable offence under the laws of the Parties and the extradition treaties between them.

2. If a Party which makes extradition conditional on the existence of an extradition treaty receives a request for extradition from another Party with which it has no extradition treaty, it may consider this Convention to be the legal basis for extradition in respect of the offence of bribery of a foreign public official.

3. Each Party shall take any measures necessary to assure either that it can extradite its nationals or that it can prosecute its nationals for the offence of bribery of a foreign public official. A Party which declines a request to extradite a person for bribery of a foreign public official solely on the ground that the person is its national shall submit the case to its competent authorities for the purpose of prosecution.

4. Extradition for bribery of a foreign public official is subject to the conditions set out in the domestic law and applicable treaties and arrangements of each Party. Where a Party makes extradition conditional upon the existence of dual criminality, that condition shall be deemed to be fulfilled if the offence for which extradition is sought is within the scope of Article 1 of this Convention.

Article 11
Responsible Authorities

For the purposes of Article 4, paragraph 3, on consultation, Article 9, on mutual legal assistance and Article 10, on extradition, each Party shall notify to the Secretary-

General of the OECD an authority or authorities responsible for making and receiving requests, which shall serve as channel of communication for these matters for that Party, without prejudice to other arrangements between Parties.

Article 12
Monitoring and Follow-up

The Parties shall co-operate in carrying out a programme of systematic follow-up to monitor and promote the full implementation of this Convention. Unless otherwise decided by consensus of the Parties, this shall be done in the framework of the OECD Working Group on Bribery in International Business Transactions and according to its terms of reference, or within the framework and terms of reference of any successor to its functions, and Parties shall bear the costs of the programme in accordance with the rules applicable to that body.

Article 13
Signature and Accession

1. Until its entry into force, this Convention shall be open for signature by OECD members and by non-members which have been invited to become full participants in its Working Group on Bribery in International Business Transactions.

2. Subsequent to its entry into force, this Convention shall be open to accession by any non-signatory which is a member of the OECD or has become a full participant in the Working Group on Bribery in International Business Transactions or any successor to its functions. For each such non-signatory, the Convention shall enter into force on the sixtieth day following the date of deposit of its instrument of accession.

Article 14
Ratification and Depositary

1. This Convention is subject to acceptance, approval or ratification by the Signatories, in accordance with their respective laws.

2. Instruments of acceptance, approval, ratification or accession shall be deposited with the Secretary-General of the OECD, who shall serve as Depositary of this Convention.

Article 15
Entry into Force

1. This Convention shall enter into force on the sixtieth day following the date upon which five of the ten countries which have the ten largest export shares, and which represent by themselves at least sixty per cent of the combined total exports of those ten countries, have deposited their instruments of acceptance, approval, or ratification. For each signatory depositing its instrument after such entry into force, the Convention shall enter into force on the sixtieth day after deposit of its instrument.

2. If, after 31 December 1998, the Convention has not entered into force under paragraph 1 above, any signatory which has deposited its instrument of acceptance, approval or ratification may declare in writing to the Depositary its readiness to accept entry into force of this Convention under this paragraph 2. The Convention shall enter into force for such a signatory on the sixtieth day following the date upon which such declarations have been deposited by at least two signatories. For each signatory depositing its declaration after such entry into force, the Convention shall enter into force on the sixtieth day following the date of deposit.

Article 16
Amendment

Any Party may propose the amendment of this Convention. A proposed amendment shall be submitted to the Depositary which shall communicate it to the other Parties at least sixty days before convening a meeting of the Parties to consider the proposed amendment. An amendment adopted by consensus of the Parties, or by such other means as the Parties may determine by consensus, shall enter into force sixty days after the deposit of an instrument of ratification, acceptance or approval by all of the Parties, or in such other circumstances as may be specified by the Parties at the time of adoption of the amendment.

Article 17
Withdrawal

A Party may withdraw from this Convention by submitting written notification to the Depositary. Such withdrawal shall be effective one year after the date of the receipt of the notification. After withdrawal, co-operation shall continue between the Parties and the Party which has withdrawn on all requests for assistance or extradition made before the effective date of withdrawal which remain pending.

Commentaries on the Convention on Combating Bribery of Officials in International Business Transactions

Adopted by the Negotiating Conference on 21 November 1997

General:

1. This Convention deals with what, in the law of some countries, is called "active corruption" or "active bribery", meaning the offence committed by the person who promises or gives the bribe, as contrasted with "passive bribery", the offence committed by the official who receives the bribe. The Convention does not utilise the term "active bribery" simply to avoid it being misread by the non-technical reader as implying that the briber has taken the initiative and the recipient is a passive victim. In fact, in a number of situations, the recipient will have induced or pressured the briber and will have been, in that sense, the more active.

2. This Convention seeks to assure a functional equivalence among the measures taken by the Parties to sanction bribery of foreign public officials, without requiring uniformity or changes in fundamental principles of a Party's legal system.

Article 1. The Offence of Bribery of Foreign Public Officials:

Re paragraph 1:

3. Article 1 establishes a standard to be met by Parties, but does not require them to utilise its precise terms in defining the offence under their domestic laws. A Party may use various approaches to fulfil its obligations, provided that conviction of a person for the offence does not require proof of elements beyond those which would be required to be proved if the offence were defined as in this paragraph. For example, a statute prohibiting the bribery of agents generally which does not specifically address bribery of a foreign public official, and a statute specifically limited to this case, could both comply with this Article. Similarly, a statute which defined the offence in terms of payments "to induce a breach of the official's duty" could meet the standard provided that it was understood that every public official had a duty to exercise judgement or discretion impartially and this was an "autonomous" definition not requiring proof of the law of the particular official's country.

4. It is an offence within the meaning of paragraph 1 to bribe to obtain or retain business or other improper advantage whether or not the company concerned was the best qualified bidder or was otherwise a company which could properly have been awarded the business.

5. "Other improper advantage" refers to something to which the company concerned was not clearly entitled, for example, an operating permit for a factory which fails to meet the statutory requirements.

6. The conduct described in paragraph 1 is an offence whether the offer or promise is made or the pecuniary or other advantage is given on that person's own behalf or on behalf of any other natural person or legal entity.

7. It is also an offence irrespective of, inter alia, the value of the advantage, its results, perceptions of local custom, the tolerance of such payments by local authorities, or the alleged necessity of the payment in order to obtain or retain business or other improper advantage.

8. It is not an offence, however, if the advantage was permitted or required by the written law or regulation of the foreign public official's country, including case law.

9. Small "facilitation" payments do not constitute payments made "to obtain or retain business or other improper advantage" within the meaning of paragraph 1 and, accordingly, are also not an offence. Such payments, which, in some countries, are made to induce public officials to perform their functions, such as issuing licenses or permits, are generally illegal in the foreign country concerned. Other countries can and should address this corrosive phenomenon by such means as support for programmes of good governance. However, criminalisation by other countries does not seem a practical or effective complementary action.

10. Under the legal system of some countries, an advantage promised or given to any person, in anticipation of his or her becoming a foreign public official, falls within the scope of the offences described in Article 1, paragraph 1 or 2. Under the legal system of many countries, it is considered technically distinct from the offences covered by the present Convention. However, there is a commonly shared concern and intent to address this phenomenon through further work.

Re paragraph 2:

11. The offences set out in paragraph 2 are understood in terms of their normal content in national legal systems. Accordingly, if authorisation, incitement, or one of the other listed acts, which does not lead to further action, is not itself punishable under a Party's legal system, then the Party would not be required to make it punishable with respect to bribery of a foreign public official.

Re paragraph 4:

12. "Public function" includes any activity in the public interest, delegated by a foreign country, such as the performance of a task delegated by it in connection with public procurement.

13. A "public agency" is an entity constituted under public law to carry out specific tasks in the public interest.

14. A "public enterprise" is any enterprise, regardless of its legal form, over which a government, or governments, may, directly or indirectly, exercise a dominant influence. This is deemed to be the case, inter alia, when the government or governments hold the majority of the enterprise's subscribed capital, control the majority of votes attaching to shares issued by the enterprise or can appoint a majority of the members of the enterprise's administrative or managerial body or supervisory board.

15. An official of a public enterprise shall be deemed to perform a public function unless the enterprise operates on a normal commercial basis in the relevant market, i.e., on a basis which is substantially equivalent to that of a private enterprise, without preferential subsidies or other privileges.

16. In special circumstances, public authority may in fact be held by persons (e.g., political party officials in single party states) not formally designated as public officials. Such persons, through their *de facto* performance of a public function, may, under the legal principles of some countries, be considered to be foreign public officials.

17. "Public international organisation" includes any international organisation formed by states, governments, or other public international organisations, whatever the form of organisation and scope of competence, including, for example, a regional economic integration organisation such as the European Communities.

18. "Foreign country" is not limited to states, but includes any organised foreign area or entity, such as an autonomous territory or a separate customs territory.

19. One case of bribery which has been contemplated under the definition in paragraph 4.c is where an executive of a company gives a bribe to a senior official of a government, in order that this official use his office—though acting outside his competence—to make another official award a contract to that company.

Article 2. Responsibility of Legal Persons:

20. In the event that, under the legal system of a Party, criminal responsibility is not applicable to legal persons, that Party shall not be required to establish such criminal responsibility.

Article 3. Sanctions:

Re paragraph 3:

21. The "proceeds" of bribery are the profits or other benefits derived by the briber from the transaction or other improper advantage obtained or retained through bribery.

22. The term "confiscation" includes forfeiture where applicable and means the permanent deprivation of property by order of a court or other competent authority. This paragraph is without prejudice to rights of victims.

23. Paragraph 3 does not preclude setting appropriate limits to monetary sanctions.

Re paragraph 4:

24. Among the civil or administrative sanctions, other than non-criminal fines, which might be imposed upon legal persons for an act of bribery of a foreign public official are: exclusion from entitlement to public benefits or aid; temporary or permanent disqualification from participation in public procurement or from the practice of other commercial activities; placing under judicial supervision; and a judicial winding-up order.

Article 4. Jurisdiction:

Re paragraph 1:

25. The territorial basis for jurisdiction should be interpreted broadly so that an extensive physical connection to the bribery act is not required.

Re paragraph 2:

26. Nationality jurisdiction is to be established according to the general principles and conditions in the legal system of each Party. These principles deal with such matters as dual criminality. However, the requirement of dual criminality should be deemed to be met if the act is unlawful where it occurred, even if under a different criminal statute. For countries which apply nationality jurisdiction only to certain types of offences, the reference to "principles" includes the principles upon which such selection is based.

Article 5. Enforcement:

27. Article 5 recognises the fundamental nature of national regimes of prosecutorial discretion. It recognises as well that, in order to protect the independence of prosecution, such discretion is to be exercised on the basis of professional motives and is not to be subject to improper influence by concerns of a political nature. Article 5 is complemented by paragraph 6 of the Annex to the 1997 OECD Revised Recommendation on Combating Bribery in International Business Transactions, C(97)123/FINAL (hereinafter, "1997 OECD Recommendation"), which recommends, inter alia, that complaints of bribery of foreign public officials should be seriously investigated by competent authorities and that adequate resources should be provided by national governments to permit effective prosecution of such bribery. Parties will have accepted this Recommendation, including its monitoring and follow-up arrangements.

Article 7. Money Laundering:

28. In Article 7, "bribery of its own public official" is intended broadly, so that bribery of a foreign public official is to be made a predicate offence for money laundering legislation on the same terms, when a Party has made either active or passive bribery of its own public official such an offence. When a Party has made only passive bribery of its own public officials a predicate offence for money laundering purposes, this article requires that the laundering of the bribe payment be subject to money laundering legislation.

Article 8. Accounting:

29. Article 8 is related to section V of the 1997 OECD Recommendation, which all Parties will have accepted and which is subject to follow-up in the OECD Working Group on Bribery in International Business Transactions. This paragraph contains a series of recommendations concerning accounting requirements, independent external audit and internal company controls the implementation of which will be important to the overall effectiveness of the fight against bribery in international business. However, one immediate consequence of the implementation of this Convention by the Parties will be that companies which are required to issue financial statements disclosing their material contingent liabilities will need to take into account the full potential liabilities under this Convention, in particular its Articles 3 and 8, as well as other losses which might flow from conviction of the company or its agents for bribery. This also has implications for the execution of professional responsibilities of auditors regarding indications of bribery of foreign public officials. In addition, the accounting offences referred to in Article 8 will generally occur in the company's home country, when the bribery offence itself may have been committed in another country, and this can fill gaps in the effective reach of the Convention.

Article 9. Mutual Legal Assistance:

30. Parties will have also accepted, through paragraph 8 of the Agreed Common Elements annexed to the 1997 OECD Recommendation, to explore and undertake means to improve the efficiency of mutual legal assistance.

Re paragraph 1:

31. Within the framework of paragraph 1 of Article 9, Parties should, upon request, facilitate or encourage the presence or availability of persons, including persons in custody, who consent to assist in investigations or participate in proceedings. Parties should take measures to be able, in appropriate cases, to transfer temporarily such a person in custody to a Party requesting it and to credit time in custody in the requesting Party to the transferred person's sentence in the requested Party. The Parties wishing to use this mechanism should also take measures to be able, as a requesting Party, to keep a transferred person in custody and return this person without necessity of extradition proceedings.

Re paragraph 2:

32. Paragraph 2 addresses the issue of identity of norms in the concept of dual criminality. Parties with statutes as diverse as a statute prohibiting the bribery of agents generally and a statute directed specifically at bribery of foreign public officials should be able to co-operate fully regarding cases whose facts fall within the scope of the offences described in this Convention.

Article 10. Extradition:

Re paragraph 2:

33. A Party may consider this Convention to be a legal basis for extradition if, for one or more categories of cases falling within this Convention, it requires an extradition treaty. For example, a country may consider it a basis for extradition of its nationals if it requires an extradition treaty for that category but does not require one for extradition of non-nationals.

Article 12. Monitoring and Follow-up:

34. The current terms of reference of the OECD Working Group on Bribery which are relevant to monitoring and follow-up are set out in Section VIII of the 1997 OECD Recommendation. They provide for:

i) receipt of notifications and other information submitted to it by the [participating] countries;

ii) regular reviews of steps taken by [participating] countries to implement the Recommendation and to make proposals, as appropriate, to assist [participating] countries in its implementation; these reviews will be based on the following complementary systems:
   - a system of self evaluation, where [participating] countries' responses on the basis of a questionnaire will provide a basis for assessing the implementation of the Recommendation;
   - a system of mutual evaluation, where each [participating] country will be examined in turn by the Working Group on Bribery, on the basis of a report which will provide an objective assessment of the progress of the [participating] country in implementing the Recommendation.

iii) examination of specific issues relating to bribery in international business transactions;

. . .

v) provision of regular information to the public on its work and activities and on implementation of the Recommendation.

35. The costs of monitoring and follow-up will, for OECD Members, be handled through the normal OECD budget process. For non-members of the OECD, the current rules create an equivalent system of cost sharing, which is described in the Resolution of the Council Concerning Fees for Regular Observer Countries and Non-Member Full Participants in OECD Subsidiary Bodies, C(96)223/FINAL.

36. The follow-up of any aspect of the Convention which is not also follow-up of the 1997 OECD Recommendation or any other instrument accepted by all the participants in the OECD Working Group on Bribery will be carried out by the Parties to the Convention and, as appropriate, the participants party to another, corresponding instrument.

Article 13. Signature and Accession:

37. The Convention will be open to non-members which become full participants in the OECD Working Group on Bribery in International Business Transactions. Full participation by non-members in this Working Group is encouraged and arranged under simple procedures. Accordingly, the requirement of full participation in the Working Group, which follows from the relationship of the Convention to other aspects of the fight against bribery in international business, should not be seen as an obstacle by countries wishing to participate in that fight. The Council of the OECD has appealed to non-members to adhere to the 1997 OECD Recommendation and to participate in any institutional follow-up or implementation mechanism, i.e., in the Working Group. The current procedures regarding full participation by non-members in the Working Group may be found in the Resolution of the Council concerning the Participation of Non-Member Economies in the Work of Subsidiary Bodies of the Organisation, C(96)64/REV1/FINAL. In addition to accepting the Revised Recommendation of the Council on Combating Bribery, a full participant also accepts the Recommendation on the Tax Deductibility of Bribes of Foreign Public Officials, adopted on 11 April 1996, C(96)27/FINAL.

17
The Extractive Industries Transparency Initiative

> Lack of transparency undermines the confidence of the public in the legitimacy of those who hold the minerals in their trust. Wherever there is corruption, it is always the poor and marginalized who suffer most. It is therefore important to harness transparency in revenue and financial management to hold people in authority to account and help build public trust.
>
> *Joyce Aryee, CEO, Ghana Chamber of Mines*[1]

> The solution starts with transparency. A famous judge in my country once said that sunlight is the best disinfectant, and there is a lot of sunlight in Africa. African countries are starting to embrace this view through participation in the EITI. Creating a favorable investment climate requires countries to translate politics into governing.
>
> *Hillary Clinton*[2]

Type Principles, Performance, Process, Multi-stakeholder

Strength Applies to both companies and governments

Keywords Extractive • Mining • Oil • Gas validation • Validation

1 Dave Prescott, *EITI Business Guide: How Companies Can Support Implementation* (EITI and IBLF, 2008).

2 8th Forum of the African Growth and Opportunity Act, Nairobi, Kenya, 5 August 2009; US Department of State website, www.state.gov/secretary/rm/2009a/08/126902.htm.

17.1 Background

The Extractive Industries Transparency Initiative (EITI) has created a global standard for transparency in oil, gas and mining. In 2003, the EITI developed a list of principles that describe how companies and governments can promote transparency. Companies publish what they pay to mineral-rich governments in taxes and other payments. Receiving governments then publish what they receive. An independent auditor then compares the two figures.

The EITI promotes the use of systems and procedures that enable the transparent use of resources. Mineral-rich countries are asked to report on the revenues they receive. There are two categories for mineral-rich countries: candidate and compliant. Candidate countries have fully complied with four indicators approved by the EITI Board. One of the four indicators is to develop a work plan for implementation in consultation with stakeholders. Candidate countries have two years in which to become compliant.

To achieve compliant status, countries must receive an EITI validation. A validation is not an audit. The independent assessment reviews the country's progress and delineates which steps need to be taken to improve the process. A national multi-stakeholder group selects the Independent Validator, according to the EITI Validation Guide. As of Spring 2010, there are two compliant countries: Azerbaijan and Liberia.

Opened in 2007, the EITI secretariat is based in Oslo and oversees the implementation of the programme, and four regional offices.

17.2 Strengths and weaknesses

The EITI addresses itself to both governments and companies, creating a new framework for promoting transparency. The EITI's multi-stakeholder nature determines its success, but also poses challenges. In some of the candidate countries, civil society is not well developed.

There has been some controversy regarding how the data is presented, and whether data should be aggregated or disaggregated. The EITI Principles allow stakeholders to define what is appropriate for each country. Experience from the EITI suggests that 'in many countries this issue has been one of the most controversial discussed by stakeholders and, good company practice suggests that having an agreed and public statement on the matter can be helpful'.[3]

Edward Bickham of Anglo American praises the EITI but complains about its pace: 'The EITI has been slow in developing but is gaining momentum. One of the limits of the EITI is that most of the countries [Anglo American] operates in do not implement it.'[4]

3 *EITI Business Guide.*

4 Interview by D. Leipziger with Edward Bickham, cited in *Guide to Industry Initiatives in Corporate Social Responsibility: Your Guide to Selecting the Right Multi-stakeholder Initiative for your Company* (Ethical Corporation Institute, May 2009), p. 77.

17.3 Challenges and opportunities

One of the challenges and opportunities of the EITI is that candidate countries must define their own process. By providing this degree of flexibility, the EITI has created a viable and effective process.

Confidentiality may present a challenge to countries implementing the EITI. In some countries, confidentiality clauses exist that prevent disclosure of information that may be termed sensitive.[5] In cases where a confidentiality clause exists, parties may sign a Memorandum of Understanding which allows for a waiver of elements of the clause.

Funding for implementing EITI principles can come from several sources, including the national government or international agencies. For example, the World Bank manages a Multi-Donor Trust Fund, which provides technical assistance. Funding is available to candidate countries to assist in the implementation process. National development agencies, such as Germany's GTZ and the UK's Department for International Development provide financial resources for candidate countries. Multilateral agencies can also provide resources, including the African Development Bank and Norway's Oil for Development Initiative.

17.4 Companies to which the EITI applies

The EITI applies to companies that operate in the mining, oil and gas fields. However, it can also apply to companies within the supply chain: for example, companies providing logistics, human resources, information service, transportation, security, management, accountancy and auditing companies. Both upstream and downstream companies in the supply chain may participate in the EITI, even if they are not part of the extractive sector.[6]

Additional resources

Website

Extractive Industries Transparency Initiative: http://eitransparency.org

5 *EITI Business Guide*, p. 19.

6 *Ibid.*, p. 14.

The Extractive Industries Transparency Initiative*

THE EITI PRINCIPLES

1. We share a belief that the prudent use of natural resource wealth should be an important engine for sustainable economic growth that contributes to sustainable development and poverty reduction, but if not managed properly, can create negative economic and social impacts.
2. We affirm that management of natural resource wealth for the benefit of a country's citizens is in the domain of sovereign governments to be exercised in the interests of their national development.
3. We recognise that the benefits of resource extraction occur as revenue streams over many years and can be highly price dependent.
4. We recognise that a public understanding of government revenues and expenditure over time could help public debate and inform choice of appropriate and realistic options for sustainable development.
5. We underline the importance of transparency by governments and companies in the extractive industries and the need to enhance public financial management and accountability.
6. We recognise that achievement of greater transparency must be set in the context of respect for contracts and laws.
7. We recognise the enhanced environment for domestic and foreign direct investment that financial transparency may bring.
8. We believe in the principle and practice of accountability by government to all citizens for the stewardship of revenue streams and public expenditure.
9. We are committed to encouraging high standards of transparency and accountability in public life, government operations and in business,
10. We believe that a broadly consistent and workable approach to the disclosure of payments and revenues is required, which is simple to undertake and to use.
11. We believe that payments' disclosure in a given country should involve all extractive industry companies operating in that country.

12. In seeking solutions, we believe that all stakeholders have important and relevant contributions to make — including governments and their agencies, extractive industry companies, service companies, multilateral organisations, financial organisations, investors, and non-governmental organisations.

THE EITI CRITERIA

Implementation of EITI must be consistent with the criteria below:

1. Regular publication of all material oil, gas and mining payments by companies to governments ("payments") and all material revenues received by governments from oil, gas and mining companies ("revenues") to a wide audience in a publicly accessible, comprehensive and comprehensible manner.
2. Where such audits do not already exist, payments and revenues are the subject of a credible, independent audit, applying international auditing standards.
3. Payments and revenues are reconciled by a credible, independent administrator, applying international auditing standards and with publication of the administrator's opinion regarding that reconciliation including discrepancies, should any be identified.
4. This approach is extended to all companies including state-owned enterprises.
5. Civil society is actively engaged as a participant in the design, monitoring and evaluation of this process and contributes towards public debate.
6. A public, financially sustainable work plan for all the above is developed by the host government, with assistance from the international financial institutions where required, including measurable targets, a timetable for implementation, and an assessment of potential capacity constraints.

18 The Business Principles for Countering Bribery

> **Corruption has no respect for national boundaries. In an increasingly globalised world, corruption seriously distorts economic activity and denies people at large the benefits of their efforts. The scourge of corruption has to be confronted through increased cross-border co-operation. Focusing on countering bribery in the private sector is an important contribution to this endeavour.**
>
> *Peter Eigen, Chairman, Transparency International*[1]

Type Framework for companies, multi-stakeholder; process- and performance-oriented

Strength Flexibility

Keywords Bribery • Transparency International • Social Accountability International • Multi-stakeholder • Consultation • Non-governmental organisations • Policies • Procedures • Facilitation payments

18.1 Background

Published in December 2002, the Business Principles for Countering Bribery (hereafter referred to as the Principles) were developed through a multi-stakeholder dialogue including trade unions, companies, non-governmental organisations (NGOs) and academics, from many countries. The convenors of the dialogue are Transparency International and Social Accountability International (SAI). Transparency International was founded in 1993 to build coalitions to fight corruption.

1 www.transparency.org, accessed 2003

With some 90 chapters around the world, Transparency International views corruption as a barrier to development and human rights. SAI is an NGO, founded in 1997 to develop and promote workplace standards through multi-stakeholder dialogue. SAI has developed the Social Accountability 8000 (SA8000) standard and a process for accrediting certifiers to audit against SA8000 (see Chapter 8).

Companies are encouraged to apply (rather than adopt) the Principles by initiating their own internal process of setting policies and procedures within the company through consultation with stakeholders.

According to Transparency International and SAI, the Principles are still at an early stage of what promises to be a long-term process. The intent was to develop principles that could guide companies through a difficult terrain rather than to establish a difficult standard that few companies could meet. As such, the Principles are a 'living document' that will evolve as the field changes. For now, the Principles chart a course for companies on what constitutes good practice rather than best practice.

18.2 Strengths and weaknesses

The Principles are based on the OECD Convention on Combating Bribery of Foreign Public Officials in International Business Transactions (see Chapter 16) and the US Foreign Corrupt Practices Act (FCPA 1977). However, they go further than these foundation standards in that they also focus on private-to-private bribery, whereas the foundation standards focus exclusively on bribery of foreign government officials.

Practical, concise and comprehensive, the Principles require companies to comply with legislation. Companies need to create a 'trust-based and inclusive internal culture in which bribery is not tolerated' (see page 337). Companies are given parameters for setting their own anti-bribery systems and procedures.

The Principles set important definitions and systems for companies. They assert that senior managers of companies 'should monitor the Programme and periodically review the Programme's suitability, adequacy and effectiveness and implement improvements as appropriate' (see page 342). The Principles encourage companies to invest ultimate responsibility for anti-bribery programmes with the chief executive officer.

18.3 Companies to which the Business Principles for Countering Bribery apply

The Principles are designed for small, medium-sized and large companies.

18.4 Questions posed and answered

The Principles pose and answer the following question:

- Which parameters are useful for companies seeking to develop their own internal systems for combating corruption?

18.5 The promise and the challenge

Launched at a time of considerable 'code fatigue', the Principles will need to promote awareness of and provide training on the Principles around the world. As with other 'living documents', the Principles will need to evolve so as to promote accountability.

Reference

FCPA (Foreign Corrupt Practices Act) (1977) Current through Pub.L 105-366 (November 10, 1998) (Washington, DC: US Government Printing Office).

Additional resources

Websites

Business Principles for Countering Bribery:
www.transparency.org/global_priorities/private_sector/business_principles
Social Accountability International (SAI): www.sa-intl.org
Transparency International: www.transparency.org

The Business Principles for Countering Bribery*

1 INTRODUCTION

The Business Principles for Countering Bribery (the "Business Principles") have been developed by a group of private sector interests, non-governmental organisations and trade unions as a tool to assist enterprises to develop effective approaches to countering bribery in all of their activities.

The Business Principles also give practical effect to recent initiatives such as the OECD Convention on Combating Bribery of Foreign Public Officials in International Business Transactions, the ICC Rules of Conduct to Combat Extortion and Bribery and the anti-bribery provisions of the revised OECD Guidelines for Multinationals.

The Business Principles have been designed for use by large, medium and small enterprises. They apply to bribery of public officials and to private-to-private transactions. The purpose of the document is to provide practical guidance for countering bribery, creating a level playing field and providing a long-term business advantage.

2 THE BUSINESS PRINCIPLES

- **The enterprise shall prohibit bribery in any form whether direct or indirect**
- **The enterprise shall commit to implementation of a Programme to counter bribery**

These Business Principles are based on a commitment to fundamental values of integrity, transparency and accountability. Enterprises shall aim to create and maintain a trust-based and inclusive internal culture in which bribery is not tolerated.

The Programme is the entirety of an enterprise's anti-bribery efforts including values, policies, processes, training and guidance.

---

* Reproduced with the permission of Social Accountability International and Transparency International.

3 AIMS

The aims of the Business Principles are to:

- provide a framework for good business practices and risk management strategies for countering bribery.
- assist enterprises to:
    a) eliminate bribery
    b) demonstrate their commitment to countering bribery
    c) make a positive contribution to improving business standards of integrity, transparency and accountability wherever they operate.

4 DEVELOPMENT OF A PROGRAMME FOR COUNTERING BRIBERY

4.1 An enterprise should develop a Programme reflecting its size, business sector, potential risks and locations of operation, which should, clearly and in reasonable detail, articulate values, policies and procedures to be used to prevent bribery from occurring in all activities under its effective control.

4.2 The Programme should be consistent with all laws relevant to countering bribery in all the jurisdictions in which the enterprise operates, particularly laws that are directly relevant to specific business practices.

4.3 The enterprise should develop the Programme in consultation with employees, trade unions or other employee representative bodies.

4.4 The enterprise should ensure that it is informed of all matters material to the effective development of the Programme by communicating with relevant interested parties.

5 SCOPE OF THE PROGRAMME

In developing its Programme for countering bribery, an enterprise should analyse which specific areas pose the greatest risks from bribery.

The Programme should address the most prevalent forms of bribery relevant to the enterprise but at a minimum should cover the following areas:

5.1 Bribes

5.1.1 The enterprise should prohibit the offer, gift, or acceptance of a bribe in any form, including kickbacks, on any portion of a contract payment, or the use of other routes or channels to provide improper benefits to customers, agents, contractors, suppliers or employees of any such party or government officials.

5.1.2 The enterprise should also prohibit an employee from arranging or accepting a bribe or kickback from customers, agents, contractors, suppliers, or employees of any such party or from government officials, for the employee's benefit or that of the employee's family, friends, associates or acquaintances.

5.2 Political contributions

5.2.1 The enterprise, its employees or agents should not make direct or indirect contributions to political parties, organisations or individuals engaged in politics, as a way of obtaining advantage in business transactions.

5.2.2 The enterprise should publicly disclose all its political contributions.

5.3 Charitable contributions and sponsorships

5.3.1 The enterprise should ensure that charitable contributions and sponsorships are not being used as a subterfuge for bribery.

5.3.2 The enterprise should publicly disclose all its charitable contributions or sponsorships.

5.4 Facilitation payments

5.4.1 Recognising that facilitation payments[1] are a form of bribery, the enterprise should identify, minimise and preferably eliminate them.

5.5 Gifts, hospitality and expenses

5.5.1 The enterprise should prohibit the offer or receipt of gifts, hospitality or expenses whenever such arrangements could affect the outcome of business transactions and are not reasonable and bona fide expenditures.

6 PROGRAMME IMPLEMENTATION REQUIREMENTS

The following section sets out the requirements that enterprises should meet, at a minimum, when implementing the Programme.

6.1 Organisation and responsibilities

6.1.1 The Board of Directors or equivalent body should base their policy on the Business Principles and provide leadership, resources and active support for management's implementation of the Programme.

6.1.2 The Chief Executive Officer is responsible for ensuring that the Programme is carried out consistently with clear lines of authority.

6.1.3 The Board of Directors, Chief Executive Officer and senior management should demonstrate visible and active commitment to the implementation of the Business Principles.

6.2 Business relationships

The enterprise should apply its Programme in its dealings with subsidiaries, joint venture partners, agents, contractors and other third parties with whom it has business relationships.

6.2.1 *Subsidiaries and joint ventures*

6.2.1.1 The enterprise should conduct due diligence before entering into a joint venture.

6.2.1.2 The enterprise should ensure that subsidiaries and joint ventures over which it maintains effective control adopt its Programme. Where an enterprise does not have effective control it should make known its Programme and use its best efforts to monitor that the conduct of such subsidiaries and joint ventures is consistent with the Business Principles.

6.2.2 *Agents*

6.2.2.1 The enterprise should not channel improper payments through an agent.

6.2.2.2 The enterprise should undertake due diligence before appointing an agent.

6.2.2.3 Compensation paid to agents should be appropriate and justifiable remuneration for legitimate services rendered.

6.2.2.4 The relationship should be documented.

6.2.2.5 The agent should contractually agree to comply with the enterprise's Programme.

6.2.2.6 The enterprise should monitor the conduct of its agents and should have a right of termination in the event that they pay bribes.

6.2.3 *Contractors and suppliers*

6.2.3.1 The enterprise should conduct its procurement practices in a fair and transparent manner.

6.2.3.2 The enterprise should undertake due diligence in evaluating major prospective contractors and suppliers to ensure that they have effective anti-bribery policies.

6.2.3.3 The enterprise should make known its anti-bribery policies to contractors and suppliers. It should monitor the conduct of major contractors and suppliers and should have a right of termination in the event that they pay bribes.

6.2.3.4 The enterprise should avoid dealing with prospective contractors and suppliers known to be paying bribes.

6.3 Human resources

6.3.1 Recruitment, promotion, training, performance evaluation and recognition should reflect the enterprise's commitment to the Programme.

6.3.2 The human resources policies and practices relevant to the Programme should be developed and undertaken in consultation with employees, trade unions or other employee representative bodies as appropriate.

6.3.3 The enterprise should make it clear that no employee will suffer demotion, penalty, or other adverse consequences for refusing to pay bribes even if it may result in the enterprise losing business.

6.3.4 The enterprise should apply appropriate sanctions for violations of its Programme.

6.4 Training

6.4.1 Managers, employees and agents should receive specific training on the Programme.

6.4.2 Where appropriate, contractors and suppliers should receive training on the Programme.

6.5 Raising concerns and seeking guidance

6.5.1 To be effective, the Programme should rely on employees and others to raise concerns and violations as early as possible. To this end, the enterprise should provide secure and accessible channels through which employees and others should feel able to raise concerns and report violations ("whistle-blowing") in confidence and without risk of reprisal.

6.5.2 These channels should also be available for employees and others to seek advice or suggest improvements to the Programme. To support this process, the enterprise should provide guidance to employees and others with respect to the interpretation of the Programme in individual cases.

6.6 Communication

6.6.1 The enterprise should establish effective internal and external communication of the Programme.

6.6.2 The enterprise should, on request, publicly disclose the management systems it employs in countering bribery.

6.6.3 The enterprise should be open to receiving communications from relevant interested parties with respect to the Programme.

6.7 Internal controls and audit

6.7.1 The enterprise should maintain accurate books and records, available for inspection, which properly and fairly document all financial transactions. The enterprise should not maintain off-the-books accounts.

6.7.2 The enterprise should establish feedback mechanisms and other internal processes supporting the continuous improvement of the Programme.

6.7.3 The enterprise should subject the internal control systems, in particular the accounting and record keeping practices, to regular audits to provide assurance that they are effective in countering bribery.

6.8 Monitoring and review

6.8.1 Senior management of the enterprise should monitor the Programme and periodically review the Programme's suitability, adequacy and effectiveness and implement improvements as appropriate. They should periodically report to the Audit Committee or the Board the results of the Programme review.

6.8.2 The Audit Committee or the Board should make an independent assessment of the adequacy of the Programme and disclose its findings in the Annual Report to shareholders.

Note:

[1] Facilitation payments: Also called "facilitating", "speed" or "grease" payments, these are small payments made to secure or expedite the performance of a routine or necessary action to which the payer of the facilitation payment has legal or other entitlement.

Part VII
Corporate governance

> **Society sets the ethical framework within which those who run companies have to work out their own codes of conduct. Responsibility for decisions, therefore, runs both ways. Business has to take account of its responsibilities to society in coming to decisions, but society has to accept its responsibilities for setting the standards against which those decisions are made.**
>
> *Sir Adrian Cadbury, Ethics prize-winner, 1987*[1]

The majority of the codes and principles in this book relate to corporate responsibility, but Part VII discusses corporate governance—a theme that is inherently linked to corporate responsibility, yet a field apart. As corporate responsibility drills deeper into companies, the linkages between corporate governance and corporate responsibility are becoming more pronounced. As managers develop mechanisms for embedding social and environmental issues into the structure and 'DNA' of companies, they will need to interface with issues of corporate governance. To institutionalise corporate responsibility, companies will need to consider issues of corporate governance, including:

- What are the responsibilities of the board of directors in terms of social and environmental issues?
- How can the company develop reporting that makes it more accountable?

1 Cadbury 1987: 73.

Both corporate responsibility and corporate governance share a common vocabulary, with both fields making frequent references to 'accountability', 'transparency' and 'disclosure'. One of the challenges for corporate responsibility is to develop linkages to the field of corporate governance. The Enron and Ahold scandals demonstrate the increased need for this kind of integration. Both companies had well-developed codes of practice in corporate responsibility, but they had poor corporate governance structures, which permitted abuse.[2]

Corporate governance relates to the 'relationship between business and society' (McIntosh *et al.* 1998: 284). Corporate governance involves the relationship between boards of directors, senior management and shareholders, involving the way in which companies are controlled.[3]

According to the International Business Leaders' Forum (IBLF undated), corporate governance poses the following types of questions:

- **Accountability**. To whom are company directors accountable—to shareholders, or to a wider group of stakeholders, including, but not exclusively, shareholders?
- **Responsibility**. For what are company directors responsible or accountable: their financial performance alone, or their wider social, economic and environmental performance?
- **'Globality'**. Where are company directors accountable: in the home or base country of the company, or in all countries where the company operates?
- **Standard-setting**. Who is responsible for setting standards for corporate governance: government legislators, business bodies, non-governmental organisations (NGOs)—and how widely do they apply in terms of issues and geographies covered?
- **Monitoring** and **disclosure**. How is corporate behaviour against these standards monitored and disclosed to the public, and who does the monitoring?
- **Enforcement**. Related to the above points, how are standards for corporate governance most effectively, efficiently and fairly implemented—by regulation, voluntary approaches or some combination of both?'

There are hundreds of voluntary policies and recommendations on corporate governance. Several countries have issued guidelines on corporate governance, including: Australia, Canada, France, Japan, South Africa and the United Kingdom.[4] According to the OECD Principles of Corporate Governance, 'there is no single model of good corporate governance' (OECD 1999: 12). There is a great deal of variation in how companies are run, depending on their location, size and

2 For an excellent analysis of the Enron debacle and its lessons for corporate responsibility, see Sullivan 2002; for the Ahold scandal, see *Economist* 2003.

3 For more information on corporate governance, see Cheffins 2000; Elkington 1997.

4 For a full list of all guidelines see www.ecgi.org/codes/all_codes.php, accessed 11 June 2010.

sector and on other factors. Different countries face different regulatory structures, and different sectors face different constraints.

Progress in the field of corporate governance has been achieved through national committees, internationally agreed principles and a series of voluntary standards. Here, some of the work conducted at the national level is first examined. A number of UK committees have addressed corporate governance and have made significant contributions to the field:

- The Cadbury Committee (Committee on the Financial Aspects of Corporate Governance 1992) drafted the Cadbury Report and a Code of Best Practice on corporate governance. The Code makes recommendations about boards, non-executive directors, executives, controls and reporting.
- The Greenbury Committee (1995) in its report focused on the issue of setting executive pay, at the same time acknowledging the importance of shareholder participation.
- The Hampel Committee (1998), charged with reviewing the Cadbury and Greenbury reports, also identified principles of good corporate governance.

The London Stock Exchange then adopted many elements of the Hampel Report by integrating these recommendations into the Combined Code (LSE 1998 [revised 2002][5]), which includes Principles of Good Governance and a Code of Best Practice. Companies listed on the London Stock Exchange must include in their annual reports and accounts a description of how they are applying the OECD Principles of Good Governance.

In South Africa, the King Report made important contributions to the field of corporate governance. It includes The King Code on Corporate Governance for South Africa (reproduced at the end of this section, page 347), which encourages all South African companies to adopt a code of ethics and to develop affirmative action programmes. In 2009, the Institute of Directors issued the latest version, generally referred to as 'King III'.

The Commonwealth Association for Corporate Governance Guidelines (reproduced at the end of this section, page 374) also are among the key guides available to companies. These Guidelines are useful in linking corporate responsibility with corporate governance issues.

The next chapter presents a discussion of key sections of the OECD Principles of Corporate Governance.

5 See www.fsa.gov.uk/pubs/ukla/lr_comcode3.pdf.

References

Cadbury, A. (1987) 'Ethical Managers Make Their Own Rules', *Harvard Business Review* (September/October 1987).

Cheffins, B. (2000) 'Current Trends in Corporate Governance: Going from London to Milan via Toronto', *Duke Journal of Comparative and International Law* 10.

Committee on the Financial Aspects of Corporate Governance (1992) *Report with Code of Best Practice* ('The Cadbury Report'; London: Gee Publishing).

Economist (2003) 'Europe's Enron: Ahold's Shocking Accounting', *The Economist*, 1 March 2003.

Elkington, J. (1997) *Cannibals with Forks: The Triple Bottom Line of 21st Century Business* (Oxford, UK: Capstone Publishing).

IBLF (International Business Leaders' Forum) (undated) 'Business Standards and Corporate Governance Framing the Issue', www.iblf.org, accessed 2003.

Institute of Directors in Southern Africa (1994) *The King Report on Corporate Governance for South Africa* (Johannesburg: Institute of Directors in Southern Africa).

McIntosh, M., D. Leipziger, K. Jones and G. Coleman (1998) *Corporate Citizenship: Successful Strategies of Responsible Companies* (London: FT Pitman).

OECD (Organisation for Economic Co-operation and Development) (1999) *Principles of Corporate Governance* (Paris: OECD).

Sullivan, R. (2002) 'One Step Forward or Two Steps Back for Effective Self-regulation?', *Journal of Corporate Citizenship* 8 (Winter 2002): 91-104.

The King Code on Corporate Governance for South Africa (The Institute of Directors in Southern Africa) September 2009*

Corporate governance principles and practices are dynamic and evolve.

This Code of governance, which deals with the Principles, should be studied with the Report in which recommendations of the best practices for each principle are provided.

All entities should apply the principles in the Code and consider the best practice recommendations in the Report. All entities should

by way of explanation make a positive statement about how the principles have been applied or have not been applied. This level of disclosure will allow stakeholders to comment on and challenge the board on the quality of its governance. The application will differ for each entity and is likely to change as the aspirational nature of the Code should drive entities to continuously improve governance practices. It is important to understand that the 'apply or explain' approach requires more consideration and explanation of what has actually been done to implement the principles and best practice recommendations of governance.

Each principle is of equal importance and together forms a holistic approach to governance. Consequently, 'substantial' application of this Code and the Report does not achieve compliance.

Detailed implementation guidance and tools are provided in the Practice Notes.

Although the terms 'company', 'boards' and 'directors' are used, this Code and the Report refer to the functional responsibility of those charged with governance in any entity and should be adapted as appropriate.

* Reprinted with the permission of the Institute of Directors, South Africa. Known widely as 'King III'.

Governance element	Principle(s)	Recommended practice
1. Ethical leadership and corporate citizenship		
Responsible leadership	1.1 The board should provide effective leadership based on an ethical foundation	Ethical leaders should: 1.1.1. direct the strategy and operations to build a sustainable business; 1.1.2. consider the short- and long-term impacts of the strategy on the economy, society and the environment; 1.1.3. do business ethically; 1.1.4. do not compromise the natural environment; and 1.1.5. take account of the company's impact on internal and external stakeholders
The board's responsibilities		The board should: 1.1.6. be responsible for the strategic direction of the company and for the control of the company; 1.1.7. set the values to which the company will adhere formulated in its code of conduct; 1.1.8. ensure that its conduct and that of management aligns to the values and is adhered to in all aspects of its business; and 1.1.9. promote the stakeholder-inclusive approach of governance.
Ethical foundation		The board should: 1.1.10. ensure that all deliberations, decisions and actions are based on the four values underpinning good governance; and 1.1.11. ensure that each director adheres to the duties of a director.
	1.2. The board should ensure that the company is and is seen to be a responsible corporate citizen	The board should: 1.2.1. consider not only on financial performance but also the impact of the company's operations on society and the environment; 1.2.2. protect, enhance and invest in the wellbeing of the economy, society and the environment; 1.2.3. ensure that the company's performance and interaction with its stakeholders is guided by the Constitution and the Bill of Rights;

Governance element	Principle(s)	Recommended practice
		1.2.4. ensure that collaborative efforts with stakeholders are embarked upon to promote ethical conduct and good corporate citizenship; 1.2.5. ensure that measurable corporate citizenship programmes are implemented; and 1.2.6. ensure that management develops corporate citizenship policies.
	1.3. The board should ensure that the company's ethics are managed effectively	The board should ensure that: 1.3.1. it builds and sustains an ethical corporate culture in the company; 1.3.2. it determines the ethical standards which should be clearly articulated and ensures that the company takes measures to achieve adherence to them in all aspects of the business; 1.3.3. adherence to ethical standards is measured; 1.3.4. internal and external ethics performance is aligned around the same ethical standards; 1.3.5. ethical risks and opportunities are incorporated in the risk management process; 1.3.6. a code of conduct and ethics-related policies are implemented; 1.3.7. compliance with the code of conduct is integrated in the operations of the company; and 1.3.8. the company's ethics performance should be assessed, monitored, reported and disclosed.
2. Boards and directors		
Role and function of the board	2.1. The board should act as the focal point for and custodian of corporate governance	The board should: 2.1.1. have a charter setting out its responsibilities; 2.1.2. meet at least four times per year; 2.1.3. monitor the relationship between management and the stakeholders of the company; and 2.1.4. ensure that the company survives and thrives.

Governance element	Principle(s)	Recommended practice
	2.2. The board should appreciate that strategy, risk, performance and sustainability are inseparable	The board should: 2.2.1. inform and approve the strategy; 2.2.2. ensure that the strategy is aligned with the purpose of the company, the value drivers of its business and the legitimate interests and expectations of its stakeholders; 2.2.3. satisfy itself that the strategy and business plans are not encumbered by risks that have not been thoroughly examined by management; and 2.2.4. ensure that the strategy will result in sustainable outcomes taking account of people, planet and profit.
	2.3. The board should provide effective leadership based on an ethical foundation	Refer principle 1.1
	2.4. The board should ensure that the company is and is seen to be a responsible corporate citizen	Refer principle 1.2
	2.5. The board should ensure that the company's ethics are managed effectively	Refer principle 1.3
	2.6. The board should ensure that the company has an effective and independent audit committee	Refer to chapter 3
	2.7. The board should be responsible for the governance of risk	Refer to chapter 4
	2.8. The board should be responsible for information technology (IT) governance	Refer to chapter 5
	2.9. The board should ensure that the company complies with applicable laws and considers adherence to non-binding rules, codes and standards	Refer to chapter 6

Governance element	Principle(s)	Recommended practice
	2.10. The board should ensure that there is an effective risk-based internal audit	Refer to chapter 7
	2.11. The board should appreciate that stakeholders' perceptions affect the company's reputation	Refer to chapter 8
	2.12. The board should ensure the integrity of the company's integrated report	Refer to chapter 9
	2.13. The board should report on the effectiveness of the company's system of internal controls	Refer to chapters 7 and 9
	2.14. The board and its directors should act in the best interests of the company	2.14.1. The board must act in the best interests of the company. 2.14.2. Directors must adhere to the legal standards of conduct. 2.14.3. Directors or the board should be permitted to take independent advice in connection with their duties following an agreed procedure. 2.14.4. Real or perceived conflicts should be disclosed to the board and managed. 2.14.5. Listed companies should have a policy regarding dealing in securities by directors, officers and selected employees.
	2.15. The board should consider business rescue proceedings or other turnaround mechanisms as soon as the company is financially distressed as defined in the Act	The board should ensure that: 2.15.1. the solvency and liquidity of the company is continuously monitored; 2.15.2. its consideration is fair to save a financially distressed company either by way of workouts, sale, merger, amalgamation, compromise with creditors or business rescue; 2.15.3. a suitable practitioner is appointed if business rescue is adopted; and

Governance element	Principle(s)	Recommended practice
		2.15.4. the practitioner furnishes security for the value of the assets of the company.
	2.16. The board should elect a chairman of the board who is an independent non-executive director. The CEO of the company should not also fulfil the role of chairman of the board	2.16.1. The members of the board should elect a chairman on an annual basis. 2.16.2. The chairman should be independent and free of conflict upon appointment. 2.16.3. A lead independent director should be appointed in the case where an executive chairman is appointed or where the chairman is not independent or conflicted. 2.16.4. The appointment of a chairman, who is not independent, should be justified in the integrated report. 2.16.5. The role of the chairman should be formalised. 2.16.6. The chairman's ability to add value, and his performance against what is expected of his role and function, should be assessed every year. 2.16.7. The CEO should not become the chairman until 3 years have lapsed. 2.16.8. The chairman together with the board, should consider the number of outside chairmanships held. 2.16.9. The board should ensure a succession plan for the role of the chairman.
	2.17. The board should appoint the chief executive officer and establish a framework for the delegation of authority	The board should: 2.17.1. appoint the CEO; 2.17.2. provide input regarding senior management appointments; 2.17.3. define its own level of materiality and approve a delegation of authority framework; 2.17.4. ensure that the role and function of the CEO is formalised and the performance of the CEO is evaluated against the criteria specified; and

Governance element	Principle(s)	Recommended practice
		2.17.5. ensure succession planning for the CEO and other senior executives and officers is in place.
Composition of the board	2.18. The board should comprise a balance of power, with a majority of non-executive directors. The majority of non-executive directors should be independent	2.18.1. The majority of board members should be non-executive directors. 2.18.2. The majority of the non-executive directors should be independent. 2.18.3. When determining the number of directors serving on the board, the knowledge, skills and resources required for conducting the business of the board should be considered. 2.18.4. Every board should consider whether its size, diversity and demographics make it effective. 2.18.5. Every board should have a minimum of two executive directors of which one should be the CEO and the other the director responsible for finance. 2.18.6. At least one third of the non-executive directors should rotate every year. 2.18.7. The board, through its nomination committee, should recommend the eligibility of prospective directors. 2.18.8. Any independent non-executive directors serving more than 9 years should be subjected to a rigorous review of his independence and performance by the board. 2.18.9. The board should include a statement in the integrated report regarding the assessment of the independence of the independent non-executive directors. 2.18.10. The board should be permitted to remove any director without shareholder approval.
Board appointment process	2.19. Directors should be appointed through a formal process	2.19.1. A nomination committee should assist with the process of identifying suitable members of the board.

Governance element	Principle(s)	Recommended practice
		2.19.2. Background and reference checks should be performed before the nomination and appointment of directors. 2.19.3. The appointment of non-executive directors should be formalised through a letter of appointment. 2.19.4. The board should make full disclosure regarding individual directors to enable shareholders to make their own assessment of directors.
Director development	2.20. The induction of and ongoing training and development of directors should be conducted through formal processes	The board should ensure that: 2.20.1. a formal induction programme is established for new directors; 2.20.2. inexperienced directors are developed through mentorship programmes; 2.20.3. continuing professional development programmes are implemented; and 2.20.4. directors receive regular briefings on changes in risks, laws and the environment.
Company secretary	2.21. The board should be assisted by a competent, suitably qualified and experienced company secretary	2.21.1. The board should appoint and remove the company secretary. 2.21.2. The board should empower the individual to enable him to properly fulfil his duties. The company secretary should: 2.21.3. have an arm's-length relationship with the board; 2.21.4. not be a director of the company; 2.21.5. assist the nominations committee with the appointment of directors; 2.21.6. assist with the director induction and training programmes; 2.21.7. provide guidance to the board on the duties of the directors and good governance; 2.21.8. ensure board and committee charters are kept up to date; 2.21.9. prepare and circulate board papers;

Governance element	Principle(s)	Recommended practice
		2.21.10. elicit responses, input, feedback for board and board committee meetings; 2.21.11. assist in drafting yearly work plans; 2.21.12. ensure preparation and circulation of minutes of board and committee meetings; and 2.21.13. assist with the evaluation of the board, committees and individual directors.
Performance assessment	2.22. The evaluation of the board, its committees and the individual directors should be performed every year	2.22.1. The board should determine its own role, functions, duties and performance criteria as well as that for directors on the board and board committees to serve as a benchmark for the performance appraisal. 2.22.2. Yearly evaluations should be performed by the chairman or an independent provider. 2.22.3. The results of performance evaluations should identify training needs for directors. 2.22.4. An overview of the appraisal process, results and action plans should be disclosed in the integrated report. 2.22.5. The nomination for the re-appointment of a director should only occur after the evaluation of the performance and attendance of the director.
Board committees	2.23. The board should delegate certain functions to well-structured committees but without abdicating its own responsibilities	2.23.1. Formal terms of reference should be established and approved for each committee of the board. 2.23.2. The committees' terms of reference should be reviewed yearly. 2.23.3. The committees should be appropriately constituted and the composition and the terms of reference should be disclosed in the integrated report. 2.23.4. Public and state-owned companies must appoint an audit committee.

Governance element	Principle(s)	Recommended practice
		2.23.5. All other companies should establish an audit committee and define its composition, purpose and duties in the memorandum of incorporation. 2.23.6. Companies should establish risk, nomination and remuneration committees. 2.23.7. Committees, other than the risk committee, should comprise a majority of non-executive directors of which the majority should be independent. 2.23.8. External advisers and executive directors should attend committee meetings by invitation. 2.23.9. Committees should be free to take independent outside professional advice at the cost of the company subject to an approved process being followed.
Group boards	2.24. A governance framework should be agreed between the group and its subsidiary boards	2.24.1. Listed subsidiaries must comply with the rules of the relevant stock exchange in respect of insider trading. 2.24.2. The holding company must respect the fiduciary duties of the director serving in a representative capacity on the board of the subsidiary. 2.24.3. The implementation and adoption of policies, processes or procedures of the holding company should be considered and approved by the subsidiary company. 2.24.4. Disclosure should be made on the adoption of the holding company's policies in the integrated report of the subsidiary company.
Remuneration of directors and senior executives	2.25. Companies should remunerate directors and executives fairly and responsibly	2.25.1. Companies should adopt remuneration policies aligned with the strategy of the company and linked to individual performance. 2.25.2. The remuneration committee should assist the board in setting and administering remuneration policies.

Governance element	Principle(s)	Recommended practice
		2.25.3. The remuneration policy should address base pay and bonuses, employee contracts, severance and retirement benefits and share-based and other long-term incentive schemes. 2.25.4. Non-executive fees should comprise a base fee as well as an attendance fee per meeting.
	2.26. Companies should disclose the remuneration of each individual director and certain senior executives	The remuneration report, included in the integrated report, should include: 2.26.1. all benefits paid to directors; 2.26.2. the salaries of the three most highly-paid employees who are not directors; 2.26.3. the policy on base pay; 2.26.4. participation in share incentive schemes; 2.26.5. the use of benchmarks; 2.26.6. incentive schemes to encourage retention; 2.26.7. justification of salaries above the median; 2.26.8. material payments that are ex-gratia in nature; 2.26.9. policies regarding executive employment; and 2.26.10.the maximum expected potential dilution as a result of incentive awards.
	2.27. Shareholders should approve the company's remuneration policy	2.27.1. Shareholders should pass a non-binding advisory vote on the company's yearly remuneration policy. 2.27.2. The board should determine the remuneration of executive directors in accordance with the remuneration policy put to shareholder's vote.
3. Audit committees		
	3.1. The board should ensure that the company has an effective and independent audit committee	3.1.1. Listed and state-owned companies must establish an audit committee. 3.1.2. All other companies should establish an audit committee and define its composition, purpose and duties in the memorandum of incorporation.

Governance element	Principle(s)	Recommended practice
		3.1.3. The board should approve the terms of reference of the audit committee. 3.1.4. The audit committee should meet as often as is necessary to fulfil its functions but at least twice a year. 3.1.5. The audit committee should meet with internal and external auditors at least once a year without management being present.
Membership and resources of the audit committee	3.2. Audit committee members should be suitably skilled and experienced independent non-executive directors	3.2.1. All members of the audit committee should be independent non-executive directors. 3.2.2. The audit committee should consist of at least three members. 3.2.3. The chairman of the board should not be the chairman or member of the audit committee. 3.2.4. The committee collectively should have sufficient qualifications and experience to fulfil its duties. 3.2.5. The audit committee members should keep up-to-date with developments affecting the required skill-set. 3.2.6 The committee should be permitted to consult with specialists or consultants subject to a board-approved process. 3.2.7 The board must fill any vacancies on the audit committee.
	3.3. The audit committee should be chaired by an independent non-executive director	3.3.1. The board should elect the chairman of the audit committee. 3.3.2. The chairman of the audit committee should participate in setting and agreeing the agenda of the committee. 3.3.3. The chairman of the audit committee should be present at the AGM.
Responsibilities of the audit committee	3.4. The audit committee should oversee integrated reporting	3.4.1. The audit committee should have regard to all factors and risks that may impact on the integrity of the integrated report. 3.4.2. The audit committee should review and comment on the financial statements included in the integrated report.

Governance element	Principle(s)	Recommended practice
		3.4.3. The audit committee should review the disclosure of sustainability issues in the integrated report to ensure that it is reliable and does not conflict with the financial information. 3.4.4. The audit committee should recommend to the board to engage an external assurance provider on material sustainability issues. 3.4.5. The audit committee should consider the need to issue interim results. 3.4.6. The audit committee should review the content of the summarised information. 3.4.7. The audit committee should engage the external auditors to provide assurance on the summarised financial information.
	3.5. The audit committee should ensure that a combined assurance model is applied to provide a coordinated approach to all assurance activities	3.5.1. The audit committee should ensure that the combined assurance is received is appropriate to address all the significant risks facing the company. 3.5.2. The relationship between the external assurance providers and the company should be monitored by the audit committee.
Internal assurance providers	3.6. The audit committee should satisfy itself of the expertise, resources and experience of the company's finance function	3.6.1. Every year a review of the finance function should be performed by the audit committee. 3.6.2. The results of the review should be disclosed in the integrated report.
	3.7. The audit committee should be responsible for overseeing of internal audit	3.7.1. The audit committee should be responsible for the appointment, performance assessment and/or dismissal of the CAE. 3.7.2. The audit committee should approve the internal audit plan. 3.7.3. The audit committee should ensure that the internal audit function is subject to an independent quality review as and when the committee determines it appropriate.

Governance element	Principle(s)	Recommended practice
	3.8. The audit committee should be an integral component of the risk management process	3.8.1. The charter of the audit committee should set out its responsibilities regarding risk management. 3.8.2. The audit committee should specifically have oversight of: 3.8.2.1. financial reporting risks; 3.8.2.2. internal financial controls; 3.8.2.3. fraud risks as it relates to financial reporting; and 3.8.2.4. IT risks as it relates to financial reporting.
External assurance providers	3.9. The audit committee is responsible for recommending the appointment of the external auditor and overseeing the external audit process	The audit committee: 3.9.1. must nominate the external auditor for appointment; 3.9.2. must approve the terms of engagement and remuneration for the external audit engagement; 3.9.3. must monitor and report on the independence of the external auditor; 3.9.4. must define a policy for non-audit services provided by the external auditor and must approve the contracts for non-audit services; 3.9.5. should be informed of any Reportable Irregularities identified and reported by the external auditor; and 3.9.6. should review the quality and effectiveness of the external audit process.
Reporting	3.10. The audit committee should report to the board and shareholders on how it has discharged its duties	3.10.1. The audit committee should report internally to the board on its statutory duties and duties assigned to it by the board. 3.10.2. The audit committee must report to the shareholders on its statutory duties: 3.10.2.1. how its duties were carried out; 3.10.2.2. if the committee is satisfied with the independence of the external auditor; 3.10.2.3. the committee's view on the financial statements and the accounting practices; and 3.10.2.4. whether the internal financial controls are effective.

Governance element	Principle(s)	Recommended practice
		3.10.3. The audit committee should provide a summary of its role and details of its composition, number of meetings and activities, in the integrated report. 3.10.4. The audit committee should recommend the integrated report for approval by the board.
4. The governance of risk		
The board's responsibility for risk governance	4.1. The board should be responsible for the governance of risk	4.1.1. A policy and plan for a system and process of risk management should be developed. 4.1.2. The board should comment in the integrated report on the effectiveness of the system and process of risk management. 4.1.3. The board's responsibility for risk governance should be expressed in the board charter. 4.1.4. The induction and ongoing training programmes of the board should incorporate risk governance. 4.1.5. The board's responsibility for risk governance should manifest in a documented risk management policy and plan. 4.1.6. The board should approve the risk management policy and plan. 4.1.7. The risk management policy should be widely distributed throughout the company. 4.1.8. The board should review the implementation of the risk management plan at least once a year. 4.1.9. The board should ensure that the implementation of the risk management plan is monitored continually.
	4.2. The board should determine the levels of risk tolerance	4.2.1. The board should set the levels of risk tolerance once a year. 4.2.2. The board may set limits for the risk appetite. 4.2.3. The board should monitor that risks taken are within the tolerance and appetite levels.

Governance element	Principle(s)	Recommended practice
	4.3. The risk committee or audit committee should assist the board in carrying out its risk responsibilities	4.3.1. The board should appoint a committee responsible for risk. 4.3.2. The risk committee should: 4.3.2.1. consider the risk management policy and plan and monitor the risk management process; 4.3.2.2. have as its members executive and non-executive directors, members of senior management and independent risk management experts to be invited, if necessary; 4.3.2.3. have a minimum of three members; and 4.3.2.4. convene at least twice per year. 4.3.3. The performance of the committee should be evaluated once a year by the board.
Management's responsibility for risk management	4.4. The board should delegate to management the responsibility to design, implement and monitor the risk management plan	4.4.1. The board's risk strategy should be executed by management by means of risk management systems and processes. 4.4.2. Management is accountable for integrating risk in the day-to-day activities of the company. 4.4.3. The CRO should be a suitably experienced person who should have access and interact regularly on strategic matters with the board and/or appropriate board committee and executive management.
Risk assessment	4.5. The board should ensure that risk assessments are performed on a continual basis	4.5.1. The board should ensure effective and ongoing risk assessments are performed. 4.5.2. A systematic, documented, formal risk assessment should be conducted at least once a year. 4.5.3. Risks should be prioritised and ranked to focus responses and interventions. 4.5.4. The risk assessment process should involve the risks affecting the various income streams of the company, the critical dependencies of the business, the sustainability and the legitimate

Governance element	**Principle(s)**	**Recommended practice**
		interests and expectations of stakeholders. 4.5.5. Risk assessments should adopt a top-down approach. 4.5.6. The board should regularly receive and review a register of the company's key risks. 4.5.7. The board should ensure that key risks are quantified where practicable.
	4.6. The board should ensure that frameworks and methodologies are implemented to increase the probability of anticipating unpredictable risks	4.6.1. The board should ensure that a framework and processes are in place to anticipate unpredictable risks.
Risk response	4.7. The board should ensure that management considers and implements appropriate risk responses	4.7.1. Management should identify and note in the risk register the risk responses decided upon. 4.7.2. Management should demonstrate to the board that the risk response provides for the identification and exploitation of opportunities to improve the performance of the company.
Risk monitoring	4.8. The board should ensure continual risk monitoring by management	4.8.1. The board should ensure that effective and continual monitoring of risk management takes place. 4.8.2. The responsibility for monitoring should be defined in the risk management plan.
Risk assurance	4.9. The board should receive assurance regarding the effectiveness of the risk management process	4.9.1. Management should provide assurance to the board that the risk management plan is integrated in the daily activities of the company. 4.9.2. Internal audit should provide a written assessment of the effectiveness of the system of internal controls and risk management to the board.

Governance element	Principle(s)	Recommended practice
Risk disclosure	4.10. The board should ensure that there are processes in place enabling complete, timely, relevant, accurate and accessible risk disclosure to stakeholders	4.10.1. Undue, unexpected or unusual risks should be disclosed in the integrated report. 4.10.2. The board should disclose its view on the effectiveness of the risk management process in the integrated report.
5. The governance of information technology		
	5.1. The board should be responsible for information technology (IT) governance	5.1.1. The board should assume the responsibility for the governance of IT and place it on the board agenda. 5.1.2. The board should ensure that an IT charter and policies are established and implemented. 5.1.3. The board should ensure promotion of an ethical IT governance culture and awareness and of a common IT language. 5.1.4. The board should ensure that an IT internal control framework is adopted and implemented. 5.1.5. The board should receive independent assurance on the effectiveness of the IT internal controls.
	5.2. IT should be aligned with the performance and sustainability objectives of the company	5.2.1. The board should ensure that the IT strategy is integrated with the company's strategic and business processes. 5.2.2. The board should ensure that there is a process in place to identity and exploit opportunities to improve the performance and sustainability of the company through the use of IT.
	5.3. The board should delegate to management the responsibility for the implementation of an IT governance framework	5.3.1. Management should be responsible for the implementation of the structures, processes and mechanisms for the IT governance framework. 5.3.2. The board may appoint an IT steering committee of similar function to assist with its governance of IT.

Governance element	Principle(s)	Recommended practice
		5.3.3. The CEO should appoint a Chief Information Officer responsible for the management of IT. 5.3.4. The CIO should be a suitably qualified and experienced person who should have access and interact regularly on strategic IT matters with the board and/or appropriate board committee and executive management.
	5.4. The board should monitor and evaluate significant IT investments and expenditure	5.4.1. The board should oversee the value delivery of IT and monitor the return on investment from significant IT projects. 5.4.2. The board should ensure that intellectual property contained in information systems are protected. 5.4.3. The board should obtain independent assurance on the IT governance and controls supporting outsourced IT services.
	5.5. IT should form an integral part of the company's risk management	5.5.1. Management should regularly demonstrate to the board that the company has adequate business resilience arrangements in place for disaster recovery. 5.5.2. The board should ensure that the company complies with IT laws and that IT related rules, codes and standards are considered.
	5.6. The board should ensure that information assets are managed effectively	5.6.1. The board should ensure that there are systems in place for the management of information which should include information security, information management and information privacy. 5.6.2. The board should ensure that all personal information is treated by the company as an important business asset and is identified. 5.6.3. The board should ensure that an Information Security Management System is developed and implemented.

Governance element	Principle(s)	Recommended practice
		5.6.4. The board should approve the information security strategy and delegate and empower management to implement the strategy.
	5.7. A risk committee and audit committee should assist the board in carrying out its IT responsibilities	5.7.1. The risk committee should ensure that IT risks are adequately addressed. 5.7.2. The risk committee should obtain appropriate assurance that controls are in place and effective in addressing IT risks. 5.7.3. The audit committee should consider IT as it relates to financial reporting and the going concern of the company. 5.7.4. The audit committee should consider the use of technology to improve audit coverage and efficiency.
6. Compliance with laws, rules, codes and standards		
	6.1. The board should ensure that the company complies with applicable laws and considers adherence to nonbinding rules, codes and standards	6.1.1. Companies must comply with all applicable laws. 6.1.2. Exceptions permitted in law, shortcomings and proposed changes expected should be handled ethically. 6.1.3. Compliance should be an ethical imperative. 6.1.4. Compliance with applicable laws should be understood not only in terms of the obligations that they create, but also for the rights and protection that they afford. 6.1.5. The board should understand the context of the law, and how other applicable laws interact with it. 6.1.6. The board should monitor the company's compliance with applicable laws, rules, codes and standards. 6.1.7. Compliance should be a regular item on the agenda of the board. 6.1.8. The board should disclose details in the integrated report on how it discharged its responsibility to establish an effective compliance framework and processes.

Governance element	Principle(s)	Recommended practice
	6.2. The board and each individual director should have a working understanding of the effect of the applicable laws, rules, codes and standards on the company and its business	6.2.1. The induction and ongoing training programmes of directors should incorporate an overview of and any changes to applicable laws, rules, codes and standards. 6.2.2. Directors should sufficiently familiarise themselves with the general content of applicable laws, rules, codes and standards to discharge their legal duties.
	6.3. Compliance risk should form an integral part of the company's risk management process	6.3.1. The risk of non-compliance should be identified, assessed and responded to through the risk management processes. 6.3.2. Companies should consider establishing a compliance function.
	6.4. The board should delegate to management the implementation of an effective compliance framework and processes	6.4.1. The board should ensure that a legal compliance policy, approved by the board, has been implemented by management. 6.4.2. The board should receive assurance on the effectiveness of the controls around compliance with laws, rules, codes and standards. 6.4.3. Compliance with laws, rules, codes and standards should be incorporated in the code of conduct of the company. 6.4.4. Management should establish the appropriate structures, educate and train, and communicate and measure key performance indicators relevant to compliance. 6.4.5. The integrated report should include details of material or often repeated instances of non-compliance by either the company or its directors in their capacity as such. 6.4.6. An independent, suitably skilled compliance officer may be appointed. 6.4.7. The compliance officer should be a suitably skilled and experienced person who should have access and interact regularly on strategic compliance matters with the board and/or appropriate board

Governance element	Principle(s)	Recommended practice
		committee and executive management. 6.4.8. The structuring of the compliance function, its role and its position in terms of reporting lines should be a reflection of the company's decision on how compliance is to be integrated with its ethics and risk management. 6.4.9. The compliance function should have adequate resources to fulfil its function.
7. Internal audit		
The need for and role of internal audit	7.1. The board should ensure that there is an effective risk based internal audit	7.1.1. Companies should establish an internal audit function. 7.1.2. Internal audit should perform the following functions: 7.1.2.1. evaluate the company's governance processes; 7.1.2.2. perform an objective assessment of the effectiveness of risk management and the internal control framework; 7.1.2.3. systematically analyse and evaluating business processes and associated controls; and 7.1.2.4. provide a source of information as appropriate, regarding instances of fraud, corruption, unethical behaviour and irregularities. 7.1.3. An internal audit charter should be defined and approved by the board. 7.1.4. The internal audit function should adhere to the IIA Standards and code of ethics.
Internal audit's approach and plan	7.2. Internal audit should follow a risk based approach to its plan	7.2.1. The internal audit plan and approach should be informed by the strategy and risks of the company. 7.2.2. Internal audit should be independent from management. 7.2.3. Internal audit should be an objective provider of assurance that considers:

Governance element	Principle(s)	Recommended practice
		7.2.3.1. the risks that may prevent or slow down the realisation of strategic goals; 7.2.3.2. whether controls are in place and functioning effectively to mitigate these; and 7.2.3.3. the opportunities that will promote the realisation of strategic goals that are identified, assessed and effectively managed by the company's management team.
	7.3. Internal audit should provide a written assessment of the effectiveness of the company's system of internal controls and risk management	7.3.1. Internal audit should form an integral part of the combined assurance model as internal assurance provider. 7.3.2. Internal controls should be established not only over financial matters, but also operational, compliance and sustainability issues. 7.3.3. Companies should maintain an effective governance, risk management and internal control framework. 7.3.4. Management should specify the elements of the control framework. 7.3.5. Internal audit should provide a written assessment of the system of internal controls and risk management to the board. 7.3.6. Internal audit should provide a written assessment of internal financial controls to the audit committee.
	7.4. The audit committee should be responsible for overseeing internal audit	7.4.1. The internal audit plan should be agreed and approved by the audit committee. 7.4.2. The audit committee should evaluate the performance of the internal audit function. 7.4.3. The audit committee should ensure that the internal audit function is subjected to an independent quality review. 7.4.4. The CAE should report functionally to the audit committee chairman.

Governance element	Principle(s)	Recommended practice
		7.4.5. The audit committee should be responsible for the appointment, performance assessment and dismissal of the CAE. 7.4.6. The audit committee should ensure that the internal audit function is appropriately resourced and has appropriate budget allocated to the function. 7.4.7. Internal audit should report at all audit committee meetings.
Internal audit's status in the company	7.5. Internal audit should be strategically positioned to achieve its objectives	7.5.1. The internal audit function should be independent and objective. 7.5.2. The internal audit function should report functionally to the audit committee. 7.5.3. The CAE should have a standing invitation to attend executive committee meetings. 7.5.4. The internal audit function should be skilled and resourced as is appropriate for the complexity and volume of risk and assurance needs. 7.5.5. The CAE should develop and maintain a quality assurance and improvement programme.
8. Governing stakeholder relationships		
	8.1. The board should appreciate that stakeholders' perceptions affect a company's reputation	8.1.1. The gap between stakeholder perceptions and the performance of the company should be managed and measured to enhance or protect the company's reputation. 8.1.2. The company's reputation and its linkage with stakeholder relationships should be a regular board agenda item. 8.1.3. The board should identify important stakeholder groupings.
	8.2. The board should delegate to management to proactively deal with stakeholder relationships	8.2.1. Management should develop a strategy and formulate policies for the management of relationships with each stakeholder grouping. 8.2.2. The board should consider whether it is appropriate to publish its stakeholder policies.

Governance element	Principle(s)	Recommended practice
		8.2.3. The board should oversee the establishment of mechanisms and processes that support stakeholders in constructive engagement with the company. 8.2.4. The board should encourage shareholders to attend AGMs. 8.2.5. The board should consider not only formal, but also informal, processes for interaction with the company's stakeholders. 8.2.6. The board should disclose in its integrated report the nature of the company's dealings with stakeholders and the outcomes of these dealings.
	8.3. The board should strive to achieve the appropriate balance between its various stakeholder groupings, in the best interests of the company	8.3.1. The board should take account of the legitimate interests and expectations of its stakeholders in its decision-making in the best interests of the company.
	8.4. Companies should ensure the equitable treatment of shareholders	8.4.1 There must be equitable treatment of all holders of the same class of shares issued. 8.4.2. The board should ensure that minority shareholders are protected.
	8.5. Transparent and effective communication with stakeholders is essential for building and maintaining their trust and confidence	8.5.1. Complete, timely, relevant, accurate, honest and accessible information should be provided by the company to its stakeholders whilst having regard to legal and strategic considerations. 8.5.2. Communication with stakeholders should be in clear and understandable language. 8.5.3. The board should adopt communication guidelines that support a responsible communication programme. 8.5.4. The board should consider disclosing in the integrated report the number and reasons for refusals of requests of information that were lodged with the company in terms of the Promotion of Access to Information Act, 2000.

Governance element	Principle(s)	Recommended practice
Dispute resolution	8.6. The board should ensure that disputes are resolved as effectively, efficiently and expeditiously as possible	8.6.1. The board should adopt formal dispute resolution processes for internal and external disputes. 8.6.2. The board should select the appropriate individuals to represent the company in ADR.
9. Integrated reporting and disclosure		
Transparency and accountability	9.1. The board should ensure the integrity of the company's integrated report	9.1.1. A company should have controls to enable it to verify and safeguard the integrity of its integrated report. 9.1.2. The board should delegate to the audit committee to evaluate sustainability disclosures. The integrated report should: 9.1.3. be prepared every year; 9.1.4. convey adequate information regarding the company's financial and sustainability performance; and 9.1.5. focus on substance over form.
	9.2. Sustainability reporting and disclosure should be integrated with the company's financial reporting	9.2.1. The board should include commentary on the company's financial results. 9.2.2. The board must disclose if the company is a going concern. 9.2.3. The integrated report should describe how the company has made its money. 9.2.4. The board should ensure that the positive and negative impacts of the company's operations and plans to improve the positives and eradicate or ameliorate the negatives in the financial year ahead are conveyed in the integrated report.
	9.3. Sustainability reporting and disclosure should be independently assured	9.3.1. General oversight and reporting of sustainability should be delegated by the board to the audit committee. 9.3.2. The audit committee should assist the board by reviewing the integrated report to ensure that the information contained in it is reliable and that it does not contradict the financial aspects of the report.

Governance element	Principle(s)	Recommended practice
		9.3.3. The audit committee should oversee the provision of assurance over sustainability issues.

Encouraging Good Governance: Commonwealth Corporate Governance Principles

The Commonwealth Business Council has published corporate governance principles in association with the Commonwealth Association for Corporate Governance in the publication *Principles for Corporate Governance in the Commonwealth: Towards Global Competitiveness and Economic Accountability*. The Commonwealth corporate governance principles are given below.

COMMONWEALTH CORPORATE GOVERNANCE PRINCIPLES

The board should:

Principle 1: Exercise leadership, enterprise, integrity and judgement in directing the corporation so as to achieve continuing prosperity for the corporation and to act in the best interest of the business enterprise in a manner based on transparency, accountability and responsibility;

Principle 2: Ensure that through a managed and effective process board appointments are made that provide a mix of proficient directors, each of whom is able to add value and to bring independent judgement to bear on the decision-making process;

Principle 3: Determine the corporation's purpose and values, determine the strategy to achieve its purpose and to implement its values in order to ensure that it survives and thrives, and ensure that procedures and practices are in place that protect the corporation's assets and reputation;

Principle 4: Monitor and evaluate the implementation of strategies, policies, management performance criteria and business plans;

Principle 5: Ensure that the corporation complies with all relevant laws, regulations and codes of best business practice;

Principle 6: Ensure that the corporation communicates with shareholders and other stakeholders effectively;

Principle 7: Serve the legitimate interests of the shareholders of the corporation and account to them fully;

Principle 8: Identify the corporation's internal and external stakeholders and agree a policy, or policies, determining how the corporation should relate to them;

Principle 9: Ensure that no one person or block of persons has unfettered power and that there is an appropriate balance of power and authority on the board which is, inter alia, usually reflected by separating the roles of chief executive officer and chairman, and by having a balance between executive and non-executive directors;

Principle 10: Regularly review processes and procedures to ensure the effectiveness of its internal systems of control, so that its decision-making capability and the accuracy of its reporting and financial results are maintained at a high level at all times;

Principle 11: Regularly assess its performance and effectiveness as a whole, and that of the individual directors, including the chief executive officer;

Principle 12: Appoint the chief executive officer and at least participate in the appointment of senior management, ensure the motivation and protection of intellectual capital intrinsic to the corporation, ensure that there is adequate training in the corporation for management and employees, and a succession plan for senior management;

Principle 13: Ensure that all technology and systems used in the corporation are adequate to properly run the business and for it to remain a meaningful competitor;

Principle 14: Identify key risk areas and key performance indicators of the business enterprise and monitor these factors;

Principle 15: Ensure annually that the corporation will continue as a going concern for its next fiscal year.

19
The OECD Principles of Corporate Governance

> **Corporate governance can be defined in a dual context. On the one hand it is a set of behavioural relationships through which enterprises are directed and controlled. Organisational know-how, managerial talent and personal incentives are important elements in this web. But it can also be described in terms of the public and private rules that specify the distribution of rights and responsibilities among different participants in an enterprise, such as managers, the board, the shareholders, the employees and other stakeholders. I believe that one of the key advantages of the OECD Principles of Corporate Governance is that they address both the behavioural and regulatory aspects of the corporate governance debate.**
>
> ***Seiichi Kondo, Deputy Secretary-General of the OECD***[1]

Type Non-binding principles; process- and performance-oriented

Strength Clarity

Keywords Shareholders • Stakeholders • Disclosure • Transparency • Board of directors • Corporate governance

1 'Opening Remarks to the Eurasian Corporate Governance Roundtable', 2000, www.gaap.ru, accessed 2003.

19.1 Background

Endorsed in 1999 by the Organisation for Economic Co-operation and Development (OECD), the Principles of Corporate Governance (hereafter in this chapter referred to as the Principles) represent the first initiative by an intergovernmental organisation to develop guiding principles in the field of corporate governance. The Principles are directed at a wide audience, including governments, companies, investors, business groups and others. The Principles are accepted by the Financial Stability Forum as one of its 12 key international standards[2] and have also been endorsed by the World Bank and the International Monetary Fund (IMF). Moreover, they have formed the basis for many national principles.

The OECD promotes policies that contribute to economic growth and development. Founded in 1961, the OECD is an organisation of governments from 30 countries (for a full list of member countries, see footnote 3 on page 61). The OECD has also made a significant contribution to corporate responsibility by developing several CR-related principles, including the OECD Guidelines for Multinational Enterprises (see Chapter 2) and the OECD Convention on Combating Bribery of Foreign Public Officials in International Business Transactions (see Chapter 16).

The OECD makes it clear that the Principles represent minimum standards. The Principles address the following issues:

- The rights of shareholders
- The equitable treatment of shareholders
- The role of stakeholders
- Disclosure and transparency
- The responsibilities of the board of directors

19.2 Strengths and weaknesses

The Principles were drafted so as to be a clear and accessible reference point for considering corporate governance arrangements. They are drafted in the form of aspirational principles and avoid prescription. They are therefore applicable in countries with widely varying institutions, legal systems and corporate governance traditions. The Principles were agreed following extensive consultation among key stakeholders so that they enjoy widespread support.

2 www.oecd.org/document/49/0,3343,en_2649_34813_31530865_1_1_1_1,00.html, accessed May 2010

19.3 Companies to which the OECD Principles of Corporate Governance apply

The OECD Principles apply to all companies, but are most relevant to publicly traded companies.

19.4 Questions posed and answered

The OECD Principles address the following questions:

- What are the fundamental rights of shareholders?
- What is the role of stakeholders in the corporate governance framework?
- What constitutes adequate disclosure and transparency standards for companies?
- What are the responsibilities and functions of the board of directors or the supervisory board?

19.5 The promise and the challenge

The G8 and the G22 have asked the OECD and the World Bank to promote corporate governance in emerging markets. To achieve this, the OECD and the World Bank have developed roundtables to discuss corporate governance standards,[3] resulting in white papers setting priorities for each region.[4] The challenge is now for the countries in each region to design, implement and enforce policies to improve their corporate governance arrangements. The work of the roundtables, supported by the OECD, will now shift to monitoring implementation and comparing experiences (www.oecd.org).

The challenge for the OECD Principles (and for corporate governance in general) will be to evolve to deal adequately with new issues arising in the corporate landscape. To this end, the Principles were revised in 2004, following a period of consultation with the private sector, trade unions and NGOs and a period of public comments.

The revised version of the Principles includes important clauses concerning stakeholders:

> Stakeholders, including individual employees and their representative bodies, should be able to freely communicate their concerns

3 www.oecd.org/department/0,2688,en_2649_34813_1_1_1_1_1,00.html
4 *Ibid.*

about illegal or unethical practices to the board and their rights should not be compromised for doing this.

The 2004 revision also provides additional guidance on shareholders:

> Shareholders, including institutional shareholders, should be allowed to consult with each other on issues concerning their basic shareholder rights as defined in the Principles, subject to exceptions to prevent abuse. Impediments to cross border voting should be eliminated.

Additional resources

Websites

OECD Corporate Governance Principles:
www.oecd.org/department/0,2688,en_2649_34813_1_1_1_1_1,00.html.

OECD Corporate Governance Principles (text):
www.oecd.org/document/49/0,3343,en_2649_34813_31530865_1_1_1_1,00.html

OECD Principles of Corporate Governance*

I. ENSURING THE BASIS FOR AN EFFECTIVE CORPORATE GOVERNANCE FRAMEWORK

The corporate governance framework should promote transparent and efficient markets, be consistent with the rule of law and clearly articulate the division of responsibilities among different supervisory, regulatory and enforcement authorities.

A. The corporate governance framework should be developed with a view to its impact on overall economic performance, market integrity and the incentives it creates for market participants and the promotion of transparent and efficient markets.

B. The legal and regulatory requirements that affect corporate governance practices in a jurisdiction should be consistent with the rule of law, transparent and enforceable.

C. The division of responsibilities among different authorities in a jurisdiction should be clearly articulated and ensure that the public interest is served.

D. Supervisory, regulatory and enforcement authorities should have the authority, integrity and resources to fulfil their duties in a professional and objective manner. Moreover, their rulings should be timely, transparent and fully explained.

II. THE RIGHTS OF SHAREHOLDERS AND KEY OWNERSHIP FUNCTIONS

The corporate governance framework should protect and facilitate the exercise of shareholders' rights.

A. Basic shareholder rights should include the right to: 1) secure methods of ownership registration; 2) convey or transfer shares; 3) obtain relevant and material information on the corporation on a timely and regular basis; 4) participate and vote in general shareholder meetings; 5) elect and remove members of the board; and 6) share in the profits of the corporation.

B. Shareholders should have the right to participate in, and to be sufficiently informed on, decisions concerning fundamental corporate changes such as: 1) amendments to the statutes, or articles of incorporation or similar governing documents of the company; 2) the authorisation of additional shares; and 3) extraordinary transactions, including the transfer of all or substantially all assets, that in effect result in the sale of the company.

C. Shareholders should have the opportunity to participate effectively and vote in general shareholder meetings and should be informed of the rules, including voting procedures, that govern general shareholder meetings:

1. Shareholders should be furnished with sufficient and timely information concerning the date, location and agenda of general meetings, as well as full and timely information regarding the issues to be decided at the meeting.
2. Shareholders should have the opportunity to ask questions to the board, including questions relating to the annual external audit, to place items on the agenda of general meetings, and to propose resolutions, subject to reasonable limitations.
3. Effective shareholder participation in key corporate governance decisions, such as the nomination and election of board members, should be facilitated. Shareholders should be able to make their views known on the remuneration policy for board members and key executives. The equity component of compensation schemes for board members and employees should be subject to shareholder approval.
4. Shareholders should be able to vote in person or in absentia, and equal effect should be given to votes whether cast in person or in absentia.

D. Capital structures and arrangements that enable certain shareholders to obtain a degree of control disproportionate to their equity ownership should be disclosed.

E. Markets for corporate control should be allowed to function in an efficient and transparent manner.

1. The rules and procedures governing the acquisition of corporate control in the capital markets, and extraordinary transactions such as mergers, and sales of substantial portions of corporate assets, should be clearly articulated and disclosed so that investors understand their rights and recourse. Transactions should occur at transparent prices and under fair conditions that protect the rights of all shareholders according to their class.
2. Anti-take-over devices should not be used to shield management and the board from accountability.

F. The exercise of ownership rights by all shareholders, including institutional investors, should be facilitated.

1. Institutional investors acting in a fiduciary capacity should disclose their overall corporate governance and voting policies with respect to their

investments, including the procedures that they have in place for deciding on the use of their voting rights.

2. Institutional investors acting in a fiduciary capacity should disclose how they manage material conflicts of interest that may affect the exercise of key ownership rights regarding their investments.

G. Shareholders, including institutional shareholders, should be allowed to consult with each other on issues concerning their basic shareholder rights as defined in the Principles, subject to exceptions to prevent abuse.

III. THE EQUITABLE TREATMENT OF SHAREHOLDERS

The corporate governance framework should ensure the equitable treatment of all shareholders, including minority and foreign shareholders. All shareholders should have the opportunity to obtain effective redress for violation of their rights.

A. All shareholders of the same series of a class should be treated equally.

1. Within any series of a class, all shares should carry the same rights. All investors should be able to obtain information about the rights attached to all series and classes of shares before they purchase. Any changes in voting rights should be subject to approval by those classes of shares which are negatively affected.
2. Minority shareholders should be protected from abusive actions by, or in the interest of, controlling shareholders acting either directly or indirectly, and should have effective means of redress.
3. Votes should be cast by custodians or nominees in a manner agreed upon with the beneficial owner of the shares.
4. Impediments to cross border voting should be eliminated.
5. Processes and procedures for general shareholder meetings should allow for equitable treatment of all shareholders. Company procedures should not make it unduly difficult or expensive to cast votes.

B. Insider trading and abusive self-dealing should be prohibited.

C. Members of the board and key executives should be required to disclose to the board whether they, directly, indirectly or on behalf of third parties, have a material interest in any transaction or matter directly affecting the corporation.

IV. THE ROLE OF STAKEHOLDERS IN CORPORATE GOVERNANCE

The corporate governance framework should recognise the rights of stakeholders established by law or through mutual agreements and

encourage active co-operation between corporations and stakeholders in creating wealth, jobs, and the sustainability of financially sound enterprises.

A. The rights of stakeholders that are established by law or through mutual agreements are to be respected.

B. Where stakeholder interests are protected by law, stakeholders should have the opportunity to obtain effective redress for violation of their rights.

C. Performance-enhancing mechanisms for employee participation should be permitted to develop.

D. Where stakeholders participate in the corporate governance process, they should have access to relevant, sufficient and reliable information on a timely and regular basis.

E. Stakeholders, including individual employees and their representative bodies, should be able to freely communicate their concerns about illegal or unethical practices to the board and their rights should not be compromised for doing this.

F. The corporate governance framework should be complemented by an effective, efficient insolvency framework and by effective enforcement of creditor rights.

V. DISCLOSURE AND TRANSPARENCY

The corporate governance framework should ensure that timely and accurate disclosure is made on all material matters regarding the corporation, including the financial situation, performance, ownership, and governance of the company.

A. Disclosure should include, but not be limited to, material information on:

1. The financial and operating results of the company.
2. Company objectives.
3. Major share ownership and voting rights.
4. Remuneration policy for members of the board and key executives, and information about board members, including their qualifications, the selection process, other company directorships and whether they are regarded as independent by the board.
5. Related party transactions.
6. Foreseeable risk factors.
7. Issues regarding employees and other stakeholders.
8. Governance structures and policies, in particular, the content of any corporate governance code or policy and the process by which it is implemented.

B. Information should be prepared and disclosed in accordance with high quality standards of accounting and financial and non-financial disclosure.

C. An annual audit should be conducted by an independent, competent and qualified, auditor in order to provide an external and objective assurance to the board and shareholders that the financial statements fairly represent the financial position and performance of the company in all material respects.

D. External auditors should be accountable to the shareholders and owe a duty to the company to exercise due professional care in the conduct of the audit.

E. Channels for disseminating information should provide for equal, timely and cost-efficient access to relevant information by users.

F. The corporate governance framework should be complemented by an effective approach that addresses and promotes the provision of analysis or advice by analysts, brokers, rating agencies and others, that is relevant to decisions by investors, free from material conflicts of interest that might compromise the integrity of their analysis or advice.

VI. THE RESPONSIBILITIES OF THE BOARD

The corporate governance framework should ensure the strategic guidance of the company, the effective monitoring of management by the board, and the board's accountability to the company and the shareholders.

A. Board members should act on a fully informed basis, in good faith, with due diligence and care, and in the best interest of the company and the shareholders.

B. Where board decisions may affect different shareholder groups differently, the board should treat all shareholders fairly.

C. The board should apply high ethical standards. It should take into account the interests of stakeholders.

D. The board should fulfil certain key functions, including:

1. Reviewing and guiding corporate strategy, major plans of action, risk policy, annual budgets and business plans; setting performance objectives; monitoring implementation and corporate performance; and overseeing major capital expenditures, acquisitions and divestitures.
2. Monitoring the effectiveness of the company's governance practices and making changes as needed.
3. Selecting, compensating, monitoring and, when necessary, replacing key executives and overseeing succession planning.
4. Aligning key executive and board remuneration with the longer term interests of the company and its shareholders.

5. Ensuring a formal and transparent board nomination and election process.

6. Monitoring and managing potential conflicts of interest of management, board members and shareholders, including misuse of corporate assets and abuse in related party transactions.

7. Ensuring the integrity of the corporation's accounting and financial reporting systems, including the independent audit, and that appropriate systems of control are in place, in particular, systems for risk management, financial and operational control, and compliance with the law and relevant standards.

8. Overseeing the process of disclosure and communications.

E. The board should be able to exercise objective independent judgement on corporate affairs.

1. Boards should consider assigning a sufficient number of non-executive board members capable of exercising independent judgement to tasks where there is a potential for conflict of interest. Examples of such key responsibilities are ensuring the integrity of financial and non-financial reporting, the review of related party transactions, nomination of board members and key executives, and board remuneration.

2. When committees of the board are established, their mandate, composition and working procedures should be well defined and disclosed by the board.

3. Board members should be able to commit themselves effectively to their responsibilities.

F. In order to fulfil their responsibilities, board members should have access to accurate, relevant and timely information.

Part VIII
Company codes of conduct

Company codes or unilaterally declared codes of conduct vary greatly in the degree to which they are embedded in the organisation. Although some statements are afterthoughts, some are becoming integrated into day-to-day decision-making. These statements also vary greatly in length, scope, audience, auditability and accessibility. Another important criterion is the degree to which they do or do not reference key foundation standards, such as the Universal Declaration of Human Rights (Chapter 5).

Company codes vary greatly by sector. Companies in the retail and/or clothing sector have codes of conduct for suppliers, whereas petroleum companies are more likely to have codes addressing human rights. Regardless of the sector, companies with unilaterally declared codes benefit greatly from the process standards and tools described in Part X, such as the AccountAbility 1000 Series (AA1000; Chapter 26 and the Global Reporting Initiative (GRI; Chapter 28).

The Human Rights Library of the University of Minnesota lists company codes of conduct,[1] all of which are accessible through the websites of these companies (see Table viii.1). It is an irony that the list begins with Ahold, considering the recent allegations that Ahold's operations in the USA have behaved unethically (see also page 344).

1 See the Library's web page at www1.umn.edu/humanrts/links/sicc.html; see also www.shell.com/home/content/aboutshell/who_we_are/our_values/sgbp/sgbp_30032008.html.

Company	***Code or tool***	***Web address***
Ahold	Mission, Vision and Common Values	ahold.com
The Body Shop	'Our Values'	thebodyshop.com
Boeing Company	Ethics and Business Conduct	boeing.com
BP Amoco	On the Side of Human Rights	bpamoco.com
Dillard Department Stores	Business Policy	dillards.com
The Dress Barn Inc. and its subsidiaries	Standards of Engagement	dressbarn.com
ExxonMobil	Corporate Guiding Principles	exxonmobil.com
Exxon	Environment, Health and Safety Policies, 1999	
Federated Department Stores	Statement of Corporate Policy	federated-fds.com
Fruit of the Loom	Contractor Code of Conduct	fruit.com
Gap Inc.	Code of Vendor Conduct	gap.com
Georgia-Pacific	Corporate Principles	gp.com
Halliburton Company and its subsidiaries	Code of Business Conduct	halliburton.com
Hartmarx*	Corporation Policy: Statement of Responsibility	hartmarx.com
Hennes & Mauritz (H&M)	Code of Conduct	hm.com
ITT Industries	Corporate Code of Conduct: Basic Principles	itt.com
JC Penney	Foreign Sourcing Requirements	jcpenney.com
Jones Apparel Group Inc.	Business Partner Standards, May 1996	jny.com
Kellwood	Policy on Business Conduct	kellwood.com
Kmart Corporation	Vendor Agreement, 13 June 1996	kmartcorp.com
Lands' End, Inc.	Standards of Business Conduct	landsend.com
Levi Strauss & Co.	Code of Conduct Global Sourcing and Operating Guidelines	levi.com
Liz Claiborne	Workplace Code of Conduct	lizclaiborne.com

* Hartmarx's policy is that of the American Apparel Manufacturers' Association (AAMA; americanapparel.com).

Table viii.1 **Examples of self-imposed company codes of conduct** (continued opposite)

Source: adapted from Human Rights Library, University of Minnesota, Minneapolis, MN, www1.umn.edu/humanrts/links/sicc.html

Company	*Code or tool*	*Web address*
Lockheed Martin	Corporation Code of Ethics and Business Conduct	lockheedmartin.com
Mobil	Environment, Health and Safety Statement, 1998	mobil.com
Oxford Industries Inc.	Contractor Sourcing Policy	oxfordinc.com
Reebok International Ltd	Human Rights Production Standards	reebok.com
Royal Dutch/Shell	Statement of General Business Principles Use-of-force Guidelines	shell.com
Russell Corporation	Vendor Policy	rusellcorp.com
Sara Lee Corporation	Supplier Selection Guidelines	saralee.com
Sears, Roebuck & Co.	Import Buying Policy and Procedures	sears.com
South African Beers (SAB)	Corporate Code of Conduct	sabmiller.com
Spiegel	Standards for Business Partnerships	spiegel.com
TotalFina	Health, Safety and Environment Charter	
Total	General Policy Regarding the Management of Human Resources	totalfinaelf.com
Total Myanmar Exploration and Production	Code of Conduct	totalfinaelf.com/us/html/de/ya/deya4-1c.htm
Unocal	Statement of Principles	unocal.com
VF Corporation	Contractor Terms of Engagement, 8 July 1996	vfc.com
Wal-Mart Stores Inc.	Standards for Vendor Partners	walmart.com
WARNACO	Business Partner Terms of Engagement and Guidelines for Country Selection	warnaco.com
WMC	Code of Conduct Indigenous Peoples Policy	wmc.com
Woolworth Corporation	Contractor Certificate	woolworths.co.uk

Table viii.1 (continued)

20
Shell's Business Principles

> **What is remarkable about Shell's Business Principles is the degree to which Shell staff around the world are aware of the Principles and the values of the company. This is quite unusual.**
>
> *Gemma Crijns, Nyenrode University and Amnesty International Business Group*[1]

Type Principles, company-specific; performance-oriented

Strength Clarity

Keywords Economic principles • Business integrity • Political activities • Health, safety and environment • Community • Competition • Stakeholders

20.1 Background

First published in 1976, Shell's General Business Principles constitute a living document that has evolved over time. The Principles are derived from values of honesty, integrity and respect for people. One of the most significant aspects of the Principles is the section on 'responsibilities', in which Shell identifies its five key stakeholders: shareholders, customers, employees, those with whom Shell does business, and society.

The Principles cover a very wide range of issues, including economic principles, business integrity, political activities, health, safety, environment, community and competition. According to Mark Wade of Shell:

1 Personal communication with the author by Gemma Crijns, Nyenrode University, Breukelen, The Netherlands, 22 May 2003.

> the Principles represent the magnetic north of the company, giving the employees a benchmark on what the company stands for and making clear the behaviour expected of all Shell employees in their business dealings large or small wherever Shell operates around the world).[2]

With operations in 140 countries, Shell has to ensure its Principles resonate with staff worldwide, with wide-ranging cultural and religious differences.

The Principles have broken new ground in several respects. According to Geoffrey Chandler, a key force behind the Principles:

> We were pioneers among transnational companies in doing this. It took a year's discussion. The process of involving both the centre and the operating companies in that discussion was as important as the eventual product.[3]

20.2 Strengths and weaknesses

The Principles are a living document in that they continue to change over time. They have been through six revisions. Shell's Principles are grounded in management systems. For example, on health and safety and the environment, the Principles state that 'Shell companies have a systematic approach to health, safety and environmental management in order to achieve continuous performance improvement' (Principle #6; see page 396).

Shell is active in an array of corporate responsibility (CR) initiatives (see Fig. 20.1) and organisations, including, among others, the UN Global Compact (see Chapter 3) the World Business Council for Sustainable Development (WBCSD, www.wbcsd.org), the Voluntary Principles on Security and Human Rights (see Chapter 6) and the Business Principles for Countering Bribery (see Chapter 18).

It would be helpful to stakeholders if the Principles were to list commitments to other codes and standards, or to provide information on this in a document attached to the Principles. (Note, however, that Shell does list the main codes and standards that it supports in its *Shell Report*.) It is unfortunate that Shell's Principles do not reference the Universal Declaration of Human Rights (Chapter 5).

Additional resource

Website

Royal Dutch/Shell: www.shell.com.

2 Interview with Mark Wade, Shell Learning–Leadership Development, London, 11 April 2003.

3 E-mail to author from Sir Geoffrey Chandler, formerly of Shell and Amnesty International's Business Group, 18 April 2003.

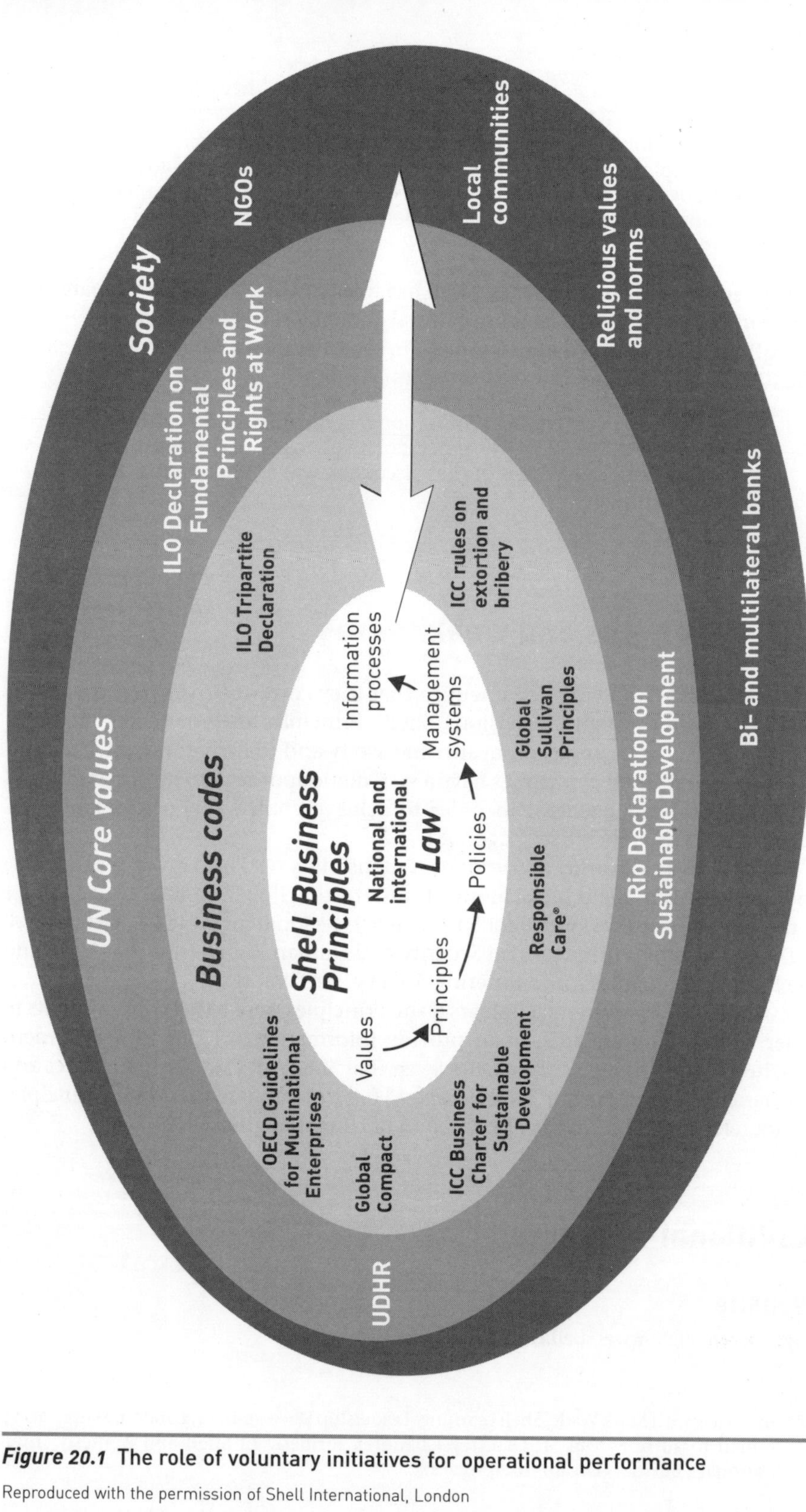

Figure 20.1 **The role of voluntary initiatives for operational performance**

Reproduced with the permission of Shell International, London

Shell General Business Principles*

Royal Dutch Shell plc

Our Values

Shell employees share a set of core values — honesty, integrity and respect for people. We also firmly believe in the fundamental importance of trust, openness, teamwork and professionalism, and pride in what we do.

Sustainable Development

As part of the Business Principles, we commit to contribute to sustainable development. This requires balancing short and long term interests, integrating economic, environmental and social considerations into business decision-making.

Responsibilities

Shell companies recognise five areas of responsibility. It is the duty of management continuously to assess the priorities and discharge these inseparable responsibilities on the basis of that assessment.

a. To shareholders

To protect shareholders' investment, and provide a long-term return competitive with those of other leading companies in the industry.

b. To customers

To win and maintain customers by developing and providing products and services which offer value in terms of price, quality, safety and environmental impact, which are supported by the requisite technological, environmental and commercial expertise.

c. To employees

To respect the human rights of our employees and to provide them with good and safe working conditions, and competitive terms and conditions of employment.

To promote the development and best use of the talents of our employees; to create an inclusive work environment where every employee has an equal opportunity to develop his or her skills and talents.

To encourage the involvement of employees in the planning and direction of their work; to provide them with channels to report concerns.

We recognise that commercial success depends on the full commitment of all employees.

d. To those with whom we do business

To seek mutually beneficial relationships with contractors, suppliers and in joint ventures and to promote the application of these Shell General Business Principles or equivalent principles in such relationships. The ability to promote these principles effectively will be an important factor in the decision to enter into or remain in such relationships.

e. To society

To conduct business as responsible corporate members of society, to comply with applicable laws and regulations, to support fundamental human rights in line with the legitimate role of business, and to give proper regard to health, safety, security and the environment.

Principle 1: Economic

Long-term profitability is essential to achieving our business goals and to our continued growth. It is a measure both of efficiency and of the value that customers place on Shell products and services. It supplies the necessary corporate resources for the continuing investment that is required to develop and produce future energy supplies to meet customer needs. Without profits and a strong financial foundation, it would not be possible to fulfil our responsibilities.

Criteria for investment and divestment decisions include sustainable development considerations (economic, social and environmental) and an appraisal of the risks of the investment.

Principle 2: Competition

Shell companies support free enterprise. We seek to compete fairly and ethically and within the framework of applicable competition laws; we will not prevent others from competing freely with us.

Principle 3: Business Integrity

Shell companies insist on honesty, integrity and fairness in all aspects of our business and expect the same in our relationships with all those with whom we do business. The direct or indirect offer, payment, soliciting or acceptance of bribes in any form is unacceptable. Facilitation payments are also bribes and should not be made. Employees must avoid conflicts of interest between their private activities and their part in the conduct of company business. Employees must also declare to their employing company potential conflicts of interest. All business transactions on behalf of a Shell company must be reflected accurately and fairly in the accounts of the company in accordance with established procedures and are subject to audit and disclosure.

Principle 4: Political Activities

a. Of companies

Shell companies act in a socially responsible manner within the laws of the countries in which we operate in pursuit of our legitimate commercial objectives.

Shell companies do not make payments to political parties, organizations or their representatives. Shell companies do not take part in party politics. However, when dealing with governments, Shell companies have the right and the responsibility to make our position known on any matters which affect us, our employees, our customers, our shareholders or local communities in a manner which is in accordance with our values and the Business Principles.

b. Of employees

Where individuals wish to engage in activities in the community, including standing for election to public office, they will be given the opportunity to do so where this is appropriate in the light of local circumstances.

Principle 5: Health, Safety, Security and the Environment

Shell companies have a systematic approach to health, safety, security and environmental management in order to achieve continuous performance improvement.

To this end, Shell companies manage these matters as critical business activities, set standards and targets for improvement, and measure, appraise and report performance externally.

We continually look for ways to reduce the environmental impact of our operations, products and services

Principle 6: Local Communities

Shell companies aim to be good neighbours by continuously improving the ways in which we contribute directly or indirectly to the general well-being of the communities within which we work.

We manage the social impacts of our business activities carefully and work with others to enhance the benefits to local communities, and to mitigate any negative impacts from our activities.

In addition, Shell companies take a constructive interest in societal matters, directly or indirectly related to our business.

Principle 7: Communication and Engagement

Shell companies recognise that regular dialogue and engagement with our stakeholders is essential. We are committed to reporting of our performance by providing full relevant information to legitimately interested parties, subject to any overriding considerations of business confidentiality.

In our interactions with employees, business partners and local communities, we seek to listen and respond to them honestly and responsibly.

Principle 8: Compliance

We comply with all applicable laws and regulations of the countries in which we operate.

21 Johnson & Johnson's 'Credo'

> **The Credo has become a trust mark. The public trusts the company to operate ethically and to create products that will help them live longer and more healthily. Similarly, potential recruits and existing staff have faith in the organisation to provide gainful employment and shareholders understand that taking care of people and the planet can lead to profits.**
>
> *Ralph S. Larsen, Former Chairman, Johnson & Johnson*[1]

Type Principles, company-specific, aspirational

Strength Stakeholder focus

Keywords Values • Responsibilities • Stakeholders

21.1 Background

At Johnson & Johnson there is no mission statement that hangs on the wall. Instead, for more than 50 years, a simple, one-page document—'Our Credo'—has guided the company's actions in fulfilling its responsibilities to customers, employees, the community and stockholders.

General Robert Wood Johnson, who guided Johnson & Johnson from a small, family-owned business to a worldwide enterprise, had a very perceptive view of a corporation's responsibilities beyond the manufacturing and marketing of products.

As early as 1935, in a pamphlet titled 'Try Reality', he urged his fellow industrialists to embrace what he termed 'a new industrial philosophy'. Johnson defined

1 www.jjeurope-csr.com, accessed 2003

this as the corporation's responsibility to customers, employees, the community and stockholders.

But it was not until eight years later, in 1943, that Johnson wrote and first published the Johnson & Johnson Credo, a one-page document outlining these responsibilities in greater detail. Johnson ensured that the Credo was embraced by his company, and he urged his management to apply it as part of their everyday business philosophy.

The Credo, seen by business leaders and the media as being far-sighted, received wide public attention and acclaim. Putting customers first, and stockholders last, was a refreshing approach to the management of a business. But it should be noted that Johnson was a practical-minded businessman. He believed that by putting the customer first the business would be well served, and it was.

The corporation has drawn heavily on the strength of the Credo for guidance through the years, and at no time was this more evident than during the Tylenol® crises of 1982 and 1986, when the McNeil Consumer & Specialty Pharmaceuticals product (the number-one over-the-counter analgesic in the US market) was adulterated with cyanide by an extortioner and used as a murder weapon. With Johnson & Johnson's good name and reputation at stake, company managers and employees made countless decisions that were inspired by the philosophy embodied in the Credo. Company managers alerted consumers via the media not to purchase any type of Tylenol product until the extent of the tampering was known and withdrew 31 million bottles of the product with a retail value of more than US$100 million from the market. The company's reputation was preserved and the Tylenol acetaminophen business was regained.

Today the Credo lives on in Johnson & Johnson stronger than ever. Company employees now participate in a periodic survey and evaluation of how well the company performs its Credo responsibilities. These assessments are then fed back to the senior management, and, where there are shortcomings, corrective action is promptly taken.

Over the years, some of the language of the Credo has been updated and new areas recognising the environment and the balance between work and family have been added. But the spirit of the document remains the same today as when it was first written.

The Johnson & Johnson Credo is available in 36 languages spreading across Africa, Asia-Pacific, Eastern Europe, Europe, Latin America, Middle East and North America.

21.2 Strengths and weaknesses

Managers at Johnson & Johnson believe that the Credo:[2]

- Helps to unify the management team and the company's employees in achieving the corporate objectives

2 See www.jnj.com/connect/about-jnj/jnj-credo.

- Provides a common set of values
- Serves as a constant reminder of the company's responsibilities to its customers, employees, communities and shareowners

The company's stock is included in the Dow Jones Sustainability Index (DJSI).

Additional resource

Website

Johnson & Johnson, 'Our citizenship': www.jnj.com/connect/about-jnj/our-citizenship

Our Credo*

We believe our first responsibility is to the doctors, nurses and patients,
to mothers and fathers and all others who use our products and services.
In meeting their needs everything we do must be of high quality.
We must constantly strive to reduce our costs
in order to maintain reasonable prices.
Customers' orders must be serviced promptly and accurately.
Our suppliers and distributors must have an opportunity
to make a fair profit.

We are responsible to our employees,
the men and women who work with us throughout the world.
Everyone must be considered as an individual.
We must respect their dignity and recognize their merit.
They must have a sense of security in their jobs.
Compensation must be fair and adequate,
and working conditions clean, orderly and safe.
We must be mindful of ways to help our employees fulfill
their family responsibilities.
Employees must feel free to make suggestions and complaints.
There must be equal opportunity for employment, development
and advancement for those qualified.
We must provide competent management,
and their actions must be just and ethical.

We are responsible to the communities in which we live and work
and to the world community as well.
We must be good citizens—support good works and charities
and bear our fair share of taxes.
We must encourage civic improvements and better health and education.
We must maintain in good order
the property we are privileged to use,
protecting the environment and natural resources.

* Reprinted with the permission of Johnson & Johnson.

Our final responsibility is to our stockholders.
Business must make a sound profit.
We must experiment with new ideas.
Research must be carried on, innovative programs developed and mistakes paid for.
New equipment must be purchased, new facilities provided and new products launched.
Reserves must be created to provide for adverse times.
When we operate according to these principles,
the stockholders should realize a fair return.

Part IX
Framework, sectoral and regional agreements

Codes of conduct require new social alliances.

Ingeborg Wick[1]

Part IX will focus on:

- Framework agreements
- Sectoral and regional agreements

In the following chapters, a general discussion of such agreements will be provided, followed by case-study examples.

Framework agreements, like sectoral and regional agreements, are forming new social alliances between stakeholders. These social alliances serve to foster trust and promote enhanced and more regular communication between a diverse range of actors. If well formulated, these new partnerships will succeed in preventing conflicts before they arise.

1 *Workers' Tool or PR Ploy? A Guide to Codes of International Labour Practice* (Bonn/Siegburg: Friedrich Ebert Foundation and Südwind Institut für Ökonomie und Ökumene, 3rd rev. edn, 2003, www.fes.de): 24.

22
Framework agreements

> **[Framework] agreements provide the basis for future global dialogue and a framework for tackling individual problems as they crop up. They are the way forward in democratising the multi-nationals.**
>
> ***Philip Jennings, General Secretary, Union Network International*[1]**

Type Negotiated agreement, performance-oriented

Strength Institutionalises consultation and builds trust

Keywords Labour • Trade unions • ILO conventions

22.1 Background

Global framework agreements are bilateral agreements between a multinational company (MNC) and the international trade union, or global union federation (GUF), that represents workers within the company. In a number of cases, the agreement also involves as a signatory the national union within the country in which the MNC has its home base. Since 1988, 71 companies have signed framework agreements, and they are becoming more common (see Table 22.1).

These agreements are based on conventions of the International Labour Organisation (ILO) and seek to establish a 'continual working relationship and dialogue' (IFBWW 2003: 2) between the trade union and the MNC. According to the International Federation of Building and Wood Workers (IFBWW),[2] which accounts for a quarter of all such agreements (see Table 22.1):

1 Quoted in Graham and Bibby 2002.

2 Since 2005 merged into Building and Wood Workers International (www.bwint.org/default.asp?Language=EN)

Year	*MNC*	*Country*	*Sector*	*Union*	*Language*
2009	Wilkhahn	Germany	Office & furniture	BWI	English
2009	Elanders	Sweden	Printing	UNI	English
2008	Group 4 Securicor (G4S)	UK	Cleaning & services	UNI	English
2008	Takashimaya	Japan	Retail	UNI	English
2008	Ability	Brazil	Telecoms	UNI	Portuguese
2008	Aker	Norway	Shipbuilding	IMF	English
2008	Icomon	Brazil	Telecoms	UNI	Portuguese
2008	Danske Bank	Denmark	Bank	UNI	English
2008	ISS	Denmark	Cleaning & services	UNI	English
2008	Italcementi	Italy	Construction	BWI	English
2008	Vallourec	France	Metalworking industry	IMF	English
2008	Rhodia	France	Chemical	ICEM	English
2008	Arcelor Mittal	Luxembourg	Metalworking industry	IMF	English
2007	Inditex	Spain	Textile	ITGLWF	English
2007	Umicore	Belgium	Metalworking industry	IMF, ICEM	English
2007	WAZ	Germany	Media	IFJ/EFJ	English
2007	Quebecor	Canada	Printing	UNI	
2007	Brunel	Netherlands	Metalworking industry	IMF, ICEM	English
2007	VolkerWessels	Netherlands	Building	BWI	English
2006	France Telecom	France	Telecommunications	UNI	English
2006	National	Australia	Bank	UNI	English

BWI Building and Wood Workers International
ICEM International Federation of Chemical, Energy, Mine and General Workers' Unions
IFJ/EFJ International Federation of Journalists/European Federation of Journalists
IFME International Federation of Mining and Energy
IMF International Metalworkers' Federation
ITGLWF International Textile Garment and Leather Workers' Federation
IUF International Union of Food, Agricultural, Hotel, Restaurant, Catering, Tobacco and Allied Workers' Associations
PSI Public Services International
UNI Union Network International

Table 22.1 **International framework agreements** *(continued over)*

Source: Sustainlabour; www.sustainlabour.org/index.php?option=com_content&task=view&id=431&Itemid=329, accessed 10 May 2010

Year	MNC	Country	Sector	Union	Language
2006	Staedtler	Germany	Office	BWI	English
2006	Euradius	Netherlands	Printing	UNI	English
2006	Nampak	South Africa	Packaging	UNI	English
2006	Royal Bam	Netherlands	Building	BWI	English
2006	Securitas	Sweden	Services	UNI	English
2006	PSA Peugeot Citroën	France	Automotive	IMF	English
2006	Portugal Telecom	Portugal	Telecommunications	UNI	English
2005	Lafarge	France	Building	BWI, ICEM	English
2005	Stabilo	Germany	Office	BWI	English
2005	EADS	Netherlands	Spatial	IMF	English
2005	BMW	Germany	Automotive	IMF	English
2005	Veidekke	Norway	Building	BWI	English
2005	Universal Postal Union	Switzerland	Post	UNI	English
2005	Falck	Denmark	Property service	UNI	English
2005	EDF	France	Energy	ICEM, PSI, IFME	English
2004	Röchling	Germany	Automotive	IMF	English
2004	Impregilo	Italy	Building	BWI	English
2004	Renault	France	Automotive	IMF	English
2004	Lukoil	Russia	Energy	ICEM	English
2004	Club Mediterranee	France	Tourism	IUF	English
2004	SCA	Sweden	Paper	ICEM	English
2004	Bosch	Germany	Automotive	IMF	English
2004	H&M	Sweden	Retail	UNI	English
2003	Prym	Germany	Automotive	IMF	French
2003	SKF	Sweden	Manufacturing	IMF	English

Table 22.1 *(from previous page; continued opposite)*

Year	*MNC*	*Country*	*Sector*	*Union*	*Language*
2003	Rheinmetall	Germany	Automotive	IMF	English
2003	Evonik	Germany	Chemical	ICEM	English
2003	GEA	Germany	Engineering	IMF	English
2003	Leoni	Germany	Automotive/electricity	IMF	English
2002	ENI	Italy	Energy	ICEM	English
2002	Anglogold	South Africa	Mines	ICEM	English
2002	DaimlerChrysler	Germany	Automotive	IMF	English
2002	Norske Skog	Norway	Paper	ICEM	English
2002	Volkswagen	Germany	Automotive	IMF	English
2002	Fonterra	New Zealand	Dairy industry	IUF	English
2002	Ballast Nedam	Netherlands	Building	BWI	English
2002	Endesa	Spain	Energy	ICEM	English
2001	Indesit	Italy	Metalworking industry	IMF	English
2001	OTE	Greece	Telecommunications	UNI	French
2001	Chiquita	United States	Agriculture	IUF	English
2001	Carrefour	France	Retail	UNI	French
2001	Skanska	Sweden	Building	BWI	English
2000	Freudenberg	Germany	Textile	ICEM	English
2000	Telefonica	Spain	Telecommunications	UNI	French
2000	Faber-Castell	Germany	Office equipment	BWI	English
2000	Hochtief	Germany	Building	BWI	English
1999	Metro	Germany	Retail	UNI	French
1998	Statoil	Norway	Energy	ICEM	English
1998	IKEA: Code of conduct; IWAY; Child Labour	Sweden	Furniture	BWI	English
1995	Accor	France	Tourism	IUF	English
1988	Danone	France	Food industry	IUF	English

Table 22.1 *(from previous page)*

> framework agreements are not intended to substitute for national law or collective bargaining; they are intended to create a framework within which all workers are guaranteed established international minimum standards for work (IFBWW 2003: 2).

Framework agreements generally commit the company to comply with national legislation and ILO conventions and recommendations that relate to the company's work. Such agreements usually acknowledge that the MNC bears responsibility for the conditions under which its products are made, even if the company outsources a majority of its products.

Framework agreements can include provisions on monitoring. For example, the agreement between Ikea and the BWI (formerly known as IFBWW) established a monitoring group composed of Ikea and trade-union employees, who conduct site visits to Ikea suppliers. With 318 affiliates in 130 countries, the BWI has a strong network to assist in monitoring (see www.bwint.org). These monitoring arrangements serve to prevent conflict; when problems arise, the framework agreement allows for resolution without leading to damaging exposure. Secretary-General of of BWI's precursor, the IFBWW, Anita Normark, says that most problems are resolved internally, between the partners, of the agreement.[3]

22.2 Strengths and weaknesses

Framework agreements complement company codes of conduct and other standards by providing mechanisms for monitoring and institutionalising dialogue. The relationship between Accor and the International Union of Food, Agricultural, Hotel, Restaurant, Catering, Tobacco and Allied Workers Associations (IUF) helped to reduce the anti-trade union nature of the company's operations in the USA and Australia (Wick 2003: 20).

22.3 Companies to which framework agreements apply

It is interesting to note that the majority of the framework agreements are signed by Scandinavian and Northern European companies with a strong tradition of social dialogue. Also, the companies signing such agreements tend to have strong trade unions, whereas sectors where trade unions are weak tend to rely more on codes of conduct than on framework agreements. The forestry sector has been successful in developing framework agreements because it is building on the success

3 Interview with Anita Normark, Secretary-General, International Federation of Building and Wood Workers, 14 March 2003.

of the sustainable forestry movement, which has already fostered awareness about social and environmental issues.

22.4 Questions posed and answered

Framework agreements pose the following question:

- What are the key areas of agreement between a multinational company and its global union federation?

22.5 The promise and the challenge

The challenge for framework agreements will be to gain visibility and recognition. They are not well known or well understood, despite their effectiveness. When successful, such agreements can serve as confidence-building measures.

22.6 Case study: Global Agreement between the ICEM and Statoil

With 29,000 employees in 40 countries, Statoil is a Norwegian company.[4] According to its website (www.statoil.com), Statoil is one of the world's largest net sellers of crude oil and is also a key supplier of natural gas within the European market. According to its website, 'We are determined to make Statoil known for its high ethical standards.'[5]

In 1998, Statoil signed an agreement with the International Federation of Chemical, Energy, Mine and General Workers' Unions (ICEM). The agreement covers labour, human rights and the environment. The goal of the agreement is to:

> create an open channel of information between ICEM and Statoil management about industrial relations issues in order to continuously improve and develop good work practice in Statoil's worldwide operations (Statoil undated: 5).

The agreement was first revised in 2001 in order to comply with the Global Compact (Chapter 3). The agreement was again revised in August 2003 and June 2005.

4 Source: www.statoil.com.

5 www.statoil.com/en/About/EthicsValues/Pages/default.aspx, accessed May 2010.

The most significant aspect of the agreement is that it sets a global policy to guide and empower decisions at the local level. Labour issues need to be resolved as close as possible to the plant or worksite—but local practice is varied. With an agreement in place, each operation knows the company's policy and can make decisions and negotiate with a consistent message.

The GUF concerned, ICEM, represents 20 million workers globally.[6] The agreement was negotiated between the Norwegian Oil and Petrochemical Workers' Union (NOPEF), the central union in Norway and a part of ICEM. NOPEF is no longer involved, having been replaced by Industri Energi.

Through the agreement, Statoil provides assurances that it will:

1. Protect the rights of workers to be represented by a trade union of their own choice and to bargain collectively (Principle 3 of the Global Compact [see page 85], and ILO Conventions 87 and 98)
2. Avoid use of forced labour or bonded labour (Principle 4 of the Global Compact, and ILO Conventions 29 and 105)
3. Avoid use of child labour (Principle 5 of the Global Compact, and ILO Convention 138)
4. Promote diversity and avoid discrimination (Principle 6 of the Global Compact, and ILO Conventions 100 and 111)
5. Commit to paying fair wages and benefits according to good industry standards in each country
6. Provide a safe and healthy work environment
7. Support a precautionary approach to environmental challenges (Principle 7 of the Global Compact)
8. Undertake initiatives to promote greater environmental responsibility (Principle 8 of the Global Compact)
9. Encourage the development and diffusion of environmentally friendly technologies (Principle 9 of the Global Compact)
10. Ensure that the company provides a clear and supportive policy on HIV/AIDS and that this policy is effectively implemented throughout Statoil operations

The agreement includes provisions for effective management and oversight. These include:

- Annual meetings at a senior level of the parties to the agreement
- Training programmes in health, safety and environment for trade-union representatives, and management training

6 www.icem.org/?id=12&doc=1225, accessed May 2010.

- A commitment to notify subcontractors and licensees of the agreement and to seek their compliance

The business benefits of such an agreement are significant. According to Geir Westgaard, Vice-President of Statoil, the agreement helps the company to manage complexity (Westgaard 2001). For a global company, such an agreement makes it easier to deal with local challenges by developing a global approach. Other benefits include decreasing risk and thereby increasing protection of the Statoil reputation and licence to operate (Westgaard 2001: 25). By securing good industrial relations, Statoil has faced few conflicts and has increased its retention of employees and job satisfaction (Statoil undated: 5).

Reg Green, responsible for health, safety and environmental affairs at ICEM, believes that global agreements highlight the importance of—and the need for agreements to be based on—genuine transparency, honesty, co-operation, participation and conflict identification and resolution, vital elements of any corporate social responsibility commitment. Signatories to such agreements recognise that there are two sides to such agreements: the commitments and obligations of the company on the one hand, and those of the relevant GUF on the other. According to Reg Green, for any framework agreement to be effective, it is a *sine qua non* that both sides to the agreement derive benefit from it.[7]

References

Graham, I., and A. Bibby (2000) 'Global Labour Agreements: A Framework for Rights', *The World of Work* 45 (December 2002, www.ilo.org/wcmsp5/groups/public/---dgreports/---dcomm/documents/publication/dwcms_080610.pdf).

IFBWW (International Federation of Building and Wood Workers) (2003) *IFBWW Strategy on Multinational Corporations (MNC): A Co-ordinated Approach to Framework Agreements and Company Codes of Conduct, Corporate Campaigns and European Works Councils* (Carouge, Switzerland: IFBWW).

Statoil (undated) *The Exchange of Information and the Development of Good Working Practice within Statoil Worldwide Operations* (submission to the Global Compact Learning Forum; Stavanger, Norway: Statoil).

Westgaard, G. (2001) 'Charting the Way Forward', presentation at the meeting of the Global Compact Learning Forum, Denham, UK, 29–30 October 2001.

Wick, I. (2003) *Workers' Tool or PR Ploy? A Guide to Codes of International Labour Practice* (Bonn/Siegburg: Friedrich Ebert Foundation and Südwind Institut für Ökonomie und Ökumene, 3rd rev. edn, www.fes.de).

Wilke, Peter, André Sobczak and Isabelle Schömann, 'Code of Conduct and International Framework Agreements: New Forms of Governance at Company Level. Case Study: Ikea', February 2008, www.eurofound.europa.eu/publications/htmlfiles/ef07927.htm, accessed May 2010.

7 Personal communication with the author.

Global Agreement between the ICEM and Statoil*

1 PREAMBLE

This agreement is set up by NOPEF (Norsk Olje og Petrokjemisk Fagforbund), as the central bargaining union for Statoil operations in Norway and NOPEF on behalf of ICEM (International Federation of Chemical, Energy, Mine and General Workers' Unions) which represents trade unions organising Statoil employees in the Company worldwide, and Statoil.

The purpose of the agreement is to create an open channel of information between NOPEF/ICEM and Statoil Management about industrial relations issues in order to continuously improve and develop good work practices in Statoil's worldwide operations.

This agreement covers all activities where Statoil has direct control. Where Statoil does not have overall control, it will exercise its best efforts in order to secure compliance with the standards set out in this agreement. Statoil will notify its subcontractors and licensees of this agreement and encourage compliance with the standards.

Based on the Parties' common recognition of fundamental human rights and Statoil's own values, the purpose is to monitor the practical application of the agreed principles and to discuss any improvements in the working practices or any positive contribution the Parties may make to the eradication of poverty through economic and social progress.

2 HUMAN RIGHTS, INDUSTRIAL RELATIONS AND HSE ISSUES

Statoil and NOPEF/ICEM affirm their support for fundamental human rights in the community and in the place of work. Furthermore, the Parties recognise the importance of protecting safety, health and well-being at work, and share the concern about the impact of exploitation that production, use and disposal may have upon the natural and human environment. This agreement is intended to ensure the best possible standards of protection for those employed in our business.

---

* Reprinted with the permission of ICEM.

The respect of human rights includes:

- the right of every employee to be represented by a union of his or her own choice and the basic trade union rights as defined by ILO Convention 87 and 98 covering freedom of association and the right to organise, as well as the right to engage in collective bargaining. Statoil therefore agrees not to oppose efforts to unionise its employees
- a commitment not to employ forced or bonded labour as proscribed in the ILO Conventions 29 and 105 or otherwise
- a commitment to employ no child labour as proscribed by ILO Convention 138
- a commitment to exercise equality of opportunity and treatment in employment, including equal remuneration for men and women for work of equal value, and the prevention of discrimination* in respect of employment and occupation as required by ILO Conventions 100 and 111 respectively
- a commitment to pay fair wages and benefits according to good industry standards in the country concerned
- a commitment to provide a safe and healthy work environment, deploying common "best practice" standards.

3 ENVIRONMENTAL ISSUES

Statoil and NOPEF/ICEM will cooperate to ensure that Statoil activities are carried out with the fullest possible regard for the environment. In particular this will include:

- supporting a precautionary approach to environmental challenges
- undertaking initiatives to promote greater environmental responsibility
- encouraging the development and diffusion of environmentally friendly technologies.

4 IMPLEMENTATION

4.1 Annual Meeting

Statoil and NOPEF/ICEM will meet annually to review practice in the area of the agreed principles and follow up this Agreement. The purpose shall be to discuss the issues covered by this agreement with a view to jointly agreeing actions that will further develop good working practices. In addition to the general industrial issues and HSE matters, the following topics may be addressed:

- general corporate policy on employment, occupational health, safety and environmental issues affecting those within the company and, as appropriate, between the company and its related companies including suppliers and subcontractors

- the economic and financial position of the company and the development of its business and related activities
- training matters
- issues affecting the exercise of trade union rights
- any other issues mutually agreed upon.

Participants at these annual meetings will normally be 4-5 senior officials from NOPEF/ICEM and relevant managers from Statoil.

4.2 Local Industrial Relations Practice

The agreement between the Parties shall be applied consistently throughout Statoil operations but is not intended to replace or interfere with local industrial relations practice related to information, problem-solving and negotiations. The Parties to the agreement respect the principle that industrial relations issues are best resolved as close as possible to the place of work.

4.3 Training Programmes

NOPEF/ICEM and Statoil will cooperate in developing joint training arrangements covering those issues—and their implementation—dealt with in this agreement. This will include appropriate training in health, safety and environmental best practice for union delegates from countries where Statoil is the operator. It will also include Management training programmes within Statoil. The cost of NOPEF/ICEM involvement in Statoil training programmes may be covered by Statoil, subject to agreement.

4.4 Union Delegates

Statoil will refrain from dismissing or otherwise discriminating against union delegates, identified as such by the Parties, or employees providing information relevant to the observance and implementation of this Agreement. All union delegates must agree to respect the commercial confidentiality of information disclosed in the exercise of their duties.

Statoil will assist union delegates in the performance of their functions by making available relevant information and other agreed facilities. When it is necessary to take time off from work to perform these functions this will be agreed upon locally and may be given as paid time off within the framework of local agreements.

Statoil may also facilitate the opportunity for union representatives from Statoil operations to meet as necessary to discuss the application and future development of this agreement.

4.5 Information

NOPEF/ICEM will distribute copies of this Agreement to all its member unions that organise employees in Statoil companies around the world, and will broadly publicise the existence of the Agreement and explain its implications to its unions in the Company.

Statoil will in the same manner distribute copies of this Agreement to all Statoil offices in local languages of the countries concerned and will inform local management of the existence and contents of this Agreement.

Any external information about this Agreement shall be mutually agreed by the Parties.

4.6 Administration

The President of NOPEF on behalf of ICEM and the Vice President Labour Relations in Statoil are responsible for the administration of this Agreement.

5 DURATION AND EVALUATION

The duration of this agreement is two years, after which this Agreement will be evaluated and may be prolonged for a new period.

Signed in Stavanger on 15th March 2001

Lars Myhre	Jostein Gaasemyr	Fred Higgs
NOPEF	**STATOIL**	**ICEM**

Note:

* Discrimination is defined as any distinction, exclusion, or preference made on the basis of race, colour, sex, religion, political opinion, national extraction or social origin, which has the effect of nullifying or impairing equality of opportunity or treatment.

23
Sectoral and regional agreements

This chapter includes initiatives from the first edition. The following two chapters (25 and 26) feature two new sector initiatives: the Equator Principles and the Principles for Responsible Investment.

> **Corporate responsibility will live or die based on the ability of codes and standards to address industry-specific concerns. To date, much work has been done to build global initiatives within a general context, but more work is needed to build expertise on sectoral and regional dimensions of corporate responsibility.**
>
> ***Deborah Leipziger*[1]**

Type Generally performance-oriented, with commitments to take joint action

Strength Foster dialogue and alliances

23.1 Background

Of all of the types of initiatives profiled in this book, sectoral and regional agreements are the most difficult to track from outside the industry and/or region involved. Sectoral agreements often develop as a result of intense media pressure. A useful example is the case of the cocoa industry developing a joint project to address forced child labour in West Africa for the harvesting of cocoa (see Section 23.6.1).

1 Leipziger 2003.

23.2 Strengths and weaknesses

Sectoral and regional agreements are able to forge partnerships and networks that can build trust and awareness. Such agreements can serve to deepen the understanding of how particular issues in corporate responsibility affect a specific group of companies. Sectoral agreements can spawn organisations, such as the Marine Stewardship Council in the fisheries sector and the Forest Stewardship Council in the timber industry, described in Sections 23.6.3 and 23.6.4, respectively. Industry standards, such as Responsible Care® (Section 23.6.2), which is focused on the chemical industry, can be effective tools for industry associations for use in membership criteria.

Because of their specificity, sectoral tools can achieve a greater depth than can the more aspirational standards and can achieve a greater sense of cohesion and common purpose. At their worst, sectoral codes may serve the lowest common denominator within an industry body.

According to Jane Nelson of the John F. Kennedy School at Harvard University, sectoral codes are becoming more and more significant.[2] Because they cover a more narrowly defined group, regional and sectoral initiatives can develop common protocols, accreditation and certification systems, product labels and cases of best practice. The specificity of sectoral agreements can lead to standards that are prescriptive and specific.

23.3 Companies to which sectoral and regional agreements apply

Sectoral and regional agreements can be forged in any industry and within any region.

23.4 Questions posed and answered

Are there measures the industry or region can take to promote corporate responsibility (CR)? What types of mechanisms can institutionalise these measures (e.g. reporting, pilots, new organisations)?

23.5 The promise and the challenge

Global principles and guidelines will require more specific guidelines along sectoral lines. For example, the Global Reporting Initiative (Chapter 28) and Social

2 Interview with Jane Nelson, John F. Kennedy School, Harvard University, Cambridge, MA, 9 April 2003; at the time of the interview Jane Nelson was still working with the International Business Leaders' Forum.

Accountability 8000 (SA8000, Chapter 8) are among the many global and multi-sectoral initiatives that are developing sectoral supplements. Another challenge is communication between the industry and the public. Sectoral agreements may be less transparent than tools developed by non-governmental organisations (NGOs) or multilateral organisations.

23.6 Sectoral agreements: case studies

Sectoral agreements include (see Ethical Corporation Institute 2009):

- Those of the Fair Labor Association for the apparel and retail sectors (on the Fair Labor Association, see Chapter 9)
- Voluntary Principles on Human Rights and Security (see Chapter 6)
- That of the cocoa industry (see Section 23.6.1)
- Responsible Care® (see Section 23.6.2)
- That of the Marine Stewardship Council (see Section 23.6.3)
- That of the Forest Stewardship Council (see Section 23.6.4)
- Industry Model Code of the World Federation of Sporting Goods[3]
- The Electronics Industry Citizenship Coalition[4]

23.6.1 The International Cocoa Initiative: Working towards Responsible Labour Standards for Cocoa Growing

For a brief interval in April 2001, the world's attention focused on a boat thought to be carrying between 180 and 250 child slaves. Afloat in the Bight of Benin, the boat *MV Etireno* had left Cotonou, the capital of Benin, and had gone missing. When the boat was eventually located, there were only 43 children on board. Aid workers from Terre des Hommes interviewed some of the children on board and reported that the children were being sent to work in Gabon (ASI 2001). Although much about this case remains a mystery, the incident did serve to focus attention on forced child labour in West Africa.

Initial claims that there were tens of thousands of children trafficked to work in cocoa in West Africa in 2001 (see Raghavan and Chatterjee 2001) caused considerable concern and resulted in a ground-breaking commitment to change. Since that time considerable effort has been made to better understand the reality on the ground and put in place programmes that seek to eliminate child labour from cocoa.

The linkage between what occurs at the global and national level and its impact at the rural level is critical for understanding that sustainable change in the

3 www.wfsgi.org/articles/71, accessed May 2010

4 www.eicc.info

situation will require partnerships across countries and sectors. The cocoa industry mobilised a response to the crisis that can serve as an example to other industries on how to deal with complex social issues. Often, the greatest difficulty is access to accurate information on what is happening. The cocoa industry responded to calls for action by agreeing to a voluntary Protocol assuring the world community of its commitment to ILO Convention 182 concerning the Prohibition and Immediate

The following organisations brokered the International Cocoa Initiative in July 2002:

- From the cocoa and chocolate industry:
  - The Association of the Chocolate, Biscuit and Confectionery Industries of the European Union
  - The Chocolate Manufacturers' Association of the USA and the National Confectioners' Association
  - The World Cocoa Foundation
  - The European Cocoa Association and others
  - The International Confectionery Association
  - The International Office of Cocoa, Chocolate and Confectionery
  - The Federation for Cocoa Commerce, London
  - The Cocoa Association of London
  - The Cocoa Merchants' Association of America
  - The Confectionery Manufacturers' Association of Canada
- From trade unions, international organisations and non-governmental organisations (NGOs):
  - The International Labour Organisation (ILO)
  - Free the Slaves
  - The Child Labour Coalition
  - The National Consumers League
  - Global March against Child Labour
  - The International Union of Food, Agricultural, Hotel, Restaurant, Catering, Tobacco and Allied Workers' Associations

The organisations listed above developed a plan to address working conditions in the cocoa industry in West Africa, to include (Candy USA 2001):

- A study on working conditions
- An advisory group for that study
- A consultative group and the signing of a joint statement
- Pilot programmes in West Africa
- Enforcement, monitoring and public reporting
- A joint foundation
- A public certification system

Box 23.1 **Organisations involved in the International Cocoa Initiative**

Action for the Elimination of the Worst Forms of Child Labour.[5] Although there has been criticism of missed deadlines and false starts, there is no doubt that there is now much better information available through national surveys supported by the cocoa industry and independently verified, as well as national plans and programmes in place in the two most important cocoa-exporting countries.

In many ways, the cocoa industry has been breaking new ground. There has never been a comprehensive investigation of working conditions on West African cocoa farms and the studies that have been done have helped drive actions by governments, NGOs and industry itself.

> The Ghana report illustrates what cocoa farming certification is about—identifying important challenges and then driving efforts to address them[6] . . . It is critical that programs supported by the government of Côte d'Ivoire, industry and other organizations address these priority issues, building upon work already underway.[7]

The two major producing governments have been supported as they create their own national programmes, while industry has funded an independent foundation, the International Cocoa Initiative, which has worked on the ground since 2004 to build national capacity, provide effective models of change and share lessons learned. Indicative of how this action has directly affected industry is the number of initiatives that companies themselves have launched. These very from typical CSR-type projects to bold initiatives that change the company's relationship with its supply chain. Some of the most notable examples in the sector are the Cadbury Cocoa Partnership; the commitment of MARS Inc. to a certified supply chain by 2020; the commitment of Nestlé to investment in the cocoa supply chain through its Cocoa Plan; and the launch by major brands of fair trade products in the UK market. There are many other examples of increased investment in the cocoa sector—some that is driven by commercial considerations and some such as those managed by the World Cocoa Foundation that are partnership efforts.

With hindsight, the cocoa industry partnership probably set unreal expectations and had much to learn, but this model offers several important lessons on how to respond in a crisis:

- Work within a multi-stakeholder framework, involving NGOs, industry, government and so on
- Refer to ILO conventions
- Take immediate action and set a timetable for action

23.6.2 Responsible Care®

Responsible Care (www.responsiblecare.org) was first conceived in Canada in 1985 to address public concern about the manufacture, distribution and use of chemi-

5 www.ilo.org/ilolex/cgi-lex/convde.pl?C182.

6 David Zimmer, Secretary General of the Association of the Chocolate, Biscuit and Confectionery Industries of the EU (CAOBISCO), quoted in World Cocoa Foundation 2008a.

7 David Zimmer, quoted in World Cocoa Foundation 2008b.

cals. In 1988, the American Chemistry Council launched Responsible Care in the US. The focus of Responsible Care is to minimise risk by addressing environment, health and safety issues in an industry characterised as high-risk from a social and environmental perspective. A voluntary programme, Responsible Care includes: Guiding Principles, a management system, an independent third-party verification system, and performance indicators. Companies certified to the Responsible Care system can use the logo. At time of writing, Responsible Care has been adopted in 53 countries.

Responsible Care has become *de rigueur* for the chemical industry. While the initiative is 'voluntary', it has become the industry norm. This is due to the fact that, in order to join the American Chemistry Council, companies must adhere to Responsible Care. The programme also requires significant community outreach through the development of Community Advisory Panels. Companies benefit from sharing best practices (www.americanchemistry.com).

23.6.3 MSC Fishery Standard: Principles and Criteria for Sustainable Fishing

Founded in 1997 by Unilever and WWF, the Marine Stewardship Council (MSC, www.msc.org) became an independent organisation in 1999. The MSC is a multi-stakeholder organisation that is 'seeking to harness consumer purchasing power to generate change and promote environmentally responsible stewardship of the world's most important renewable food source'.[8] Certification bodies accredited by the MSC undertake independent assessments of fisheries to its environmental standard for sustainable fishing. Products from fisheries that pass this assessment can display the MSC's logo once the company wishing to do so has had undertaken a chain of custody certification to ensure traceability of the product from the fishery to the consumer .

Customer Licence Code MSCI0187
www.msc.org

The MSC has developed principles and criteria for sustainable fishing.[9]

23.6.4 Forest Stewardship Council

As a multi-stakeholder organisation, the Forest Stewardship Council (FSC, www.fsc.org) includes a wide range of views, from the timber trade to NGOs representing environmental and social concerns, indigenous peoples and certifiers. Founded in 1993, the FSC promotes sustainable forestry by accrediting certifiers that audit wood producers to assure that those producers pass the FSC Principles and

8 www.msc.org, accessed 2003
9 www.msc.org/about-us/standards, and www.msc.org/documents/scheme-documents/msc-standards/MSC_environmental_standard_for_sustainable_fishing.pdf, both accessed May 2010

Criteria.[10] Certified companies can display the FSC logo on their products and in their promotional materials.

23.7 Regional agreements: case study

23.7.1 Asia–Pacific Economic Co-operation (APEC) Code of Business Conduct

The Asia–Pacific Economic Co-operation (APEC, www.apec.org) seeks to promote open trade and co-operation in the Asia–Pacific region. With 21 members in Asia and the Americas, APEC countries account for 43.7% of global trade (as of 2010).

In 1999, a group of Asian business leaders issued a draft of the APEC Code of Business Conduct. This initiative is intended to serve as a model or aspirational code, but it also includes recommendations for concrete steps that companies can take to adopt the code and focuses on the area of corruption, referencing the Rules of Conduct to Combat Extortion and Bribery of the International Chamber of Commerce,[11] the Caux Round Table 'Principles for Business'[12] and the OECD's Principles of Corporate Governance (see Chapter 19). The APEC Code articulates seven standards for corporate conduct:

1. **International and local communities.** A company must recognise its responsibilities toward the international and local communities within which it operates and the individuals that make up those communities.
2. **Respect for laws.** A company must respect international and domestic rules and recognise that some behaviour, although legal, may still have adverse consequences.
3. **Stakeholder responsibility.** A company must recognise the rights of stakeholders as established by laws and encourage active co-operation between companies and stakeholders in creating wealth, jobs, and the sustainability of financially sound enterprises.
4. **Responsibility for the environment.** A company must protect and, where possible, improve the environment within which it operates, promote sustainable development and prevent the wasteful use of natural resources.
5. **Free and fair competition.** A company must support free and fair competition in our industries and avoid anti-competitive actions.
6. **Company governance.** A company should implement a company governance framework that ensures timely and accurate disclosure on all material matters regarding the company.

10 www.fsc.org/pc.html
11 www.iccwbo.org/id904/index.html
12 www.cauxroundtable.org

7. **Illicit actions.** A company must not participate in or condone extortion, bribery, money laundering, or other corrupt practices.

While intended to supplement company codes of conduct, 'it is expected that the CEO of any enterprise using the APEC Business Code would sign the Code and formally agree to uphold the moral obligations it expresses'. The APEC code also includes policy recommendations for governments.

The APEC Code is limited in the area of accountability. It does not require companies to report to anyone but shareholders, nor does it include verification or monitoring of any kind.

The Code is very general about human rights and does not address child or forced labour. In 2007, APEC released the Business Integrity and Transparency Principles for the Private Sector.[13]

References

ASI (Anti-Slavery International) (2001) 'Trafficked Children were on Benin "Slave Ship" ', 1 May 2001, www.antislavery.org, accessed 2003.

Candy USA (2001) 'Global Chocolate Industry Plan to Combat Abusive Child Labour', 1 October 2001, www.candyusa.org, accessed 2003.

Ethical Corporation Institute (2009) *The Guide to Industry Initiatives in CSR*, www.ethicalcorporationinstitute.com/reports/voluntaryinitiatives/?t=ecihprhs, accessed May 2010.

Leipziger, D. (2003) *Sustainable Futures* (London: Morley Fund Management, Winter 2003).

Raghavan, S., and S. Chatterjee (2001) 'A Slave Labour Force of Youths', *Philadelphia Inquirer*, 24 June 2001.

World Cocoa Foundation (2008a) 'Ghana Certification. Report Highlights Important Issues; Will Guide Future Efforts. Based on Survey Covering 60% of Ghana's Cocoa Production'; www.worldcocoafoundation.org/addressing-child-labor/ghana-certification.html, accessed 11 June 2010.

—— (2008b) 'Côte d'Ivoire Certification. Results Will Help Children, Adults, Farming Communities. Survey Covers More than 50% of Country's Cocoa Production'; www.worldcocoafoundation.org/addressing-child-labor/cotedivoire-certification.html, accessed 11 June 2010.

Additional resources

Websites

Forest Stewardship Council: www.fsc.org
Marine Stewardship Council: www.msc.org
Responsible Care®: www.icca-chem.org/en/Home/ICCA-initiatives/Responsible-care

13 www.apec.org/apec/news___media/2007_media_releases/060907_aus_bizcodeconduct.html, accessed May 2010

Statement on Responsible Care®

of the International Council of Chemical Associations*

Responsible Care is the voluntary initiative of the global chemical industry in which companies, through their national associations, commit to work together to:

- continuously improve their company's and the chemical industry's performance in protecting people and the environment throughout the life cycle of their products and processes;
- contribute to the sustainable development of local communities and of society as a whole;
- inform their publics of the risks and benefits of what they make and do, and about their performance, achievements and challenges;
- dialogue and work with their stakeholders at the local, national and international level to understand and address their concerns and aspirations;
- cooperate with governments and organizations at all levels in the development and implementation of effective regulations and standards, and to meet or exceed those requirements;
- extend Responsible Care to all those who manage chemicals.

* Reprinted with the permission of the International Council of Chemical Associations.

24
The Equator Principles

> **The Equator Principles have become the global standard for project finance and have transformed the funding of major projects globally.**
>
> *Business Wire*[1]

Type Principles

Strength Critical mass

Linkages International Finance Corporation's Performance Standards

Keywords Social • Environmental assessment • Project financing • Equator Principle • Financial institution

24.1 Overview

The Equator Principles (EPs) are a set of guidelines for financial institutions which provide a benchmark on social and environmental issues for project financing. Adopted in 2003, by ten international banks, the Equator Principles apply across all sectors and countries, addressing all project financing with capital costs over $10 million.

The Equator Principles have been successful in achieving critical mass. Nearly 70 financial institutions in 16 countries have signed on to the Principles, covering 71% of all project finance debt in emerging markets. Participating financial institutions range from banks and insurance companies to bilateral development

1 'Equator Principles celebrates five years of environmental impact and improved business practices', *Business Wire*, 8 May 2008; www.highbeam.com/doc/1G1-178741191.html.

agencies and export credit agencies. Adopters of the Equator Principles are known as Equator Principle Financial Institutions (EPFIs).

Under the Principles, borrowers must conduct a Social and Environmental Assessment of a proposed project. Projects are rated into three categories: 'A', 'B' and 'C', with 'A' projects having the highest degree of social and environmental impact. For all projects designated as either 'A' or 'B' in non-OECD countries or non-high-income countries, borrowers must establish a Social and Environmental Management System. When there is a 'significant adverse' impact on a community, consultation with affected parties is required and must be conducted in a 'structured and culturally appropriate manner'.

The Equator Principles contain measures for addressing grievance and requires an independent review of all Category A projects, and, as appropriate, for Category B projects. Equator Banks report annually on their progress in meeting the Principles.

The Principles state: 'We will not provide loans to projects where the borrower will not or is unable to comply with our respective social and environmental policies and procedures that implement the Equator Principles.'

According to Béatrice de Montleau, of ABN-AMRO, an EPFI, the EPs have been successful for several reasons: first, large projects have a significant impact on the environment and on society. The high risk to reputation galvanised companies to take action. This led to a critical mass. NGO involvement has also made the initiative successful.[2]

In 2006, the EPFIs met to revise the Principles to incorporate the lessons learned and feedback from key stakeholders. The Principles were also aligned with the International Finance Corporation's Performance Standards. The EPFIs are working to formalise voting procedures and to monitor public reporting requirements. The EP website serves as a portal, providing direct links to the annual reports of its 53 EPFIs.

24.2 Strengths and weaknesses

The Equator Principles is one of very few voluntary sector initiatives to have succeeded in reaching critical mass in its sector, the market for project financing. One of the challenges ahead is to expand into banking sectors in emerging markets. The EPFIs have created an Outreach Committee to actively engage with banks in China, Russia and India.

2 Interview by Deborah Leipziger with Béatrice de Montleau, ABN-AMRO, 14 November 2008.

24.3 Challenges

Several of the EPFIs have come under criticism for financing the $3.6 billion Baku–Tbilisi–Ceyhan (BTC) oil pipeline. A report entitled *Principles, Profits, or Just PR? Triple P Investments under the Equator Principles* states that the EPFIs have financed projects that violate the Equator Principles. NGOs have expressed concern about a lack of transparency about how decision-making around the Equator Principles occurs.

While the Equator Principles are currently available in Chinese, French, Japanese, Russian, Portuguese and Spanish, there is a need for additional translations.

Additional resources

Website

Equator Principles: www.equator-principles.com

The 'Equator Principles'*

A financial industry benchmark for determining, assessing and managing social and environmental risk in project financing

PREAMBLE

Project financing, a method of funding in which the lender looks primarily to the revenues generated by a single project both as the source of repayment and as security for the exposure, plays an important role in financing development throughout the world.[1] Project financiers may encounter social and environmental issues that are both complex and challenging, particularly with respect to projects in the emerging markets.

The Equator Principles Financial Institutions (EPFIs) have consequently adopted these Principles in order to ensure that the projects we finance are developed in a manner that is socially responsible and reflect sound environmental management practices. By doing so, negative impacts on project-affected ecosystems and communities should be avoided where possible, and if these impacts are unavoidable, they should be reduced, mitigated and/or compensated for appropriately. We believe that

1 Project finance is "a method of funding in which the lender looks primarily to the revenues generated by a single project, both as the source of repayment and as security for the exposure. This type of financing is usually for large, complex and expensive installations that might include, for example, power plants, chemical processing plants, mines, transportation infrastructure, environment, and telecommunications infrastructure. Project finance may take the form of financing of the construction of a new capital installation, or refinancing of an existing installation, with or without improvements. In such transactions, the lender is usually paid solely or almost exclusively out of the money generated by the contracts for the facility's output, such as the electricity sold by a power plant. The borrower is usually an SPE (Special Purpose Entity) that is not permitted to perform any function other than developing, owning, and operating the installation. The consequence is that repayment depends primarily on the project's cash flow and on the collateral value of the project's assets." Source: Basel Committee on Banking Supervision, *International Convergence of Capital Measurement and Capital Standards* ("Basel II"), November 2005; www.bis.org/publ/bcbs118.pdf.

* July 2006; www.equator-principles.com

adoption of and adherence to these Principles offers significant benefits to ourselves, our borrowers and local stakeholders through our borrowers' engagement with locally affected communities. We therefore recognise that our role as financiers affords us opportunities to promote responsible environmental stewardship and socially responsible development. As such, EPFIs will consider reviewing these Principles from time-to-time based on implementation experience, and in order to reflect ongoing learning and emerging good practice.

These Principles are intended to serve as a common baseline and framework for the implementation by each EPFI of its own internal social and environmental policies, procedures and standards related to its project financing activities. We will not provide loans to projects where the borrower will not or is unable to comply with our respective social and environmental policies and procedures that implement the Equator Principles.

SCOPE

The Principles apply to all new project financings globally with total project capital costs of US$10 million or more, and across all industry sectors. In addition, while the Principles are not intended to be applied retroactively, we will apply them to all project financings covering expansion or upgrade of an existing facility where changes in scale or scope may create significant environmental and/or social impacts, or significantly change the nature or degree of an existing impact.

The Principles also extend to project finance advisory activities. In these cases, EPFIs commit to make the client aware of the content, application and benefits of applying the Principles to the anticipated project, and request that the client communicate to the EPFI its intention to adhere to the requirements of the Principles when subsequently seeking financing.

STATEMENT OF PRINCIPLES

EPFIs will only provide loans to projects that conform to Principles 1–9 below:

Principle 1: Review and Categorisation

When a project is proposed for financing, the EPFI will, as part of its internal social and environmental review and due diligence, categorise such project based on the magnitude of its potential impacts and risks in accordance with the environmental and social screening criteria of the International Finance Corporation (IFC) (Exhibit I).

Principle 2: Social and Environmental Assessment

For each project assessed as being either Category A or Category B, the borrower has conducted a Social and Environmental Assessment ("Assessment") process[2] to address, as appropriate and to the EPFI's satisfaction, the relevant social and environmental impacts and risks of the proposed project (which may include, if relevant, the illustrative list of issues as found in Exhibit II). The Assessment should also propose mitigation and management measures relevant and appropriate to the nature and scale of the proposed project.

Principle 3: Applicable Social and Environmental Standards

For projects located in non-OECD countries, and those located in OECD countries not designated as High-Income, as defined by the World Bank Development Indicators Database, the Assessment will refer to the then applicable IFC Performance Standards (Exhibit III) and the then applicable Industry Specific EHS Guidelines ("EHS Guidelines") (Exhibit IV). The Assessment will establish to a participating EPFI's satisfaction the project's overall compliance with, or justified deviation from, the respective Performance Standards and EHS Guidelines.

The regulatory, permitting and public comment process requirements in High-Income OECD Countries, as defined by the World Bank Development Indicators Database, generally meet or exceed the requirements of the IFC Performance Standards (Exhibit III) and EHS Guidelines (Exhibit IV). Consequently, to avoid duplication and streamline EPFI's review of these projects, successful completion of an Assessment (or its equivalent) process under and in compliance with local or national law in High-Income OECD Countries is considered to be an acceptable substitute for the IFC Performance Standards, EHS Guidelines and further requirements as detailed in Principles 4, 5 and 6 below. For these projects, however, the EPFI still categorises and reviews the project in accordance with Principles 1 and 2 above.

The Assessment process in both cases should address compliance with relevant host country laws, regulations and permits that pertain to social and environmental matters.

Principle 4: Action Plan and Management System

For all Category A and Category B projects located in non-OECD countries, and those located in OECD countries not designated as High-Income, as defined by the World

2 **Social and Environmental Assessment** is a process that determines the social and environmental impacts and risks (including labour, health, and safety) of a proposed project in its area of influence. For the purposes of Equator Principles compliance, this will be an adequate, accurate and objective evaluation and presentation of the issues, whether prepared by the borrower, consultants or external experts. Depending on the nature and scale of the project, the assessment document may comprise a full-scale social and environmental impact assessment, a limited or focused environmental or social assessment (e.g. audit), or straight-forward application of environmental siting, pollution standards, design criteria, or construction standards. One or more specialised studies may also need to be undertaken.

Bank Development Indicators Database, the borrower has prepared an Action Plan (AP)[3] which addresses the relevant findings, and draws on the conclusions of the Assessment. The AP will describe and prioritise the actions needed to implement mitigation measures, corrective actions and monitoring measures necessary to manage the impacts and risks identified in the Assessment. Borrowers will build on, maintain or establish a Social and Environmental Management System that addresses the management of these impacts, risks, and corrective actions required to comply with applicable host country social and environmental laws and regulations, and requirements of the applicable Performance Standards and EHS Guidelines, as defined in the AP.

For projects located in High-Income OECD countries, EPFIs may require development of an Action Plan based on relevant permitting and regulatory requirements, and as defined by host-country law.

Principle 5: Consultation and Disclosure

For all Category A and, as appropriate, Category B projects located in non-OECD countries, and those located in OECD countries not designated as High-Income, as defined by the World Bank Development Indicators Database, the government, borrower or third party expert has consulted with project affected communities in a structured and culturally appropriate manner.[4] For projects with significant adverse impacts on affected communities, the process will ensure their free, prior and informed consultation and facilitate their informed participation as a means to establish, to the satisfaction of the EPFI, whether a project has adequately incorporated affected communities' concerns.[5]

3 The **Action Plan** may range from a brief description of routine mitigation measures to a series of documents (e.g., resettlement action plan, indigenous peoples plan, emergency preparedness and response plan, decommissioning plan, etc). The level of detail and complexity of the Action Plan and the priority of the identified measures and actions will be commensurate with the project's potential impacts and risks. Consistent with Performance Standard 1, the internal **Social and Environmental Management System** will incorporate the following elements: (i) Social and Environmental Assessment; (ii) management program; (iii) organisational capacity; (iv) training; (v) community engagement; (vi) monitoring; and (vii) reporting.

4 **Affected communities** are communities of the local population within the project's area of influence who are likely to be adversely affected by the project. Where such consultation needs to be undertaken in a structured manner, EPFIs may require the preparation of a Public Consultation and Disclosure Plan (PCDP).

5 **Consultation** should be "free" (free of external manipulation, interference or coercion, and intimidation), "prior" (timely disclosure of information) and "informed" (relevant, understandable and accessible information), and apply to the entire project process and not to the early stages of the project alone. The borrower will tailor its consultation process to the language preferences of the affected communities, their decision-making processes, and the needs of disadvantaged or vulnerable groups. Consultation with Indigenous Peoples must conform to specific and detailed requirements as found in Performance Standard 7. Furthermore, the special rights of Indigenous Peoples as recognised by host-country legislation will need to be addressed.

In order to accomplish this, the Assessment documentation and AP, or non-technical summaries thereof, will be made available to the public by the borrower for a reasonable minimum period in the relevant local language and in a culturally appropriate manner. The borrower will take account of and document the process and results of the consultation, including any actions agreed resulting from the consultation. For projects with adverse social or environmental impacts, disclosure should occur early in the Assessment process and in any event before the project construction commences, and on an ongoing basis.

Principle 6: Grievance Mechanism

For all Category A and, as appropriate, Category B projects located in non-OECD countries, and those located in OECD countries not designated as High-Income, as defined by the World Bank Development Indicators Database, to ensure that consultation, disclosure and community engagement continues throughout construction and operation of the project, the borrower will, scaled to the risks and adverse impacts of the project, establish a grievance mechanism as part of the management system. This will allow the borrower to receive and facilitate resolution of concerns and grievances about the project's social and environmental performance raised by individuals or groups from among project-affected communities. The borrower will inform the affected communities about the mechanism in the course of its community engagement process and ensure that the mechanism addresses concerns promptly and transparently, in a culturally appropriate manner, and is readily accessible to all segments of the affected communities.

Principle 7: Independent Review

For all Category A projects and, as appropriate, for Category B projects, an independent social or environmental expert not directly associated with the borrower will review the Assessment, AP and consultation process documentation in order to assist EPFI's due diligence, and assess Equator Principles compliance.

Principle 8: Covenants

An important strength of the Principles is the incorporation of covenants linked to compliance. For Category A and B projects, the borrower will covenant in financing documentation:

a) to comply with all relevant host country social and environmental laws, regulations and permits in all material respects;

b) to comply with the AP (where applicable) during the construction and operation of the project in all material respects;

c) to provide periodic reports in a format agreed with EPFIs (with the frequency of these reports proportionate to the severity of impacts, or as required by law, but not less than annually), prepared by in-house staff or third party experts, that i) document compliance with the AP (where applicable), and ii) provide representation of compliance with relevant local, state and host country social and environmental laws, regulations and permits; and

d) to decommission the facilities, where applicable and appropriate, in accordance with an agreed decommissioning plan.

Where a borrower is not in compliance with its social and environmental covenants, EPFIs will work with the borrower to bring it back into compliance to the extent feasible, and if the borrower fails to re-establish compliance within an agreed grace period, EPFIs reserve the right to exercise remedies, as they consider appropriate.

Principle 9: Independent Monitoring and Reporting

To ensure ongoing monitoring and reporting over the life of the loan, EPFIs will, for all Category A projects, and as appropriate, for Category B projects, require appointment of an independent environmental and/or social expert, or require that the borrower retain qualified and experienced external experts to verify its monitoring information which would be shared with EPFIs.

Principle 10: EPFI Reporting

Each EPFI adopting the Equator Principles commits to report publicly at least annually about its Equator Principles implementation processes and experience, taking into account appropriate confidentiality considerations.[6]

DISCLAIMER

The adopting EPFIs view these Principles as a financial industry benchmark for developing individual, internal social and environmental policies, procedures and practices. As with all internal policies, these Principles do not create any rights in, or liability to, any person, public or private. Institutions are adopting and implementing these Principles voluntarily and independently, without reliance on or recourse to IFC or the World Bank.

Exhibit I: Categorisation of projects

As part of their review of a project's expected social and environmental impacts, EPFIs use a system of social and environmental categorisation, based on IFC's environmental and social screening criteria, to reflect the magnitude of impacts understood as a result of assessment. These categories are:

- **Category A** – Projects with potential significant adverse social or environmental impacts that are diverse, irreversible or unprecedented;

6 Such reporting should at a minimum include the number of transactions screened by each EPFI, including the categorisation accorded to transactions (and may include a breakdown by sector or region), and information regarding .

- **Category B** – Projects with potential limited adverse social or environmental impacts that are few in number, generally site-specific, largely reversible and readily addressed through mitigation measures; and
- **Category C** – Projects with minimal or no social or environmental impacts.

Exhibit II: Illustrative list of potential social and environmental issues to be addressed in the Social and Environmental Assessment documentation

In the context of the business of the project, the Assessment documentation will address, where applicable, the following issues:

a) assessment of the baseline social and environmental conditions

b) consideration of feasible environmentally and socially preferable alternatives

c) requirements under host country laws and regulations, applicable international treaties and agreements

d) protection of human rights and community health, safety and security (including risks, impacts and management of project's use of security personnel)

e) protection of cultural property and heritage

f) protection and conservation of biodiversity, including endangered species and sensitive ecosystems in modified, natural and critical habitats, and identification of legally protected areas

g) sustainable management and use of renewable natural resources (including sustainable resource management through appropriate independent certification systems)

h) use and management of dangerous substances

i) major hazards assessment and management

j) labour issues (including the four core labour standards), and occupational health and safety

k) fire prevention and life safety

l) socio-economic impacts

m) land acquisition and involuntary resettlement

n) impacts on affected communities, and disadvantaged or vulnerable groups

o) impacts on indigenous peoples, and their unique cultural systems and values

p) cumulative impacts of existing projects, the proposed project, and anticipated future projects

q) consultation and participation of affected parties in the design, review and implementation of the project

r) efficient production, delivery and use of energy

s) pollution prevention and waste minimisation, pollution controls (liquid effluents and air emissions) and solid and chemical waste management

Note: The above list is for illustrative purposes only. The Social and Environmental Assessment process of each project may or may not identify all issues noted above, or be relevant to every project.

Exhibit III: IFC Performance Standards on Social and Environmental Sustainability

As of April 30, 2006, the following list of IFC Performance Standards were applicable:

- Performance Standard 1: Social & Environmental Assessment & Management System
- Performance Standard 2: Labor and Working Conditions
- Performance Standard 3: Pollution Prevention and Abatement
- Performance Standard 4: Community Health, Safety and Security
- Performance Standard 5: Land Acquisition and Involuntary Resettlement
- Performance Standard 6: Biodiversity Conservation and Sustainable Natural Resource Management
- Performance Standard 7: Indigenous Peoples
- Performance Standard 8: Cultural Heritage

Note: The IFC has developed a set of **Guidance Notes** to accompany each Performance Standard. While not formally adopting the Guidance Notes, EPFIs or borrowers may use the Guidance Notes as useful points of reference when seeking further guidance on or interpretation of the Performance Standards. The IFC Performance Standards, Guidance Notes and Industry Sector EHS Guidelines can be found at www.ifc.org/enviro.

Exhibit IV: Industry-Specific Environmental, Health and Safety (EHS) Guidelines

EPFIs will utilise the appropriate environmental, health and safety (EHS) guidelines used by IFC which are now in place, and as may be amended from time-to-time.

IFC is using two complementary sets of EHS Guidelines available at the IFC website (www.ifc.org/enviro). These sets consist of all the environmental guidelines contained in Part III of the World Bank's Pollution Prevention and Abatement Handbook (PPAH) which went into official use on July 1, 1998 and a series of environmental, health and safety guidelines published on the IFC website between 1991 and 2003. Ultimately new guidelines, incorporating the concepts of cleaner production and environmental management systems, will be written to replace this series of industry sector, PPAH and IFC guidelines.

Where no sector specific guideline exists for a particular project then the PPAH's General Environmental Guidelines and the IFC Occupational Health and Safety Guidelines (2003) are applied, with modifications as necessary to suit the project.*

The table below lists both the World Bank Guidelines and the IFC Guidelines as of March 1, 2006.

Industry Specific EHS Guidelines:

World Bank Guidelines (PPAH)	IFC Guidelines
1. Aluminum Manufacturing	1. Airports
2. Base Metal and Iron Ore Mining	2. Ceramic Tile Manufacturing
3. Breweries	3. Construction Materials Plants
4. Cement Manufacturing	4. Electric Power Transmission and Distribution
5. Chlor-Alkali Plants	5. Fish Processing
6. Coal Mining and Production	6. Food and Beverage Processing
7. Coke Manufacturing	7. Forestry Operations: Logging
8. Copper Smelting	8. Gas Terminal Systems
9. Dairy Industry	9. Geothermal Projects
10. Dye Manufacturing	10. Hazardous Materials Management
11. Electronics Manufacturing	11. Health Care
12. Electroplating Industry	12. Life & Fire Safety
13. Foundries	13. Occupational Health and Safety
14. Fruit and Vegetable Processing	14. Office Buildings
15. General Environmental Guidelines	15. Offshore Oil & Gas
16. Glass Manufacturing	16. Polychlorinated Biphenyls (PCBs)
17. Industrial Estates	17. Pesticide Handling and Application
18. Iron and Steel Manufacturing	18. Plantations
19. Lead and Zinc Smelting	19. Port and Harbor Facilities
20. Meat Processing and Rendering	20. Rail Transit Systems
21. Mini Steel Mills	21. Roads and Highways
22. Mixed Fertilizer Plants	22. Telecommunications
23. Monitoring	23. Tourism and Hospitality Development
24. Nickel Smelting and Refining	24. Waste Management Facilities
25. Nitrogenous Fertilizer Plants	25. Wastewater Reuse
26. Oil and Gas Development (Onshore)	26. Wildland Management
27. Pesticides Formulation	27. Wind Energy Conversion Systems
28. Pesticides Manufacturing	28. Wood Products Industries
29. Petrochemicals Manufacturing	
30. Petroleum Refining	
31. Pharmaceutical Manufacturing	
32. Phosphate Fertilizer Plants	
33. Printing Industry	
34. Pulp and Paper Mills	
35. Sugar Manufacturing	
36. Tanning and Leather Finishing	
37. Textiles Industry	
38. Thermal Power Guidelines for New Plants	
39. Thermal Power Rehabilitation of Existing Plants	
40. Vegetable Oil Processing	
41. Wood Preserving Industry	

* Exception (the following are World Bank Guidelines not contained in the PPAH and currently in use)
Mining and Milling – Underground
Mining and Milling – Open Pit

25
The Principles for Responsible Investment

> **The PRI is becoming a de facto industry standard for responsible investment.**
>
> *Alain Dromer, CEO, Aviva*[1]

Type Principles

Strength Linkages with other initiatives

Linkages UN Global Compact; EITI; Carbon Disclosure Project

Keywords Environmental • Social • Governance • Disclosure • Reporting

25.1 Overview

The Principles for Responsible Investment (PRI) provide a framework for investors on how to incorporate environmental, social and governance (ESG) issues into investment decisions. The goal of the PRI is to affect change throughout the mainstream investment community, not only within the socially responsible investment community. The PRI contains six principles which address a broad range of issues, from disclosure to effectiveness of implementation. The PRI uses investment as leverage to drill ESG aims into companies across the board.

1 Investor Keynote Speech, Triple Bottom Line Investment (TBLI) Conference, 13 November 2008.

Rather than exclude or divest from socially and environmentally irresponsible companies, the PRI creates opportunities for engagement across a wide range of investment categories. The PRI process was convened in 2005 by the UN Secretary-General. Since then, it has enjoyed rapid growth, and in only two years grew to cover $14 trillion in assets. This asset base provides support for implementation and dissemination. PRI signatories are encouraged to provide a voluntary contribution of $10,000 to assist the secretariat.

The initial focus of the PRI is on 'innovation, collaboration and learning by doing'. All signatories must report on progress. The PRI's flexible structure allows for a wide range of complementary and innovative ventures.

The PRI provides an excellent example of how a voluntary initiative can allow for systemic change and how principles can provide clarity and momentum. The PRI have benefited from the experiences of other initiatives and created a very good model for change management within a sector. It provides an excellent example of how an initiative can deliver results through collaboration by pooling resources and sharing best practices. Engagement across a wide spectrum of investors is far more effective than within a country or sector.

The PRI is governed by a 13-person Board, which includes 11 elected members from among the asset owners and two representatives from the UN system (to include one from UNEP and one from the Global Compact).

There are three categories of signatories:

- **Asset owners:** including pension funds, government reserve funds, foundations, insurance and reinsurance companies as well as depository organisations
- **Investment managers**
- **Professional service partners** are organisations that function as providers of services.

Signatories decide which category they belong in, but the PRI Board reserves the right to advise and make a final determination on which is the best category. An important benchmark for the PRI is defining an investor *vis-à-vis* a manager. An entity is an investor if it manages more of its own funds than of third-party clients.

25.2 Strengths and weaknesses

The PRI benefits from the direct involvement of the UN Global Compact (UNGC) and the UN Environment Programme (UNEP). The UNGC and UNEP provide leadership and expertise, as well as support and models of best practice.

The PRI requires commitment from top leadership within investment bodies. This is critical for affecting change within organisations and also within companies in which the organisations invest and within their supplier base.

The PRI has integrated a wide range of issues: from environmental and social, to governance. It has also worked synergistically with a range of other initiatives, including the EITI (see Chapter 17).

In its reporting, the PRI has been very transparent, providing data on how the PRI signatories are implementing the principles. Rapid growth allows for a rapidly expanding source of revenues. Like many initiatives, the PRI is geared towards large investors; however, there is a Small Funds Initiative which helps smaller investors to collaborate on implementation. (Small investors are considered to be those with assets of less than $2 billion.)

25.3 Challenges and opportunities

Like the Equator Principles, the PRI has undergone very rapid growth. Managing such growth can be a challenge to the provision of services. (In a 12-month period, the PRI nearly doubled its number of signatories.)

Another challenge facing PRI (and other initiatives) is to attract signatories from the developing world. Aware of this challenge, the PRI has formed an Emerging Markets Project, which features workshops in South Africa and activities in Brazil and Thailand. The PRI is developing region-specific tools which will include more materials in local languages.

The turbulence in financial markets may also pose a challenge, or it may provide a catalyst for action and renewed focus on governance issues.

The PRI is utilising technology to create mechanisms for dialogue. For example, it has created an Engagement Clearinghouse, an online forum for collaboration between and among signatories. There is also an Implementation Blog.

An example of how PRI signatories co-ordinate their engagement includes the rapid response to allegations that the steel industry was confronted by the issue of forced labour in its supply chain in Brazil. By developing a concerted response, the PRI signatories were able to mobilise change by showing the steel industry that concern was widespread.

Additional resources

Website

Principles for Responsible Investment: www.unpri.org

The Principles for Responsible Investment*

As institutional investors, we have a duty to act in the best long-term interests of our beneficiaries. In this fiduciary role, we believe that environmental, social, and corporate governance (ESG) issues can affect the performance of investment portfolios (to varying degrees across companies, sectors, regions, asset classes and through time). We also recognise that applying these Principles may better align investors with broader objectives of society. Therefore, where consistent with our fiduciary responsibilities, we commit to the following:

1 **We will incorporate ESG issues into investment analysis and decision-making processes.**

Possible actions:

- Address ESG issues in investment policy statements
- Support development of ESG-related tools, metrics, and analyses
- Assess the capabilities of internal investment managers to incorporate ESG issues
- Assess the capabilities of external investment managers to incorporate ESG issues
- Ask investment service providers (such as financial analysts, consultants, brokers, research firms, or rating companies) to integrate ESG factors into evolving research and analysis
- Encourage academic and other research on this theme
- Advocate ESG training for investment professionals

* www.unpri.org/principles

2 We will be active owners and incorporate ESG issues into our ownership policies and practices.

Possible actions:

- Develop and disclose an active ownership policy consistent with the Principles
- Exercise voting rights or monitor compliance with voting policy (if outsourced)
- Develop an engagement capability (either directly or through outsourcing)
- Participate in the development of policy, regulation, and standard setting (such as promoting and protecting shareholder rights)
- File shareholder resolutions consistent with long-term ESG considerations
- Engage with companies on ESG issues
- Participate in collaborative engagement initiatives
- Ask investment managers to undertake and report on ESG-related engagement

3 We will seek appropriate disclosure on ESG issues by the entities in which we invest.

Possible actions:

- Ask for standardised reporting on ESG issues (using tools such as the Global Reporting Initiative)
- Ask for ESG issues to be integrated within annual financial reports
- Ask for information from companies regarding adoption of/adherence to relevant norms, standards, codes of conduct or international initiatives (such as the UN Global Compact)
- Support shareholder initiatives and resolutions promoting ESG disclosure

4 We will promote acceptance and implementation of the Principles within the investment industry.

Possible actions:

- Include Principles-related requirements in requests for proposals (RFPs)
- Align investment mandates, monitoring procedures, performance indicators and incentive structures accordingly (for example, ensure investment management processes reflect long-term time horizons when appropriate)
- Communicate ESG expectations to investment service providers
- Revisit relationships with service providers that fail to meet ESG expectations
- Support the development of tools for benchmarking ESG integration

- Support regulatory or policy developments that enable implementation of the Principles

5 We will work together to enhance our effectiveness in implementing the Principles.

Possible actions:

- Support/participate in networks and information platforms to share tools, pool resources, and make use of investor reporting as a source of learning
- Collectively address relevant emerging issues
- Develop or support appropriate collaborative initiatives

6 We will each report on our activities and progress towards implementing the Principles.

Possible actions:

- Disclose how ESG issues are integrated within investment practices
- Disclose active ownership activities (voting, engagement, and/or policy dialogue)
- Disclose what is required from service providers in relation to the Principles
- Communicate with beneficiaries about ESG issues and the Principles
- Report on progress and/or achievements relating to the Principles using a 'Comply or Explain'[1] approach
- Seek to determine the impact of the Principles
- Make use of reporting to raise awareness among a broader group of stakeholders

The Principles for Responsible Investment were developed by an international group of institutional investors reflecting the increasing relevance of environmental, social and corporate governance issues to investment practices. The process was convened by the United Nations Secretary-General.

In signing the Principles, we as investors publicly commit to adopt and implement them, where consistent with our fiduciary responsibilities. We also commit to evaluate the effectiveness and improve the content of the Principles over time. We believe this will improve our ability to meet commitments to beneficiaries as well as better align our investment activities with the broader interests of society.

We encourage other investors to adopt the Principles.

1 The Comply or Explain approach requires signatories to report on how they implement the Principles, or provide an explanation where they do not comply with them.

Part X
Implementation

Parts I–IX of this book have addressed performance standards, defining acceptable norms for companies. Part X addresses process standards and guidelines that can assist companies in the implementation of corporate responsibility.

Part X will be looking at the 'how-to' side of corporate responsibility, covering:

- Stakeholder engagement
- Reporting
- Environmental management systems
- Assurance
- Professional qualifications

This part contains, in order of presentation, the following process standards and guidelines:

- AccountAbility 1000 (AA1000) Series
- AA1000 Assurance Standard
- Global Reporting Initiative
- ISO 14001

26
The AccountAbility 1000 Series: AA1000 AccountAbility Principles Standard 2008

> **The AA1000 [Series] provides the requisite flexibility that is essential to achieve innovation and continuous improvement.**
>
> ***Judith M. Mullins, Director of Emerging Issues and Process Integration, General Motors***[1]

> **The biggest challenge for the assurance professionals in responding to the increasing demands of corporate accountability and transparency, whether from a financial, environmental or other audit background, is to take an open and flexible approach and to dare to experiment. The AccountAbility 1000 [Series] provides an excellent structure for this experimentation by bringing together a multistakeholder view on what constitutes current best practice—both in terms of the principles and the processes our experimentation should be guided by and aspire to . . . Auditors must be prepared to work in new alliances and dialogue with our stakeholders.**
>
> ***David Coles, Partner, KPMG, Sustainability Advisory Services***[2]

Type Foundation standard

Strength It provides an overarching framework for corporate responsibility

Keywords Principles • Inclusivity • Materiality • Responsiveness • Accountability • Stakeholders • Assurance

1 'Launch of AccountAbility 1000: Endorsement Quotes', in *Notes for AccountAbility's Council Meeting in Copenhagen, 14 November, 1999.*

2 *Ibid.*

26.1 Background

The AA1000 Series includes three standards:

- AA1000APS (2008) Accountability Principles (page 444)
- AA1000AS (2008) Assurance Standard (page 455)
- AA1000SES (2005) Stakeholder Engagement Standard

The AccountAbility 1000 (AA1000) Series defines accountability as:

> acknowledging, assuming responsibility for and being transparent about the impacts of your policies, decisions, actions, products and associated performance.

Launched in 1999, the AA1000 Series is designed to assist companies, stakeholders, auditors, consultants and standard-setting bodies. The AA1000 Series can be used in two ways: on its own, or in conjunction with other corporate responsibility (CR) standards. It provides a roadmap for companies on key CR issues, explaining points of divergence and convergence with other major standards.

Founded in 1995, AccountAbility is a global, non-profit organisation that works to promote accountability innovation for sustainable development.

The AA1000 Series has as its premise three principles:

- The foundation principle of inclusivity
- The principles of materiality
- The principle of responsiveness

26.2 Companies to which the AccountAbility 1000 Principles Standard applies

The AA1000 AccountAbility Principles Standard is designed for organisations of all sizes in any country or sector. It can be used in conjunction with the Global Reporting Initiative (GRI, Chapter 28), ISO standards (on ISO 14001, see Chapter 29) and Social Accountability (SA8000, Chapter 8), among others.

26.3 Questions posed and answered

Given the complexity and breadth of issues covered, the AA1000 Series poses and answers many questions. Among the key questions addressed are:

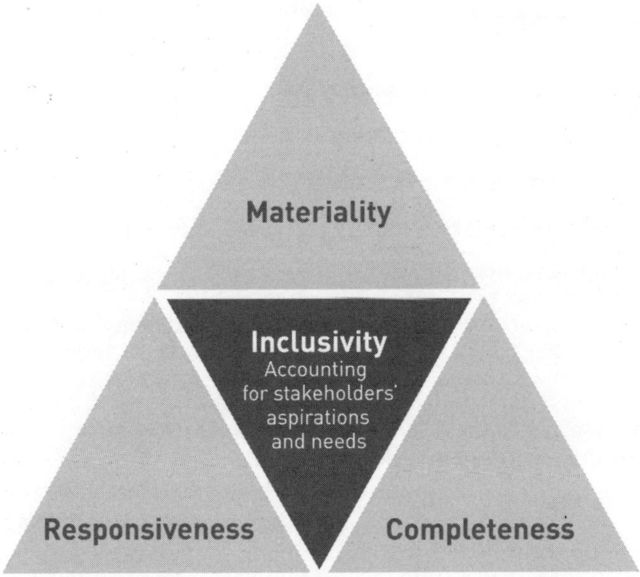

AA1000 Series: Commitment and Principles

- What is accountability? What is transparency?
- What are the principles that underpin accountability?

Reference

Smith, D. (2002) *Demonstrating Corporate Values: Which standard for your company?* (London: Institute for Business Ethics).

Additional resource

Website

AccountAbility: www.accountability.org

AA1000 AccountAbility Principles Standard 2008

FOREWORD

i. Evolution of the AA1000 AccountAbility Principles

The AccountAbility Principles for Sustainable Development first appeared in the AA1000 AccountAbility Framework Standard published in 1999. During the consultations for the development of the first edition of the AA1000 Assurance Standard, which was published in 2003, the principles underwent significant debate and revision. The result was the Commitment to Inclusivity supported by the three principles of Materiality, Completeness and Responsiveness. These principles were at the heart of the AA1000 Assurance Standard published in 2003, AA1000AS (2003), and the AA1000 Stakeholder Engagement Standard published in 2005, AA1000SES (2005). They were further clarified in a Guidance Note on the application of the principles in relation to AA1000AS (2003) published in 2006.

During the consultation process for the 2008 revision of the AA1000 Assurance Standard there was consensus that the AA1000 AccountAbility Principles be placed in a separate standard in order to allow for broader application and to facilitate their use during sustainability assurance engagements. This standard, the AA1000 AccountAbility Principles Standard, AA1000APS (2008), is the product of this consensus and includes three principles: the foundation principle of Inclusivity and the principles of Materiality and Responsiveness. While completeness is not included as an AccountAbility Principle it remains key to providing sustainability assurance, since it refers to the extent to which these three principles have been achieved.

The AA1000 AccountAbility Principles in this standard supersede all previous versions published by AccountAbility.

ii. Development process

The AA1000APS (2008) was developed using a broad-based, multi-stakeholder process. A period of initial research that included a widely broadcast e-survey was followed by face-to-face consultations in 20 countries with a comprehensive range of

---

stakeholders and a series of workshops with specific stakeholder groups. All of the input received was considered by the AccountAbility Standards Technical Committee, which prepared a draft standard for public review. There were three periods of public review of 60-90 days each. All public review took the form of collaborative drafting with full transparency using wiki software. Between each of these periods of public review and following the final period, the AccountAbility Standards Technical Committee reviewed and revised the draft. The final draft was agreed by the AccountAbility Standards Technical Committee and submitted to the AccountAbility Operating Board which approved it for publication.

The evolving nature of learning in the standards field means that the process of developing standards is ongoing. By continually engaging with AA1000 AccountAbility Principles users and stakeholders, AccountAbility is able to reflect learning in the form of additional guidance and revisions to its standards. AccountAbility invites you to share your AA1000 AccountAbility Principles experiences with us so that we can continue to improve the AA1000 Series.

INTRODUCTION

i. Aims and Benefits of the AA1000 AccountAbility Principles

Accountability is acknowledging, assuming responsibility for and being transparent about the impacts of your policies, decisions, actions, products and associated performance.

It obliges an organisation to involve stakeholders in identifying, understanding and responding to sustainability issues and concerns, and to report, explain and be answerable to stakeholders for decisions, actions and performance. It includes the way in which an organisation governs, sets strategy and manages performance.

The basic premise is that an accountable organisation will take action to:

- establish a strategy based on a comprehensive and balanced understanding of and response to material issues and stakeholder issues and concerns;
- establish goals and standards against which the strategy and associated performance can be managed and judged, and
- disclose credible information about strategy, goals, standards and performance to those who base their actions and decisions on this information.

These actions provide the basis for establishing, evaluating and communicating accountability. The AA1000 AccountAbility Principles set out in this standard drive these actions.

The value of these principles lies in their comprehensive coverage and the flexibility of their application. They demand that an organisation actively engages with its stakeholders, fully identifies and understands the sustainability issues that will have an impact on its performance, including economic, environmental, social and longer term financial performance, and then uses this understanding to develop responsible business strategies and performance objectives. As principles rather than prescriptive rules, they allow the organisation to focus on what is material to its own vision and provide a framework for identifying and acting on opportunities as well as managing non-financial risk and compliance.

ii. Scope of the standard

This standard covers the purpose, meaning, interrelationship and application of the AA1000 AccountAbility Principles.

1. PURPOSE OF THE AA1000APS (2008)

The purpose of the AA1000APS (2008) is to provide organisations with an internationally accepted, freely available set of principles to frame and structure the way in which they understand, govern, administer, implement, evaluate and communicate their accountability.

The AA1000 AccountAbility Principles are primarily intended for use by organisations developing an accountable and strategic approach to sustainability. They will help such an organisation understand, manage and improve its sustainability performance.

In addition, users of other standards in the AA1000 Series use these principles according to the requirements of the relevant AA1000 standard.

Note: The AA1000 AccountAbility Principles provide the basis for understanding and achieving sustainability assurance according to the AA1000AS (2008) and accountable stakeholder engagement according to the AA1000SES (2005).

2. THE ACCOUNTABILITY PRINCIPLES

There are three AA1000 AccountAbility Principles, one of which is a foundation principle.

- **The Foundation Principle of Inclusivity**
- **The Principle of Materiality**
- **The Principle of Responsiveness**

The foundation principle of Inclusivity is necessary for the achievement of Materiality and Responsiveness. Together the three principles support the realisation of accountability.

Inclusivity is the starting point for determining materiality. The materiality process determines the most relevant and significant issues for an organisation and its stakeholders. Responsiveness is the decisions, actions and performance related to those material issues.

2.1 The Foundation Principle of Inclusivity

Principle

An organisation shall be inclusive.

Definition

For an organisation that accepts its accountability to those on whom it has an impact and who have an impact on it, inclusivity is the participation of stakeholders in developing and achieving an accountable and strategic response to sustainability.

Stakeholders are those individuals, groups of individuals or organisations that affect and/or could be affected by an organisation's activities, products or services and associated performance.

Explanation

Inclusivity is much more than a stakeholder engagement process. It is the commitment to be accountable to those on whom the organisation has an impact and who have an impact on it, and to enable their participation in identifying issues and finding solutions. It is about collaborating at all levels, including governance, to achieve better outcomes.

Accepting accountability to those it has an impact on (its stakeholders) does not mean that an organisation has to do everything that a stakeholder requests, nor that it loses the responsibility to make its own decisions.

Inclusivity requires a defined process of engagement and participation that provides comprehensive and balanced involvement and results in strategies, plans, actions and outcomes that address and respond to issues and impacts in an accountable way.

An organisation seeks to have a comprehensive understanding of who its stakeholders are and a comprehensive and balanced understanding of their needs and concerns and the ways in which they engage.

The way in which an organisation engages with stakeholders will depend on the capacities of both and the maturity of the existing relationship.

Criteria

An organisation will adhere to the principle of inclusivity when:

- It has made a commitment to be accountable to those on whom it has an impact or who have an impact on it.
- It has in place a process of stakeholder participation that:
    - is applied across the organisation (e.g. group and local level);
    - is integrated in the organisation, and
    - is ongoing and not 'one off'.

- It has in place, or has access to, the necessary competencies and resources to operate the process of stakeholder participation.
- The stakeholder participation process:
  - identifies and understands stakeholders, their capacity to engage, and their views and expectations;
  - identifies, develops and implements appropriate, robust and balanced engagement strategies, plans and modes of engagement for stakeholders;
  - facilitates understanding, learning and improvement of the organisation;
  - establishes ways for stakeholders to be involved in decisions that will improve sustainability performance;
  - builds the capacity of internal stakeholders and supports building capacity for external stakeholders to engage, and
  - addresses conflicts or dilemmas between different stakeholder expectations.
- The stakeholder engagement results in the involvement of stakeholders in developing and achieving an accountable and strategic response to sustainability.

2.2 The Principle of Materiality

Principle

An organisation shall identify its material issues.

Definitions

Materiality is determining the relevance and significance of an issue to an organisation and its stakeholders.

A material issue is an issue that will influence the decisions, actions and performance of an organisation or its stakeholders.

Explanation

To make good decisions and actions an organisation and its stakeholders need to know what issues are material to the sustainability performance of the organisation.

To determine what is material requires a materiality determination process. The process is designed to ensure that comprehensive and balanced information is input and then analysed. An organisation needs to input the right types of information from the right sources, covering an appropriate time period. Such inputs include information other than financial information: information on non-financial, sustainability drivers and their impact on stakeholders. The sources of information will include information from stakeholders. The time period encompasses the short, medium and long-term.

The analysis of the information takes into consideration sustainability drivers and accounts for the needs, concerns and expectations of the organisation and its stakeholders. It is the organisation that is ultimately responsible for the determination of its material issues. This process is aligned with the processes for organisational decision making and strategy development.

An organisation develops a comprehensive understanding of its sustainability context and what its material issues are, as well as those issues that, while not material to the organisation, still require a response, and a balanced and robust understanding of who they are material to and why.

The determination of material issues will change over time as issues mature and understanding improves.

Criteria

An organisation will adhere to the principle of materiality when:

- It has in place a materiality determination process that:
  - is applied across the organisation (e.g. group and local level);
  - is integrated in the organisation, and
  - is ongoing and not 'one off'.
- It has in place, or has access to, the necessary competencies and resources to apply the materiality determination process.
- The materiality determination process:
  - identifies and fairly represents issues from a wide range of sources including the needs and concerns of stakeholders, societal norms, financial considerations, peer-based norms and policy-based performance and understands their sustainability context;
  - evaluates the relevance of the identified sustainability issues based on suitable and explicit criteria that are credible, clear and understandable as well as replicable, defensible and assurable;
  - determines the significance of the identified sustainability issues using criteria and thresholds that are credible, clear and understandable as well as replicable, defensible and assurable;
  - takes into account the changing sustainability context and maturity of issues and concerns, and
  - includes a means of addressing conflicts or dilemmas between different expectations regarding materiality.
- The materiality determination process results in a comprehensive and balanced understanding and prioritisation of its material sustainability issues.

2.3 The Principle of Responsiveness

Principle

An organisation shall respond to stakeholder issues that affect its performance.

Definition

Responsiveness is an organisation's response to stakeholder issues that affect its sustainability performance and is realised through decisions, actions and performance, as well as communication with stakeholders.

Explanation

Responsiveness is how an organisation demonstrates it responds to its stakeholders and is accountable to them. This may include: establishing policies, objectives and targets, governance structure, management systems and processes, action plans, stakeholder engagement, measurement and monitoring of performance or assurance. An organisation's responses may not agree with the views of all stakeholders. Stakeholders participate in developing responses.

Since responses will compete for available resources, responses are necessarily prioritised. This prioritisation needs to be consistent with other strategies and operations, as well as with stakeholder interests, and communicated to stakeholders. An organisation seeks to allocate adequate resources for responses. Resources are adequate when they allow the organisation to achieve its stated commitments within the stated time period and to communicate its responses in a way that is consistent with stakeholder interests and expectations.

An organisation communicates responses in a manner that meets the needs and expectations of its stakeholders so they can take informed decisions. An organisation puts in place the necessary competencies, capacity and processes to achieve the responses it commits to. An organisation responds in a timely way.

A responsive organisation will respond to its material issues and to its stakeholders in a comprehensive and balanced manner, however, the way in which an organisation responds to an issue will depend on the maturity of the issue as well as the maturity of the organisation.

Criteria

An organisation will adhere to the principle of responsiveness when:

- It has in place a process for developing appropriate responses that:
    - is applied across the organisation (e.g. group and local level);
    - is integrated in the organisation;
    - is ongoing and not 'one off';

  - is based on a comprehensive and balanced understanding of the response to material issues expected by stakeholders;
  - involves stakeholders as appropriate;
  - considers the relationship between the maturity of an issue and the appropriateness of a response;
  - prioritises responses taking materiality and resource requirements into account, and
  - considers the timeliness of response.
- It has in place, or has access to, the necessary competencies and resources to achieve its commitments.
- It responds in a comprehensive and balanced way to material issues.
- It responds in a way that addresses the needs, concerns and expectations of stakeholders.
- It responds in a timely way.
- It has in place a process to communicate with stakeholders that:
  - is applied across the organisation (e.g. group and local level);
  - is integrated in the organisation, and
  - is ongoing and not 'one off'.
- The communications process:
  - reflects the needs and expectations of stakeholders;
  - is comprehensive and balanced, identifies shortcomings and prevents material misstatements, and
  - is accessible to stakeholders.
- It uses suitable reporting principles, frameworks or guidelines for sustainability reporting.
- The communications process results in comprehensive and balanced communications to stakeholders that are consistent with the nature and extent of the organisation's adherence to the AA1000 AccountAbility Principles.

3. REFERENCES TO THE AA1000 ACCOUNTABILITY PRINCIPLES

The AA1000 AccountAbility Principles are used to guide sustainability assurance in accordance with the AA1000AS (2008) and stakeholder engagement in accordance with the AA1000SES (2005). Any reference to the use of these principles shall be acknowledged. The term AA1000 AccountAbility Principles shall not be used in relation to principles that are significantly modified, supplemented or referred to in isolation, as this may mislead users.

27
The AccountAbility 1000 Assurance Standard

> **The AA1000 Assurance Standard offers a unique opportunity to resurrect assurance, phoenix-like, from the ashes of Enron, WorldCom and other trust-eroding corporate disasters.**
>
> *John Elkington, Chairperson, SustainAbility Ltd*[1]

Type Process standard

Strength It promotes the development of professional qualifications

Keywords Assurance • Assurance providers • AccountAbility • Principles • Competence

27.1 Background

In an age of cynicism, one of the key challenges for corporate responsibility is the need to demonstrate that social and environmental programmes are making a difference. Consumers and investors are less inclined to trust companies after the scandals of WorldCom, Enron (Fox 2002; Sullivan 2002) and Ahold (*Economist* 2003). The assurance of corporate responsibility (CR) initiatives plays a key role in building the trust necessary to sustain these programmes. According to AccountAbility:

> The concern that more data does not always equate to accurate or useful information is damaging the credibility and effectiveness of today's progressive drive to increase social and sustainability accounting and reporting (AccountAbility 2002).

1 Speaking at the launch of the AA1000 Assurance Standard, London, 25 March 2003 (www.accountability.org.uk, accessed 2003).

AccountAbility has turned the field of corporate responsibility into a discipline, setting out professional qualifications, providing training and developing methodologies—'the how'—of corporate responsibility.

According to the AA1000 Assurance Standard, assurance can be defined as:

> . . . the methods and processes employed by an assurance provider to evaluate an organisation's public disclosure about its performance as well as underlying systems, data and processes against suitable criteria and standards in order to increase the credibility of public disclosure. Assurance includes the communication of the results of the assurance process in an assurance statement (AA1000 AS 2008: 23).

The AA1000 Assurance Standard includes four elements:

- Core assurance principles
- Practice and quality standards and guidelines
- Guidelines for organisations
- Qualifications of assurance providers

Owing to space constraints only some sections of the AA1000 Assurance Standard are included.

27.2 Strengths and weaknesses

The AA1000 Assurance Standard is designed to cover assurance processes across the spectrum of sustainability issues. It is compatible with the Global Reporting Initiative (GRI, Chapter 28) in that it provides guidance to global reporters using the GRI guidelines. The AA1000 Assurance Standard can also be used with audits of factory compliance with labour standards and carbon emissions.

The AA1000 Assurance Standard is accessible online at no cost. This accessibility of the standard is important, as it facilitates consultation with stakeholders. The consultation process for the AA1000 Assurance Standard has been thorough, benefiting from input from a wide range of organisations.

27.3 Organisations to which the AA1000 Assurance Standard applies

The AA1000 Assurance Standard is designed to assist assurance practitioners and providers. Companies developing reports may find the standard useful as well as they develop assurance mechanisms. Stakeholders can also benefit from an understanding of how the assurance process works.

27.4 Questions posed and answered

The AA1000 Assurance Standard asks:

- What are the different levels of assurance?
- What constitutes a competent assurance statement?
- How should the assurance provider plan and perform the engagement?

27.5 The challenge and the promise

As more and more companies and assurance providers are guided by the AA1000 Assurance Standard, the credibility of corporate responsibility will increase, with a corresponding decrease in apathy. Reporting should become more focused, credible and, most importantly, useful to stakeholders. The AA1000 Assurance Standard should limit conflicts of interest between service providers and the organisations to which they provide assurance. These benefits will also promote the field of socially responsible investment (SRI), making the decision-making process within the SRI community more likely to be based on credible and accurate information. Furthermore, the AA1000 Assurance Standard, if implemented broadly, will promote the comparability of reports across different sectors.

A major challenge facing the field of assurance will be to build capacity among assurance providers. The AA1000 Assurance Standard provides useful guidance in this emerging field.

References

AccountAbility (2002) 'Closing the Assurance Gap: The AA1000 Series Quality Assurance Framework' (London: AccountAbility, April 2002).

—— (2003) *AccountAbility 1000 Assurance Standard* (London: AccountAbility).

Economist (2003) 'Europe's Enron: Ahold's Shocking Accounting', *The Economist*, 1 March 2003.

Fox, L. (2002) *Enron: The Rise and Fall* (New York; John Wiley).

Sullivan, R. (2002) 'One Step Forward or Two Steps Back for Effective Self-regulation?', *Journal of Corporate Citizenship* 8 (Winter 2002): 91-104.

Additional resource

Website

AccountAbility: www.accountability.org

AA1000 Assurance Standard*

1. PURPOSE OF THE AA1000AS (2008)

The AA1000AS (2008) is an internationally accepted, freely available standard that provides the requirements for conducting sustainability assurance.

Sustainability assurance in accordance with the AA1000AS (2008) evaluates and provides conclusions on:

- the nature and extent of adherence to the AA1000 AccountAbility Principles, and where applicable
- the quality of publicly disclosed information on sustainability performance.

This standard is primarily intended for use by sustainability assurance practitioners and providers. This standard may also be useful to report preparers seeking assurance in accordance with this standard, as well as to users of sustainability assurance reports and statements and other standards developers.

Note: The AA1000 AccountAbility Principles are presented in the AA1000 AccountAbility Principles Standard.

2. USING THE AA1000AS (2008)

2.1. Types of AA1000AS (2008) engagement

There are two types of AA1000AS (2008) sustainability assurance engagement:

Type 1 – AccountAbility Principles

The assurance provider shall evaluate the nature and extent of the organisation's adherence to all three AA1000 AccountAbility Principles.

Assurance on the AA1000 AccountAbility Principles is intended to give stakeholders assurance on the way an organisation manages sustainability performance, and how it communicates this in its sustainability reporting, without verifying the reliability of the reported information.

The assurance provider evaluates publicly disclosed information, the systems and processes the organisation has in place to ensure adherence to the principles and the performance information that demonstrates adherence. For Type 1 assurance, the evaluation of performance information does not require the assurance provider to provide conclusions on the reliability of the performance information. Rather, it uses information on performance as a source of evidence when evaluating adherence to the principles. An assurance provider is not restricted in the types of information it seeks as evidence.

The evaluation does not need to be based on explicit management assertions about adherence to the Principles, although an assertion based approach to assurance accords with the AA1000AS (2008).

For assurance on adherence to the AA1000 AccountAbility Principles an assurance provider provides findings and conclusions relating to the nature and extent of an organisation's adherence to the Principles.

Type 2 – AccountAbility Principles and Performance Information

The assurance provider shall evaluate the nature and extent of the organisation's adherence to the AA1000 AccountAbility Principles, as for Type 1.

When conducting a Type 2 engagement, the assurance provider shall also evaluate the reliability of specified sustainability performance information. Specified sustainability performance information is the information the assurance provider and the reporting organisation agree to include in the scope of the assurance engagement. Specified information is selected based on the materiality determination and needs to be meaningful to the intended users of the assurance statement. An assurance engagement that only includes an evaluation of the reliability of specified publicly disclosed sustainability performance information is not in accordance with the AA1000AS (2008).

The evaluation of the reliability of specified sustainability performance information is based on explicit management assertions about sustainability performance and includes a review of their completeness and accuracy.

For assurance on specified sustainability performance information an assurance provider provides findings and conclusions relating to the reliability of the sustainability performance information.

If an organisation provides in its report an assertion concerning compliance with a specified reporting framework, and compliance with this reporting framework is included with the scope of the specified sustainability performance information to be assured, the assurance provider provides findings and conclusions on compliance with the reporting framework.

2.2. Levels of AA1000AS (2008) assurance

An assurance engagement may be carried out to provide a high level of assurance or a moderate level of assurance. Since different subject matter may be addressed in one assurance engagement, a high level of assurance may be provided for some subject matter while a moderate level of assurance may be provided for other subject matter in the same assurance statement.

The following table outlines the characteristics of high and moderate assurance and the related assurance procedures.

<table>
<tr><th colspan="3">Characteristics of High and Moderate assurance</th></tr>
<tr><th></th><th>High assurance</th><th>Moderate assurance</th></tr>
<tr><td>Objective</td><td>The assurance provider achieves high assurance where sufficient evidence has been obtained to support their statement such that the risk of their conclusion being in error is very low but not zero.

High assurance will provide users with a high level of confidence in an organisation's disclosures on the subject matter it refers to.</td><td>The assurance provider achieves moderate assurance where sufficient evidence has been obtained to support their statement such that the risk of their conclusion being in error is reduced but not reduced to very low but not zero.

Moderate assurance will enhance the user's confidence in an organisation's disclosures on the subject matter it refers to.</td></tr>
<tr><td>Evidence characteristics</td><td>Unrestricted

For the principles

Evidence from internal and external sources and parties including stakeholders; evidence gathering at all levels of the organisation.

For the specified performance information

Extensive depth of evidence gathering including corroborative evidence and sufficient sampling at lower levels in the organisation. Emphasis is on the reliability of the information.</td><td>Less extensive

For the principles

Evidence from internal sources and parties; evidence gathering generally restricted to corporate/management levels in the organisation.

For the specified performance information

Limited depth of evidence gathering including inquiry and analytical procedures and limited sampling at lower levels in the organisation as necessary. Emphasis is on the plausibility of the information.</td></tr>
<tr><td>Statement</td><td>For principles

Conclusion on the nature and extent of adherence relating to disclosures by the organisation.

For the specified performance information

Conclusion on reliability.</td><td>For principles

Conclusion, based on work undertaken, on the nature and extent of adherence relating to disclosures by the organisation.

For the specified performance information

Conclusion on reliability based on procedures undertaken.</td></tr>
</table>

2.3. References to the use of the standard

Only assurance engagements that meet the requirements of this standard shall state that assurance has been provided in accordance with the AA1000AS (2008).

2.4. Relationship to other standards and guidance

The AA1000APS (2008) provides the criteria for evaluating adherence to the AccountAbility Principles.

Conventions, legal requirements, standards, guidelines and other frameworks may provide criteria to be used to evaluate sustainability performance information. These may be designed for specific performance issues, systems, processes, physical characteristics or behaviours. These may be subject matter or systems specific and may have associated verification or certification programs. In such cases it may be acceptable to use these verifications and certifications as evidence.

The AA1000AS (2008) is supported by a Guidance Note, *Guidance for the use of AA1000AS (2008)* which is intended to be used by assurance practitioners, reporting organisations seeking assurance and stakeholders using assurance statements.

3. ACCEPTING AN AA1000AS (2008) ENGAGEMENT

3.1. Scope of the engagement

The assurance provider shall agree the scope of the engagement with the reporting organisation based on the requirements in clause 2.1. The agreement shall be in writing.

When accepting a Type 2 engagement the assurance provider shall take into consideration the material issues so that the specified performance information covered by the assurance engagement is meaningful to the intended user of the assurance statement.

Before accepting an engagement the assurance provider shall be satisfied that the requirements of the AA1000AS (2008) can be met and that the reporting organisation is acting in good faith. In particular, the assurance provider shall be satisfied that the engagement subject matter is appropriate, and the practitioner will have access to sufficient evidence to support findings and conclusions.

3.1.1. Disclosures covered

The assurance provider shall identify and agree with the reporting organisation on all disclosures (e.g. reports and other forms of communication) to be covered by the assurance engagement.

3.1.2. Suitable criteria

The assurance provider shall use the criteria in AA1000APS (2008) to evaluate adherence to the AccountAbility Principles.

The assurance provider shall not accept a Type 2 engagement unless there are suitable criteria for evaluating specified performance information.

Suitable criteria are those that are relevant, complete, reliable, neutral and understandable. All criteria shall be publicly available.

Criteria can be either established or specifically developed. Established criteria may be found in regulatory requirements, as well as other standards, guidelines or frameworks and have been developed by an independent peer reviewed or multi-stakeholder processes. The preference is to use established criteria.

3.1.3. Level of assurance

The assurance provider shall agree the level of assurance to be provided with the reporting organisation. This may be a combination of levels, for example high or moderate in relation to the principles (Type 1 and Type 2) and high or moderate, or a combination, for a Type 2 engagement on specified performance information. The levels shall be documented in the assurance agreement.

The assurance provider shall be sufficiently confident that the agreed level is achievable (e.g. that systems, processes and evidence exist) before the engagement begins. The engagement shall be planned and conducted to obtain sufficient evidence to achieve the agreed level.

The assurance provider shall not agree to a change to a lower level of assurance during an engagement without good reason. This change shall be explained in the assurance statement.

The assurance statement shall reflect the agreed level of assurance for the engagement. If, for any reason, this is not achieved during the engagement, the reasons shall be explained in the assurance statement.

3.2. Independence and impartiality

An assurance provider shall not accept an engagement if it will be unduly limited by its relationship with the organisation or its stakeholders in reaching and publishing an independent and impartial assurance statement.

The assurance provider shall make a public statement of independence and impartiality that includes disclosure of:

- any relationships (including financial, commercial, preparation of the report, governance and ownership positions) that could be perceived to affect the assurance providers ability to provide an independent and impartial statement, and
- any mechanisms or professional codes of practice designed to ensure independence to which the assurance provider or assurance practitioner are bound.

3.3. Competence

An assurance provider shall not accept an engagement if it does not possess the necessary competencies.

Assurance providers shall ensure that the individual assurance practitioners and organisations, including external experts, involved in an assurance engagement are demonstrably competent.

The assurance provider shall be prepared, given the absence of any undue risk and upon request by a reporting organisation, to make information available to interested stakeholders about the competencies of the assurance practitioners involved in its assurance engagement.

3.3.1. Assurance practitioner competence

The assurance provider shall ensure that the individual assurance practitioners, as well as the external experts, involved in the assurance engagement are, as a team, demonstrably competent in the following areas as a minimum:

- the AccountAbility Principles;
- application of reporting and assurance practices and standards;
- sustainability subject matter (including the specific subject matter of the engagement), and
- stakeholder engagement.

3.3.2. Assurance provider competence

The organisational assurance provider shall be able to demonstrate adequate institutional competencies.

Competencies shall include:

- assurance oversight mechanism to ensure quality of provision;
- understanding of the legal aspects of the assurance process, and
- infrastructure and systems to ensure quality delivery of assurance.

3.4. Due care

Assurance providers and individual assurance practitioners shall exercise due care at all times in accordance with the needs of the users of their assurance statement, the importance of the task and the competencies required.

3.5. Engagement Agreement (contract)

The terms and conditions of the engagement shall be agreed in writing.

The use of existing organisational procurement practices and agreements shall be acceptable if at a minimum an agreement covers:

- responsibilities of the reporting organisation and assurance provider;
- subject matter;

- scope (including Type and Level), and
- the intention to provide assurance in accordance with the AA1000AS (2008).

4. CONDUCTING AN AA1000AS (2008) ENGAGEMENT

4.1. Planning the engagement

The assurance provider shall plan the assurance engagement so that it will be performed effectively. Planning involves developing a clear strategy for evidence gathering and evaluation for the agreed scope.

Adequate planning ensures a sufficiently comprehensive, robust and balanced assurance process. Planning is an iterative process and will occur throughout the engagement as an assurance provider may have to revise its plan due to evidence obtained.

The nature and extent of the planning process will vary depending on the size and complexity of the engagement. In planning an assurance provider shall consider:

- the tasks and activities to be performed;
- the evidence gathering requirements, sampling methods and associated risks;
- the resources requirements, and
- the schedule for the engagement.

The assurance provider shall document this in an engagement plan that includes as a minimum:

- objectives of the engagement;
- assurance standard/s to be used;
- roles and relationships;
- scope of the engagement;
- criteria to be used;
- level of assurance;
- assurance strategy, including:
  - risk assessment, and
  - evidence requirements;
- tasks and activities, including:
  - gathering methods;
  - resources requirements, and
  - schedule.

4.2. Performing the engagement

The assurance provider shall perform the engagement with an attitude of professional scepticism. This means assessing and questioning the validity of evidence obtained and the implications of this evidence.

4.2.1. Evaluation of adherence to the AA1000 AccountAbility Principles

During the assurance engagement the assurance provider shall evaluate and report findings and conclusions on the nature and extent of an organisation's adherence to the AA1000 AccountAbility Principles (Inclusivity, Materiality and Responsiveness). The assurance provider shall use the criteria in the AA1000APS (2008).

Minimum evidence gathering for evaluating adherence to the AA1000 AccountAbility Principles at a moderate level of assurance shall include:

- understanding and testing on a sample basis the processes used to adhere to and evaluate adherence to the AccountAbility Principles;
- inquiring of management, including senior management at executive and functional levels, and of relevant management responsible for the day to day management of sustainability, about the effectiveness of processes used to adhere to the AA1000 AccountAbility Principles;
- observing and inspecting management practices, process testing and evidence gathering across the organisation on a sample basis, and
- collecting and evaluating documentary evidence and management representations that support adherence to the principles.

For a high level of assurance the assurance provider shall also seek more extensive evidence in all areas as well as corroborative evidence where available, including through direct engagement with stakeholders.

For a high level of assurance the assurance provider shall obtain sufficient evidence such that the risk of their conclusion being in error is very low but not zero.

Further guidance can be found in the Guidance Note, *Guidance for the use of AA1000AS (2008)*.

4.2.2. Evaluation of specified sustainability performance information

If included in the scope of the assurance engagement, the assurance provider shall evaluate and report findings and conclusions on the reliability of specified sustainability performance information.

The assurance provider shall evaluate the systems, processes, information and data used to support sustainability performance disclosures on the issues agreed for inclusion in the scope of the assurance engagement. The scope of the evaluation of sustainability performance information shall state the performance information to be concluded upon, which may include compliance with a reporting framework if specified.

The assurance provider shall evaluate the quality of the public disclosures and the underlying systems, processes, information and data.

Minimum evidence gathering for evaluating the reliability of specified performance information at a moderate level of assurance shall include:

- understanding the management of specified performance information and information collection processes;
- reviewing the design of systems and processes for managing specified information;
- inquiring on a sample basis of individuals with overall responsibility for information measurement and collection (from source to aggregation) and reporting about the information collection processes;
- carrying out analytical procedures (e.g. trend analysis);
- observing and inspecting on a sample basis management practices, process testing and evidence gathering (from source to aggregation);
- limited testing of detail on a sample basis (e.g. re-performance of calculations);
- collecting and evaluating documentary evidence and management representations to support the assurance work undertaken, and
- confirming that what is disclosed is consistent with the findings of the assurance process.

For a high level of assurance the assurance provider shall also seek more extensive evidence in all relevant areas as well as corroborative evidence where available.

For a high level of assurance the assurance provider shall obtain sufficient evidence such that the risk of their conclusion being in error is very low but not zero.

Further guidance can be found in the Guidance Note, *Guidance for the use of AA1000AS (2008)*.

4.2.3. Limitations

Any limitations in the scope of the disclosures on sustainability, the assurance engagement or the evidence gathering shall be addressed in the assurance statement and reflected in the report to management if one is prepared.

Where the scope of a disclosure is limited the assurance provider shall indicate in its statement this limitation and the need for communications to address other sustainability issues and stakeholders.

The assurance provider shall determine if limitations encountered during the engagement make it impossible to continue the engagement, and shall take appropriate action.

4.2.4. Documentation

The assurance provider shall document evidence, retaining necessary copies of relevant evidence. The assurance provider shall also document the assurance plan, material assessments and judgements made, and conclusions.

4.3. Reporting by the assurance provider

4.3.1. Assurance statement

The result of the assurance process is a set of findings, conclusions and recommendations provided by the assurance provider in a publicly issued assurance statement.

Any limitations to the scope of a disclosure or the assurance engagement shall be addressed in the assurance statement.

To claim accordance with the AA1000AS (2008) in the assurance statement the assurance provider shall meet all the requirements of this standard, including the requirements for the assurance statement.

An AA1000AS (2008) assurance statement may also include any other legally required statements that may apply as well as the requirements of any standard used during the engagement.

An assurance statement shall include the following information as a minimum:

- intended users of the assurance statement;
- the responsibility of the reporting organisation and of the assurance provider;
- assurance standard/s used, including reference to the AA1000AS (2008);
- description of the scope, including the Type of assurance provided;
- description of disclosures covered;
- description of methodology;
- any limitations;
- reference to criteria used;
- statement of level of assurance;
- findings and conclusions concerning adherence to the AA1000 AccountAbility Principles of Inclusivity, Materiality and Responsiveness (in all instances);
- findings and conclusions concerning the reliability of specified performance information (for Type 2 assurance only);
- observations and/or recommendations;
- notes on competencies and independence of the assurance provider;
- name of the assurance provider, and
- date and place.

4.3.2. Report to Management

If agreed in the engagement agreement, the assurance provider shall prepare a report to management.

The report to management shall not communicate materially different conclusions than those found in the publicly available assurance statement. Where relevant, the report to management shall include any limitations in the scope of the disclosures on sustainability, the assurance engagement or the evidence gathering.

28 The Global Reporting Initiative

> **GRI may well become the Securities and Exchange Commission for worldwide economic, environmental and social sustainability reporting.**
>
> ***Peter Downing, The Corporate Board*[1]**

> **The GRI Guidelines have been a great help for us in understanding and translating the changing global agenda into topics and issues that Novo Nordisk should report on to the public.**
>
> ***Lise Kingo, Senior Vice President, Stakeholder Relations, Novo Nordisk*[2]**

Type Process-oriented tool, multi-stakeholder tool

Strength Its comprehensive and standardised reporting framework

Keywords Sustainability • Guidelines • Reporting • Social reports • Environment • Framework • Indicators • Multi-stakeholder

28.1 Background

The Global Reporting Initiative (GRI) has pioneered sustainability reporting, providing guidelines that serve as a framework for economic, social and environmental reporting. The mission of GRI is 'to elevate the quality of reporting to a higher level of comparability, consistency and utility' (GRI 2002a: 9).

1 Quoted on GRI website, www.globalreporting.org, accessed 2003.

2 GRI 2002b: 3.

In 1997, the Coalition for Environmentally Responsible Economies (Ceres) (see Chapter 14), in collaboration with the Tellus Institute, convened the GRI. The UN Environment Programme (UNEP) has also played an important role in the formation of the GRI. The Guidelines are the product of an intensive, multi-stakeholder, consultation process, involving thousands of non-governmental organisations (NGOs), companies, business groups, trade unions and accountancy organisations (United Nations 2002).

In June 2000, GRI launched the Sustainability Reporting Guidelines, and a fully revised and updated version was released in September 2002 during the World Summit on Sustainable Development. In 2006, the GRI launched the G3 Guidelines, parts of which are included in this book. Thousands of companies in 60 countries issue GRI reports.[3]

Although the GRI Guidelines are not a code of conduct, a management system or a standard, they are extremely useful to companies working on code implementation. The Guidelines promote the communication of (GRI 2002a: 11):

- Actions taken to improve economic, environmental and social performance
- The outcomes of such actions
- Future strategies for improvement

The G3 Guidelines are structured in two parts. Part 1 includes Principles to define report content: materiality, stakeholder inclusiveness, sustainability context, and completeness and guidance on how to set boundaries for the report. Part 2 includes standard disclosures, strategy and profile, management approach and performance indicators.

Due to space limitations, only the following excerpts from the Guidelines are included in this book:

- Principles for defining report content
- Principles for defining report quality
- Guidance for report boundary setting
- Options for reporting

The Guidelines set a framework for GRI reporters. Reporting organisations can strive to have their reports be 'in accordance' with the Guidelines or simply use the Guidelines informally. If companies select the former approach, they must meet certain set criteria. There is no formal verification by GRI to ensure that these criteria have been met.

3 For a list of companies see: www.globalreporting.org/GRIReports/GRIReportsList (accessed 9 June 2010).

28.2 Strengths and weaknesses

The GRI has strong support from companies and NGOs around the world. One of the factors that has led to its strong position as a brand leader among corporate responsibility (CR) initiatives, among all sectors, is the degree to which GRI has been very inclusive of its many stakeholder groups. In the first three years of its existence, GRI engaged with 10,000 stakeholders from more than 50 countries (United Nations 2002: 5). The 2000 version of the Guidelines was distributed to 12,000 people in eight different languages (United Nations 2002: 5). This unprecedented degree of outreach is one of the greatest achievements of the GRI. This level of engagement sets an important standard for consultation for new initiatives.

The GRI encourages companies to set targets and then to report on whether or not those targets have been met. If the company has not met its targets, it should give reasons. By encouraging companies to set and report on targets, stakeholders have 'standards' to which they can hold the company accountable. The GRI also encourages organisations to engage with stakeholders and to select organisation-specific performance indicators most relevant both to the reporting organisation and to its key stakeholders.

Many companies find the large number of indicators within the GRI framework daunting. Reporting can also be expensive, especially for large organisations. For Rio Tinto, the cost of reporting in 2001 was more than US$1 million (Downing 2003: 32). For Agilent Technologies the costs were approximately US$240,000, and for Ford Motor Company, they were US$350,000 (Downing 2003: 33). These costs do not include data collection and verification.

The GRI is a very valuable tool—it serves as an 'internal tool for evaluating the consistency between corporate sustainability policy and strategy on the one hand, and actual performance on the other' (GRI 1999: 5). Research is needed to demonstrate the link between reporting and improved social and environmental performance.

28.3 Organisations to which the Global Reporting Initiative Sustainability Reporting Guidelines apply

Although in the long term the GRI Guidelines are intended to be applicable to all types of organisations, the initial development work of the GRI has been focused on reporting by business organisations. The GRI recognises that smaller organisations may have more difficulty in becoming GRI reporters and, as such, encourages them to adopt an incremental approach to using the Guidelines.

According to Simon Zadek, 'the GRI is most useful for the companies that are not leaders in the [CR] field' (quoted in Maitland 2002). The Guidelines can be used as a complement to many of the codes and standards profiled in this book.

28.4 Questions posed and answered

The questions that GRI asks include:

- How can a company communicate to its stakeholders?
- On what issues should a company report?
- What are the boundaries of a company?

28.5 The promise and the challenge

Verification is one of the greatest challenges facing the GRI. Increasingly, external verification is seen as an important tool for guaranteeing the credibility of a report. External verification is not required by the GRI. However, GRI is convening a multi-stakeholder group to examine verification issues in general (www.globalreporting.org).

The GRI is among the most visionary of the CR tools profiled in this book. It will take decades for the GRI to become mainstream. According to Robert Massie, a GRI board member, they are in 'year 5 of a 30-year process' (quoted in Maitland 2002). In the course of the next few years, GRI is planning to harmonise reporting requirements, develop sectoral supplements and to improve the Guidelines (www.globalreporting.org). The challenge for the GRI is to make sustainability reporting not only mainstream but also useful to stakeholders and to the reporters.

According to Teo Lessidrenska, who has worked with GRI for many years, 'One of the recent outcomes of the [recent financial] crisis is the changing role of national governments as supporters of sustainability reporting. The French, Dutch, and most recently the UK, Swedish and Danish, have been influenced by GRI.'[4]

28.6 Strengths

The GRI is to be commended for making the Guidelines available in 23 languages. The GRI has made a wide range of sector supplements available, including:[5]

- Financial services
- Electric utilities
- Mining and metals

4 Interview with Teo Lessidrenska, an associate at GRI, 18 January 2009.

5 The following sectors are also being discussed within GRI but are not finalised at the time of publication: airports, apparel and footwear, automotive, construction and real estate, event organisers, logistics and transportation, media, oil and gas, public agencies, and telecom.

- Food processing
- NGOs

References

Downing, P. (2003) 'The GRI and Corporate Reporting', *Ethical Corporation* 13 (January 2003): 32-35.

GRI (Global Reporting Initiative) (1999) *Sustainability Reporting Guidelines* (Boston, MA: GRI).

—— (2002a) *Sustainability Reporting Guidelines* (Boston, MA: GRI).

—— (2002b) *What Others Are Saying* (Boston, MA: GRI).

Maitland, A. (2002) 'Businesses are Called to Account', *Financial Times*, 28 March 2002.

United Nations (2002) *A Historic Collaborative Achievement: Inauguration of the Global Reporting Initiative* (New York: United Nations, 4 April 2002).

Additional resource

Website

Global Reporting Initiative: www.globalreporting.org

GRI Sustainability Reporting Guidelines*

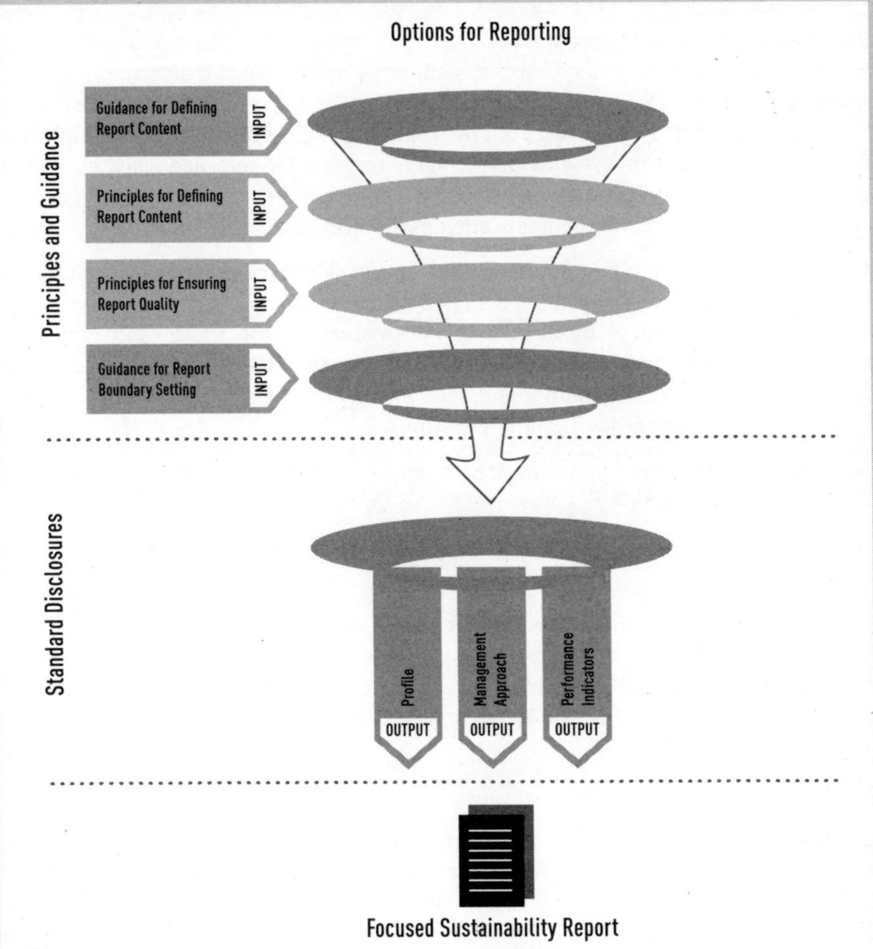

Figure 2: Overview of the GRI Guidelines

Source: GRI G3 Guidelines, p. 4. © Global Reporting Initiative (2006). www.globalreporting.org

* GRI G3 Guidelines, pp. 6-19. © Global Reporting Initiative (2006). www.globalreporting.org. Reproduced with permission.

PART 1: DEFINING REPORT CONTENT, QUALITY, AND BOUNDARY

This section provides Reporting Principles and Reporting Guidance regarding defining report content, ensuring the quality of reported information, and setting the Report Boundary.

Reporting Guidance describes actions that can be taken, or options that the reporting organization can consider when making decisions on what to report on, and generally helps interpret or govern the use of the GRI Reporting Framework. Guidance is provided for defining report content and setting report Boundary.

Reporting Principles describe the outcomes a report should achieve and guide decisions throughout the reporting process, such as selecting which topics and Indicators to report on and how to report on them. Each of the Principles consists of a definition, an explanation, and a set of tests for the reporting organization to assess its use of the Principles. The tests are intended to serve as tools for self-diagnosis, but not as specific disclosures to report against. Tests can, however, serve as a reference for explaining decisions about the application of the Principles

Together, the Principles are intended to help achieve transparency – a value and a goal that underlies all aspects of sustainability reporting. Transparency can be defined as the complete disclosure of information on the topics and Indicators required to reflect impacts and enable stakeholders to make decisions, and the processes, procedures, and assumptions used to prepare those disclosures. The Principles themselves are organized into two groups:

- Principles for determining the topics and Indicators on which the organization should report; and
- Principles for ensuring the quality and appropriate presentation of reported information.

The Principles have been grouped in this way to help clarify their role and function, but this does not impose a rigid restriction on their use. Each Principle can support a range of decisions, and may prove useful in considering questions beyond just defining report content or ensuring the quality of reported information.

1.1 Defining Report Content

In order to ensure a balanced and reasonable presentation of the organization's performance, a determination must be made about what content the report should cover. This determination should be made by considering both the organization's purpose and experience, and the reasonable expectations and interests of the organization's stakeholders. Both are important reference points when deciding what to include in the report.

Reporting Guidance for Defining Content

The following approach governs the use of the GRI Reporting Framework in preparing sustainability reports.

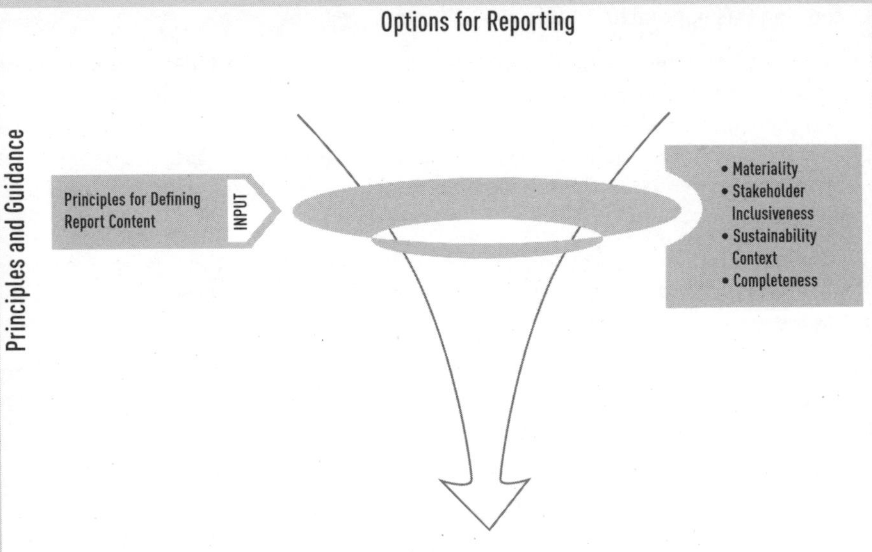

Figure 3: Principles for defining report Content

Source: GRI G3 Guidelines, p. 7. © Global Reporting Initiative (2006). www.globalreporting.org

- Identify the topics and related Indicators that are relevant, and therefore might be appropriate to report, by undergoing an iterative process using the Principles of materiality, stakeholder inclusiveness, sustainability context, and guidance on setting the Report Boundary.
- When identifying topics, consider the relevance of all Indicator Aspects identified in the GRI Guidelines and applicable Sector Supplements. Also consider other topics, if any, that are relevant to report.
- From the set of relevant topics and Indicators identified, use the tests listed for each Principle to assess which topics and Indicators are material, and therefore should be reported[3].
- Use the Principles to prioritize selected topics and decide which will be emphasized.
- The specific methods or processes used for assessing materiality should:
  - Differ for, and can be defined by, each organization;
  - Always take into account the guidance and tests found in the GRI Reporting Principles; and
  - Be disclosed.

3 GRI Organizational Profile Disclosures (1–4) apply to all reporting organizations.

In applying this approach:

- Differentiate between Core and Additional Indicators. All Indicators have been developed through GRI's multi-stakeholder processes, and those designated as Core are generally applicable Indicators and are assumed to be material for most organizations. An organization should report on these unless they are deemed not material on the basis of the Reporting Principles. Additional Indicators may also be determined to be material.
- The Indicators in final versions of Sector Supplements are considered to be Core Indicators, and should be applied using the same approach as the Core Indicators found in the Guidelines.
- All other information (e.g., company specific Indicators) included in the report should be subject to the same Reporting Principles and have the same technical rigor as GRI Standard Disclosures.
- Confirm that the information to be reported and the Report Boundary are appropriate by applying the Principle of completeness.

Reporting Principles for Defining Content

Each of the Reporting Principles consists of a definition, an explanation, and a set of tests to guide the use of the Principles. The tests are intended to serve as tools for self-diagnosis, but not as specific Disclosure items to report against. The Principles should be used together with the guidance on defining content.

Materiality

Definition: The information in a report should cover topics and Indicators that reflect the organization's significant economic, environmental, and social impacts, or that would substantively influence the assessments and decisions of stakeholders.

Explanation: Organizations are faced with a wide range of topics on which it could report. Relevant topics and Indicators are those that may reasonably be considered important for reflecting the organization's economic, environmental, and social impacts, or influencing the decisions of stakeholders, and, therefore, potentially merit inclusion in the report. Materiality is the threshold at which an issue or Indicator becomes sufficiently important that it should be reported. Beyond this threshold, not all material topics will be of equal importance and the emphasis within a report should reflect the relative priority of these material topics and Indicators.

In financial reporting, materiality is commonly thought of as a threshold for influencing the economic decisions of those using an organization's financial statements, investors in particular. The concept of a threshold is also important in sustainability reporting, but it is concerned with a wider range of impacts and stakeholders. Materiality for sustainability reporting is not limited only to those sustainability topics that have a significant financial impact on the organization. Determining materiality for a sustainability report also includes considering economic, environmental, and social impacts that cross a threshold in affecting the ability to meet the needs of the present without compromising the needs of future generations.[4] These material issues will often have a significant financial impact in the near-term or long-term on an organization. They will therefore also be relevant for stakeholders who focus strictly on the financial condition of an organization.

A combination of internal and external factors should be used to determine whether information is material, including factors such as the organization's overall mission and competitive strategy, concerns expressed directly by stakeholders, broader social expectations, and the organization's influence on upstream (e.g., supply chain) and downstream (e.g., customers) entities. Assessments of materiality should also take into account the basic expectations expressed in the international standards and agreements with which the organization is expected to comply.

These internal and external factors should be considered when evaluating the importance of information for reflecting significant economic, environmental, and social impacts, or stakeholder decision making.[5] A range of established methodologies can be used to assess the significance of impacts. In general, 'significant impacts' refer to those that are a subject of established concern for expert communities, or that have been identified using established tools such as impact assessment methodologies or life cycle assessments. Impacts that are considered important enough to require active management or engagement by the organization can likely be considered to be significant.

The report should emphasize information on performance regarding the most material topics. Other relevant topics can be included, but should be given less prominence in the report. The process by which the relative priority of topics was determined should be explained.

In addition to guiding the selection of topics to report, the Materiality Principle also applies to the use of Performance Indicators. When disclosing performance data, there are varying degrees of comprehensiveness and detail that could be provided in a report. In some cases, GRI guidance exists on the level of detail generally considered appropriate for a specific Indicator. Overall, decisions on how to report data should be guided by the importance of the information for assessing the performance of the organization, and facilitating appropriate comparisons. Reporting on material topics may involve disclosing information used by external stakeholders that differs from the information used internally for day-to-day management purposes. However, such information does indeed belong in a report, where it can inform assessments or decision-making by stakeholders, or support engagement with stakeholders that can result in actions that would significantly influence performance or address key topics of stakeholder concern.

4 World Commission on Environment and Development. Our Common Future. Oxford: Oxford University Press, 1987, p. 43.

5 See the principle of stakeholder inclusion for a discussion of stakeholders.

Tests:

External Factors

In defining material topics, take into account external factors, including:

✓ Main sustainability interests/topics and Indicators raised by stakeholders.

✓ The main topics and future challenges for the sector reported by peers and competitors.

✓ Relevant laws, regulations, international agreements, or voluntary agreements with strategic significance to the organization and its stakeholders.

✓ Reasonably estimable sustainability impacts, risks, or opportunities (e.g., global warming, HIV-AIDS, poverty) identified through sound investigation by people with recognized expertise, or by expert bodies with recognized credentials in the field.

Internal Factors

In defining material topics, take into account internal factors, including:

✓ Key organizational values, policies, strategies, operational management systems, goals, and targets.

✓ The interests/expectations of stakeholders specifically invested in the success of the organization (e.g., employees, shareholders, and suppliers).

✓ Significant risks to the organization.

✓ Critical factors for enabling organizational success.

✓ The core competencies of the organization and the manner in which they can or could contribute to sustainable development.

Prioritizing

✓ The report prioritizes material topics and Indicators.

Stakeholder Inclusiveness

Definition: The reporting organization should identify its stakeholders and explain in the report how it has responded to their reasonable expectations and interests.

Explanation: Stakeholders are defined as entities or individuals that can reasonably be expected to be significantly affected by the organization's activities, products, and/or services; and whose actions can reasonably be expected to affect the ability of the organization to successfully implement its strategies and achieve its objectives. This includes entities or individuals whose rights under law or international conventions provide them with legitimate claims vis-à-vis the organization.

Stakeholders can include those who are invested in the organization (e.g., employees, shareholders, suppliers) as well as those who are external to the organization (e.g., communities).

The reasonable expectations and interests of stakeholders are a key reference point for many decisions in the preparation of a report, such as the scope, boundary, application of Indicators, and assurance approach. However, not all of an organization's stakeholders will use the report. This presents challenges in balancing the specific interests/expectations of stakeholders who can reasonably be expected to use the report with broader expectations of accountability to all stakeholders.

For some decisions, such as the report scope or boundary of a report, the reasonable expectations and interests of a wide range of stakeholder will need to be considered. There may be, for example, stakeholders who are unable to articulate their views on a report and whose concerns are presented by proxies. There may also be stakeholders who choose not to express views on reports because they rely on different means of communication and engagement. The reasonable expectations and interests of these stakeholders should still be acknowledged in decisions about the content of the report. However, other decisions, such as the level of detail required to be useful to stakeholders, or expectations of different stakeholders about what is required to achieve clarity, may require greater emphasis on those who can reasonably be expected to use the report. It is important to document the processes and approach taken in making these decisions.

Stakeholder engagement processes can serve as tools for understanding the reasonable expectations and interests of stakeholders. Organizations typically initiate different types of stakeholder engagement as part of their regular activities, which can provide useful inputs for decisions on reporting. These may include, for example, stakeholder engagement for the purpose of compliance with internationally-agreed standards, or informing ongoing organizational/ business processes. In addition, stakeholder engagement may also be implemented specifically to inform the report preparation process. Organizations can also use other means such as the media, the scientific community, or collaborative activities with peers and stakeholders. These means can help the organization better understand stakeholders' reasonable expectations and interests.

For a report to be assurable, the process of stakeholder engagement should be documented. When stakeholder engagement processes are used for reporting purposes, they should be based on systematic or generally-accepted approaches, methodologies, or principles. The overall approach should be sufficiently effective to ensure that stakeholders' information needs are properly understood. The reporting organization should document its approach for defining which stakeholders it engaged with, how and when it engaged with them, and how engagement has influenced the report content and the organization's sustainability activities. These processes should be capable of identifying direct input from stakeholders as well as legitimately established societal expectations. An organization may encounter conflicting views or differing expectations among its stakeholders, and will need to be able to explain how it balanced these in reaching its reporting decisions.

Failure to identify and engage with stakeholders is likely to result in reports that are not suitable, and therefore not fully credible, to all stakeholders. In contrast, systematic stakeholder engagement enhances stakeholder receptivity and the usefulness of the report. Executed properly, it is likely to result in ongoing learning within the organization and by external parties, as well as increase accountability to a range of stakeholders. Accountability strengthens trust between the reporting organization and its stakeholders. Trust, in turn, fortifies report credibility.

Tests:

- ✓ The organization can describe the stakeholders to whom it considers itself accountable.
- ✓ The report content draws upon the outcomes of stakeholder engagement processes used by the organization in its ongoing activities, and as required by the legal and institutional framework in which it operates.
- ✓ The report content draws upon the outcomes of any stakeholder engagement processes undertaken specifically for the report.
- ✓ The stakeholder engagement processes that inform decisions about the report are consistent with the scope and boundary of the report.

Sustainability Context

Definition: The report should present the organization's performance in the wider context of sustainability.

Explanation: Information on performance should be placed in context. The underlying question of sustainability reporting is how an organization contributes, or aims to contribute in the future, to the improvement or deterioration of economic, environmental, and social conditions, developments, and trends at the local, regional, or global level. Reporting only on trends in individual performance (or the efficiency of the organization) will fail to respond to this underlying question. Reports should therefore seek to present performance in relation to broader concepts of sustainability. This will involve discussing the performance of the organization in the context of the limits and demands placed on environmental or social resources at the sectoral, local, regional, or global level. For example, this could mean that in addition to reporting on trends in eco-efficiency, an organization might also present its absolute pollution loading in relation to the capacity of the regional ecosystem to absorb the pollutant.

This concept is often most clearly articulated in the environmental arena in terms of global limits on resource use and pollution levels. However, it can also be relevant with respect to social and economic objectives such as national or international socio-economic and sustainable development goals. For example, an organization could report on employee wages and social benefit levels in relation to nation-wide minimum and median income levels and the capacity of social safety nets to absorb those in poverty or those living close to the poverty line. Organizations operating in a diverse range of locations, sizes, and sectors will need to consider how to best frame their overall organizational performance in the broader context of sustainability. This may require distinguishing between topics or factors that drive global impacts (such as climate change) and those that have more regional or local impacts (such as community development). Similarly, distinctions might need to be made between trends or patterns of impacts across the range of operations versus contextualizing performance location by location.

The organization's own sustainability and business strategy provides the context in which to discuss performance. The relationship between sustainability and organizational strategy should be made clear, as should the context within which performance is reported.

Tests:

- ✓ The organization presents its understanding of sustainable development and draws on objective and available information as well as measures of sustainable development for the topics covered in the report.
- ✓ The organization presents its performance with reference to broader sustainable development conditions and goals, as reflected in recognized sectoral, local, regional, and/or global publications.
- ✓ The organization presents its performance in a manner that attempts to communicate the magnitude of its impact and contribution in appropriate geographical contexts.
- ✓ The report describes how sustainability topics relate to long-term organizational strategy, risks, and opportunities, including supply-chain topics.

Completeness

Definition: Coverage of the material topics and Indicators and definition of the report boundary should be sufficient to reflect significant economic, environmental, and social impacts and enable stakeholders to assess the reporting organization's performance in the reporting period.

Explanation: Completeness primarily encompasses the dimensions of scope, boundary, and time. The concept of completeness can also be used to refer to practices in information collection (for example, ensuring that compiled data includes results from all sites within the Report Boundary) and whether the presentation of information is reasonable and appropriate. These topics are related to report quality, and are addressed in greater detail under the Principles of accuracy and balance later in Part 1.

Scope refers to the range of sustainability topics covered in a report. The sum of the topics and Indicators reported should be sufficient to reflect significant economic, environmental, and social impacts. It should also enable stakeholders to assess the organization's performance. In determining whether the information in the report is sufficient, the organization should consider both the results of stakeholder engagement processes and broad-based societal expectations that may not have surfaced directly through stakeholder engagement processes.

'Boundary' refers to the range of entities (e.g., subsidiaries, joint ventures, sub-contractors, etc.) whose performance is represented by the report. In setting the boundary for its report, an organization must consider the range of entities over which it exercises control (often referred to as the 'organizational boundary', and usually linked to definitions used in financial reporting) and over which it exercises influence (often called the 'operational boundary'). In assessing influence, the organization will need to consider its ability to influence entities upstream (e.g., in its supply chain) as well as entities downstream (e.g., distributors and users of its products and services). The boundary may vary based on the specific Aspect or type of information being reported.

'Time' refers to the need for the selected information to be complete for the time period specified by the report. As far as practicable, activities, events, and impacts should be presented for the reporting period in which they occur. This includes reporting on activities that produce minimal short-term impact, but which have a significant and reasonably foreseeable cumulative effect that may become unavoidable or irreversible in the longer term (e.g., bio-accumulative or persistent pollutants). In making estimates of future impacts (both positive and negative), the reported information should be based on well-reasoned estimates that reflect the likely size, nature, and scope of impacts. Although such estimates are by nature subject to uncertainty, they can provide useful information for decision-making as long as the basis for estimates is clearly disclosed and the limitations of the estimates are clearly acknowledged. Disclosing the nature and likelihood of such impacts, even if they may only materialize in the future, is consistent with the goal of providing a balanced and reasonable representation of the organization's economic, environmental, and social performance.

Tests:

- ✓ The report was developed taking into account the entire chain of entities upstream and downstream, and covers and prioritizes all information that should reasonably be considered material on the basis of the principles of materiality, sustainability context, and stakeholder inclusiveness.
- ✓ The report includes all entities that meet the criteria of being subject to control or significant influence of the reporting organization unless otherwise declared.
- ✓ The information in the report includes all significant actions or events in the reporting period, and reasonable estimates of significant future impacts of past events when those impacts are reasonably foreseeable and may become unavoidable or irreversible.
- ✓ The report does not omit relevant information that would influence or inform stakeholder assessments or decisions, or that would reflect significant economic, environmental, and social impacts.

1.2 Reporting Principles for Defining Quality

This section contains Principles that guide choices on ensuring the quality of reported information, including its proper presentation. Decisions related to the process of preparing information in a report should be consistent with these Principles. All of these Principles are fundamental for effective transparency. The quality of information enables stakeholders to make sound and reasonable assessments of performance, and take appropriate action.

Reporting Principles for Defining Quality

Balance

Definition: The report should reflect positive and negative aspects of the organization's performance to enable a reasoned assessment of overall performance.

Explanation: The overall presentation of the report's content should provide an unbiased picture of the reporting organization's performance. The report should avoid selections, omissions, or presentation formats that are reasonably likely to unduly or inappropriately influence a decision or judgment by the report reader. The report should include both favorable and unfavorable results, as well as topics that can influence the decisions of stakeholders in proportion to their materiality. Reports should clearly distinguish between factual presentation and the reporting organization's interpretation of information.

Tests:

- ✓ The report discloses both favorable and unfavorable results and topics.
- ✓ The information in the report is presented in a format that allows users to see positive and negative trends in performance on a year-to-year basis.
- ✓ The emphasis on the various topics in the report is proportionate to their relative materiality.

Comparability

Definition: Issues and information should be selected, compiled, and reported consistently. Reported information should be presented in a manner that enables stakeholders to analyze changes in the organization's performance over time, and could support analysis relative to other organizations.

Explanation: Comparability is necessary for evaluating performance. Stakeholders using the report should be able to compare information reported on economic, environmental, and social performance against the organization's past performance, its objectives, and, to the degree possible, against the performance of other organizations. Consistency in reporting allows internal and external parties to benchmark performance and assess progress as part of rating activities, investment decisions, advocacy programs, and other activities. Comparisons between organizations require sensitivity to factors such as differences in organizational size, geographic influences, and other considerations that may affect the relative performance of an organization. Where necessary, report preparers should consider providing context that will help report users understand the factors that may contribute to differences in performance between organizations.

Maintaining consistency with the methods used to calculate data, with the layout of the report, and with explaining the methods and assumptions used to prepare information, all facilitates comparability over time. As the relative importance of topics to a given organization and its stakeholders change over time, the content of reports will also evolve. However, within the confines of the Principle of Materiality, organizations should aim for consistency in their reports over time. An organization

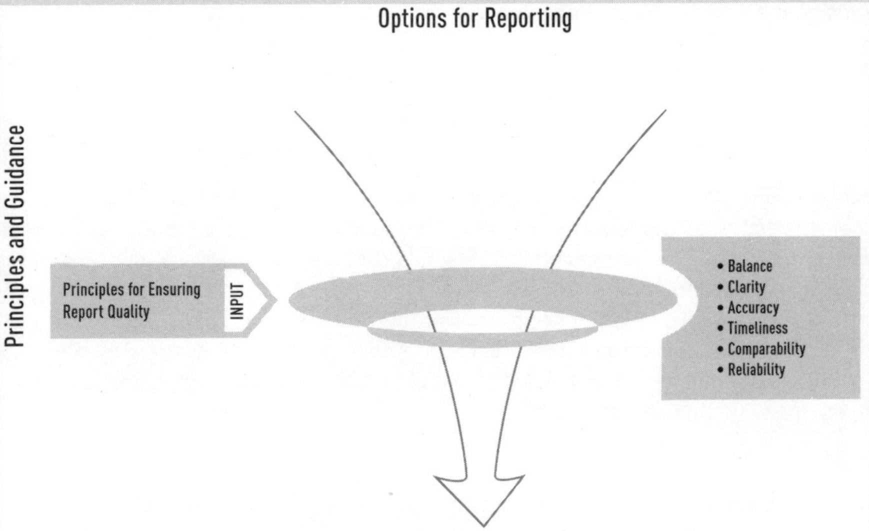

Figure 5: Principles for Ensuring Report Quality

Source: GRI G3 Guidelines, p. 14. © Global Reporting Initiative (2006). www.globalreporting.org

should include total numbers (i.e., absolute data such as tons of waste) as well as ratios (i.e., normalized data such as waste per unit of production) to enable analytical comparisons.

When changes occur with the boundary, scope, length of the reporting period, or content (including the design, definitions, and use of any Indicators in the report), reporting organizations should, whenever practicable, restate current disclosures alongside historical data (or vice versa). This ensures that information and comparisons are both reliable and meaningful over time. Where such restatements are not provided, the report should explain the reasons and implications for interpreting current disclosures.

Tests:

- ✓ The report and the information contained within it can be compared on a year-to-year basis.
- ✓ The organization's performance can be compared with appropriate benchmarks.
- ✓ Any significant variation between reporting periods in the boundary, scope, length of reporting period, or information covered in the report can be identified and explained.
- ✓ Where they are available, the report utilizes generally accepted protocols for compiling, measuring, and presenting information, including the GRI Technical Protocols for Indicators contained in the Guidelines.
- ✓ The report uses GRI Sector Supplements, where available.

Accuracy

Definition: The reported information should be sufficiently accurate and detailed for stakeholders to assess the reporting organization's performance.

Explanation: Responses to economic, environmental, and social topics and Indicators can be expressed in many different ways, ranging from qualitative responses to detailed quantitative measurements. The characteristics that determine accuracy vary according to the nature of the information and the user of the information. For example, the accuracy of qualitative information is largely determined by the degree of clarity, detail, and balance in presentation within the appropriate Report Boundary. The accuracy of quantitative information, on the other hand, may depend on the specific methods used to gather, compile, and analyze data. The specific threshold of accuracy that is necessary will depend partly on the intended use of the information. Certain decisions will require higher levels of accuracy in reported information than others.

Tests:

- ✓ The report indicates the data that has been measured.
- ✓ The data measurement techniques and bases for calculations are adequately described, and can be replicated with similar results.
- ✓ The margin of error for quantitative data is not sufficient to substantially influence the ability of stakeholders to reach appropriate and informed conclusions on performance.
- ✓ The report indicates which data has been estimated and the underlying assumptions and techniques used to produce the estimates, or where that information can be found.
- ✓ The qualitative statements in the report are valid on the basis of other reported information and other available evidence.

Timeliness

Definition: Reporting occurs on a regular schedule and information is available in time for stakeholders to make informed decisions.

Explanation: The usefulness of information is closely tied to whether the timing of its disclosure to stakeholders enables them to effectively integrate it into their decision-making. The timing of release refers both to the regularity of reporting as well as its proximity to the actual events described in the report.

Although a constant flow of information is desirable for meeting certain purposes, reporting organizations should commit to regularly providing a consolidated disclosure of their economic, environmental, and social performance at a single point in time. Consistency in the frequency of reporting and the length of reporting periods is also necessary to ensure comparability of information over time and accessibility of the report to stakeholders. It can be of value for stakeholders if the schedules for sustainability reporting and financial reporting are aligned. The organization should balance the need to provide information in a timely manner with the importance of ensuring that the information is reliable.

Tests:

- ✓ Information in the report has been disclosed while it is recent relative to the reporting period.
- ✓ The collection and publication of key performance information is aligned with the sustainability reporting schedule.
- ✓ The information in the report (including web-based reports) clearly indicates the time period to which it relates, when it will be updated, and when the last updates were made.

Clarity

Definition: Information should be made available in a manner that is understandable and accessible to stakeholders using the report.

Explanation: The report should present information in a way that is understandable, accessible, and usable by the organization's range of stakeholders (whether in print form or through other channels). A stakeholder should be able to find desired information without unreasonable effort. Information should be presented in a manner that is comprehensible to stakeholders who have a reasonable understanding of the organization and its activities. Graphics and consolidated data tables can help make the information in the report accessible and understandable. The level of aggregation of information can also affect the clarity of a report if it is either significantly more or less detailed than stakeholders expect.

Tests:

- ✓ The report contains the level of information required by stakeholders, but avoids excessive and unnecessary detail.
- ✓ Stakeholders can find the specific information they want without unreasonable effort through tables of contents, maps, links, or other aids.
- ✓ The report avoids technical terms, acronyms, jargon, or other content likely to be unfamiliar to stakeholders, and should include explanations (where necessary) in the relevant section or in a glossary.
- ✓ The data and information in the report is available to stakeholders, including those with particular accessibility needs (e.g., differing abilities, language, or technology).

Reliability

Definition: Information and processes used in the preparation of a report should be gathered, recorded, compiled, analyzed, and disclosed in a way that could be subject to examination and that establishes the quality and materiality of the information.

Explanation: Stakeholders should have confidence that a report could be checked to establish the veracity of its contents and the extent to which it has appropriately applied Reporting Principles. The information and data included in a report should be supported by internal controls or documentation that could be reviewed by individuals other than those who prepared the report. Disclosures about performance that are not substantiated by evidence should not appear in a sustainability report unless they represent material information, and the report provides unambiguous explanations of any uncertainties associated with the information. The decision-making processes underlying a report should be documented in a manner that allows the basis of key decisions (such as processes for determining the report content and boundary or stakeholder engagement) to be examined. In designing information systems, reporting organizations should anticipate that the systems could be examined as part of an external assurance process.

Tests:

- ✓ The scope and extent of external assurance is identified.
- ✓ The original source of the information in the report can be identified by the organization.
- ✓ Reliable evidence to support assumptions or complex calculations can be identified by the organization.
- ✓ Representation is available from the original data or information owners, attesting to its accuracy within acceptable margins of error.

1.3 Reporting Guidance for Boundary Setting6

In parallel with defining the content of a report, an organization must determine which entities' (e.g., subsidiaries and joint ventures) performance will be represented by the report. The Sustainability Report Boundary should include the entities over which the reporting organization exercises control or significant influence both in and through its relationships with various entities upstream (e.g., supply chain) and downstream (e.g., distribution and customers).

For the purpose of setting boundaries, the following definitions should apply[7]:

- Control: the power to govern the financial and operating policies of an enterprise so as to obtain benefits from its activities.
- Significant influence: the power to participate in the financial and operating policy decisions of the entity but not the power to control those policies.

The guidance below on setting the Report Boundary pertains to the report as a whole as well as setting the boundary for individual Performance Indicators.

Not all entities within the Report Boundary must be reported on in the same manner. The approach to reporting on an entity will depend on a combination of the reporting

6 The guidance on Report Boundary has been derived from the Boundary Protocol. Future updates to the Guidelines will incorporate any further lessons or guidance developed from experience with the Reporting Boundary Protocol.

7 Further discussion of these terms can be found in the Boundary Protocol.

organization's control or influence over the entity, and whether the disclosure relates to operational performance, management performance, or narrative/descriptive information.

The Report Boundary guidance is based on the recognition that different relationships involve differing degrees of access to information and the ability to affect outcomes. For example, operational information such as emissions data can be reliably compiled from entities under the control of an organization, but may not be available for a joint venture or a supplier. The Report Boundary guidance below sets minimum expectations for the inclusion of entities upstream and downstream when reporting on Indicators and management disclosures. However, an organization may determine that it is necessary to extend the boundary for an Indicator(s) to include entities upstream or downstream. Determining the significance of an entity when collecting information or considering the extension of a boundary depends on the scale of its sustainability impacts. Entities with significant impacts typically generate the greatest risk or opportunity for an organization and its stakeholders, and therefore are the entities for which the organization is most likely to be perceived as being accountable or responsible.

Reporting Guidance for Boundary Setting

- A sustainability report should include in its boundary all entities that generate significant sustainability impacts (actual and potential) and/or all entities over which the reporting organization exercises control or significant influence with regard to financial and operating policies and practices.
- These entities can be included using either Indicators of operational performance, Indicators of management performance, or narrative descriptions.
- At a minimum, the reporting organization should include the following entities in its report using these approaches:
  - Entities over which the organization exercises control should be covered by Indicators of Operational Performance; and
  - Entities over which the organization exercises significant influence should be covered by Disclosures on Management Approach.
- The boundaries for narrative disclosures should include entities over which the organization does not exercise control/significant influence, but which are associated with key challenges for the organization because their impacts are significant
- The report should cover all entities within its Report Boundary. In the process of preparing its report, an organization may choose not to gather data on a particular entity or group of entities within the defined boundary on the basis of efficiency as long as such a decision does not substantively change the final result of a Disclosure or Indicator.

29
ISO 14001

> [ISO 14001 is] the gold medal winner among environmental management systems: liked by the market, internationally available and recognised, not too difficult to achieve (especially if you are a big company) and it satisfies the users.
>
> *Ruth Hillary, Network for Environmental Management and Auditing* [1]

> Baxter Healthcare's adherence to ISO 14001 will definitely help to sustain our long-term competitiveness, as discerning customers around the world are becoming more environmentally conscious.
>
> *Jay Rajangam, Senior Environmental Engineer, Baxter Healthcare (Singapore)* [2]

Type Process-oriented standard, certification standard

Strength Management systems

Keywords Environmental management systems • ISO • Auditors • Certification • Standard • Overview

29.1 Background

The ISO 14000 series is a family of standards for creating environmental management systems (EMSs; for a definition of an EMS, see Box 29.1).

1 Hillary 2001: 11.
2 Quoted in ISO 1998.

- **Environmental management system**: the part of the overall management system that includes organisational structure, planning activities, responsibilities, practices, procedures, processes and resources for developing, implementing, achieving, reviewing and maintaining the environmental policy.

Box 29.1 **Definition**

Source: www.iso14000.com, accessed 2003

The International Organisation for Standardisation (ISO) has developed over 13,000 standards, working with standard-setting bodies in 145 countries. The ISO 9000 and ISO14000 series are among the most well known of the ISO standards. As with all ISO standards, companies that have successfully undergone an ISO 14001 audit by a trained auditor receive an ISO 14001 certificate. The ISO standards can also be used internally, without external auditors.

Since its launch in 1996, and up to the end of December 2008, at least 188,815 ISO 4001 certificates have been issued in 155 countries and economies. The 2008 total represents an increase of 22% over 2007 (ISO 2008).

Companies in compliance with ISO 14001 must develop the following (McIntosh *et al.* 2003: 104):

- An environmental policy
- An assessment of environmental aspects
- An assessment of legal and voluntary obligations
- A management system
- A series of periodic internal audits and reports to top management

29.2 Strengths and weaknesses

The management systems of ISO 14001 provide a useful framework for organisations to address environmental issues. Through training, employees gain an understanding of how to prevent environmental problems. However, one of the most serious shortcomings of ISO 14001 is that it has no performance criteria. Hence, an organisation can implement excellent management systems to address environmental issues yet still cause serious environmental problems. ISO 14001 does not focus on sustainability.

ISO 14001 has attained a critical mass of companies around the world. The advantage for companies of such a well-known and well-accepted certification standard is that companies can opt to work only with certified facilities.

A flexible standard:

> ISO 14001 is not a thoroughbred. It is a workhorse of a standard, designed to get you started and going down the right path . . . it motivates and allows those implementing it to do with it what they want. This is ISO 14001's greatest strength—and weakness (Hillary 2001: 15).

The costs associated with implementing ISO 14001 can be significant (but subsidies are available in some regions to offset the cost—for example, local governments in Japan have provided subsidies). However, these costs can be seen as an investment, in that most companies find that such investments lead to business benefits. A survey of 18 Danish companies found that companies received new business as a result of their work on environmental issues. In addition, some companies reported a reduction in their environmental impact, with some negative environmental impacts removed altogether (Pedersen and Nielsen 2000: 37).

In recent years, there have been demands that ISO become more accountable to stakeholders and more transparent. A number of developing countries have complained to the World Trade Organisation that ISO does not take their needs into account when developing standards (ISO 2002). Mike Smith, the ISO Director for the ISO Standard Department, believes that electronic telecommunications will make it easier for enhanced participation at ISO by developing countries (ISO 2002).

29.3 Companies to which ISO 14001 applies

ISO 14001 is well suited to large companies with well-developed management systems.

29.4 Questions posed and answered

ISO 14001 poses the following question:

- How can a company develop management systems to address environmental issues?

29.5 The promise and the challenge

The management systems of ISO have the potential to provide useful analogues for the field of corporate responsibility. Although these management systems are increasingly being modelled in standards such as Social Accountability 8000 (SA8000, Chapter 8), the ISO system will also need to learn from the corporate responsibility (CR) community about multi-stakeholder dialogue. The challenge for ISO will be to find mechanisms for including greater participation of stakeholders in decision-making.

29.6 Compatibility with other standards

ISO 14001 is very compatible with a range of standards, including those within the ISO family of standards, such as the ISO 9000 series. Once a company has developed the management systems for the ISO 14001 certificate, it becomes easier to implement SA8000 as well.

ISO 14001 is also becoming more compatible with the Eco-Management and Audit Scheme (EMAS) of the European Union (see page 251). Developed by the European Union, EMAS is a tool for public and private organisations and requires a company to:

- Conduct an environmental review
- Establish an effective management system
- Conduct an environmental audit
- Write a statement about its environmental performance

In 2001, the Council of Europe and the European Parliament revised EMAS, specifying that organisations should adopt the ISO 14001 management systems to meet the second EMAS criterion listed above.

References

Hillary, R. (2001) 'Introduction', in R. Hillary (ed.), *ISO 14001: Case Studies and Practical Experiences* (Sheffield, UK: Greenleaf Publishing): 9-16.

ISO (International Organisation for Standardisation) (1999) *The ISO 14001 Information Guide* (Geneva: ISO).

—— (2002) 'ISO is no "Sleeping Beauty" says ISO Director of Standards', news item, June 2002, www.iso.ch, accessed 2003.

—— (2003) 'ISO weighs up work on social responsibility of organizations', press release 843, 12 February 2003.

—— (2008) 'The ISO Survey—2008'; www.iso.org/iso/survey2008.pdf, accessed 11 June 2010.

McIntosh, M., D. Leipziger and G. Coleman (2003) *Living Corporate Citizenship: Strategic Routes to Socially Responsible Business* (London: FT Pearson).

Pedersen, C., and B. Nielsen (2000) 'Maintaining the Momentum: EMS after the Certifier has Left', in R. Hillary (ed.), *ISO 14001: Case Studies and Practical Experiences* (Sheffield, UK: Greenleaf Publishing): 31-38.

Additional resources

Website

International Organisation for Standardisation (ISO): www.iso.org

ISO 14001:1996
Environmental Management Systems: Specifications with Guidance for Use*

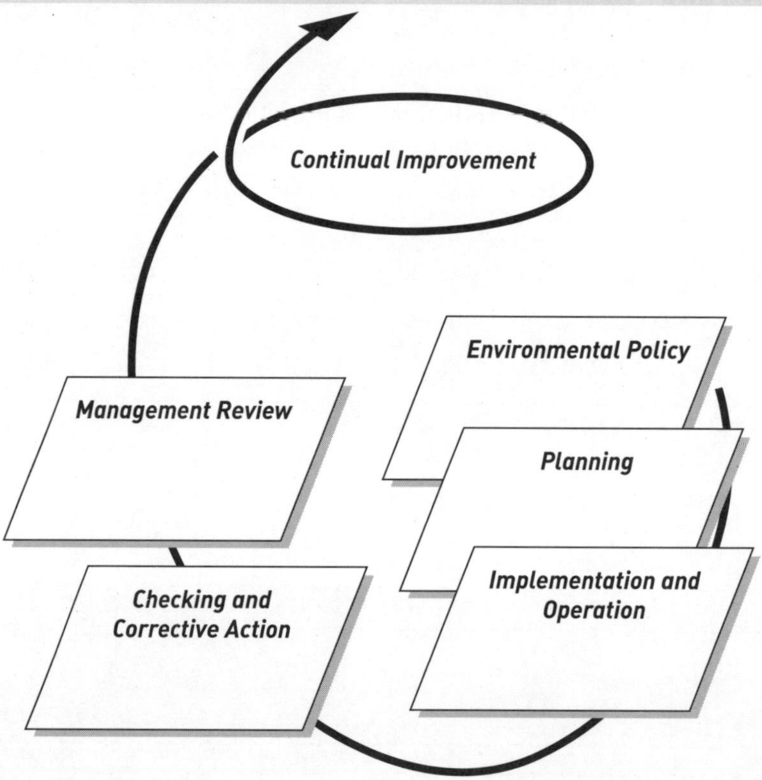

Figure 1: Environmental management system model for this International Standard

* Selected extracts only are reproduced here. Extracts from BS EN ISO 14001: 1996 reproduced with the permission of the British Standards Institution under licence number 2003SK/069. BSI publications can be obtained from BSI Customer Services, 389 Chiswick High Road, London W4 4AL. UK (tel: +44 [0]20 8996 9001; e-mail: cservices@bsi-global.com).

4 ENVIRONMENTAL MANAGEMENT SYSTEM REQUIREMENTS

4.1 *General requirements*

The organization shall establish and maintain an environmental management system, the requirements of which are described in the whole of clause **4**.

4.2 *Environmental policy*

Top management shall define the organization's environmental policy and ensure that it

a) is appropriate to the nature, scale and environmental impacts of its activities, products or services;

b) includes a commitment to continual improvement and prevention of pollution;

c) includes a commitment to comply with relevant environmental legislation and regulations, and with other requirements to which the organization subscribes;

d) provides the framework for setting and reviewing environmental objectives and targets;

e) is documented, implemented and maintained and communicated to all employees;

f) is available to the public.

4.3 *Planning*

4.3.1 Environmental aspects

The organization shall establish and maintain (a) procedure(s) to identify the environmental aspects of its activities, products or services that it can control and over which it can be expected to have an influence, in order to determine those which have or can have significant impacts on the environment. The organization shall ensure that the aspects related to these significant impacts are considered in setting its environmental objectives.

The organization shall keep this information up-to-date.

4.3.2 Legal and other requirements

The organization shall establish and maintain a procedure to identify and have access to legal and other requirements to which the organization subscribes, that are applicable to the environmental aspects of its activities, products or services.

4.3.3 Objectives and targets

The organization shall establish and maintain documented environmental objectives and targets, at each relevant function and level within the organization.

When establishing and reviewing its objectives, an organization shall consider the legal and other requirements, its significant environmental aspects, its technological options and its financial, operational and business requirements, and the views of interested parties.

The objectives and targets shall be consistent with the environmental policy, including the commitment to prevention of pollution.

4.3.4 Environmental management programme(s)

The organization shall establish and maintain (a) programme(s) for achieving its objectives and targets. It shall include

a) designation of responsibility for achieving objectives and targets at each relevant function and level of the organization;

b) the means and time-frame by which they are to be achieved.

If a project relates to new developments and new or modified activities, products or services, programme(s) shall be amended where relevant to ensure that environmental management applies to such projects.

4.4 *Implementation and operation*

4.4.1 Structure and responsibility

Roles, responsibility and authorities shall be defined, documented and communicated in order to facilitate effective environmental management.

Management shall provide resources essential to the implementation and control of the environmental management system. Resources include human resources and specialized skills, technology and financial resources.

The organization's top management shall appoint (a) specific management representative(s) who, irrespective of other responsibilities, shall have defined roles, responsibilities and authority for

a) ensuring that environmental management system requirements are established, implemented and maintained in accordance with this International Standard;

b) reporting on the performance of the environmental management system to top management for review and as a basis for improvement of the environmental management system.

4.4.2 Training, awareness and competence

The organization shall identify training needs. It shall require that all personnel whose work may create a significant impact upon the environment, have received appropriate training.

It shall establish and maintain procedures to make its employees or members at each relevant function and level aware of

a) the importance of conformance with the environmental policy and procedures and with the requirements of the environmental management system;

b) the significant environmental impacts, actual or potential, of their work activities and the environmental benefits of improved personal performance;

c) their roles and responsibilities in achieving conformance with the environmental policy and procedures and with the requirements of the environmental management system, including emergency preparedness and response requirements;

d) the potential consequences of departure from specified operating procedures.

Personnel performing the tasks which can cause significant environmental impacts shall be competent on the basis of appropriate education, training and/or experience.

4.4.3 Communication

With regard to its environmental aspects and environmental management system, the organization shall establish and maintain procedures for

a) internal communication between the various levels and functions of the organization;

b) receiving, documenting and responding to relevant communication from external interested parties.

The organization shall consider processes for external communication on its significant environmental aspects and record its decision.

4.4.4 Environmental management system documentation

The organization shall establish and maintain information, in paper or electronic form, to

a) describe the core elements of the management system and their interaction;

b) provide direction to related documentation.

4.4.5 Document control

The organization shall establish and maintain procedures for controlling all documents required by this International Standard to ensure that

a) they can be located;

b) they are periodically reviewed, revised as necessary and approved for adequacy by authorized personnel;

c) the current versions of relevant documents are available at all locations where operations essential to the effective functioning of the environmental management system are performed;

d) obsolete documents are promptly removed from all points of issue and points of use, or otherwise assured against unintended use;

e) any obsolete documents retained for legal and/or knowledge preservation purposes are suitably identified.

Documentation shall be legible, dated (with dates of revision) and readily identifiable, maintained in an orderly manner and retained for a specified period. Procedures and responsibilities shall be established and maintained concerning the creation and modification of the various types of document.

4.4.6 Operational control

The organization shall identify those operations and activities that are associated with the identified significant environmental aspects in line with its policy, objectives and targets. The organization shall plan these activities, including maintenance, in order to ensure that they are carried out under specified conditions by

a) establishing and maintaining documented procedures to cover situations where their absence could lead to deviations from the environmental policy and the objectives and targets;

b) stipulating operating criteria in the procedures;

c) establishing and maintaining procedures related to the identifiable significant environmental aspects of goods and services used by the organization and communicating relevant procedures and requirements to suppliers and contractors.

4.4.7 Emergency preparedness and response

The organization shall establish and maintain procedures to identify potential for and respond to accidents and emergency situations, and for preventing and mitigating the environmental impacts that may be associated with them.

The organization shall review and revise, where necessary, its emergency preparedness and response procedures, in particular, after the occurrence of accidents or emergency situations.

The organization shall also periodically test such procedures where practicable.

4.5 *Checking and corrective action*

4.5.1 Monitoring and measurement

The organization shall establish and maintain documented procedures to monitor and measure, on a regular basis, the key characteristics of its operations and activities that can have a significant impact on the environment. This shall include the recording of information to track performance, relevant operational controls and conformance with the organization's environmental objectives and targets.

Monitoring equipment shall be calibrated and maintained and records of this process shall be retained according to the organization's procedures.

The organization shall establish and maintain a documented procedure for periodically evaluating compliance with relevant environmental legislation and regulations.

4.5.2 Nonconformance and corrective and preventive action

The organization shall establish and maintain procedures for defining responsibility and authority for handling and investigating nonconformance, taking action to mitigate any impacts caused and for initiating and completing corrective and preventive action.

Any corrective or preventive action taken to eliminate the causes of actual and potential nonconformances shall be appropriate to the magnitude of problems and commensurate with the environmental impact encountered.

The organization shall implement and record any changes in the documented procedures resulting from corrective and preventive action.

4.5.3 Records

The organization shall establish and maintain procedures for the identification, maintenance and disposition of environmental records. These records shall include training records and the results of audits and reviews.

Environmental records shall be legible, identifiable and traceable to the activity, product or service involved. Environmental records shall be stored and maintained in such a way that they are readily retrievable and protected against damage, deterioration or loss. Their retention times shall be established and recorded.

Records shall be maintained, as appropriate to the system and to the organization, to demonstrate conformance to the requirements of this International Standard.

4.5.4 Environmental management system audit

The organization shall establish and maintain (a) programme(s) and procedures for periodic environmental management system audits to be carried out, in order to

a) determine whether or not the environmental management system
   1) conforms to planned arrangements for environmental management including the requirements of this International Standard; and
   2) has been properly implemented and maintained; and

b) provide information on the results of audits to management.

The organization's audit programme, including any schedule, shall be based on the environmental importance of the activity concerned and the results of previous audits. In order to be comprehensive, the audit procedures shall cover the audit scope, frequency and methodologies, as well as the responsibilities and requirements for conducting audits and reporting results.

4.6 *Management review*

The organization's top management shall, at intervals that it determines, review the environmental management system, to ensure its continuing suitability, adequacy and effectiveness. The management review process shall ensure that the necessary information is collected to allow management to carry out this evaluation. This review shall be documented.

The management review shall address the possible need for changes to policy, objectives and other elements of the environmental management system, in the light of environmental management system audit results, changing circumstances and the commitment to continual improvement.

ANNEX A (INFORMATIVE) GUIDANCE ON THE USE OF THE SPECIFICATION

This annex gives additional information on the requirements and is intended to avoid misinterpretation of the specification. This annex only addresses the environmental management system requirements contained in clause 4.

A.1 *General requirements*

It is intended that the implementation of an environmental management system described by the specification will result in improved environmental performance. The specification is based on the concept that the organization will periodically review and evaluate its environmental management system in order to identify opportunities for improvement and their implementation. Improvements in its environmental management system are intended to result in additional improvements in environmental performance.

The environmental management system provides a structured process for the achievement of continual improvement, the rate and extent of which will be determined by the organization in the light of economic and other circumstances. Although some improvement in environmental performance can be expected due to the adoption of a systematic approach, it should be understood that the environmental management system is a tool which enables the organization to achieve and systematically control the level of environmental performance that it sets itself. The establishment and operation of an environmental management system will not, in itself, necessarily result in an immediate reduction of adverse environmental impact.

An organization has the freedom and flexibility to define its boundaries and may choose to implement this International Standard with respect to the entire organization, or to specific operating units or activities of the organization. If this International Standard is implemented for a specific operating unit or activity, policies and procedures developed by other parts of the organization can be used to meet the requirements of this International Standard, provided that they are applicable to the specific operating unit or activity that will be subject to it. The level of detail and complexity of the environmental management system, the extent of documentation and the resources devoted to it will be dependent in the size of an organization and the nature of its activities. This may be the case in particular for small and medium-sized enterprises. Integration of environmental matters with the overall management system can contribute to the effective implementation of the environmental management system, as well as to efficiency and to clarity of roles.

This International Standard contains management system requirements, based on the dynamic cyclical process of "plan, implement, check and review".

The system should enable an organization to

a) establish an environmental policy appropriate to itself;

b) identify the environmental aspects arising from the organization's past, existing or planned activities, products or services, to determine the environmental impacts of significance;

c) identify the relevant legislative and regulatory requirements;

d) identify priorities and set appropriate environmental objectives and targets;

e) establish a structure and (a) programme(s) to implement the policy and achieve objectives and targets;

f) facilitate planning, control, monitoring, corrective action, auditing and review activities to ensure both that the policy is complied with and that the environmental management system remains appropriate;

g) be capable of adapting to changing circumstances.

A.2 *Environmental policy*

The environmental policy is the driver for implementing and improving the organization's environmental management system so that it can maintain and potentially improve its environmental performance. The policy should therefore reflect the commitment of top management to compliance with applicable laws and continual improvement. The policy forms the basis upon which the organization sets its objectives and targets. The policy should be sufficiently clear to be capable of being understood by internal and external interested parties and should be periodically reviewed and revised to reflect changing conditions and information. Its area of application should be clearly identifiable.

The organization's top management should define and document its environmental policy within the context of the environmental policy of any broader corporate body of which it is a part and with the endorsement of that body, if there is one.

NOTE: Top management may consist of an individual or group of individuals with executive responsibility for the organization.

A.3 *Planning*

A.3.1 Environmental aspects

Subclause **4.3.1** is intended to provide a process for an organization to identify significant environmental aspects that should be addressed as a priority by the organization's environmental management system. This process should take into account the cost and time of undertaking the analysis and the availability of reliable data. Information already developed for regulatory or other purposes may be used in this process. Organizations may also take into account the degree of practical control they may have over the environmental aspects being considered. Organizations should determine what their environmental aspects are, taking into account the inputs and outputs associated with their current and relevant past activities, products and/or services.

An organization with no existing environmental management system should, initially, establish its current position with regard to the environment by means of a review. The aim should be to consider all environmental aspects of the organization as a basis for establishing the environmental management system.

Those organizations with operating environmental management systems do not have to undertake such a review.

The review should cover four key areas:

a) legislative and regulatory requirements;

b) an identification of significant environmental aspects;

c) an examination of all existing environmental management practices and procedures;

d) an evaluation of feedback from the investigation of previous incidents.

In all cases, consideration should be given to normal and abnormal operations within the organization, and to potential emergency conditions.

A suitable approach to the review may include check-lists, interviews, direct inspection and measurement, results of previous audits or other reviews depending on the nature of the activities.

The process to identify the significant environmental aspects associated with the activities at operating units should, where relevant, consider,

a) emissions to air;

b) releases to water;

c) waste management;

d) contamination of land;

e) use of raw materials and natural resources;

f) other local environmental and community issues.

This process should consider normal operating conditions, shut-down and start-up conditions, as well as the realistic potential significant impacts associated with reasonably foreseeable or emergency situations.

The process is intended to identify significant environmental aspects associated with activities, products or services, and is not intended to require a detailed life cycle assessment. Organizations do not have to evaluate each product, component or raw material input. They may select categories of activities, products or services to identify those aspects most likely to have a significant impact.

The control and influence over the environmental aspects of products vary significantly, depending on the market situation of the organization. A contractor or supplier to the organization may have comparatively little control, while the organization responsible for product design can alter the aspects significantly by changing, for example, a single input material. Whilst recognizing that organizations may have limited control over the use and disposal of their products, they should consider, where practical, proper handling and disposal mechanisms. This provision is not intended to change or increase an organisation's legal obligations.

A.3.2 Legal and other requirements

Examples of other requirements to which the organization may subscribe are

a) industry codes of practice;

b) agreements with public authorities;

c) non-regulatory guidelines.

A.3.3 Objectives and targets

The objectives should be specific and targets should be measurable wherever practicable, and where appropriate take preventative measures into account.

When considering their technological options, an organization may consider the use of the best available technology where economically viable, cost-effective and judged appropriate.

The reference to the financial requirements of the organization is not intended to imply that organizations are obliged to use environmental cost-accounting methodologies.

A.3.4 Environmental management programme(s)

The creation and use of one or more programmes is a key element to the successful implementation of an environmental management system. The programme should describe how the organization's objectives and targets will be achieved, including time-scales and personnel responsible for implementing the organization's environmental policy. This programme may be subdivided to address specific elements of the organization's operations. The programme should include an environmental review for new activities.

The programme may include, where appropriate and practical, consideration of planning, design, production, marketing and disposal stages. This may be undertaken for both current and new activities, products or services. For products this may address design, materials, production processes, use and ultimate disposal. For installations or significant modifications of processes this may address planning, design, construction, commissioning, operation and, at the appropriate time determined by the organization, decommissioning.

A.4 *Implementation and operation*

A.4.1 Structure and responsibility

The successful implementation of an environmental management system calls for the commitment of all employees of the organization. Environmental responsibilities therefore should not be seen as confined to the environmental function, but may also include other areas of an organization, such as operational management or staff functions other than environmental.

This commitment should begin at the highest levels of management. Accordingly, top management should establish the organization's environmental policy and ensure that the environmental management system is implemented. As part of this commitment, the top management should designate (a) specific management representative(s) with defined responsibility and authority for implementing the environmental management system. In large or complex organizations there may be more than one designated representative. In small or medium sized enterprises, these responsibilities may be undertaken by one individual. Top management should also ensure that appropriate resources are provided to ensure that the environmental management system is implemented and maintained. It is also important that the key environmental management system responsibilities are well defined and communicated to the relevant personnel.

A.4.2 Training, awareness and competence

The organization should establish and maintain procedures for identifying training needs. The organization should also require that contractors working on its behalf are able to demonstrate that their employees have the requisite training.

Management should determine the level of experience, competence and training necessary to ensure the capability of personnel, especially those carrying out specialized environmental management functions.

A.4.3 Communication

Organizations should implement a procedure for receiving, documenting and responding to relevant information and requests from interested parties. This procedure may include a dialogue with interested parties and consideration of their relevant concerns. In some circumstances, responses to interested parties' concerns may include relevant information about the environmental impacts associated with the organization's operations. These procedures should also address necessary communications with public authorities regarding emergency planning and other relevant issues.

A.4.4 Environmental management system documentation

The level of detail of the documentation should be sufficient to describe the core elements of the environmental management system and their interaction and provide direction on where to obtain more detailed information on the operation of specific parts of the environmental management system. This documentation may be integrated with documentation of other systems implemented by the organization. It does not have to be in the form of a single manual.

Related documentation may include

a) process information;

b) organizational charts;

c) internal standards and operational procedures;

d) site emergency plans.

A.4.5 Document control

The intent of **4.4.5** is to ensure that organizations create and maintain documents in a manner sufficient to implement the environmental management system. However, the primary focus of organizations should be on the effective implementation of the environmental management system and on environmental performance and not on a complex documentation control system.

A.4.6 Operational control

Text may be included here in a future revision.

A.4.7 Emergency preparedness and response

Text may be included here in a future revision.

A.5 *Checking and corrective action*

A.5.1 Monitoring and measurement

Text may be included here in a future revision.

A.5.2 Nonconformance and corrective and preventive action

In establishing and maintaining procedures for investigating and correcting nonconformance, the organization should include these basic elements:

a) identifying the cause of the nonconformance;

b) identifying and implementing the necessary corrective action;

c) implementing or modifying controls necessary to avoid repetition of the nonconformance;

d) recording any changes in written procedures resulting from the corrective action.

Depending on the situation, this may be accomplished rapidly and with a minimum of formal planning or it may be a more complex and long-term activity. The associated documentation should be appropriate to the level of corrective action.

A.5.3 Records

Procedures for identification, maintenance and disposition of records should focus on those records needed for the implementation and operation of the environmental management system and for recording the extent to which planned objectives and targets have been met.

Environmental records may include

a) information on applicable environmental laws or other requirements;

b) complaint records;

c) training records;

d) process information;

e) product information;

f) inspection, maintenance and calibration records;

g) pertinent contractor and supplier information;

h) incident reports;

i) information on emergency preparedness and response;

j) information on significant environmental aspects;

k) audit results;

l) management reviews.

Proper account should be taken of confidential business information.

A.5.4 Environmental management system audit

The audit programme and procedures should cover

a) the activities and areas to be considered in audits;

b) the frequency of audits;

c) the responsibilities associated with managing and conducting audits;

d) the communication of audit results;

e) auditor competence;

f) how audits will be conducted.

Audits may be performed by personnel from within the organization and/or by external persons selected by the organization. In either case, the persons conducting the audit should be in a position to do so impartially and objectively.

A.6 *Management review*

In order to maintain continual improvement, suitability and effectiveness of the environmental management system, and thereby its performance, the organization's management should review and evaluate the environmental management system at defined intervals. The scope of the review should be comprehensive, though not all elements of an environmental management system need to be reviewed at once and the review process may take place over a period of time.

The review of the policy, objectives and procedures should be carried out by the level of management that defined them.

Reviews should include

a) results from audits;

b) the extent to which objectives and targets have been met;

c) the continuing suitability of the environmental management system in relation to changing conditions and information;

d) concerns amongst relevant interested parties.

Observations, conclusions and recommendations should be documented for necessary action.

Part XI
Visions for the future

30 An emerging consensus

Many of the 34 tools profiled in this book represent a synthesis of different approaches, a crystallising of the visions of companies, non-governmental organisations (NGOs), trade unions and governments into a new paradigm. According to Mark Wade of Shell, a consolidation is necessary among the [bewildering array] of codes and guidelines.[1] Many of the standard-setting bodies have worked in relative isolation:

> A new relationship is evolving between companies, NGOs and governments. The barriers between these sectors is growing more porous, with different actors more willing to step outside the confines of their sector.[2]

This book explores the 'space between' the various sectors, the fertile ground in which convergence can germinate.

The corporate responsibility (CR) movement faces a struggle between the need for convergence among standards and the need to promote innovation. The other key challenge is to develop trust through verification in the face of growing cynicism from a range of stakeholders. In order to reach a critical mass, the initiatives described in this volume will need to demonstrate the business benefits of these codes.

30.1 Pathways to convergence

If the 1990s were the age of codes of conduct, the first decade of the 21st century has become the age of convergence. Although the need for convergence of

1 Interview with Mark Wade, Shell Learning–Leadership Development, London, 11 April 2003.

2 *Ibid.*

standards has never been greater, the consensus necessary for achieving convergence can be elusive. Codes of conduct and standards are the result of intense negotiations between stakeholders and strongly reflect the organisation(s) that developed them. As a result, there are important cultural, historical, sectoral and/or geographic nuances to each code that make it unique. These different points of departure can be barriers to convergence. The convergence debate can open up items that have already been debated and decided, causing a need to revisit politically sensitive issues. Furthermore, there is often a strong sense of competition among some initiatives, which can make co-operation unlikely.

There are two types of convergence: convergence of performance standards, and procedural convergence. In the convergence of performance standards, the expectations of companies are harmonised. For example, convergence of CR performance standards might merge requirements and definitions around such issues as use of child labour, or discrimination. Procedural convergence refers to the convergence of processes such as reporting, external verification and accreditation. The first category defines parameters of performance for corporate responsibility; the second defines its new disciplines. The disciplines of corporate responsibility will be established in answering the following types of question:

- What constitutes social auditing?
- What constitutes best practice in social reporting?

It is easier to achieve convergence on procedural issues than it is on performance standards. Whereas performance standards have been negotiated with great difficulty, procedural mechanisms are still evolving, and standard-setters may be more open to sharing lessons learned. Procedural convergence is a key goal in order to increase the transparency of CR initiatives.

There are several initiatives working towards procedural convergence. The International Social and Environmental Accreditation and Labelling (ISEAL) Alliance (see www.isealalliance.org; for the membership of ISEAL, see Box 30.1) includes accreditation bodies covering fair trade, social accountability, organic agriculture and sustainable fishing and forestry. The ISEAL Alliance is working on a common methodology for social and environmental accreditation procedures. Rather than creating a new standard, the goal of the project is to learn from other initiatives through pilot projects and to develop common frameworks, definitions and protocols. The ISEAL Alliance is researching the overlap of standards and is developing a framework for increasing compatibility. Joint training programmes are another priority. The ISEAL Alliance is an excellent model for convergence. Rather than creating a single standard, the goal is to learn and share experiences and to develop common procedures and protocols that will make each of the participating initiatives stronger.

Convergence is also being promoted among the following procedural standards:

- The AccountAbility 1000 (AA1000) Assurance Standard (Chapter 27)
- The Global Reporting Initiative (GRI, Chapter 28)

Current members of the ISEAL Alliance are:

- The Fair Trade Labelling Organisation (FLO) (www.fairtrade.net)
- The Forest Stewardship Council (FSC) (www.fsc.org)
- The International Federation of Organic Agriculture Movements (IFOAM) (www.ifoam.org)
- The International Organic Accreditation Service (IOAS) (www.ioas.org)
- The Marine Aquarium Council (MAC) (www.aquariumcouncil.org)
- The Marine Stewardship Council (MSC) (www.msc.org)
- The Social Accountability International (SAI) (www.sa-intl.org)
- The Sustainable Agriculture Network (SAN) (www.rainforest-alliance.org/agriculture.cfm?id=san)
- Rainforest Alliance (www.rainforest-alliance.org)
- Social Accountability Accreditation Services (www.saasaccreditation.org)
- Union for Ethical Biotrade (www.ethicalbiotrade.org)
- Utz Certified (www.utzcertified.org)

Note: There are also now associate members, including the 4C Association, Alliance for Water Stewardship, and the Better Sugarcane Initiative, among many others. To see the full list, go to: www.isealalliance.org/portrait/associate%20member

Box 30.1 **Members of the International Social and Environmental Accreditation and Labelling (ISEAL) Alliance**

Source: www.isealalliance.org

- The Eco-Management and Audit Scheme (EMAS) of the European Union (see page 251)
- Q-Res[3]

The aim is to develop a common platform and template of key elements. These organisations plan to develop a handbook for companies.

In addition to these multilateral types of convergence, there is an increase in the number of bilateral forms of convergence taking place. For example, the GRI and the UN Global Compact (Chapter 3) have signed a formal statement of mutual recognition. These statements are making it easier for companies to make their CR strategies more coherent, integrated and significant to a broader array of stakeholders. At best, procedural convergence among CR initiatives can lead to forms of

3 Developed in Italy in 1999 by the Centre for Ethics, Law and Economics at the University of Castellanza in Italy, Q-Res addresses the social and ethical issues facing companies (www.biblio.liuc.it, accessed 2003).

accreditation and verification that are widely accepted. This in turn will promote the credibility of corporate responsibility.

30.2 Promoting trust through verification

We are in an age of accountability, where society holds companies and governments increasingly accountable for their actions. Hence, one of the key challenges within the field of CR relates to the issue of credibility and transparency. How can stakeholders trust what a company says about its social record in social reports? One of the major challenges for the field is the development of institutions and procedures for independent verification of social reports. What types of organisations can verify company reports and statements, and how will this be done? Under what conditions can a facility be termed socially responsible? Initiatives such as SA8000 (Chapter 8) and ISO 14001 (Chapter 29) are using a model of certification at the facility level to demonstrate compliance. Without credible systems for verification and certification, stakeholders may become increasingly cynical about corporate responsibility